£6-

John Ford: 'I was born in 1895, I'm American and I make W

D0412409

Contents

The Process

Gotta Dance

Farewell

Acknowledgements

The editors wish to thank M. Trarieux-Lumière, and Madame Michele Aubert of Les Archives du Film du C.N.C., Association Frères Lumière; Patricia Kelly; the heirs of Sidney Howard; and Sandra Wake from Plexus.

Stills courtesy of BFI Stills, Posters and Design. Copyright for the stills are held by the following: Association Frères Lumière, France (*Lumière photograms*); United Artists (*The Miracle Worker, Alice's Restaurant, The Missouri Breaks*); Warner Bros (*The Silver Chalice, The Left-Handed Gun, Bonnie and Clyde, Night Moves*); Columbia (*Mickey One, The Chase*); Sony Classics (*Vanya on 42nd Street*); Filmways (*Four Friends*); CBS (*Target*); Samuel Goldwyn (*Whoopee*); The Disney Corporation (*Steamboat Willie*); RKO (*King Kong*); MGM (*Doctor Zhivago, Anchors Away, An American in Paris, Singin' in the Rain, On the Town, They Were Expendable*); Newsweek (photo of Sandy Dennis by Vytas Valaitis); Republic (*Rio Grande*). Extract taken from *Federico Fellini: Je suis un grand menteur*, published in France by L'Arche éditeur. Translated from the Italian by Damien Pettigrew. Drawing entitled, 'I Adore Interviews' copyright Damien Pettigrew.

Introduction
John Boorman

Walter Donohue and I conceived of *Projections* as an annual party to which we invite film-makers we like and admire. Although the book is not topical in a journalistic sense we do try to tap into the cinematic *Zeitgeist*. I spent most of the year in the jungles and rivers of Malaysia making *Beyond Rangoon*. Walter Donohue likes to feel concrete underfoot and gets anxious if he is more than 400 yards from a movie house. Despite this, I persuaded him to come out there to help me. That left the *Zeitgeist* of the cinema sorely unattended.

Enter Tom Luddy: producer with Coppola's Zoetrope; former keeper of the Pacific Film Archive; co-director of the Telluride Film Festival for more than twenty years, Tom is a master of networking. He knows everybody, and has their numbers, phone and fax. The *Zeitgeist* would be safe in his hands and Tom agreed to help out and asked David Thomson to do it with him.

David's prodigious output of writing on the cinema is legendary. Within the last few years, apart from weekly journalism, he published a biography of Selznick which not only illuminates a life, but defines a period of movie-making; and an updated version of his idiosyncratic *Biographical Dictionary of Film*.

The starting point of *Projections* each year is the choice of diarist. I did the first one, Tavernier the second, Coppola the third. They are radically different from each other and set the tone for the rest of the book. Tom and David proposed James Toback, which was an inspired choice. His journal turns out to be more daring and dangerous than any of ours. I found it compelling, and his agonies profoundly familiar.

Meanwhile, film marches digitally on into its second century. In the 1960s if you asked young American movie-makers which directors they were influenced by, you would hear: Fellini, Kubrick, Antonioni, Bergman. Today they mostly go for Spielberg and Scorsese. And Spielberg begat Zemeckis and Tarantino sprung fully formed from Scorsese's loins. But a deeper unacknowledged influence has been at work on American films – Tex Avery. Only now have computer effects given directors the chance to achieve the speed and surreal violence that Tex got into his animation. Someone sagely said that all art aspires to the condition of music. American film, it seems, aspires to the condition of animation.

The Centenary

So here comes the centenary, with the millennium hot on its heels. From that moment when the workers spilled out of the Lumière factory, the planet had acquired a visual memory, a Welt-flick. Whatever it has become as an art form, the moving image has chronicled these hundred years.

Many years ago, when I was looking for archive film in the Imperial War Museum, I happened upon footage, not unlike that of the Lumière factory exit, that moved me to tears. In the First World War the movie camera was used as an aid to records. It was set up by the roadside while entire regiments marched past. The face of each man was seen for an instant and gone. They were all smiles and swagger as they marched to their deaths.

In the first section of the book we are delighted to have unearthed a forgotten interview with Louis Lumière in which he describes how he invented the movie camera (which also doubled as a projector) and so started the whole thing off. Martin Scorsese discusses how the screen's aspect ratio has evolved since those early days, and what the implications are for film-makers as secondary markets, such as television and video, become important sources of revenue for a film.

Our Burning Question this year also touches on the legacy of cinema's centenary: its gifts and horrors. Pauline Kael's inspired phrase 'I lost it at the movies' sums things up. Whatever delights the movies have showered upon us, they have stolen our innocence. There is no experience or situation or place that we have not felt, seen or been to on film. Does that mean the movies have condemned us to live life at second-hand? Or that we enjoy a richness and breadth of experience that no individual in the past could possibly encompass? Probably both.

The Lumière Brothers: Auguste and Louis

1   Founding Father

Louis Lumière in conversation
with Georges Sadoul
Edited and translated by
Pierre Hodgson

Introduction

Spring 1994. I have a new job, helping out in a French government agency set up to promote the centenary of film, *L'Association Premier Siècle du Cinéma*. France being France, this is a big deal. I am not quite sure what I have been hired to do. Somewhat unenthusiastically, I start rummaging through the shelves, familiarizing myself with all the videotapes people have sent in. I slot another VHS into the machine. There is no label to say what it is. Only the name of the distributor, 'Lobster Films, Paris', a firm which specializes in clearing out attics in search of old films.

An image appears on the screen. The sound is not quite in sync, the picture flickering black and white. The first words emerge: *'Monsieur Louis Lumière, dans quelles circonstances avez-vous commencé à vous intéresser aux photographies animées?'* ('Mr Louis Lumière, in what circumstances did your interest in animated photography arise?') And I realize what this is. This is the only extant television interview with the man who invented cinema, recorded on 6 January 1948.

The interview – a transcript of which is translated here in honour of the centenary – was published in France in the 1960s in book form. The original television and radio versions have almost never been seen or heard.

Many men, apart from Louis Lumière, have a claim on the title of founding father of cinema. Thomas Edison in America, for instance, or Max Skladanowski in Germany. But it was Lumière who designed, built and marketed the first all-round film machine, which worked as a camera, a projector and printer all at once. It was he who called it the 'cinematograph', the word by which in most countries the film business, or some aspect of it, is known today. And it was he who started the first continuous, fee-paying public screenings at the Grand Café in Paris just one hundred years ago.

Louis Lumière never expected cinema to be more than a passing fad (though, as he says in this interview, he was experimenting with 3-D films in 1935, forty years after the original invention). But because his camera doubled as a projector, it laid the foundations of an industry. Within months of the first fee-paying public screening, on 28 December 1895, Lumière had sent projectionists all over the world – to Mexico and St Petersburg and Saigon – where they showed footage of France to pay for the cost of shooting pictures to send home. The new fad spread like wild fire.

Most of the 1,500 or so Lumière films which have survived (average length 40–50 seconds) are documentaries of exotic places, state visits, army training courses, of comic scenes from everyday life. The subject matter is rarely of much interest. But Louis Lumière was an accomplished photographer* and he used this skill to develop cinematography of great modern beauty. The first fifty or so films in the catalogue were shot by him personally, and the rest by a handful of cameramen whom he trained. In this interview, Lumière denies he was ever a film director, but if he was not that, we can safely say he was the first *auteur*.

After the First World War, the Lumière film business declined, and the brothers' interest moved off in different directions, but the historical connection remained. When it was decided to hold a film festival in Cannes, it was thought that the president of the jury ought to be the man who, forty-five years earlier, had laid the foundations for the industry – Louis Lumière.

That was in early September 1939, quite possibly the worst timing there has ever been. War broke out, and the festival was postponed until 1946, by which time Lumière was too old to be president. Nevertheless, he attended the first Cannes Film Festival as a member of the public and there he met the historian of early cinema, Georges Sadoul. A few weeks later, Sadoul received a huge envelope through the post containing an alarming number of corrections to the definitive work he had just published.

Not long before these events, General de Gaulle had set up an organization called RTF designed to emulate or perhaps to rival the BBC. As it happened, Sadoul was on the staff of this organization, employed, partly at least, to experiment with a new form called television.

When he received Lumière's package, Sadoul did two things. He set about producing a revised edition of his book, and he decided to interview Louis Lumière for television. Perhaps the irony of it appealed to him. Here was the founding father of film, now almost on his death bed, just present at the birth of the next mass medium.

The old man had long refused to give any interviews, but on this occasion he agreed. He invited Sadoul and his wife to come and visit him at his house at Bandol, on the coast between Marseilles and Cannes, and said the television crew could come in after lunch. After a few technical mishaps, the interview

---

*The original Lumière family business was manufacturing high quality photographic plates (the firm was eventually taken over by Ilford).

was recorded and Louis Lumière died very shortly afterwards.

The interview itself is strange, not at all what we think of as television. There is no attempt at naturalism. Louis Lumière reads from a prepared typescript, rather like a cautious lawyer giving a press statement after a difficult trial. He wears a suit and a medal of high rank in the Légion d'honneur, the French equivalent of a knighthood. It seems as though the occasional cutaways to the interviewer were added later, with spurious questions designed to dress up a formal statement as a conversation. Lumière's great age and frailty are obvious. The typescript shakes in his hand. His voice is cracked. But his determination to set the record straight is impressive. Here is a man who, in his lifetime, has seen the toy he invented become by far the most popular form of entertainment in the world, wanting to tell people how it all happened; the man who invented cinema, in at the start of television.

GEORGES SADOUL: *Mr Louis Lumière, in what circumstances did your interest in animated photography arise?*
LOUIS LUMIÈRE: My brother Auguste and I started work in the summer of 1894. At this time, Marey, Edison and Demeny had conducted useful research, but no one had yet projected images on to a screen. No one had found a way of driving film through a camera. My brother Auguste experimented with a serrated cylinder, similar to that used by Léon Boully in some other invention, but this system was too violent. It could not work and it never did.
GS: *Did Mr Auguste Lumière then suggest any other solutions to the problem?*
LL: No. My brother lost interest in the technical side of cinematography as soon as I had discovered a workable method of driving film through a camera. The patent was taken out by us jointly because we always took joint credit for research and patents, regardless of whether or not each of us had made a contribution. The fact is that I am the sole author of cinematography, just as my brother was sole author of other inventions patented jointly by us.
GS: *What was your solution to the problem?*
LL: One night, sick in bed and unable to sleep, I had a brainwave. The answer was to adapt, for use in cinematography, a device similar to the presser foot which shifts cloth through a sewing-machine. I tried a circular eccentric gear, then soon replaced it with a similar, but triangular mechanism.
GS: *And so you built a prototype along these lines?*
LL: The first machine was built by Mr Moisson, chief engineer in our factories, according to a series of sketches which I gave him. There was no celluloid in France at that time, so our first experiments were conducted using strips of photographic paper manufactured in our factories. I cut the strips and perforated them myself. The first results were excellent, as you can see.
GS: *Quite. There is something very moving about that long strip of paper which you*

have donated to the Cinémathèque française. The images are perfectly sharp.

LL: Those strips were for experimental purposes only. You could not project images from such negatives because paper is too opaque. But in the laboratory I was able to imagine the effect of animation by holding paper images up to a strong light. The results were very good.

GS: *Was it long before celluloid came in?*

LL: I would have used celluloid from the beginning if I had been able to obtain sufficiently supple and transparent supplies in France. But it was available neither in France nor in England. In the end I sent one of our heads of department to America, to the New York Celluloid Company, where he found sheets of plain celluloid which we were able to coat, cut into strips and perforate in Lyons. It was Mr Moisson who devised a perforating-machine, according to the same principles as a sewing-machine.

GS: *The emulsion you produced was of a much higher quality than that made by Kodak for Edison's films. That is obvious, now we can compare the two. Photographically speaking, the earliest American films are of an indifferent quality, whereas yours are as good as today's. When did you make your first film on celluloid?*

LL: I made my first film towards the end of the summer of 1894. It is *La Sortie des usines Lumière* (Workers Leaving the Lumière Factories). You've probably noticed that the men are in straw boaters and the women in summer dresses. At that stage, I needed a great deal of sunlight to shoot such a sequence because I had only a poor quality lens. I could not have shot that sequence in autumn or winter. *La Sortie des usines Lumière* was shown for the first time in Paris, rue de Rennes, at the Society for the Encouragement of National Industry on 22 March 1895. At the end of the screening, I was invited by Mascart, an eminent physicist and member of the Académie française, to give a lecture. I also projected on to a screen a picture of a photographic image undergoing development. This presented certain difficulties I won't go into here.

GS: *Was your invention already called cinematography?*

LL: I don't think so. Our first patent, taken out on 13 February 1895, had no particular name. We called it 'a machine designed to take and show chrono-photographic prints'. The word 'cinematography' came a few weeks later.

GS: *We're all so familiar with the word 'cinema' nowadays, but at the time people thought it barbarous and unpronounceable. Did you never think of calling it anything else?*

LL: My father, Antoine Lumière, couldn't bear the word 'cinematograph'. His friend Lechère, who was a sales representative for Moët et Chandon champagne, persuaded him to call the thing 'domitor'.

GS: *What did that mean?*

LL: I'm not sure. I think Lechère thought it up. The root concept is probably something to do with domination. Neither my brother nor I ever accepted this word. We never used it.

GS: *But if you had accepted it, instead of talking about going to the cinema, we'd say going*

to the domitor, and instead of cinematography we'd say domitory, because it was the
success of the machine which you called 'cinematograph' that laid the foundations of a
new art form and a new kind of entertainment. Were there any particular technical
problems associated with the perfection of the domitor, I mean cinematograph?

LL: One thing that bothered me was: how strong is celluloid? At the time, this was an unknown quantity. We did not know what the properties of celluloid were. So I devised a series of experiments which involved piercing strips of film with needles of different diameters and suspending various weights on the needles. In this way, I discovered that the perforations could, without inconvenience, be larger than the diameter of the sprocket over which they passed. This caused no loss of strength compared to a perforation exactly the same diameter as its sprocket.

GS: *Was the cinematograph built in your factories?*

LL: No, we weren't equipped to do such work. After a lecture I gave in Paris in 1895, an engineer named Jules Carpentier asked if he could manufacture our cameras in his works, which had just started production of a first-class stills camera. Carpentier and I became close friends, and remained close friends until he died. I accepted his proposition, but he was not able to complete cameras for delivery until early in 1896, so until then I had to make do with the prototype we had built in Lyons.

GS: *Since, in 1895, you only had one instrument, which doubled up both as a camera and as a projector, you must have been personally responsible for shooting every film made that year.*

LL: That is right. All the films shown in 1895, either at the Photographic Conference in Lyons in June, or at the *Revue Générale des Sciences* in Paris in July, or in the basement of the Grand Café from 28 December on, all these films were shot by me, with one single exception: *Les Brûleuses d'herbe* (The Girls who Burn Grass), which my brother Auguste shot while on holiday at our house at La Ciotat. I should add that, not only did I shoot these films, but the first films shown at the Grand Café were developed by me in enamel hospital pails containing developer, water and fixative, and it was I who made the prints, using a white, sun-drenched wall as a light source.

GS: *For half a century now these films have been world famous. They mark the dawn of cinematography. They are:* Boat Leaving Harbour, Game of Cards, Arrival of a Train in the Station at La Ciotat, Demolishing a Wall, Lunch for Baby *and* The Gardener Takes a Shower. *Can you tell us something about* Game of Cards, *for instance.*

LL: The players are my father, Antoine Lumière, who is the one lighting a cigar; and opposite him, his friend, Trewey, dealing. Trewey was our agent in London and he organized the cinematograph screenings there. He appears in several of my films, *Assiettes tournantes* (Turning Plates) for instance. The third player, the one pouring out beer, is my father-in-law, Winkler, the brewer from Lyons. The footman was an employee. He was from Gonfaron. A true-blooded, silver-tongued southerner. He had an answer to everything and always made us laugh with his pranks.

GS: *What about* Arrival of a Train?

LL: I shot that in La Ciotat in 1895. On the platform, there is a little girl hopping. She is holding her mother's hand on one side and her nanny's on the other. That is my eldest daughter, Madame Trarieux, now four times a grandmother. My mother, Madame Antoine Lumière, is in the picture too, wearing a Scottish shawl.

GS: *The arrival of the train was your big hit at the Grand Café. When the locomotive appeared on the screen, spectators shrank back terrified. They thought they were going to be run over. What about* Demolishing a Wall?

LL: It was shot by me in our factory in Monplaisir (Lyons) while the builders were in. The man in shirt sleeves is my brother Auguste, telling the men what to do.

GS: *At the Grand Café, from January 1896 onwards, the film was shown backwards, which made it look as though a wall was building itself. A kind of special effect – the first ever. What about* Lunch for Baby?

LL: It was shot in the garden of our house in Lyons. The man is my brother Auguste, the woman is his wife and the baby is their daughter.

GS: *The first ever close-up. People were amazed not just by the expression on the baby's face, but also by the way the bushes moved in the sun. Now tell us about* The Gardener Takes a Shower.

LL: I am not 100 per cent certain, but I think the idea for the script came from a prank of my younger brother Edward. Unfortunately, he was killed as a pilot in the 1914–18 war. He was too young to play the part of the boy with his foot on the hose, so I found an apprentice in the works instead. His name was Duval and he was our chief packer for nearly forty-two years. The gardener is played by our gardener, Monsieur Clerc. He worked in the factory for forty years too, and is still alive today. He retired to somewhere near Valence.

GS: *Did you shoot any other films during 1895, apart from these eight famous ones?*

LL: I must have shot about fifty, though I can't be certain. Each film was seventeen metres in length and the screening lasted for about one minute. Seventeen metres may seem an odd sort of length, but it was governed by the capacity of the magazine containing the negative.

GS: *Can you recall the names of any other films you shot during 1895?*

LL: We produced a few comedies featuring relatives, friends and employees. One such was *Le Photographie* (The Photographer) starring my brother Auguste and Maurice, the photographer, who was to hold the franchise of our cinematograph at the Grand Café. We also made a film called *Charcuterie américaine* (American Pork Butcher), starring a sausage-making machine. The pig went in one end and sausages came out the other, and vice versa. My brother and I had great fun building the machine at our house in La Ciotat. On the side, we inscribed the words *Crack, charcutier à Marseille* (Crack of Marseilles, Pork Butcher). Perhaps I should mention *Debarquement des congressistes à Neuville-sur-Saône* (Arrival of Conference Members at Neuville-sur-Saône), which is really the first newsreel footage. I shot it during the conference in June 1895 and projected it the very next day.

GS: *Did you make any further films after 1895?*

LL: Very few. I left that to the cameramen I trained: Promio, Mesguisch, Doublier, Perrigot and others. Within a few years, they filled our catalogue with more than 1,200 films shot across five continents.

GS: *When did you abandon your cinematographic activities?*

LL: My last work was done in 1935, when I invented a form of three-dimensional cinema. I showed the results in Paris, Lyons, Marseilles and Nice. I have always been a technician and a researcher. I have never been what is called a director. I can't see myself in a modern studio. As a matter of fact, I am unable to move now. I can scarcely leave Bandol.

Workers Leaving the Lumière factory

Boat Leaving Harbour

Game of Cards

Arrival of a Train in the Station at La Ciotat

Demolishing a Wall

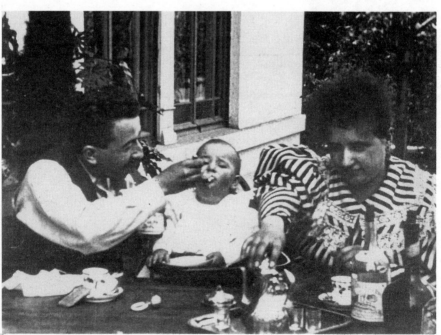

Lunch for Baby

The Gardener Takes a Shower

The Photograph

2 The Burning Question

Scott Fitzgerald said, 'Movies have taken away our dreams. Of all betrayals, that is the worst.' In this year, when we celebrate 100 years of cinema, what is the greatest gift or the worst legacy of the movies?

Arthur Penn

When you are a medium and only 100 years old at that, you must suffer the pains of scrutiny. So, a question has been asked: what is 'the greatest gift and the worst legacy to have resulted from the new medium'.

Greatest benefit: we see the world and its peoples and creatures and places. We see. A world observed is a world changed because it is observed. Pain, joy, wonder, terror come into our eyes and we believe what we 'see' even if it isn't there.

We are told tales and we believe them. It is a convincing medium; probably the most convincing. It doesn't tell the truth, not twenty-four times a second, not even once a second. It tells the truth we choose to believe. Or, as someone has said of History, it is the lies we choose to believe.

Worst legacy: it is such fun! And we believe it. Our propensity for being amazed is fed and we suspend our disbelief at the drop of the lights. Suspend? Hell, we positively litter the planet with our disbelief. It is flung every which way with reckless abandon. Cartoons, pictures, sound, special effects – we buy them all.

That's the danger. It's so much fun, that damned medium. And I sound like Scrooge: 'Bah, humbug.' Let's go to the movies.

Monte Hellman

Far from taking away our dreams, movies have given us the opportunity to continue our dreams while awake, and provided us with new characters and fantastic creatures to populate our dreams while sleeping.

And to a few lucky ones like myself, they have given a spectacular way to tell our dreams to others.

But there is a price to pay for everything. Movies have also created that monster we call Hollywood, which, with the lure of riches and fame, every year encourages hundreds of hopefuls who want to make movies, in the worst way, to do just that.

Nora Ephron
Actually, movies seem to me to be a remarkably harmless, quite lovable, virtually ineffective (in a true political sense) art form that is responsible for next to nothing but an occasional fashion trend. Whereas television can be blamed for virtually everything.

Vincent Ward
It is an instructive coincidence that the celebration of 100 years of cinema should fall in the same year that saw the death of Dennis Potter. While lauded in the UK, his works have hardly been seen on American television, even though *The Singing Detective* and *Blue Remembered Hills* are perhaps the best/ most significant television or film in the past twenty or thirty years. What Potter signifies to me – and I think for most people who appreciate his writing – is proof that personal and profound work can be realized through the mass medium of television: that much maligned off-shoot of film. His genius was to convey something important about people – to create work of the most serious intent – and yet make it accessible by presenting his vision through the dubious means of the babble box.

What all great film or television share is the personality of great authorship. Rather than take away our dreams, film – and on occasion, television – sometimes manages to reach out to an audience to share the very specific dreams of the film-maker/writer, and thus challenge and stimulate the audience's dreams and notions. The role of the film-maker is somehow, despite the massive costs involved, to create those singular dreams that tell us something about people, about the simple condition of 'being', about this strange business of living. The challenge is to make films that are accessible, yet somehow do not compromise and turn one's dreams into an emulsified, middle-of-the-road product that represents most of what is made.

Roger Corman
Indeed, to take away our dreams would be the worst betrayal. However, movies don't rob us of our dreams – they merely change how we dream. On the one hand, filmic images replace what was once only in our minds – our vision of ideal beauty, the coast of a different continent, what a medieval castle was like in its heyday. With the advent of film, we were able to look at these images 'for real', as a camera had recorded them. We looked at someone else's dream visualized and realized in a seemingly unmutual experience. But this merely enables us to create our own visions and dreams in a new way.

Perhaps the most miraculous achievement in cinema is the institution of the international film festival. It is a forum for words, ideas, sounds, moving images, dialogue and discovery. We are able to enter the dreams of those with sensibilities fundamentally unlike our own – or uncannily like ours. To share

in the consciousness of others, to exchange ideas and images with others, is not
to relinquish our own. We are not replaced, but fortified, and carry on in our
making of dreams, of films, betraying nothing but our love of cinema.

Fred Zinnemann

The greatest gift and the worst legacy of motion pictures is technology itself. It
is moving much too fast and with ever-increasing speed, with greed as the
locomotive and with responsibility non-existent to act as a brake. Where that
train is going is anybody's guess.

Andre de Toth

We are all passengers on the multimedia's interactive superhighway.

Don't be awestruck. It's not new. It's the same old road, slick from blood
and sweat, and its pot-holes are the shattered dreams of disappointments.
Only the speed limit has been removed.

It was all started long ago by a speed maniac, a daredevil fireman, who loved
to drive at breakneck speed – twenty, sometimes even as high as twenty-five
miles per hour – driving to blazes across St Louis, basking in the hero-worship
of the World's Fair crowd's ooohs and aaahs, and the questions: 'How does it
feel to go so fast?'

Enter Auguste and Louis Lumière. Under their influence and prompted by
adoration, our speed-demon fireman bought a large screen, a railroad car
which he shook violently while projecting moving scenery outside its windows.
Postscript: he became richer in a year than the *frères* Lumière in their lifetime.
That's showbiz.

Enter fireman Steven Spielberg, and the dinosaur, his railroad car. His
moth-eaten shark will be forgotten with the fireman of St Louis. But not
Spielberg. He put up the first sign of danger on the superhighway. Spielberg's
living dinosaurs wiped the human puppets off the screen and slapped us in the
face with the question, the question of tomorrow. Whom do you want to rule
the screen?

The danger doesn't lie in the fast-advancing technology. The responsibility
lies with the children in us, fascinated to play with the new toys and blinded by
them, disregarding everything else. Hillary climbed Everest 'because it was
there'. And all the intriguing new cinematic miracles are there at our finger-
tips. The temptation is tremendous. There has to be a difference, a big
difference between writing stories for the equipment and using the fabulous
equipment to tell real stories of real people (with or without dinosaurs). But
once the feast days of over-indulgence are over, the surviving passengers on
the multimedia's interactive, digital, fibre-optic superhighway will be on their
way to Utopia: the promised land of unshackled dreams, a new haven for
creative artists, money-makers and fakers. That's showbiz.

But on your way to paradise, folks, please, stop by at 25 rue du Première-Film, Lyons, France – INSTITUTE LUMIÈRE, the birthplace of *frères* Lumières' magic – and thank them for the 100 miserable years they gave us. We enjoyed every minute of it so much.

Istvan Szabo
The greatest gift is the close-up.

A living human face: thoughts born in front of us, or emotions dying in front of us – giving way to new thoughts and emotions. Art gives us energy. In film, a truly charismatic face carries this energy, conveying the message.

The worst legacy is the possibility of abusing our enormous responsibility. Talent and morality do not exclude each other: see TRIUMPH OF THE WILL.

Richard Lowenstein
The greatest gift: Arnold Schwarzenegger.
The worst legacy: Arnold Schwarzenegger.

Dusan Makavejev
The greatest gifts were the years and moments that made us believe that films could change the world for the better.

The worst was to see the world following and fulfilling the ugliest schemes and prophecies from B-movies.

Kevin Brownlow
If the movies have taken away our dreams, they have substituted nightmares. I would defend the right of film-makers to put anything on the screen without fear of censorship, but when you talk to children who have yet to be exposed to the ultra-violence of the modern cinema, you cannot fail to feel uneasy.

Of course, films have been violent from the beginning. Early actualities included graphic scenes of atrocities, like the decapitation of a Chinese rebel during the Boxer Rebellion, a still from which is lovingly reproduced in books and catalogues.

Audiences may have been accustomed to the violence of stage melodrama, but they were shaken by the early cinema because they could not always distinguish between reality and re-creation, because the screen was often so large and because they felt so much more involved. The cinema had a bad reputation from the beginning and not just because of the illicit goings on that were suddenly made possible in the dark. One criminal blamed his crime on *The Great Train Robbery* (1903) and, as far as story films are concerned, you can't go back much further than that.

I recently showed my nine-year-old daughter a Rin-Tin-Tin film of 1923. (She is crazy about dogs.) The idea that a man could even consider shooting a dog, unjustly accused of killing a baby, was so horrendous that it ruined her enjoyment of the film. I shudder to think what will hit her when she's a few years older and thinks *Reservoir Dogs* is an animal picture.

Thanks largely to the Hays (and Breen) Office, the regular run of commercial cinema was pretty bland in my youth. My nightmares were caused by far less graphic sequences than one sees today. Having scampered out of *Snow White* at the Ritz, Tunbridge Wells, in 1944 because I was terrified of the Wicked Queen, I am surprised anyone took me to the cinema again. In 1945, the Cameo-Poly, Regent Street, London, held a children's matinée with a Soviet-made fairy-tale. The accompanying newsreel carried the first pictures of Belsen. The horrified mothers besieged the manager's office, but he was as dismayed as they were. We kids paid no attention. Bulldozing corpses had no parallel in our world. On the other hand, *The Little Hump-Backed Donkey* terrified me more than I have ever been terrified in the cinema. The scene which kept me awake night after night showed the hero and heroine being forced to dive into a colossal mug of hot milk.

If children can be so upset by such a whimsical image, why bother about their reaction to graphic violence? Wouldn't that pass over their heads like the newsreel of Belsen? It may do, but there comes the point when the child is old enough to confront what we laughingly call adult entertainment and it has the effect it was intended to have. Either the child is traumatized, as anyone would be after witnessing something like a gory road accident, or they react with excitement and want more. The latter reaction is the one regarded as desirable by film people.

I object to graphic violence not only on moral grounds, but because it stops me going to the cinema. Call me feeble, unadventurous – it doesn't alter the fact that as soon as I get a whiff of ultra-violence, I avoid it like the plague. There may be many drawn to the picture because of its gore, but I'll wager there are far more repelled. I remember seeing *Bonnie and Clyde* when it first came to a cinema in suburban London. The final shoot-out was, at the time, the bloodiest sequence ever seen on the commercial screen. What puzzled me was the sound – not just the roar of police gunfire, but a stronger sound – like Oerlikon guns. Only when the gunfire faded did I realize that it was the repeated banging of the hard seats in the stalls – so many people were walking out that it sounded like the Somme. I wasn't among them, I hasten to add; I thought the film brilliantly directed and the violence at the end legitimate, even if I did watch through half-closed eyes. Since that was the beginning of ultra-violence, in a way, I forecast that the cycle would soon be over. How wrong I was!

It would make an interesting psychiatric study: who needs treatment more – the person who goes to the cinema to revel in the blood, or the person who dares not go? I admit to a certain level of hypocrisy, as I have a fascination for violence. I used to have an ambition to be a newsreel cameraman. I filmed the

Mosley marches with my 16mm camera and was thrilled when they degenerated into riots. I accompanied the Grosvenor Square demos in the 1960s and travelled to Belfast and Derry in the hope of astonishing footage. In Prague in 1968 I was arrested by the Russians for filming their military headquarters and got away only by acting like a combination of Philby, Burgess and Uriah Heep. When I returned to London, I called the American TV networks to show them my unique footage of a city under occupation.

'Where are the tanks?' demanded the producer, indignant that I had wasted his time. 'Our Austrian people got tanks firing on people. What the hell have you got?'

It was the end of my ambition and the rolls of film were put back in their cans, never to be opened again.

When I did encounter violence on these occasions, I had no hesitation in filming it, noting the extraordinary sense of detachment acquired by peering through a viewfinder. It reminded me of the story of a Swedish cameraman who was shooting an exquisitely lit landscape. 'How beautiful,' he sighed. 'I wish I was here.' Those frontline cameramen I have spoken to all mentioned the barrier to the emotions provided by the lens. Unhappily, the audience has no such barrier. In the old days they were protected by censors. Ironically, censors work hardest during a war. In retrospect, I am amazed that the Belsen footage was permitted on the public screens. Atrocities committed by our side were also filmed, but were hastily excised. At the liberation of Dachau, a team of Signal Corps men led by director George Stevens went in with the troops. They filmed what they saw and it makes terrible viewing – not only the 16mm colour footage, which the BBC turned into an excellent documentary, but the black and white footage which rests in the National Archives in Washington. Among the Signal Corps men was director Thornton Freeland, the man who made *Flying Down to Rio*. When some of the prisoners cornered an SS guard beneath a hut and were preparing to despatch him with a knife, Freeland called out: 'Bring him over here. Kill him in the light.' And his cameraman filmed the summary execution with his Mitchell, sync sound and all. The film went back to London and was destroyed by the American military. History is not well served by censors, but audiences might offer silent thanks if they knew what they were being protected from.

When I set out to be a director, I had an ambiguous attitude towards violence on the screen. I wanted to make a pacifist film about war, but I wanted to show what war was like – the usual explanation of those who make gory films. *It Happened Here** (1964) was a semi-professional film about what might have happened if we had lost the Second World War. It was not a violent film, for it, too, concentrated on occupation rather than invasion, but my co-director,

*The film is available on Connoisseur Video.

Andrew Mollo, and I needed to shock the audience at the beginning. We wanted to show a German officer being shot in such a way that the audience would be as appalled as the leading character. I talked the problem over in the cutting rooms where I worked with my assistant, Peter Watkins (who went on to make *The War Game* (1966).) He offered to do the make-up himself and he made a far more horrifying job of it than I could have imagined. When the rushes came back I could hardly look at them. The German's eye had been shot out and lay like a poached egg in the middle of his face. But I cannot describe how satisfying it was to see the film in public and to hear the gasp produced by that shot. The audience of 1964 was not accustomed to such authentic deaths – people generally threw up their arms and fell over. Where once film-makers longed to hear audiences laugh, so I felt a soaring sense of power at hearing them gasp. And one sure way to repeat that was by confronting them with horrifying images. This I was too squeamish to do and, in any case, I never made it as a feature director. Since those days, thousands of other film-makers have done the job most effectively.

However, audiences cease to gasp when something becomes familiar and film-makers have steadily had to raise the level of shock. Where once David Lean could cause heart failure with the appearance of a convict in a graveyard, now you have to follow the example of director Richard Donner, who cruelly timed a decapitation so that the most gruesome part would happen when those who had shut their eyes had opened them again.

The apparent lust for horror in mainstream films is, like everything else, driven by commercial considerations. Television in America used to be unbelievably bland, and to get people into the cinema they had to be tempted by what they could not see at home. But this has become self-defeating, since video stores now supply many jolly things which even Quentin Tarantino dare not put on the public screen. If people's tastes were once indicated by their bookshelves, their perversions are now revealed by their videos. Yet the cinema has to compete and I predict it won't be long before the manufacturers of what airlines used to call motion-discomfort bags are contracted to supply the movie houses – they'll call them motion-picture-discomfort bags, perhaps. The Latin word 'vomitorium' will take on a new meaning.

It bothers me that while many are undoubtedly horrified, millions who see these films are *not* distressed by the violence. I suppose it is comforting to remember that during the most violent era the world has ever known – Europe under the Third Reich – they saw no ultra-violence on the screen. They practised enough of it in real life. Hitler, however, was apparently assuaged for the July plot by watching film of the conspirators being hanged by piano wire – filmed in Agfacolor and shown that night at one of the big Berlin cinemas.

Psychologists tell us there is no proof that violent films lead to violent behaviour. It doesn't have to. It can have all sorts of other effects, some of them traumatic. But if, as they say, films have no effect on behaviour, what are we all doing in the business? Wasn't it the experience of going to the movies that excited us in the first place? Isn't that an effect on behaviour? In any case, if you want to see the effects of the moving image, you only have to look at the skyline of any European city. The buildings tower upwards in a desperate attempt to look glamorous and American. Once, you could tell from the architecture what part of the world you were in. Not any more. Thanks to the movies and television, modern cities more and more resemble downtown Dallas. And while once you could look at a European's clothing and tell where he came from, now everyone dresses like extras in an American movie. Young people, particularly, have adopted baseball caps and baseball gear without the slightest idea what the insignia means. European pop music is indistinguishable from American and the singers adopt American accents. All this is a powerful tribute to the American motion-picture and television industry, and if you still think these movies have no effect on behaviour, how do you explain the recent craze for joy-riding? Every second thriller has a car chase, they are invariably brilliantly shot and cut, and the excitement for a kid imprisoned on a housing estate is as great for them as for us. The difference is they want to alleviate the dullness of their lives by acting it out.

Moving pictures have a lot to answer for, and it's no use sheltering them beneath the sacred shroud of 'art' – art can kill.

The American crime film has acted as a most persuasive commercial for the handgun since George Barnes aimed his Colt .45 at the camera in *The Great Train Robbery*. It's understandable; Universal once tried the experiment of making a series of Westerns without gunplay and very unexciting they were. But now it's getting ridiculous. In the 1994 London Film Festival programme, there were no fewer than thirteen films illustrated by someone handling a gun. For that's how arguments are settled in most American films. No matter how inspired the dialogue, the cackle is cut by a hand reaching for a holster. Small children 'take the stance' with their toy guns exactly as they have seen their elders and betters on TV, on posters, on the screen. People of a criminal disposition, as we have seen on security videos, do the same, except their guns aren't toys. The fatally misinterpreted clause in the US Constitution about the right of the citizen to bear arms – which was intended to benefit the militia, not the mafia – has led to a proliferation of deadly weapons which, in a society which prefers actions to words, leads to people producing pistols more often than pencils. I remember interviewing the veteran director Sidney Franklin, who was a gentle and humane man, responsible for such films as *The Good Earth*. He suddenly noticed an unmarked car cruising around his property. He reached into a drawer and produced a pistol – a move which seemed as natural to him as if he were Humphrey Bogart.

Violence may be in bad taste, but why shouldn't people be obsessed with it? We are all threatened by it and most of us have experienced it. Is it not as unhealthy to suppress it as to suppress sex? This may be so, but all I ask is a warning. I don't want this stuff taking me unawares. I booked into a hotel room in Italy one evening, switched on the TV and watched a man being all too realistically crushed beneath the tracks of a tank – a triumph of special effects. I am still haunted by that nauseating image.

One should be grateful to the British Board of Film Classification for the idea of the 15 and 18 age categories, but it isn't much help to the likes of me. The censors are far harsher on sex than on violence and they have a strange idea of what children should keep away from. When I took my daughter to the harmless comedy *Mrs Doubtfire*, I was infuriated to find she was barred because it had a 12 classification owing to some sexual innuendo which would have meant nothing to her anyway. Other kids slipped in and the usherettes took no notice. When she got back to school, all her classmates had seen it, making nonsense of the ruling. Her classmates also have no difficulty seeing the gory pictures with an even higher classification, not to mention 'video nasties', which are some schoolchildren's idea of a treat.

I would welcome a new classification – SOS (Squeamish Out Swiftly?) – and perhaps a new kind of cinema, where they show cut versions, rather as they do on airliners. I once saw *The French Connection* on an aeroplane and told friends, 'You see, they *can* make first-class thrillers without violence ...' I would not complain if ultra-violent films were an occasional problem, like the old horror films, which arrived in England to be well advertised by an H certificate. Yet nowadays you never know when you are going to be assaulted by some repellent sequence, brilliantly executed by the special-effects storm-troopers of the Hollywood studios.

Audiences have shown they love violent pictures, and there are cheers for particularly imaginative deaths as there is applause for a soloist in a concert hall. Cinema is fantasy and ultra-violence is supposed to act as a catharsis. Perhaps many lives are saved by films like *The Texas Chainsaw Massacre*, but you only have to look at the coverage of the Los Angeles riots to see that audiences have been paying close attention to the instructional films that Hollywood has been providing, and that Hollywood was itself in grave danger. It was like the retribution in the last reel of a Cecil B. DeMille picture.

Mind you, I have a copy of a 1924 Eisenstein film called *Strike* which I have never managed to see all the way through, because the climax shows a Cossack attack on civilians which is imaginatively intercut with the killing of cattle in a slaughterhouse. Maybe we could attract a new audience for silent films by reviving this, and by showing *Sang des Bêtes* as an appetizer. Perhaps they might even get a cheer. It's a good idea, but I don't think I'll suggest it, because if it was adopted I'd have to stay away ...

Vincent Sherman

For me, cinema, including documentaries and newsreels, has made an invaluable contribution to our world: not only because of its entertainment values, but in its recording of great events, it gives us an opportunity to see and hear important and famous men and women. Wouldn't it be gratifying to be able to see and hear Lincoln deliver his Gettysburg address, or George Washington rally his troops at Valley Forge? Or the first Congress debate the Constitution? And while we should be grateful that we can see the early silent films of Chaplin, Harold Lloyd, Buster Keaton, Mary Pickford and Lillian Gish, wouldn't it also be valuable to see Bernhardt, Duse, Coquelin, Grasso, Henry Irving, Booth and Burbage?

I have had a long association with cinema – first, when it was called simply moving pictures, then movies, then films, and saw my first one in 1912, showing Indians moving about somewhere out West. I was six years old and the theatre was an empty store with wooden benches and a projector (later a piano was added). It was in Vienna, Georgia, where I was born, a small town in the southern part of the state. It was not long before stories began to be filmed in five reels, and two-reel comedies began to be made by Mack Sennett and Sunshine. I recall the pleasure I had in watching Francis X. Bushman, Harold Lockwood and Wallace Reid, as they demonstrated their manly qualities.

As I grew up, my father let me go every Saturday afternoon to see an episode of one of the many serials that kept us in suspense from one week to the next: *The Perils of Pauline* or *The Clutching Hand* or *The Diamond from the Sky*. I distinctly recall the night in 1915 that I saw *Birth of a Nation* in Cordele, Georgia, nine miles from Vienna, and began to get an inkling of the tremendous power film could exert. Later, Griffith made *Intolerance* to counteract some of the anti-black prejudice the first one had inadvertently created. And as I write this, I remember a night in 1938 or 1939 when Griffith came to a meeting of the Directors' Guild in Hollywood and was asked if he would like to say a few words to us. He stood and said simply, 'If you men would only realize – you have in your hands the means to change the world.'

When I graduated from Oglethorpe University in 1925, I became a film salesman for an independent distributor throughout the south-east where I sold Westerns at $7.50 per night. About this time, Cecil B. De Mille's *The Ten Commandments* appeared, with Rod La Rocque, Richard Dix, Estelle Taylor and a great character actor, Theodore Roberts. Along with its success, it achieved a little-known or recognized result: it made moving pictures respectable in the small towns of the south. Prior to this, the churches and their ministers regarded films as evil and the work of the devil. But this film, which condemned greed and extolled morality, was the catalyst. Then came sound and colour. By this time I was an actor in the New York theatre trying at the same time to write and direct. Finally, after ten years of struggling, I was offered a job in Hollywood at Warner Bros, in July 1937, as a writer, actor and/or director.

So I have had an opportunity to witness the development of film from its earliest days. Its greatest gifts, to me, are the reflections of the times it offers: the moral values, styles of acting and dress, and the image of the great actors and personalities of the past, in both newsreels and works of fiction.

Isn't it satisfying to be able to show your children and grandchildren Chaplin in *The Gold Rush*, Harold Lloyd in *The Freshman*, or Buster Keaton, or the Barrymores, Shirley Temple, Cagney, Bogart, Wayne, Flynn, Robinson, Bette Davis and Ingrid Bergman, or Vivien Leigh, or Joan Crawford? And dozens of other talented performers?

And let's not forget the many fine films from England, France, Italy and Russia, which have given us a sense of the life and times of those countries.

Along with every other great gift to society, there is, at times, a corruption of film, when it is used for prurience or violence. In fact, at this moment I am disturbed by the millions of dollars that are spent to exploit greater demonstrations of killing, explosions, accidents and devastation. This week alone I have seen three films that try to outdo each other in the violent-action department, and was left uninvolved and uninterested, but depressed.

Huang Mingchuan

Moving pictures are extra wings of the domestic power which constantly scan the political sky of our lives.

Moving pictures are devastating typhoons from a foreign sea, that strike everyone on the land continually without end.

Moving pictures – from inside or out – truly reveal a sign of the desire of modern Formosans who wish to be overwhelmed until they die.

Alex Cox

Greatest gift: films have the capacity to recreate our dreams.
Worst legacy: they have contrived to do it boringly.

Michael Tolkin

I hope the quote is right. I hope that Fitzgerald said 'Movies have taken away our dreams', and not, '*The* movies have taken away our dreams', because beginning with the noun restricts the thought in a much more provocative way. If the article is there, then '*the* movies' summons into the witness box the film industry as an institution, which makes the thought too easy, the maudlin rant of a bitter drunk mad at Hollywood for bringing him to the line where genius has to give way to talent. So I'm going to assume that he meant movies' effect on dreams, the way a doctor might describe vodka's effect on driving.

Which leaves another question: what did he mean by dreams? As the visions of sleep, or dreams in the traditional second sense as wishes, or private fantasies? That's also a cheap thought, as though the movies didn't complete something which the novel had already started. I'm thinking of the first chapter of *Huckleberry Finn*, when Huck and Tom play at 'ambuscading the A-rabs', which is one of Tom's exorbitant fantasies taken from books. Does Fitzgerald want to suggest that children's games, once pure, were destroyed by mass culture? Walter Scott was already a director, and his books were no less influential on the minds of children than *The Mickey Mouse Show*. So if Fitzgerald wants to whine about Hollywood's effect on some uncorrupted imagination, he's a few millennia late. The process didn't begin with the movies: any lie which someone dies for is a movie; anything where blood and death are joined to voluptuous pleasures, any form of art or enchantment that accepts cruelty as entertainment and makes the fantasy of one's own death an acceptable spectacle is a movie. But if he's really holding his own disappointments in check and not just saying that Hollywood ruined his dreams of literary triumph (which he tucks behind the presumption of collective betrayal), if the movies double-crossed him, they cheated everyone; if he's trying to say something specific about the cultural–physiological effect of movies on real dreams and not dreams as hopes, as imaginary realities – well, what a question! We're all too young to answer.

Fitzgerald was born in 1896, when the movies were two, so he probably had a good ten or fifteen years of sleep before he ever saw a real movie, not just a demonstration of a toy. Was Fitzgerald aware of a change in his dreams after he started watching movies? Could dreams have been different before the movies, maybe scarier, maybe more personal, maybe more surreal, more private? Did Fitzgerald sense that watching projected images gave the subconscious a template, where before the movies everyone had to create something for themselves? What were nightmares before the movies? The worst dreams I had as a child came when I was seven, after watching *The Bride of Frankenstein* through a crack in the door of the housekeeper's bedroom. The image that forced me under the covers for probably five years (or did I ever come up?) was Elsa Lancaster's shock at meeting Boris Karloff. I don't know if that's any worse a dream than a medieval child might have had after a pilgrimage to a cathedral with bloody saints and painted gargoyles, but the universal access to movies, their ubiquity, guarantees that singular, private dread is in shorter supply. So if the movies reduce terror to something equally accessible to all, with models and maps, then Fitzgerald also means that what has been betrayed is a glimpse into the other side of horror, which might be awe, or amazement, or genuine revelation, which has to come from the singular concentration of one person.

Which leads to the next question: why is this the worst betrayal? Here's an old dream:

In my dream I was standing on the bank of the Nile, when out of the Nile came up seven sturdy and well-formed cows and grazed in the reed grass. Presently there followed them seven other cows, scrawny, ill-formed and emaciated – never had I seen their likes for ugliness in all the land of Egypt! And the seven lean ugly cows ate up the first seven cows, the sturdy ones; but when they had consumed them, one could not tell that they had consumed them, for they looked just as bad as before.

And Joseph said to Pharaoh . . . 'God has revealed to Pharaoh what He is about to do.'

At this point, Joseph gives the interpretation of the fourteen cows as seven fat years followed by seven lean years, so, with the Pharaoh's authority, he fills the granaries and the country survives. Now in this degraded age we're all more terrified of dreams as iron-clad prophecies of things to come than of dreams as clues, and clues are the guide to the crime committed, with the self as evidence, neurosis as corpse. Would those cows have so divinely presented Pharaoh with an image of crisis that also contained the solution to the crisis if he had had to filter his dreams through a grid of sensitivities clogged with pictures of Bing Crosby and Deanna Durbin? – or even to skewer the hipoisie, Woody Strode and Jack Elam?

If the Talmud is right – and it usually is – and dreams are one-sixtieth of prophecy, then was Fitzgerald, child of the filmless age – let's borrow a movie image . . . Kevin McCarthy at the end of *Bodysnatchers* – trying to warn us? Reason enough to drink.

As to the question, 'What do you think is the greatest gift or the worst legacy of the movies?' In a sour mood today, filled with a flu and annoyed with something I missed because what I was aiming for was the wrong target, I say: the worst legacy was Bing Crosby as a priest. And the worst legacy was the plague of opinion, and all the arguments, and the vocabularies of film worship, and the ideologies that see harshly realistic movies, or even satirically realistic films, as better, because they supposedly prove the lie of *der Bingle* in a clerical collar, or that the gangster movie or the violent movie, or the movie of accurate despair is somehow better because it tells the truth, or the cinema of this genre or that genre has the answer, as though *The Professionals* in some way relieves us of the agony caused by *Pillow Talk*, as though Don Siegel is right and Stanley Kramer wrong, as though there's any real difference between Truffaut and Godard. I'm reduced to looking for movies that have no pretension, which is a pretentious quest in itself, but at least I have the Grail: the greatest gift of the movies was Laurel and Hardy. Their silly movies don't leave you with surges of adrenalin, or feelings of incompetence, or ugliness, in comparison with the swift deeds of the beautiful heroes of every other movie; they don't even make you want to go to Hollywood to make movies. *A Chump at Oxford* has a scene in a garden, where the boys sit on a bench in front of a tall hedge and Stanley tries to light his pipe. Behind him, a prankster reaches through the hedge and adds first one hand and then the other, confusing Stanley, who loses track of which hand is his. Their movies are spectacularly pointless and the anguish of the two is relentless, without either Laurel or Hardy ever asking for a feather's weight of the audience's flattery. Where even Buster Keaton wants to be loved independent of his characters, loved as the vehicle for his characters, where you see Keaton or Chaplin as actors, there is no other way to imagine Laurel and Hardy than in their roles. This isn't a trick of glamour, like Garbo's or Bogart's, but something I think only they ever achieved. For all their fame, they aren't movie stars, they don't compete with the gods. What they do is enough to qualify them as miracles: they scorn optimism without ever losing hope, which is the sort of offering that can save the world.

On the other hand, maybe the movies are great – all of them, the good and the bad. Anything to get us out of the house and give us something to chat about. Maybe Fitzgerald was blaming the wrong target. Maybe he meant radio.

Percy Adlon

I love them I hate them I love them I hate them I love them
I hate them I love them I hate them I love them I hate them
I love them I hate them I love them I hate them I love them
I hate them I love them I hate them I love them I hate them
I love them I hate them I love them I hate them I love them
I hate them I love them I hate them I love them I hate them
I love them I hate them I love them I hate them I love them
I hate them I love them I hate them I love them I hate them
I love them I hate them I love them I hate them I love them
I hate them I love them I hate them I love them I hate them
I love them I hate them I love them I hate them I love them
I hate them I love them I hate them I love them I hate them
I love them I hate them I love them I hate them I love them
I hate them I love them I hate them I love them I hate them
I love them I hate them I love them I hate them I love them
I hate them I love them I hate them I love them I hate them
I love them I hate them I love them I hate them I love them
I hate them I love them I hate them I love them I hate them
I love them I hate them I love them I hate them I love them
I hate them I love them I hate them I love them I hate them
I love them I hate them I love them I hate them I love them
I hate them I love them I hate them I love them I hate them
I love them I hate them I love them I hate them I love them

I hate them I love them I hate them I love them I hate them
I love them I hate them I love them I hate them I love them
I hate them I love them I hate them I love them I hate them
I love them I hate them I love them I hate them I love them
I hate them I love them I hate them I love them I hate them
I love them I hate them I love them I hate them I love them
I hate them I love them I hate them I love them I hate them
I love them I hate them I love them I hate them I love them
I hate them I love them I hate them I love them I hate them
I love them I hate them I love them I hate them I love them
I hate them I love them I hate them I love them I hate them
I love them I hate them I love them I hate them I love them
I hate them I love them I hate them I love them I hate them
I love them I hate them I love them I hate them I love them
I hate them I love them I hate them I love them I hate them
I love them I hate them I love them I hate them I love them
I hate them I love them I hate them I love them I hate them
I love them I hate them I love them I hate them I love them
I hate them I love them I hate them I love them I hate them
I love them I hate them I love them I hate them I love them.
I hate them I love them I hate them I love them I hate them
I love them I hate them I love them I hate them I love them
I hate them I love them I hate them I love them I hate them
I love them I hate them I love them I hate them I love them
I hate them I love them I hate them I love them I hate them
I love them I hate them I love them I hate them I love them
I hate them I love them I hate them I love them I hate them
I love them I hate them I love them I hate them I love them
I hate them I love them I hate them I love them I hate them
I love them I hate them I love them I hate them I love them
I hate them I love them I hate them I love them I hate them
I love them I hate them I love them I hate them I love them
I hate them I love them I hate them I love them I hate them
I love them I hate them I love them I hate them I love them
I hate them I love them I hate them I love them I hate them
I love them I hate them I love them I hate them I love them
I hate them I love them I hate them I love them I hate them
I love them I hate them I love them I hate them I love them
I hate them I love them I hate them I love them I hate them
I love them I hate them I love them I hate them I love them
I hate them I love them I hate them I love them I hate them
I love them I hate them I love them I hate them I love them

3   Anamorphobia
Martin Scorsese in conversation with Gregory Solman

Introduction

Up until this interview, Martin Scorsese had been one of those few film artists to whom there was so much I wanted to say, I'd have rather said nothing at all. First at college, and later in graduate film school, I analysed his work, frame by frame, immediately drawn to his sensibility. Once a production assistant allowed me a furtive view of Scorsese directing an exterior night scene on Manhattan's Upper West Side. For hours, I watched him pop in and out of a taxi cab, in which he was directing Robert De Niro, visible in the window, in *King of Comedy*. I was too distant to hear, but the intensity of his gesticulation made for a satisfying silent picture.

Finally, the right opportunity arose for our first exchange. This interview was conducted for a short piece for *Variety* on the cusp of the Artists' Rights Foundation's symposium in Beverly Hills, which Scorsese could not attend, evidently because of one of his own film-preservation causes. But earlier in the Foundation's history, he valiantly presented its case before no less formidable an audience than the US Congress. Talk about a tough house.

I'm left with an image of Scorsese that he himself conjures here: one of America's best directors and sincerest film fans, confined to his quarters, television on, restlessly distracted, no longer free to enjoy the cinema as he always had – a lifelong passion for film-making ironically thwarted by a devotion to film-making.

GREGORY SOLMAN: *I'd like to start with your comments on what I've called 'anamorphobia': a director's fear of widescreen. Since the mid-1980s, when video-cassette rentals and television sales began to supplant theatrical rentals as the studios' primary revenue stream, has there been any subtle pressure to shoot in 4:3 or spherical aspect ratios?*

MARTIN SCORSESE: Over the years, from when I saw my first widescreen movie, *The Robe*, at the Roxy Theatre in New York back in 1953, I was always very enthusiastic about the use of widescreen. I think one has to understand that the 4:3 ratio was settled upon for various different reasons at the beginning of the century. I don't think that everyone agreed that this was the best aesthetic presentation of moving images. There were certain technical pressures that resulted in the 4:3 aspect ratio. Even back in the early days of film, there were experiments with widescreen. I happened to feel that, even back in 1953, widescreen was the future. And it is now, in fact: television is going to go into widescreen presentation soon. What happened to me, though, when I finally got to make my own movies, I specifically made them in flat [spherical] formats, mainly because I knew that when they went to television, the image would be so cropped that the image would be in a sense 're-directed' technically, by a technician.

GS: *So there was a sense of self-censorship?*

MS: Absolutely. Finally, the first time I did use anamorphic lenses was only a few years ago with *Cape Fear*. So the past two films I've made have been widescreen: *Cape Fear* and *The Age of Innocence*. And I'll probably continue to use widescreen from now on because I have a feeling that television will become, to a certain extent, a widescreen format and the use of laser discs, for people who are really interested in composition, would get the original film in widescreen. And I just happen to think that, in a strange way, the use of widescreen is even more intimate than the 4:3, or even the 1.85:1 aspect ratio.

GS: *Is it perhaps explicable because of the effect on peripheral vision. One is more inside the film . . .*

MS: Exactly. Granted, it is a little hard to compose close-ups, and as much as I adore widescreen, very often when I'm thinking of a composition, I think in 4:3 aspect ratio because of my exposure to some of the old movies. I would have loved to see Orson Welles's use of widescreen, for example. When I think of the strongest compositions, I think of his films. The pressure is such that I only received a little bit of a comment, a very slight comment, about doing widescreen for *Cape Fear*. Nothing elaborate, nothing definite. Just a hint that the use of anamorphic might pose a problem for secondary markets.

GS: *One wonders how a studio might have reacted to an unknown director making the same request.*

MS: I have to say that when you are a younger director still breaking in, you may have to make concessions to get the money to make the picture. So you may not be able to use widescreen. One of the things studios don't want to hear today is widescreen black and white. That's like the kiss of death for some reason . . .

GS: *I love Philip Lathrop's work on* Lonely Are the Brave . . .

MS: Beautiful compositions and beautiful lighting. *Mean Streets* – there was no way it could have been made by a studio. It was made independently. It was picked up by a studio, but not made under studio guidance, or picked up as a script by a studio. So there are certain kinds of films you're just going to have to suffer through and claw your way through, and get as much money as you can for them.

GS: *But you're suggesting the impetus to shoot spherical is short-sighted, even when it comes to secondary distribution.*

MS: I think so. Obviously, television will be a widescreen process and widescreen TVs are already available. And when you look a few years down the line – before everything goes into a transitional state – it will finally become compatible with everything else we now have.

GS: *If it's not driven by other factors – for instance, whether or not people want to watch* Wheel of Fortune *in widescreen.*

MS: Yes, but I think news programmes might be interesting. You could put the anchor on the left or the right and then have the images going on while they're speaking over it. It could be a very, very interesting use of widescreen. And the old films, the films from 1953 on, are going to look very good; but then we're going to have the problem of showing the older films in the proper aspect ratio, called windowboxing. Who knows, maybe they'll be showing a film like *Mr Smith Goes to Washington* and Jimmy Stewart's head will be cut off because they want to do it widescreen. Well, it's impossible. But I think windowboxing is a lot easier to see as commonplace – I think it will be easier on the eyes.

GS: *We may go through a whole new round of complaints.*

MS: Right. *Citizen Kane* – Joseph Cotten's and Orson Welles's heads cut off.

GS: *'How come they're so tall and narrow?'*

MS: I know, I know. 'It looks like there's pieces missing . . .' Yes.

GS: *'I spent all this money on a widescreen TV . . .'*

MS: Right. 'And now they show all these old movies.' So we're going to have all these problems the opposite way. But pretty much every film from 1953 on will be given a really good chance to be seen in its original aspect ratio. Because the composition in widescreen – the use of the wide frame for dramatic structure, the use of a close-up in the foreground and a figure in the background, whether it is all in focus or it is slightly off on one character or the other – it all emphasizes things in a different way. And the compositions tell the story. You look at a film panned and scanned and take a look at the same film on a corresponding monitor letterboxed. You'll see the difference, because with the panned and scanned films on television, half the information is missing, which means half the story-telling is missing. The film is not as effective.

One of the things a director does is aim the lens in the direction in which he wants the audience to be able to understand the story, to make a dramatic and intellectual point. So when you only have half of that . . . Very often I look at something that is panned and scanned on TV and I see a person all the way on the left of the frame and nobody on the right. I tell the people I'm with, 'Apparently there is somebody over there, by the door to our room. He's over there, we can't see him now. Oh, there he is. Now we've lost her. She's over there. She's by the window.' A panned and scanned film on television has a strange, disturbingly inaccurate sense and aura about it. You don't really know.

You can't be involved with the film emotionally, and have a catharsis and really enjoy it dramatically . . .

GS: *You can't judge the artistic vision, either. When I'm watching a panned-scanned film, I'm always questioning, 'Is this just bad direction or bad pan-scanning?'*

MS: Right.

GS: *If I were watching the parking-lot scene from* Cape Fear, *for instance, I'd have to wonder, 'Are they just on De Niro here, when Nick Nolte is cowering in the foreground?' . . .*

MS: Exactly. That was our hardest shot to do pan and scan.

GS: *'Am I watching De Niro here because Scorsese wants me to, or only because he happens to be talking?'*

MS: The bottom line is, there is a distance, an ambiguity placed between the viewer and the director and the other artists who made the film, so that you really don't know what they want you to think or want you to feel, because there is something in every cut missing. It is a serious problem and it really affects the film. More than that, it affects the enjoyment of the film by new audiences watching it, who have not seen it in a theatre. As it is, it is different when you see a film on TV anyway. So imagine, panning and scanning takes it another three or four steps away from the original experience.

GS: *It is so bizarre. It reminds me of Godard's comments when they were considering putting* Breathless *on TV. He's supposed to have said something like, 'Sure, you can put it on TV, as long as you colourize it and insert commercials with car crashes at specified moments.' It was as if Godard were saying, 'Play* Breathless *on television, but don't pretend that it's* Breathless.'

MS: Right. Make it television. It is very hip to do that, too. He's so hip. He's ahead of everybody, all the time. Put it on TV, you know, put commercials with car crashes, colourize it, crop it, who knows? It's a good point, because it becomes something else.

GS: *New devices in broadcasting will increase the practice of time-compressing programming for commercial insertion, with digital technology masking the audio pitch shift. Isn't a film's temporality essential to it as a work of art? How about the art of editing and directorial pacing, as well as the psychological importance of a movie's internal beats and moments?*

MS: Well, this is obviously another serious problem – probably even more serious, I think, because time compression is an insidious device. The audience watching it on TV, especially on cable stations . . . films are time compressed without the audience knowing. You may say, 'What's the reason?' So they can get it into a time-slot. The [next programme] has to start at eight o'clock, so this has to end at a certain time. Now I thought, because you pay for cable, one of its attributes is supposed to be that you can see a film as it was in a theatre. This is not the case and the American audience doesn't understand this yet.

What happens with the pacing of a film is that it's altered. The timing is altered and ultimately the timing of the actors is altered. So that what happens is, you may be watching something on television and you may feel that it wasn't as effective as when you saw it in a theatre. You might just attribute that to the fact that it is being shown on television now, but that's not the case. If you can sometimes lock yourself into watching a picture on television ... It's not the best way of seeing a film, but if you don't interrupt, if you don't pick up the phone, if the lights are dimmed and you are watching this experience, maybe on a bigger screen TV, you know, you get a pretty close semblance of what it might be like to see it projected on film – maybe. You can study it. You can study composition. You can study acting.

Now imagine somebody studying acting off a time-compressed tape. Imagine even more so, that for casting a film, I have to look at some actor's work and they send me some tapes, or they say, 'Marty, this was on HBO or cable the other night, do you have a copy of it?' And I say yes. 'Well, look at this scene with this person.' So I'm watching this scene and it's off cable which has been time compressed, and the man or woman doesn't get the job.

GS: *It's affecting your ability to judge their work correctly.*

MS: Absolutely. And there is an overall emotional impact a picture has – indeed, most films have. When you speed it up, it loses its effectiveness. It really does. As it is, when a film is on television, it has to fight everything else that is going on around the room in the house. If you like a movie when you watch it on TV, that's pretty good, because the damage that is done between everything else that is in the room – the telephone ringing, people coming in and out, and people talking – even if you are alone, you look out the window and you can see certain things on the street as you are watching the film. It is very different from being in a locked environment, where the image is the only light coming off the screen, everything else dark around it, with the right kind of sound. If a film fights through all of that, it must be pretty effective. But now, add to this time compression. And, by the way, the station's not telling you that it's time compressed ... If I am not mistaken, some of this is even going on in the video industry, too, to squeeze a film all on one tape.

GS: *Yes. I've returned several videos that weren't even recorded at the highest quality speed. One of them was* Southern Comfort, *which was recorded ...*

MS: EP?

GS: *Not even EP. It was recorded at ... you know, the one for getting six hours on a regular-length tape?*

MS: SLP?

GS: *Yes.*

MS: People might wonder, 'Why are they being so picky about these things?' Well, the reality is, it goes deeper into the soul of our country, what we feel, what we can be proud of, and what we can nurture, sustain and cherish from our patrimony. And the fact that it is 100 years of cinema coming up this year ... Well, the thing about it is, to take a real sense of responsibility for this art form, which is basically American, and to be proud of it, to cherish it and to take care of it and utilize it to teach, educate, and finally to *admit* that it is an art form. That doesn't mean that everybody who makes movies has to say, 'Well, I'm an artist.' But whether you like it or not, you are. What that means is that there are good artists, bad artists and mediocre artists, but they're artists whether you like it or not.

GS: *And that makes the critical distinction between film as art and film as product. All of this tends to treat it as product. It is interesting that you talk of it as an American art form, and it leads me to wonder, if we treat film this way, what is our moral right to prevent other countries from maltreating our films worse than they're treated here, though it's hard to imagine they would.*

MS: We don't have a chance, then. It has to do with film's close proximity to commerce. I mean, a movie has to be projected, or it even has to go into software, into video, and to make a movie, it is the old story. It doesn't cost just the paints and the canvas, or the blank piece of paper that you can use a pen to write with, it costs millions of dollars in most cases. So you do have an ultimate responsibility, I think, to help the people who gave you that money, make some of that money back. That's not asking a lot. That means it has to be shown in a commercial situation, a commercial venue ...

GS: *But at any cost to the art?*

MS: That's the fine line the Artists' Rights Foundation is trying to walk. That fine line always gets overlapped, back and forth, back and forth. We have to draw some restrictions around that area. That's why the Artists' Rights Foundation is speaking up now and has done in the past few years.

GS: *Did you see the Robert Aldrich festival, by the way? One critic I talked to saw a really good print of one of the films, he enquired about it and was told that it had come from Aldrich's personal library. What's your general response to directorial stewardship? Should directors insist upon a print of any film they make?*

MS: If I can get one, I like to get a 35mm. I put it in a vault and it's not shown. I think it is more important for a director to have in his contract with the DGA that every film should have YCMs made. That is the preservation material. Since the studios do own the film and they give you anywhere from $1 million to 50 or 60 – maybe more in some cases – to make it, they are very nervous about prints being out there, outside the auspices of the studios. Rightly so, and if you ever do get a print like that, you have to be very careful not to show it. You have to sign contracts guaranteeing that the film will not be shown for

*YCM elements are black-and-white separations made from a color print for long-term storage. A film laboratory can reconstitute an exact record of the original color by passing the YCM through the primary filters of Red, Green and Blue.

commercial profit anywhere, that's most important. But I think, even more importantly, every studio should be doing YCMs on their pictures automatically. Now, this may be an issue about whether a studio wants to do it themselves as a matter of policy. As a point of honour, they may not welcome this coming down as an edict from the union. I think many of the studios today, working with the film foundation that I have, are very much aware that they have to preserve the films they have.

GS: *I was talking with Allen Daviau yesterday and he told me that one of the studios, I think it must have been Tri-Star, destroyed the original material from a Barry Levinson film. I guess that was a matter of policy. The nightmare, I remember – not fondly, because I did my master's thesis on it – was Paramount destroying an archive print of* Days of Heaven *by mistake, when they thought they were destroying extra prints of* Days of Thunder.

MS: Oh, my God.

GS: *There were probably cans of* Days of Thunder *sitting around and they were thinking, 'This is going to get out and somebody is going to have a free Tom Cruise festival.' So they destroyed one of the last-remaining originals.*

MS: These are tragedies. But I must tell you, most, not all studios – and we're only talking about five or six – are trying their best to have some sense of what's valuable, where it is, what's in each can, to start off with. *Days of Thunder* is not *Days of Heaven.* So that's a mistake somebody did in a logging situation and it's a nightmare. And imagine – that's a new film! Imagine what they do when they try to find something made in 1933 or 1942.

GS: *And this gets worse as the digital era dawns on us.*

MS: The market for films in the future, on digital, video, laser, whichever new device will come forward in the future, is only going to be as good as the elements from which they are making those films. I believe that. And granted, you can clean up bad elements on video and on laser, digitally, to a certain extent. But quite honestly, the better an image looks, the more it's going to look like a new movie. A lot of these incredible films on TNT and American Movie Classics, they have very beautiful black and white – it looks as if they were shot yesterday. It's amazing because these are either coming off the original negatives or some very good elements.

GS: *That's an important point segueing off into supervision of transfer. Would you want to sign off on a YCM, or is that too cut and dry?*

MS: The problem is, you'd have to keep a record of the original timing. And that's a problem, because you may want to restore a film or make a new print from the YCMs . . .

GS: *Maybe that's what they should use digital for, for keeping these records. Put it to good use.*

MS: Yes, if the people who made the film are no longer around, or they're dead, well, you have to go back to the original records as best you can. In one case recently, when prints were made of a widescreen colour film, some scenes were shot day-for-night and they were printed in the new films as daylight. So that the people were wondering, 'Why is everyone running around as if they can't be seen? Everybody can be seen – it's daylight.'

GS: *That must have been embarrassing, seeing people cowering and peering in the light. It's become a vampire movie, everyone afraid of the light.*

MS: Well, *that's* an interesting thing. Over the years, we've seen *Nosferatu*, the great vampire film by Murnau, only in black and white, and we wondered why everyone was running around in daylight. How could a vampire be running around in daylight? The point is that it wasn't tinted. In the original all the night scenes were tinted blue. The restoration that was made, I think in Germany, in the past five years, and that you can now see on laser disc and video, has the original tinting. The tinted blue sequences, or night sequences, create a whole other atmosphere. It is quite beautiful.

GS: *Do you supervise the tele-cine transfers of your films?*

MS: In most cases I do. Basically, I try to supervise the laser transfer and the video transfer as much as possible; when it goes to network television, it is supervised by myself or my producer; and, in all three instances, as much as possible by the director of photography.

GS: *So that is a good assignation for you?*

MS: You have to try. You have to understand, if you make the kind of film that I usually make – which has some bad language, some violence in it – when a film goes to network, it goes into people's houses unsolicited, so the film has to be cut and there has to be commercials in it, and it becomes a TV show. It's something else entirely.

GS: *Now that cable provides a viable commercial venue for the airing of motion pictures uncut and uncensored, should directors enjoy the right to restrict airings of their motion pictures to cable?*

MS: Well, that doesn't mean that directors shouldn't show their films on network television. I think that whatever outlet you can get for the film, fine. But they are different forms and that's why the Artists' Rights Foundation is dealing with the idea of labelling, to let people know that this is not the original form of the film.

GS: *And that labelling ought to be expanded, shouldn't it? Because they usually say that something's been edited for television and I'm not sure that's sufficient for me. But what would you think of a director who says that his films should only be shown on cable. Is that being too unreasonable?*

MS: Yes, well, you used the word unreasonable. It's up to them. I gotta tell you, if they give you $25 million to make a picture, you can't say that it can only be shown on cable. They'd say, 'You have to be realistic about this. We have to make some money back. What are you talking about?'

GS: *I'm talking about the possibility that when they gave me the $25 million, they were* *making a tacit assumption about how that film would do upon theatrical release.*

MS: Oh, no. There's no such thing. I think the theatre might be the least of all, unless you're making the kind of film that makes a great deal of money, like a Spielberg film and that sort of thing. The theatre presentation of a film is less money, I think. The ancillary markets are what's really important.

GS: *I know and that's very frightening to me. As they become more and more imperious about intervening in the film-making process, the secondary markets are the greater revenue streams. Do you agree, at least, that that's problematic in a sense?*

MS: It is. But you have to find your way through that maze as a film-maker. You have to be able to make the picture work in these different markets as best as possible. For me, the type of film I usually make, I find, is least represented on national television and that I can't help. Because *Taxi Driver*, at six o'clock at night while people are having dinner, unedited, for a nine-year-old kid, is not right. It just is not right. I don't particularly mind that kind of thing because . . .

GS: . . . *Because you are realist?*

MS: Pretty much. About that sort of thing, yes.

GS: *Well, when does that start intruding on the process? When does it affect the front end? When does an artist start telling himself, 'I won't make a* Taxi Driver *because for more than 60 per cent of the time, this is going to be seen on television'?*

MS: Who's saying I won't make a *Taxi Driver*: the studio or the film-maker?

GS: *When does the artist start thinking that way?*

MS: The artist can't think that way. If the artist really is an artist, they've got to make the films they've gotta make. What you may have to do is accept the fact that you may not be able to get a whole lot of money, but you find a way to make the film for very little, so there is less of a risk for the studio to give you that money, because you are dealing with certain, difficult subject matter. You have to do it, even if you have to make the film and draw the pictures yourself. You have to want to make that film really strongly. You can't let any idea of how that film is going to be presented afterwards deter you from that. When you get to that bridge, you cross it. If you are only going to make films you think are going to be shown, then I don't think you'll ever get to make a movie. You know?

GS: *I suppose the opposite problem can arise. For instance, how Paramount refused to give Peter Bogdanovich's film a theatrical release. I imagine, as an artist, that would mean a great deal to you . . .*

MS: Yes.

GS: *In this case, considering the other films that they put out last year, it's amazing they chose not to put out* The Thing Called Love.

MS: I don't know. I kind of stay here in my house. I didn't even know that the film was not put out. There are a number of pictures . . . Nick Roeg back in the early 1980s, his films were not released. Bogdanovich now. It is a dangerous situation. It seems to me they make a choice depending on how much money it will take to open a film and sometimes they feel it's not worth it. It is a very dangerous situation. That's why I feel to a certain extent film-makers have to beat everybody at their own game and make films as cheaply as possible. Unless, as I say, you are into a Spielbergian situation, where a film that you make has the potential of making $300 million. That's something else.

GS: *So, can we protect films from being compressed, for instance, or pan-scanned?*

MS: At this stage, I don't think we can. The only thing we can do is talk about it like we are now, go on television and talk about it, and put a label in front of the film. Very often studios say the audiences won't watch a film if a label goes on before it, but I find that it is not true. Especially if a film has commercials in it, you already know it's been cut. I'll look at *Midnight Cowboy*, for example, on a syndicated station, edited. I tend to look at it. It isn't the original film, but I still look at sections of it.

GS: *And if they're so convinced that what they are doing is great, why should they be ashamed of admitting it?*

MS: I know. I know.

GS: *They should be* bragging *about colourization if they think it's such a great idea.*

MS: I know.

GS: *I've made the argument in the past that even if the choice* was *economic to make a film in black and white, then that is an ideological statement on behalf of the people who put up the money: 'This subject matter doesn't merit colour.'*

MS: That, in itself, is important. Black and white is a whole other issue. It's never really black and white; it's shades of grey. Blacks, whites, shadows ... shadows mean something. The tone of the grey means something in the frame. You know what I mean? ... It creates an emotional and psychological point. It conveys an idea, by the use of tones, and greys and blacks and whites. Once you try to pump colour into it – where it just wasn't meant to be – the image just doesn't hold it. And the emotional impact of the film is diffused.

GS: *And it's no argument to say, 'Turn off the colour,' either.*

MS: That doesn't happen any more, no.

GS: *Well, it isn't true either, is it? Once they've colourized a film, they've ruined the black and white, basically.*

MS: That's right. Because if you do have a television set in which you can turn your colour down, well, of course, the greys and whites and blacks are very different from the original black and white. But I don't know how many films are being colourized any more.

GS: *I understand they have new and better ways of colourization and we're awaiting the digital onslaught. Whether or not we've stopped them with our arguments, I don't know. I think it's more likely that people don't like colourized films.*

MS: I was just going to say that people don't seem to like them, and the only thing that is going to stop them is if it doesn't make money. I think that's what's happening. I'm not quite sure, but I think it may not be as lucrative as they thought. It costs a lot of money to colourize, so what's the point?

GS: *I find it interesting that in the music-video world they tend to use black and white* . . .

MS: Constantly . . .

GS: . . . *and they also letterbox, even stuff shot in video, to give it the essence of film, which* . . .

MS: . . . Which is just amazing.

GS: *It's just completely* opposite *artistic sensibilities. You have people trying to fake that they are making films when they don't have the means to do it, then people have a film before them and the opportunity to play it as a film, and they* . . .

MS: . . . They won't do it. It's a kind of schizophrenia. It's madness . . . I have to run. You know, we could talk for hours about this, because I can see you really enjoy the movies, so we could have a lot of fun, but I've got to go.

The Journal

The centrepiece of each Projections *has been the film-maker's journal. As a diarist we needed someone — as David Thomson says in his Introduction — 'who had the haunted soul of an outsider along with the privileged position of an insider'. This perfectly describes James Toback, the writer of* The Gambler *(filmed by Karel Reisz, 1974) and* Bugsy *(filmed by Barry Levinson, 1991); writer/director of* Fingers *(1977),* Love and Money *(1980),* Exposed *(1983),* The Pick-Up Artist *(1987) and* The Big Bang *(1989).*

James Toback (photo by Brian Hamill)

4   Divisions and Dislocations:
A Journal for 1994
James Toback

Introduction – David Thomson

Not too many American film-makers would own up to keeping diaries. As in Washington, so in Hollywood, the diary can become an incriminating document – of those in power and of those who must button their public lip so as not to offend power. In so many cases a diary might reveal little more than the days of waiting, the humiliation and the impotence of the diarist. Nor should we assume that every film-maker can write well enough. There are plenty of movie directors who are failed novelists. So we needed someone who could write; who *would* write – out of pure, altruistic self-obsession; who could be dangerously candid; and who had the haunted soul of an outsider along with the privileged position of an insider. This is Jim Toback.

We have been friends a long time. For my part, this is because of his rogue charm, his endless capacity for telephone gossip, his generosity, his lack of pomp, his zest for existential limits, his humour, his relentless adhesion to youth and the entertainment of wondering how much to believe.

I guessed the diary would be crazed, insightful about the business, insolent, startling, rhapsodic and very personal. It could also celebrate Jim's fiftieth birthday. I supposed that as a practising Hollywood person, he would have to be discreet about many things – but I relied on the likelihood that his telling me those things anyway would offer a way of getting them into the diary. There always seemed the possibility that Toback, the unique yet variable film-maker, might find himself in a kind of writing that harked back to Dostoyevsky.

Getting the 'text' out of him was an education. Jim's diary describes someone who has difficulty coming to completion. By last June, Tom Luddy and I had urged him to start sending us pages. Aha, he said, and then admitted a few problems: he did not really type, and no one else could read his handwriting. So, we worked it out that he would record the diaries and we would get them typed. Thus, micro-cassettes began to arrive – after so many calls that I became admiring of Warren Beatty's icy, ingrowing patience with Jim. (We had angry rows, accusations of falsehood, with beguiling accounts of block, mishap and loss from Jim.) One day, someone should issue this diary on tape, for I think it is most itself in Jim's seductive voice, supplying punctuation while warding off bystanders, all against the mixed backgrounds of Manhattan streets, a 747 above America, the subway, the surf at Malibu and a few sounds I cannot quite identify – or believe.

Prologue

David Thomson calls to suggest that I write a film-related diary for the coming year. The idea is at once appealing and appalling – which means that I'll do it. I have a centrally rooted need to prefer 'yes' to 'no', action to inertia, aggression to passivity, initiative to response – a mode of reassurance that I'm alive rather than dead, or conspicuously dying. Of course, I *am* dying every day. (*La vie est une malaise fatale*, as my high-school French teacher, Harry Heller, used to remind us compulsively.) But I fear the death of those I love far more than I fear my own death. Mine, I suspect, I'm looking forward to a bit; ready, if not eager.

It is appealing, because I have so many interior voices at war that it can only be salubrious to give expression to one in the clear register of print for half an hour a day. My old friend, Jeremy Larner, political speech-writer and screenwriter (*The Candidate*), implored me twenty years ago to start a diary and, with an uncharacteristically detached sense of helplessness, I've regularly regretted not having taken him up on it.

It is appalling, because I've already spent far too much time talking, writing expositionally, fucking around, discussing and drifting, and far too little time writing and directing the movies which it is my deepest passion and driven responsibility to make. (What am I without it? What function do I serve? What despair lurks as the price for not delivering?) Warren Beatty, personal and cinematic communicant, would say – *will* say, I'm sure, when I tell him about this task I've undertaken, a task to which he would rather yield a pinkie than embrace – 'I'm glad you have so much free time on your hands. I guess the script you're doing for me which is now nineteen months late must be finished and ready to be shot.'

I hear that voice and agree with it. I also – *pace* James Caan's Axel Freed in my first script, *The Gambler* – agree with Dostoyevsky's underground man, who ridicules the Platonic notion that one need only demonstrate rationally that two and two equal four to get all the world in step, and who posits instead the idea that man lays claim to his own individuality precisely by reserving the right to insist that two and two equal five in the face of all contradictory proof. I am indeed working through the last stages of my nineteen-months-late *Shrink* and plan to read it to my communicant WB sometime soon. *Shrink* is a dark comedy about a psychiatrist whose complex obsessions and false fronts – whose sickness – reduce the problems of most of his patients to shame. Beatty took me and the idea to Tri-Star and got my former agent and his old friend,

Mike Medavoy (since deposed as studio head), to advance me a considerable sum of money.

'*How* soon?' he accuses.

'Sooner than you think,' I reply.

'It's already far too late to be any sooner than I think,' he responds.

Bugsy was years late. (Although I did make *The Pick-Up Artist* and my personal favourite, *The Big Bang*, along the way.) And while a perfidious sin shouldn't be cited as extenuating circumstances in defence of a venial one, I still believe that no matter how much rethinking and rewriting lies ahead in any movie which looks to have a feel of life, it is urgent to believe completely in one's work before showing it to anyone (except, perhaps, a typist). After delivery, one will never have the same luxury of unfettered reinvention.

State the fact: I am late, habitually, in all areas of my life except one – shooting a movie. (Ultimate self-preservation: sometimes two and two *do* equal four.)

At any event, a diary, or journal, *ipso facto*, cannot be in arrears. Either it exists in its ongoing syncopated regularity, or there is no diary at all. But it cannot be crafted late.

1 January

Phone talk throughout the day with my three movie regulars and great, dear friends: the aforementioned, beloved WB; the smart, witty talented *Landsmann*, Barry Levinson; and my agent of sixteen years, Jeff Berg, the chairman of ICM (it never hurts to be close to a chairman), who has throughout felt very much like a brother (of which he has three in blood and I, none). I could in fact make this movie journal little more than a compendium of the conversations I have with these three Hollywood stars, all of them more powerful in the industry – according to any of those 'hundred most' lists so favoured by glossy magazines this past decade – than your humble diarist, but I'll go for variety instead. Besides, increasingly the substance of my talks with each of these communicants has become well-intentioned queries and (excepting Barry) pressures on the two scripts I should have finished already and started shooting: *Shrink* and *Harvard Man*. (*Harvard Man*, I should note, is a script which, unlike *Shrink*, I am writing on speculation. For a writer–director, particularly one with a constitutional inability to hold on to money, this is akin to a high-wire walker performing without a net below.)

When Warren, Barry and I made *Bugsy* we were, for about a year, physically and psychologically all but inseparable. Since then, Barry has made two movies: *Toys* and the terrifically funny, skilful and engaging *Jimmy Hollywood*, several rough versions of which I have seen with great delight during the past month as his post-production journey comes to a conclusion. Warren has written, produced and starred in *Love Affair*, an elaborate and stylishly elegant remake of *An Affair to Remember* and the earlier Boyer–Dunne *Love Affair*. Jeff Berg has set and shepherded the deals of forty movies. I, on the other hand – while I did write some scenes for Warren on *A Love Affair* – have achieved, as of this moment, nothing to speak of since *Bugsy*. I do have *Shrink* and I do have *Harvard Man*. But a movie is more than a script in the hands of its author. One moves, analogically speaking, from masturbation to romance to orgy in the conception and execution of a film. I am still a step away from romance on both projects.

3 January

All these movies are coming out and I'm seeing none of them. Each time I start to go I think I should be writing instead. I should be organizing, planning, casting, budgeting. Somehow, watching basketball on TV, listening to Mahler and Bach, reading books and magazines and newspapers, running around LA, driving with the top down directionlessly in the smog-filtered sun – these don't seem like illegitimate distractions. But going to a movie does, until I've finished my own work. I see the clips of these movies and interviews. Endless self-promotion. Everybody is (or should be) embarrassed by it, but nobody seems to be and everybody does it (myself, to be sure, included). It's not unlike looking in a mirror and smiling at oneself, while flashing a wink and saying, 'Hi! You're pretty cute.' The bombardment of the E! channel, *Entertainment Tonight*, *Hard Copy*, CNN *Showbiz Today*, clips on review spots, clips on the morning shows, the guests on the morning shows, endless babble which finally makes one say, 'I've got to get out of here. I've got to escape from other movies into my own.'

14 January

Tom Luddy, Agnieszka Holland and Barbet Schroeder join me for dinner at the Peninsula Hotel in Beverly Hills, where I'm staying in lavish circumstances far beyond, as always, my chronically depleted means. (My philosophy has long been: spend or charge now, pay later, and if you don't have it, try to find a way of getting it when the time comes.) They have miles to travel, while I need simply to take an elevator down to the dining room. And yet it is I who arrive half an hour late. To explain my compulsive need to find a way to be late, to keep people waiting, in a conventional Freudian fashion (i.e., the demonstration to myself and to others of my importance) is too bald to be interesting; to explain it any other way is too evasive to be credible. So I'll move on to the meal – an occasion of genuine exhilaration, not so much for the specific philosophical or psychological content as for some odd rhythmic balance that is naturally achieved. The overriding subject is Getting Movies Financed by Studios, an entirely unremarkable topic of conversation for three directors and a producer, on the face of it. What is remarkable is the almost sensual instinct for timing in the delivery of anecdote and repartee. Each has a role in fine balance with the others. And despite his and her share of success, each is perennially on the run, never secure or sure of anything, except his, or her, own ability and needs. Curiously, I can't remember much of what is said, only how sharply I enjoy saying and hearing it. If I drank, I would suppose I was drunk. But I haven't had a sip of alcohol since 31 January 1983, and no drugs since 1965 when I flipped out for eight days on LSD, the seminal event of my life (a nearly life-ending journey which I took with the naïve intention of experiencing madness, hardly understanding that madness was, by definition, a mental state without control and, therefore, potentially without end). Declining any accusations of Alzheimer's, I suggest that the proper analogy for the dinner would be to volleyball, where each member of the team keeps tapping and popping at the right moment to stop the ball hitting the ground.

I'm not completely blank. I do ask Barbet about Idi Amin, the subject of his marvellous documentary about the paradigmatic ex-dictator of Uganda. He fills us in – the black Blimp is living in Saudi Arabia with many children and a few wives. The Saudis take good – if not great – care of him as thanks for his conversion to Islam and efforts to spread it around his sad and now AIDS-infested nation.

The evening makes me aware of how infrequently I spend time with (or, for that matter, have anything at all to do with) people who make movies – other than the law firm of Beatty, Levinson and Berg. Harvey Keitel and Karel Reisz, Don Simpson and Robert Towne, there *are* others, but I've been afraid that becoming a film *professional* and active member of the 'community' is the inevitable precursor to making movies about *movies* instead of movies about what Don Simpson, in *The Big Bang*, calls 'life in quotes'. Is a subway, in other words, preferable to a limousine? Since the self is an 'act' to begin with, does one need to remind oneself any more than is absolutely essential that one's work is, at bottom, pretence? The only reason to spend time with people making movies would, by this logic, be if one were planning to make a movie about people making movies. Otherwise, one's time would best be spent in the company of the gangsters, doctors, children, prostitutes, or priests one is next planning to explore in film.

Still, it is a ball laughing with three smart, likeable, witty, engaging film people.

The Earthquake (17 January)

Lying in my large and comfortable bed in the Peninsula Hotel, I wake up to the rumblings and shakings of ... the second Big Bang. I've been in previous earthquakes, six or seven of them, but the cumulative impact of all put together doesn't come close to the cataclysmic effect of this bomb. It's as though the shaking won't stop. And although one is later to find out that the actual duration was forty-five seconds for the first blast and fifteen for the second, since one doesn't know how long each blast is going to last, each feels as though it is going to last until the destruction is complete.

In retrospect I feel pleased to the point of smugness that I didn't panic. In fact, even with hysteria and panic just beneath the surface (a line I'm lifting from Rudolph Nureyev's role in *Exposed*), I responded with near-glacial detachment. I thought, 'What must I get hold of before I run outside?' *Harvard Man* and *Shrink*. No time for anything else. Unxeroxed, non-databased, the only copies being those resting on the hotel desk, I grabbed my notebooks and ran into the hallway. Ten or so frenzied guests in bathrobes or underwear were already screaming and bumping into each other. I, having fallen asleep in jeans, a shirt and a blazer, found the emergency exit and pointed to it as if leading a charge. 'This way!' I shouted, feeling consciously like John Wayne. The crowd followed as I opened the door and ran downstairs and outside into the courtyard in front of the hotel. Pandemonium in pitch black, with a few transistor radios in the centre of huddles of people, revealing stabs at news. But the confusion was clearly as overwhelming in the minds of the reporters as in the minds of those hungry for knowledge of their fate.

The effect of celebrity – knowing no bounds, not even those of natural disaster – is operative from the start. Whispers identify Michael Bolton, Elle MacPherson and Gerry Levin of Time Warner (scurrying about with his cellular phone trying to locate a plane). I don't exempt myself. I was quite taken by the sight of Tony Bennett, who appeared to have spent the evening preparing himself for the occasion in full and elegant coif. We looked at each other for a moment, and then I said, 'I think we met the night of the Academy Awards with Danny Aiello in the Polo Lounge.'

'That's right,' he said, 'but Danny did most of the talking.'

'Well,' I said, 'it looks as if we'll have a chance to start a relationship now.'

He laughed and I felt an immediate sense of rapport with this legendary figure, whose singing had reached me and moved me in a way that few if any popular singers had when I was in high school. I launched into riffs on the death of California as a viable state, watching earnest nods of affirmation from the man who, with 'I Left My Heart in San Francisco', was probably more responsible for the elevation of the image of the state than any other twenty singers this century. He talked about an earthquake in Japan when he was singing with Count Basie twenty years ago, an earthquake he slept through. Ian McShane, a wonderful British actor whom I used in *Exposed* in 1983 but whom I haven't seen since, appeared out of nowhere with his wife, and after introductions, he and I picked up as if there had been no interruption at all between our last day of shooting and this odd, dark moment in the Peninsula courtyard.

There was something oddly splendid about this sense of being stranded in darkness and space, but not so splendid that my primary conscious thought was other than to find a way to the airport and get out on whatever contraption might be flying. I was struck by how thin and flimsy my allegiance to this second home in fact was. I had, after all, spent half my adult life in the Los Angeles area, had done most of my setting up, much of my pre-production, most of my post-production work there, and had shot one full movie, *Love and Money*, in the area. There were also friends and a sense of camaraderie stronger than I now feel when returning to New York where, with the exception of my family, few if any remain. Clearly, this was a place of work, not a home, because I did not feel any sense of treachery, abandonment or cowardly flight which, in retrospect, should have been at least vaguely present in my mind.

With dawn, I bribed the parking attendant to get my rented Mustang convertible out of the garage, a feat he had finished only seconds before telling several people it was impossible. (Just because I'm ready to die, doesn't mean I'm willing to be buried alive in rubble.) Who knows what rage he had to face from other ship-jumpers after I sped off unaware of what holes in the earth I might be driving into. Ever since my acid flip-out, when faced with death I have been able to click into a state of readiness for it which frees me from the normal panic one observes in life-ending or life-threatening circumstances. Rather than listening to news of the catastrophe on the radio, I played tapes – Brahms's German Requiem, with Otto Klemperer conducting, and the end of the St Matthew Passion – appropriately dirgeful music. If LA isn't a wasteland under ordinary circumstances, it certainly was this morning. The only noticeable faces and bodies on the drive to the airport seemed like extras who had wandered out of *Mad Max* or its sequel. When I got to the American Airlines terminal, I parked my Mustang – or, more precisely, Budget Rent-a-Car's Mustang – at the curb and rushed in to buy a ticket. Budget would have to find its car in its own way, as I was not to be distracted by the contractual responsibilities of automobile return. The only flight to New York was full, but bribery again saved the day. (Is money, after all, the answer to crisis?) A venal ticket agent accepted a crisp hundred-dollar bill slipped into his palm and escorted me to Flight 1 to JFK. A major aftershock caused the entire terminal to shake violently just before I boarded.

Somehow, finding Matthew Modine on board rendered the entire experience reunion-like, as if going back to camp or high school to see old friends.

Matthew and his wife, Cari, had fled the Beverly Wilshire which, having been built many decades before, hadn't weathered the storm so well. The deepest fear we – and Penelope Ann Miller, another escapee – seemed to have was that somehow we had violated a certain pact, a certain sense of sportsmanship. But each reinforced the other's justifications, and by the time we landed in New York, the only reason we didn't go to a party to which we had all been invited was that the plane had arrived too late.

23 January

New York seems safer to be sure, no aftershocks – as daily, even hourly, one hears of in LA. I return to Stephanie, with whom in mystery and harmony I have shared the past thirteen years (and who edited *The Big Bang* with wit and elegance). And there's a reunion with my mother who – always there for me, an indomitable force at eighty – is recovering from a deeply gashed ankle which had her in the hospital for weeks. The Mustang has been found and retrieved by Budget, so I am safe from arrest for car theft. Still, I know my obligation is to be back, working, meeting with Beatty, and the sense of abandonment felt by Beatty, Levinson and Berg is palpable. In each of the three- or four-times-daily conversations I have with them, there is a sense that I did, in fact, show a profound failure of allegiance. Which is not to say that I don't argue passionately and, I believe, persuasively that LA simply can't remain home to anyone with an eye on a prolonged future. There will be other quakes and they will be cataclysmic. There will be destruction of monumental proportions. It isn't a question of whether; only of when.

Beatty's house is basically destroyed, the house he delayed moving into for years after buying the land and building it, the house which was the first he was to inhabit after decades of hotel life. It was a house serving as a centre, a home for a new wife and new daughter, a place for work, my base of preparation for *The Pick-Up Artist* and *Bugsy*. So now he was to be a transient again, living in the Bel Air Hotel.

In the era of the much-vaunted superhighway (an era with which I feel myself to be at profound odds), with its faxes and telecommunications, who the fuck cares where one is in preparing or posting a film? Why does LA need to be the centre of film-making any more? Movies on the run, the way they should be.

27 January

I'm back in LA.

29 January

An old friend, a novelist and critic, sends me a script. What is wanted? Advice? Help? What am I going to say if I think the script is worthless or just not good enough to make? He asks for an honest and frank response, but suppose the response is 'bury it'? I almost feel like finding an excuse not to read it at all, but by page 5 I'm relieved, and by page 50, thrilled. It's a terrific script and would – will, I hope – make a great movie. When I express all this to the writer on the phone and suggest Nastassja Kinski, whom I used in the lead in *Exposed*, he is elated.

Everyone I've ever known connected with the movies, myself profoundly included, needs and loves genuine reassurance and approval, particularly in the early stages. Am I on the right track, or have I gone mad? I write everything by hand, so the first person to see what I'm doing is invariably the typist or computer whiz. More often than not, this person has no particular affinity for movies in general or me in particular, and if she or he doesn't respond properly ('My God, what a hilarious, overwhelming, riveting, devastating work of art this is! Whom are you going to allow to finance it?'), I descend instantly into paranoia. ('You didn't find that funny? You don't think it's fascinating? You didn't love the ending?')

When I was preparing *Fingers*, my production office was part of the Fabergé Brut perfume layout in the Burlington building in New York. George Barrie, the head of the company and producer of *Fingers*, had recently put his friend Cary Grant on the Fabergé board. One day, after going over a shot list with my cameraman Michael Chapman, I was stunned suddenly to see Cary himself right there in the flesh in front of me. George introduced us. Cary shook my hand, and I came up with the only line I could think of at the moment. 'I've always loved you,' I said, 'on the screen. Everything I've ever seen you in. Whatever else is going on, if you're in it, I'm hypnotized.' There ensued what to me felt like a ten-minute silence as our eyes locked. Finally, to break the silence, I added: 'I know you must hear this sort of response to you all the time, so forgive me for embarrassing you.'

Cary continued looking straight into my eyes and spoke with great passion in a quiet voice: 'Not only do I not hear all the time what you just said, I rarely hear anything like it. And far from being embarrassed, I'm immensely pleased and gratified to hear it. And if you want to say it to me every time we meet, I'll be extremely happy to listen.' At the time, I thought he was simply being polite, but six movies later I'm more inclined to believe that, to the very end, even Cary Grant needed to know he was admired.

30 January

Flying to Las Vegas for the day, I'm sitting across the aisle from Frank
Mancuso, former head of Paramount, new head of MGM. I'm travelling
alone. He is with his wife. In 1982, when he was the head of distribution at
Paramount, *Love and Money* (my least good movie, as I tend to call it) was about
to get dribbled or dripped into the marketplace under his aegis. It wasn't that I
was able to make a strong case for the financial potential of the movie, but I did
want some answers about theatres, cities and advertising. Understandably,
Love and Money was not on the top of Mancuso's list of concerns. Still, ten of
my calls over a four-day period had gone unanswered. We had never met, so
on my eleventh call I questioned his secretary.

'Have you been giving him all my messages?'

'I certainly have, Mr Toback. Hasn't he called you back?'

'No. He hasn't.'

'That's very unusual for him. I don't know what to say.'

'Here's what to say,' I improvised, letting my anger lead me and speaking
with exaggerated slowness so that my words could be transcribed precisely.
'Tell him that unless an ice pick has just been driven into the back of his head
behind his left ear and he is bleeding to death in the gutter, I will expect a call
back from him within the next thirty seconds.'

There was a pause and then: 'I will give him the message.'

Twenty seconds later, the phone rang: 'Hi, Jim, it's Frank. What can I do for
you?'

An extremely pleasant ten-minute conversation ensued, resulting in an
unplanned New York opening, modest but reasonable, and an invitation to
lunch at the Paramount executive dining room. The lunch was also friendly
and informal, and I left liking Mancuso and figuring that our paths would cross
again. 'We should work together some day,' we said to each other. Now, twelve
years later, with no contact in between, we were meeting for the second time.
What I found most remarkable was that Mancuso was not only reading a script
on this one-hour flight, but taking avid notes in the margins. I have always
assumed that no one who runs a studio actually reads any scripts; rather that
'coverage' is skimmed – a summary in judgement by a recently graduated *cum
laude*, but not *magna* and surely not *summa*, English major from Berkeley or
Brown. It appears I was wrong. We traded anecdotes. Mancuso's wife is lively
and has a nice sense of humour. Maybe we *will* work together some day.

6 February

Harvey Keitel invites me to a gathering at his Malibu beach house, rented
from Freddie Fields. It is one of the accoutrements of Harvey's late-found,

newly arrived fame that actors and directors pay court to him now – or, more precisely, come to his court. Actors and rock musicians have formed a cult fan club since *Mean Streets*, but not in nearly the numbers nor with the unadulterated intensity that is now evident. Christopher Penn, Bruce Willis, David Caruso, Quentin Tarantino, Wayne Wang – are all happy to be in Harvey's orbit. Abel Ferrara wonders what I've been doing.

'We miss you,' he says. 'We need you. You've got to get back in action.'

I cruise on to automatic pilot: 'I'm doing two things. *Harvard Man*, which is what I've been obsessed with doing for years – acid flip-out madness, basketball-fixing, sex, crime, orgasm, love, death, oblivion; and *Shrink*, with Beatty. I'm not sure which one will be first, but both will happen, back-to-back, soon.'

He's thrilled and wishes me luck. How many more times am I going to give that little speech before I start one of these two movies?

Quentin Tarantino introduces himself, professes admiration even more for *Exposed* than for *Fingers*, tells me that his interest in Harvey stemmed from Harvey's terrorist role in *Exposed* as Rivas, a character I based on Carlos. Quentin proceeds to recite nearly the entire role by heart, which Harvey overhears. Since Harvey had never felt Rivas to be his immortalizing cinematic conception, he is amused and surprised to learn of Tarantino's enthusiasm. 'Maybe I should see it again,' he laughs.

Like Cary Grant, I am excited by flattery, particularly when it comes from a source whose work I admire. But I get flashes of panic and doubt. When? *When?* Rationally, I can satisfy myself with my standard explanation. I need to prepare at greater length than other film-makers. I have to live them, digest them, write them, research and cast them, direct them, edit them, promote them. I'm never able to go from job to job, to come in on somebody else's script, to leave the editing to another consciousness. But it's hard to convince myself that I need as much time as I've taken, as much time as I'm taking now.

16 February

Stephen Dorff comes over to the Peninsula Hotel to meet me and talk about *Harvard Man*. I've seen him act with John Gielgud in a South African movie and as the romantic lead in an Aerosmith video. He's quick, witty, sharp, funny, self-effacing, arrogant, skinny, handsome, angular, hip/cool and emblematic of the new sexual and stylistic forms of desirability (at least for late teens, which is the age world with which I'm dealing).

It is difficult to reconcile myself to the fact that I'm now condemned to writing these surrogate characters, like Jack Jericho in *The Pick-Up Artist* and my *Harvard Man* protagonist, as figures half my age. *The Pick-Up Artist* was originally conceived as a movie for a man in his mid-forties, and Bobby De Niro was to play him. After a reading at De Niro's apartment, however, it became simultaneously clear to him and to me, and independently to *The Pick-Up Artist*'s shadow producer, Warren Beatty, that the idea of a man nearing fifty compulsively repeating his obsessional cruising habits was perhaps a bit too unpalatable to warrant centrality in a sunny romantic comedy – or even in a dark romantic comedy, for that matter. So we switched gears and I reconceived the role for Robert Downey, who was twenty-five years younger. When I wrote *The Gambler* I was a couple of years younger than Axel Freed/Jimmy Caan. When I wrote and directed *Fingers* I was a couple of years younger than Jimmy Angelelli/Harvey Keitel. Now, whoever my *Harvard Man* will be, he will be young enough to be my biological grandson. Were the circumstances and psychological dramas of my life so much more fascinating in the first half than in the second that only they, rather than the events of the recent past, can serve uniquely as the inspirational material for my work?

When my grandfather was ninety-six and slipping into serious confusion, I used to ask him how old he was. Once after starting with a guess of fifty, he worked his way down until I stopped him at twenty-two. I then told him his true age, to which he replied, 'That's not possible.' I said, 'Why not?' He said, 'Because it seems like only yesterday that I was four.' It seems like only yesterday that I was nineteen, running around the streets of Cambridge with a fractured, disintegrated self. Eight days in which the Kierkegaardian, Heideggerian dread, which had up to then seemed like an appealingly brooding philosophical idea, became not only my but *the* only reality on the earth.

Of course, the question of an older man writing for a younger one who is a surrogate for the older's younger self is only a short jump away from many collaborater/competitor relations: father/son, brother/brother, boss/worker, teacher/student. There is also sexual jealousy and sexual admiration, a longing to relive through the newer, fresher, younger incarnation excitements available through personal magnetism, as well as a secret need to retain supremacy. Dorff has just completed an interview for *Movieline* in which he has managed to slight, mock, ridicule or offend nearly everybody to whom he has made reference, including friends among contemporary actors. He has been chastised by his publicist and other advisers, but seems to be cheerfully unaffected by this concern for his image as a politically sensitive member of the film community. More power to him! He asks me whether I don't feel he has stepped over the boundaries of good sense a bit, which is what he has been told. I tell him I'm not a good person to ask, having accumulated a large share of enemies regularly over the years in no small measure through my own indiscreet and often insulting comments. We seem to agree that the false sense of mutual congratulation and self-congratulation which constitutes the tone of most intra-community movie talk is nauseating. So any antidote is a fresh surprise. I tell him about *Harvard Man*, rather than reading it to him. He seems to grasp the nature of the character. We move on with a promise to speak.

20 February

Barry Levinson unveils a cut of *Jimmy Hollywood*. In a small screening room in Santa Monica, Bruno Kirby (a sensationally funny actor), Peter Giuliano (Barry's producer) and a group from the editorial crew sit through what seems to me – no surprise, since I observed much of the shooting and mini-assemblages during shooting – to be a wildly original, thoroughly enjoyable, beautifully acted, poignant work of art. I can't imagine that the movie won't go down extremely well with critics (or what is left of them), reviewers, media mavens and certainly audiences. It seems so superior to anything else around in the commercial mainstream or substream, that only an unforeseeably per-verse reaction can stop it from succeeding. And it is precisely that reaction which Barry and the others seem to fear. Maybe his public whacking at the hands of the critics of *Toys* has made him wary and permanently prepared for disaster, but I believe – and tell him so – that former heroes are eventually rewarded for persevering through humiliation. Therefore, Barry will in effect receive an even better response to *Jimmy Hollywood* than he would have, in partial compensation for the wreckage of *Toys*. I have an ongoing depression about the vast majority of movies released broadly across America – the mall movies – which is the result of seeing hardly a recognizable or interesting human being presented anywhere with any kind of personal style. My depres-sion is jolted by this freshly rendered work.

I had talked to Christian Slater two years earlier about doing *Harvard Man*. This is certainly no *Harvard Man* performance, but it is a deft, dark and suitably goofy one. I want to convince myself that there are several actors who can do *Harvard Man*. To put myself ever again in the position I was in while preparing *Love and Money*, where only one actor acceptable to financiers was available and to know that he (Ray Sharkey) was entirely off the mark, would be intolerable. I am, of course, relating everything on screen and off to *Harvard Man*, to myself.

21 February

I wake up with an awful sense of emptiness. I'm glad for Barry; I feel a sense of pride and pleasure in *Jimmy Hollywood*, almost as if I've shared in its making. But I can't shake the sense of paralysis, waste and delay. Barry is working, Warren is working, everybody is working. I am watching and in wait. Day after day is going by without concrete action. Any detached observer watching my behaviour would guess that I was a creator in crisis, a creator not creating, a creator whose work is past and whose future doesn't exist. Does every writer and director, does every artist whose vision is original, who needs to start things himself, go through such awful self-doubt?

24 February

Barry asks me to see a revised cut of *Jimmy Hollywood*. I find it difficult to say no to Barry on any matter, perhaps because I've developed the habit from our collaboration on *Bugsy* in which several times a day I would hear: 'What if we tried this?' or 'How about taking a shot at that?' I was always eager to test his ideas, usually finding them sharp even when, on occasion, I had initially doubted them. I don't feel the impact of the changes in *Jimmy Hollywood*. It strikes me on second viewing to be the same superb film I felt it to be the other day.

27 February

I can't sleep. I can't think. I can't write. I can barely speak today. This has to be the most inexplicably impotent day of my adult life. I can't wait for tomorrow to see if I will feel better.

28 February

I wake up with a similar, perhaps slightly less oppressive, sense of doom. I'm embarrassed to feel this way. I feel as if I need to be productive, I need to be working, to have a chance of blasting it away. I will sit down and start writing and let nothing distract me. Barry calls and suggests another viewing of *Jimmy Hollywood* in two days.

2 March

I see *Jimmy Hollywood* for the third time and enjoy it immensely. How many movies have I been able to sit through three times without needing to hum my way out of panic? It occurs to me that the frequent screenings of *Jimmy Hollywood* suggest some kind of uncertainty on the part of, if not Barry, other people around the film. I still can't imagine why there should be any concern. I literally can't get myself to go into a theatre to watch anything else playing. On the other hand, my taste is preternaturally aberrational. Could that bode ill for Barry?

10 March

Jay Maloney, the rising young star of CAA agents, takes me out to lunch. The war going on between ICM and CAA is of sufficient intensity that one is never unaware of the representation of whichever actor or actress one looks to hire. Jeff Berg, the aforementioned centrepiece of the Beatty, Berg and

Levinson law firm, runs ICM and is among a handful of my closest friends. However, all other things being equal and perhaps even if they aren't, he will always favour an ICM over a CAA client. This habit is shared full-bloodedly by Mike Ovitz and everyone else at CAA. Since I am both Jeff's friend and client, I am not the recipient of a bombardment of offers with CAA clients attached. But on this occasion Jay Maloney seems intent on putting the idea of Leonardo DiCaprio in my mind for *Harvard Man*. Having already decided that Leonardo is the best sheer actor of his generation by a considerable distance over whoever is second, the idea immediately appeals to me, but I've read enough about *Basketball Diaries*, which he is shooting, to suspect that there are at best many superficial similarities between that work and *Harvard Man*, and at worst, that it would be inconceivable that he would want to do back-to-back, or even in the same several-year period, two films so close in so many ways. One is after all, in *Basketball Diaries*, talking about a protagonist whose heroin addiction draws him away from basketball and introduces him to his stripped-down self. *Harvard Man* concerns the loss of identity through madness induced by LSD and takes an excursion into the criminal side of college basketball. Jay insists this will not be a problem and that I should, *must*, meet Leonardo.

Any time.

15 March

Warren calls. It is not one of our normal, banter-filled, wit-competitive, daily chats. It is rather concern in the form of reprimand or reprimand in the form of concern.

'So when do you think you'll have *Shrink* in shape for me to read it, typed neatly from beginning to end?'

'I'll read it to you,' I say.

'When? Give me a date.'

'March 22nd.'

'Is that a commitment?'

'Yes,' I answer.

'Can we say that if you do not meet that commitment that you no longer consider yourself to be a serious or responsible person?'

'Yes,' I respond.

'Can we assume that your desire to make movies will have vanished completely, and that your sense of resignation as an artist will be complete if you miss that date?'

'We can assume it,' I say.

'How many years overdue are you on this script?' he asks. 'Three and a half?'

'One and a half,' I answer.

Warren says: 'Oh, I'm sure it's more than that.'

'No, one and a half.'

Warren: 'I'm sure it's at least two.'

'No, one and a half.'

Warren: 'You repeat "one and a half" as if to be only one and half years over is something of an achievement.'

'No. I'm embarrassed. I feel bad about it. I wish it hadn't happened. But when I give it to you, both of us will be glad I've waited as long as I have.'

A long pause. 'We'll see.' Click.

21 March

The returns on *Jimmy Hollywood* are catastrophic. It seems that only I regard the film as something of a personal masterpiece. I am upset for Barry, depressed at the state of movies, a state in which the one really original film out will clearly not find a place either critically or with audiences. The only question seems to be how quickly it will be removed from the 900 theatres in which it is opening next week.

I have not forgotten my date with my esteemed benefactor. Tomorrow I must perform *Shrink*.

22 March

I wake up with a knot of dread in my stomach. *Shrink* is not finished. It is as though I expected to find that the last half of the movie had somehow written itself. I do know where I'm going with the unwritten part of the script. Perhaps I can perform it for Warren, improvising as though it were already written, make it feel true enough that it will be perceived as a ready piece of work. What exactly is wrong with me? What kind of anger am I trying to provoke? What frustration? Am I out to punish the people I love and the person in whose well-being I have my highest and finest investment, namely myself? It is hard to avoid painful answers to these questions, so why the fuck don't I just finish? What am I going to say? Do I have enough time to write the last sixty pages of the script and rewrite the first sixty in ten hours?

More bad reviews for *Jimmy Hollywood*. More frustration and anger for Barry. Warren shows up at my suite in the Peninsula Hotel at eight o'clock. He is not late. I read him and Annette the first half of the script. I am surprised, shocked, at how many flaws I find in the half that is 'finished'. I am still certain that there is a great movie about a tortured psychoanalyst, the seeds of which are here. Warren seems to concur, but only about the seeds.

'How can you have done so much good writing,' he asks, 'and at the same time so little?'

He paces about the room. It is a painful moment for both of us. There is none of the levity or sarcasm which would defuse the disappointment and the anger.

'Is it *Harvard Man?*' he asks. 'Are you spending all your time on that?'

'I'm working on *Harvard Man*,' I say.

'To the exclusion of *Shrink?*'

'No.'

'Then where is it? Where is the second half that you said you would have finished?'

I point to my head. Warren doesn't laugh.

'I don't know what to say. Do you want to do this movie?'

'Yes.'

'When do you want to do this movie?'

'I will finish.'

There are no more 'when?'s There is a shake of the head, and then he says: 'Shall we order dinner?'

I order an elaborate dinner for three and we don't refer to the uncompleted script again. I expect Annette to be uneasy during these exchanges, which are reprises of dozens I've had with WB, dating back to years before he knew her. But she is such a graceful, gracious and witty presence, entirely composed, and her smiles and laughs lead us back in sync.

30 March

Jimmy Hollywood opens to reviews even worse than recently feared and to business worse than nearly any major studio release in the past twelve months. Barry seems numb, ironic, detached. I am enraged, but there is nobody to punch. What is wrong with all these people? What movie are they watching? What movie did they miss? Perhaps the problem is that movies of a certain dark temperament, with humour in places where humour is ordinarily felt to be inappropriate, have profoundly limited audience appeal, now more than ever before. The reactions to *Fingers* when it opened sixteen years ago flood my brain. A handful of presciently idolatrous reviews were drowned out by middle-brow vitriol. Even now I experience a rush of rage and wouldn't mind at all going after a few of the slanderers with a good smack. Even now it is hard for me to keep my tongue stuck in my cheek without having it slip down into my throat. There is surely some vicarious pleasure in working up this lather of rage over the wreckage of *Jimmy Hollywood*.

I can't even work up the minimal enthusiasm for the Oscars which delivery boys, postmen and secretaries feel. Maybe I think I should have been nominated for the first half of my *Shrink* script or for Best Long Preparation for a Movie – two years for *Harvard Man*, a year and a half for *Shrink*. When I was

nominated for the script of *Bugsy* in 1991, the occasion, the ceremony, were all
great fun. The crop of movies was no better than any in the last ten or fifteen
years, but because *Bugsy* was there and I had written it, it seemed as though for
that one year, the occasion was indeed worthy of the attention. Before and
since, in my absence as a nominee, the occasion has floated like so much trashy
flotsam to the level of sublime superfluity.

7 April

Another conversation with Beatty in which banter becomes brittle. He wants a
new date. I don't give him one because I no longer have confidence that I can
reach it. All my fantasy life now is centred around *Harvard Man*. I am carrying
dialogue and images and behaviour in my mind to a point where it resembles
the very madness I experienced under acid. It is a sense that what I am seeing
and hearing internally is more real and vibrant than what I am seeing and
hearing externally. The voices, as on acid, will not shut up. Conflicting,
warring, loud and soft snippets of dialogue, incantatory phrases, warring lines
of music. This is the way I'm planning to dramatize the madness of the
character in the film, and I now seem to be walking around with that madness
in my mind. But it doesn't frighten me as true madness would. Here I justify it
as preparation. This is the psychic state I will transmit to screen.

Suicide is never entirely off my mind. I get flashes, urges to jump in front of
cars, to buy a pistol and blow my brains out in the park or in the ocean. Once
one feels death as the minute-by-minute inevitability it is, there is an ongoing
temptation to seize control of the circumstances and timing. Why should one
let some drunk driver, or idly vicious person, or even one's own vascular
system in revolt, determine one's destiny? The pain one would bring to the
people who would be in despair is the obvious and quickest answer. But it is
the unfinished *Harvard Man* which, bizarrely, pops into my mind as the reason
I must not yet die. Life is incomplete without it. I actually found myself saying
out loud today at an automatic teller machine: 'That's why I'm here!'

'I beg your pardon?' the man standing next to me said.

I looked at him and said, 'I was just talking about *Harvard Man*.'

He squinted at me as if I had three heads. Am I going nuts?

13 April

Shifting focus from *Shrink* to *Harvard Man*, making a clear decision that it is
the latter which I will do next, is not going to be so simple as I thought. I was in
fact the instigator of a rather large payment that Beatty got Tri-Star to give me
in 1991. Any contractual obligations aside, emotionally I would need assent
from Beatty to move ahead on *Harvard Man* and to leave *Shrink* behind. But

Shrink has clearly made enough of a dent in his mind that he is with strong justification expecting it and by silent implication demanding it. He has been my favourite screen presence since I first saw him in *Splendor in the Grass* when I was a junior in high school and over the past sixteen years he has become my best friend. There is no one I would rather work with. There is no one I would rather direct. I also feel more confident writing for him than I do for any other actor or actress in the world. But *Harvard Man* has seized me, particularly these last few days. It is integrated into my consciousness in a way that no movie ever has integrated itself before.

17 April

I fly from New York to Cambridge. I realize that I must start to immerse myself in the mundane realities of Harvard life. I must start to eavesdrop on conversations, to watch students of all stripes, to go to basketball games, to sit in on classes. I've done this in a spot-check way over the past three years, but now I need to do it in earnest. There is an innate flashback sense of connection with undergraduate life simply by walking these largely unchanged streets.

My old dorm rooms in Leveret Towers and Thayer North erase three decades in one second. I am stunned when I meet the present occupant of Leveret F42. He is angelic in appearance, with smooth, hairless skin and an ingratiating smile. He is well-muscled without being bulky. Could he be *Harvard Man*? I take his name and number.

He asks how long ago I lived in Leveret Towers, and I say, 'Oh, I guess it's been twenty years.' His jaw drops. 'My God,' he says, 'I wasn't even born when you were living here.'

I ask him if he has ever thought about acting and he says, with a sly smile: 'Only during the last minute when you told me you were a director.' It occurs to me that an invisible presence observing everything from my entrance in the room to this moment would suspect gay cruising on my part.

'You ever do any LSD?' I say.

'Acid?' He looks around to make sure no one else is in the 12-by-8-foot cell. 'Not recently,' he whispers.

'Is there a lot of it at Harvard now?' I ask.

He nods gravely.

'What about people flipping out?'

He looks confused.

'Going insane,' I say. 'Losing your mind.'

'Yeah, I guess so. Sure,' he says. 'You mean like for a minute or two?'

'No,' I say. 'For eight days.'

'Eight days? Wow!' He seems overwhelmed. 'You might as well just kill yourself if you feel insane for eight days. Is that what happened to you?'

I nod. And then I feel a flash of barely contained panic. I am suddenly back in the moment when it started: after several hours of ecstasy (aural and visual hallucinations of ethereal beauty), when John Rich – classmate, friend and acid vet – says, 'It never ends,' snapping me into the void. No self left. No 'I'. Just the noise of words with no inherent meaning; cacophonous voices rattling inside my head. Controlling the panic is essential. Once it takes hold, there is no control. I slap him on the shoulder, pinch his cheek, look him in the eye and say, 'You're a cute guy. You're gonna be a major force some-where. Maybe in this movie. I gotta run.' I dash out quickly to the elevator, a rickety, grey contraption, and press the lobby button.

Halfway down, it stalls. To a lifelong claustrophobic this is not a pleasant circumstance. One could even go so far as to say it is bordering on torture to be stuck in a self-service elevator with the dimensions of a kitchen closet. *Fingers* is the only movie I know of in which the protagonist is stuck in an elevator, a womb entrapment experience which Harvey Keitel took to with suitable and chilling hysteria. Here *I* am, stuck in the Leveret House elevator, close to flipping out twenty-nine years after the fact. I manage to find a perverse and nasty irony in this dreaded enclosure and actually start to laugh. I sing three 1950s rock 'n' roll songs to myself with fervour and volume. The echoing of the elevator walls conceals the limitations of my tenor voice. 'First a boy and a girl meet each other/Then they sit down to talk for a while/In your heart you want her for a lover/As each step draws you closer to the aisle/You may start with a simple conversation/Like darling, please put me on trial.'

The alarm button, on which I pound while singing, doesn't work. But my musical projection draws attention, and within ten minutes the elevator has been edged down to a point where the door can be pried open and I climb out.

Back on the streets, heading towards Holyoke Center, where I had a disastrous encounter with an inept psychiatrist who knew nothing about LSD, I realize how much readier I am to handle panic and near-hysteria than I was at the time of my blast out. Accepting one's death, meditating one's way into it, and seeing it as a natural consequence of being alive, seems to me the fundamental psychological task of this split-second journey that we're on.

24 April

Back in New York, I arrange to meet Leonardo DiCaprio at the Essex House. People are saying everywhere about him what they were saying about Bobby De Niro when he was twenty-five: the actor of our generation, the next Marlon Brando, the wave of the future. But Leonardo is nineteen, and I am struck immediately by what a young nineteen he is. I am also stunned by his beauty.

He has a poetic and romantic elegance even in the most awkward of his movements, and a radiation of intelligence and unruly favour in his smile and eyes. His hair, both in texture and colour, fits the structure of his head. He seems taller than I had imagined, six-one or -two I would guess, and has the sort of build that doesn't seem to have finished growing. Certainly it hasn't finished filling out. If he builds a bit of muscle on his upper half, he will look enough like a point guard to make the basketball scenes credible. Assuming, of course, that he can shoot and dribble and pass.

'Can you?' I ask him.

'I'm pretty good,' he says.

I tell him the story of *Harvard Man*, and act parts of the movie out. He seems taken by it, and by me. I certainly am by him. Within an hour, it is clearly becoming something we both want to do. Seven girls call him in the hour I'm up in his room, most of them models whose pictures are on the cover of magazines on various chairs and tables. He is wide-eyed and excited about it. It's obviously pretty new to him, and he asks me many questions about my own history and inclinations. He is also eager to know about Warren Beatty and Jim Brown. So was I. Listening to him deal on the phone with agents, managers, publicists, film-production people and girls, there is a deftness and sense of detached control which are admirable and surprising. An innocent who doesn't miss a trick.

28 April

Half the day is spent on the phone with Beatty, Levinson and Berg. Warren wants *Shrink*. He tries a different tactic.

'Why don't you just admit that you have no interest in finishing this movie, that you have no powers of concentration left. Why don't you admit that you just took the money and ran?'

'Because it isn't true,' I protest. 'Because you are going to get a script which you will want to do.'

'When I am how old?' Warren asks.

'You'll get it quicker than you got *Bugsy*,' I say.

'That was six years. Will this be five and a half?'

Berg, who stresses his verbs with Type-A vehemence, says, 'We've *gotta* get this Harvard movie set up. You've *gotta* get back in action making movies. You *can't* delay any longer. I know how to finance this movie now. You *must* find a way of finishing.'

Levinson, fully into *Disclosure*, plays it lighter. 'Any time you're ready with the Harvard script, I'd love to go ahead and set it up at my company,' he says quietly. It is at least the fifteenth time he has made that generous and desirable offer, each time in the same casual and relaxed tone of voice. He asks me to write a scene for Michael Douglas and Demi Moore, the central sexual harassment scene, by her of him, in the film. It is actually the first *half* of the scene he needs, the dialogue leading up to the first touch.) I agree to do it and write it in the next fifteen minutes after we get off the phone. I fax it to him, and he expresses great excitement and assures me it will be shot as written. I wouldn't be averse to a cheque for $50,000, but no such offer is forthcoming.

3 May

Just what I need, another potential distraction! Another detour! Another mode of delay! Steve Rebello, an exceptionally lively journalist friend, wants to refresh his memory of my Victoria Woodhull script in preparation for an article he's going to do for *Movieline*, 'The Ten Best Screenplays Never Made'. *Vicky*, as I have called it, was originally written for Faye Dunaway, with George Cukor to direct in 1976. It fell apart when George Barrie, chairman of Fabergé and eager backer of movies at the time (the same George Barrie who a week later rewarded me for the disappointment with the financing of *Fingers*), decided that *The Bluebird* disqualified Cukor from being funded at the lavish level *Vicky* required. It had been largely absent from my mind since then and probably would have remained so, but for Rebello's call. I read it out loud and am both impressed and embarrassed. Four or five scenes are quite good. She is a relentless, fascinating, tricky, erotic woman. But half the script appears to have been written by somebody else or by me when I was someone whom I choose not to remember. It occurs to me – why not? I have so little to do – that if I rewrite it, it can cease to remain in the never-made category. But for whom? I mention Rebello's call to Beatty, suggest that I'll send him the script and then introduce the idea that I might look to rewrite it, half expecting him to think I am playing a joke. But he surprises me by suggesting that it sounds ideal for Annette. I have enlisted the least likely collaborator in more lateral movement.

4 May

I start rewriting *Vicky*. It's fun.

5 May

For the first time in months, I speak to Pauline Kael, whom I used to speak to regularly. It isn't that we've had any kind of falling out. It's more a friendship that can tolerate lengthy interruptions and, when resumed, feels as though it has been going on throughout. We have had a chequered past. Her first review of a film of mine – *The Gambler*, Karel Reisz's film with Jimmy Caan – was negative, bordering on nasty. She singled me out for having written a screen-play with large ambitions, larger pretensions, and a wall between the world of the movie and the viewers invited to see it. Her *Fingers* review moved in six directions at the same time, and had the odd effect of propelling her into the arms of Warren Beatty and then mine, as she temporarily quit her job at the *New Yorker* to explore the idea of producing *Love and Money*, which was, as I noted earlier, eventually to become my euphemistically designated 'least favourite film'.

The collaboration was abortive, but our strange friendship survived it. Suffice it to say that I have always enjoyed reading her and never enjoyed reading a review she has written of anything I have done. Her retirement from film criticism served as the death knell of the self-conscious aspect of the form. I think she sensed that fewer and fewer movies were worth writing about. It would often appear to me that she was straining to excite herself enough to squeeze out 750 or 1,000 words on some film which she would have had no desire to see or even think about again.

'There's reviewing now and blurbing,' I say to her, 'but very little to read.'

'There's very little to see,' she says.

She's always eager for news and rarely wants to talk about her health, which is the subject I am probing. I mention three or four film critics I do enjoy reading, and we argue a bit. She seems concerned that I haven't yet got in gear and looks to egg me on. The law firm can take on a fourth member. Her opinions remain strong, bordering on violent, and when we don't share a feeling about an actor, writer or director, positive or negative, she will do whatever she can to persuade me of his or her vices and/or virtues, the ones I've missed. Like everyone, she has only good things to say about Leonardo.

8 May

I combine *Vicky* and *Harvard Man*: I rewrite *Vicky* on the plane going up to Cambridge and in my room at the Charles, but I resume my paths of renewal around Cambridge. I go back to lecture halls. I shoot some baskets in the gym. I go back to my room at Thayer. I cruise the Widener. I walk on the banks of the Charles at night. I go to three clubs – including the Blue Parrot in the Brattle Building, close to what it was in my time. Constant rushes of nostalgia. I have to remind myself of how much misery I was often in.

I visit my room again in Leverett Towers. Is this a perversity? My friend isn't in, but the door isn't locked. I lie on the bed, which is angled the same way it was when I was sleeping in it three decades ago. I fall asleep for about fifteen minutes and wake up disoriented.

12 May

Karel Reisz – probably the most fundamentally decent, wittily enjoyable figure in movies – calls upon his arrival in New York and we get together. If there is one person without whom my entire life in film would have been impossible, it is he. *The Gambler* was by no means destined to become a movie. I had been generating interest, curiosity, excitement, advances and options, but there was no go, and the chances of it ever becoming a film were close to vanishing when Karel finally got the script and read it. He read my Jim Brown book as well. He saw a connection that I didn't see, and suggested that I come to London to talk and write and work with him. Six months later he decided to tell Paramount that he was ready to shoot the movie with me as a collaborator, observer and integral part of the process. My entire technical education in film-making took place during the next year by his side. We have remained close, seeing each other whenever we are in the same city, speaking infrequently but intensely on the phone, encouraging each other constantly in our work. Ever since *Everybody Wins*, a film I consider swinishly underrated (in fact, I think I like it more than Karel does), he has turned to directing on the British stage. He seems not at all inclined to get back to the grind of making movies. He complains about the quality of scripts he is being given and about the exhausting physical process. There is no one on earth it is easier to wish well.

20 May

It strikes me as odd that I am writing a journal at all. Days and weekends, weeks and months, even years, have always tended to blur in my mind. I need to look to see what day it is, sometimes even what month. The structuring of life seems desperate and artificial. (No wonder *Harvard Man* and *Shrink* aren't done!)

24 May

What the fuck have I been doing! It seems as if this entire month has simply been passing me by. I don't like the work I'm doing. I've written three new endings for *Harvard Man* in the last three days, and none of them is right. Of all my movies, only *The Big Bang*, which had no 'story', had an ending which was clear to me from the start. Every other film has changed its ending, often radically. I don't suppose that a tragic ending is appropriate to *Harvard Man*, but I haven't yet found a way of making any kind of convincing affirmation. I feel that I must, because despite my inclination to avoid endings which don't acknowledge death, in this case death has been dealt with sufficiently along the way, and not to acknowledge some joy in being able to move into the future would feel like an unpleasant cheat.

29 May

Don Simpson, high-concept producer *extraordinaire*, frustrated stand-up comedian and co-star of *The Big Bang*, calls to ask for his money. Few people in Hollywood have exhibited anything close to the exuberant financial generosity Simpson has since he made his first score with *Flashdance* in 1983. I have avoided the subject of debt in this diary, primarily because I'm trying to keep it centred on movies, and the talk and action directly related to them. But gambling – a recurrent addiction in my life – leads ineluctably to urgent need for money and the need for money affects, if it doesn't determine, one's work. I have never – *could* never – direct a work without a passionate sense of its worth, but I have taken large sums of money to write certain scenes and rewrite certain scripts. This is as bald an act of prostitution as any sexual service exchanged plainly for cash. Debt has been an ongoing theme, perhaps one of *the* ongoing themes of my life since I started gambling when I was nineteen. A gambler needs outs. An out can be a place to bet, to take a last shot, to see if redemption from the threat of trouble or death can come in two hours. But an out is also a reliable bail-out source. Such figures are ordinarily naïve about the nature of gambling; they look to feel that their help will end the problem.

Simpson, no stranger to addiction, knows that this is not the case but has come through time and again when I have needed him. This time – for reasons I can't understand – there is an urgency for collection. I tell him the possible ways and dates, but ask him not to rely on any of them because the future is unclear. We move on to what he always refers to as the 'movie business', and I listen to half an hour of uninterrupted analysis of the state of studio politics, the diminishing role of the director, and a personal expatiation on the vast smorgasbord of future projects he is generating. Michelle Pfeiffer, Will Smith, Gene Hackman, Denzel Washington, my own Warren Beatty, Jack Nicholson, Tom Cruise – every name imaginable is a possible player in his immediate future. He wants to produce *Harvard Man* as much as Barry, and there will be no small dose of hurt feelings if it doesn't work out for him to do so. Since I intend, however, to use him as a sexually twisted detective in the movie and since acting is his deepest dream, relations shouldn't suffer too profoundly if Barry is the producer. There is very little of a scandalous nature that Simpson doesn't know about. Being connected with Heidi Fleiss and her trade in particular, or crime in Hollywood in general, is likely to be part of his inside track. His energy level when switched on is quite ferocious. There are few people he can't outlast.

What does it mean to be in debt? First, it means that people are chasing *you*, you aren't chasing *them*, and even if the purpose of the chase is potentially destructive to your health, you remain at the centre of that world's attention. Second, if one gets away without paying the debt, or if one pays it late but doesn't suffer unduly for doing so, there is a sense of escape from entrapment. In beating death one is – if only temporarily – reborn. Finally, there is the sheer joy of flirting with disaster. (A suggested definition for the separation of the human race into two categories: those who find flirting with disaster imbecilic and those who find it irresistible.)

5 June

It feels like summer. In the late 1960s, when I was married to Mimi Russell, the granddaughter of the Duke of Marlborough, her family owned and lived in the Vanderbilt estate in Southampton. The family was at the centre of all social and cultural activity in the Hamptons. Now it's Movieland from June through August, a Spielberg place. And I will spend the summer in the city, shuttling back and forth to Cambridge and, oddly, feeling good to be removed from all social movie whirl.

I like the sense of movies as something made on the run. The idea that these next movies exist only in my mind wherever I am, but that at some point they will exist on film, on a screen, in other people's minds is an exciting delight. By this logic, *The Big Bang* was the ideal film-making experience. A band of friends, colleagues, strangers, renting, stealing, borrowing equipment, some using their own, people taking subways and buses to a rented house in Tenafly, New Jersey, nobody knowing quite what was expected of them. The wonderful sense of being stranded, of being forced to come up with something to justify the time, the removal from ordinary life. It was the most extreme example of a director saying to his assembled adventurers, 'Trust me.'

12 June

O. J. Simpson. this will be the flash sensation news story of the next five years. My memories of O.J. at Jim Brown's house in situations involving a multiplicity of sexual players is that the effect was one of studied enjoyment and forced camaraderie, but that the mind behind it was filled with anxiety and competitive rage. Of course, the same could probably be said for everyone in that wild house in those erotically expressive times, not least of all (perhaps most of all) for the only white male in the joint, your diarist. But Simpson's detached conviviality made the dichotomy more glaring. He'd had a falling out with Jim, and under the Arabic notion that the enemy of your friend is your enemy, I had always felt an obligation to avoid any show of affection when I would run into him in public places. This assumes that he is guilty, which I immediately do. It raises and will probably continue to raise the thorniest of questions between the sexes, which is when anger and jealousy become physically expressed in violence, is it always purely the work of a vile bully who should be electrocuted at the stake, or is it at least in analytical terms a seductive, destructive dance of mutual provocation? I'm reminded of how much of the territory once staked out by the novel, then by film, is now held by TV news. The sense of action, excitement and surprise so artificially and feebly played out in contemporary films in not infrequently vivid on CNN.

13 June

Warren, predictably, suggests that I will use the O. J. Simpson case as a narcotic to avoid completing *Shrink*. I fly up for my weekly fix of Cambridge life. I am acting out the movie regularly in various locations, often jumping back and forth playing all roles. There is a chance that I will be carted off at some point, a wicked irony in light of my original problems on Mt Auburn Street. One man who saw me yelling at an empty space on the street came over to offer consolation.

'I know how you feel,' he said, 'it's those demons.'
'No, it's just for a movie,' I said.
He smiled knowingly.

18 June

I am trying to find a way of making the *Vicky* script feel naturalistic and 'historical' simultaneously, and I'm having a rough time of it. I resolve to abandon any notions of history proper and just worry about making the scenes feel exciting and true.

19 June

Dustin Hoffman sends me *Outbreak*, a virus script which he's going to do with Wolfgang Peterson. He feels – with justification – that the dialogue can use a good deal of help and insists I'm the only one who can do it. Just what I need! Another opportunity to spread out. Secretly, I know I have to say no. Saying yes would rip the borders of decorum into travesty. But I choose to say no by asking for an outrageous amount of money and by refusing to meet with Wolfgang Peterson before receiving a concrete offer matching my demands.

'Why,' I ask the producer arrogantly, 'should I discuss my ideas, give them away, when that's presumably what I would be paid for? If this were my own movie I would be happy to do anything for free. I would steal to get it done. But you are talking about offering me a job. Make an offer.'

'But wouldn't you just come out and meet for an afternoon with Wolfgang?' she repeats.

'I don't think that would be a good idea,' I say, and we lose each other on a mobile phone.

Scrutinizing my motives, I decide it is actually *Das Boot* which bothers me. The fact that Jews all over the world were seduced into paying tribute to this Nazi *apologia* as a little work of art doesn't, in any way I can glean, lessen its Nazi soul. Here are a bunch of loyal Nazis in uniform just doing their job, some of them good others not so good, the movie seems to say. Well, thank you but no thank you. Dustin, self-conscious philo-Semite that he is, doesn't seem to see it in that light. It's always fun to talk to him. He's smart, with a truly hilarious and filthy sense of humour. He's totally faithful to his wife and completely obsessed with sex. How many men on the planet earth can make that statement with a straight face?

21 June

Hot, muggy and oppressive. Soaked with sweat, I walk through Central Park, dribbling and twirling my basketball, wearing my crimson and black Harvard cap to cover up my pate. These props have a symbolic value in making *Harvard Man*'s imminence (how many times have I said *that* before?) real to me. But the value has not only been symbolic. Playing basketball regularly again has given me a refreshed sense of how to shoot the ten minutes or so of basketball scenes in the film. The technological atmosphere around sports is polluted by a dense haze of lazy conventions. I will shoot tight in their minds and very wide for context. They are functional scenes – certain narrative information needs to be conveyed clearly in them – but they must be psychologically expressive as well. The seduction of corruption – the protagonist's fixing of a game, playing in effect against himself and his team-mates without being detected – needs to be revealed clearly, economically and obliquely. Gliding and jerking in the park with a bunch of black leapers, all of whom are young enough to be my sons, sparks a display of images – angles, compositions, rhythms of movement – which would not have come any other way. I am both in the game and shooting it.

Dustin calls. He's still nervous about the dialogue in the virus movie (I keep blocking out the title). We talk about an under-the-table, straight deal. He'll pay me to rewrite all the dialogue in a week. His back goes out and he needs Demeral for the pain. He's off to Tahiti. Just as well. An impermissible distraction. My addiction to distractions.

After dinner, I join Norman Mailer, with his wife, Norris, Milos Forman, Patrick Swayze and Tom Luddy at Russian Samovar. Spirits are high. Norman and Norris as writers, Milos as director and Tom as producer are planning a film which takes place during the Buchanan administration (James, not Pat). Norman, having been the first and strongest literary and philosophical inspiration of my life and also the subject of my first essay to appear in print (in *Commentary*), has retained over a thirty-year period a central place in my consciousness. We've also – after a rocky first few years – become the closest of friends.

There is much *schadenfreude* in Hollywood and in the cultural media world altogether. It is such a miserable trait – of which I am certainly not free myself – that it feels positively ennobling genuinely to wish one's friends well, and I'm thrilled to see Norman in good health, cheerful and ready to make what sounds like a great film. He and Tom collaborated on *Tough Guys Don't Dance*, a terrific, bold and stupidly maligned movie adaptation of Norman's eponymous novel. I like Milos: a tough-minded Central European Jew, with a great sense of humour. Patrick also has a nice wit and seems to be a fundamentally decent fellow. We talk a lot about O.J. I bring in Jim Brown and pontificate a bit. I seem to have become the self-appointed expert on this case, which I can't get off my mind. Only later does it occur to me that no reference has been made to Norman's stabbing of his second wife forty years ago. Norris says she has seen Norman on the line between genius and madness, but never over it. I've seen him in many places and the most remarkable change is the diffusion of rage into wisdom, wit, modesty and a nearly transcendent consciousness, especially in regard to life's pain – all qualities which were there before, but which now seem even stronger.

There is a dogged, almost heroic professionalism about a writer of Norman's stature continuing to pursue the dream of the Great American Novel in his sixties. *Harlot's Ghost* and now the big new work about Lee Harvey Oswald stake a claim to territory that no one else from Norman's literary generation could conceivably stake. And surely no younger novelist would even suggest that he or she be mentioned in the same breath as Norman. This attenuation of the novelistic scene is hardly surprising, given the fashion in which film has consumed the consciousnesses (at the expense of the novel) of two generations after Mailer (even as rock and roll has seized their imaginations from the classical world). A few years ago, at one in the morning in the back of a taxi in SoHo, Norman confessed to me that if he were beginning again today as an artist out of Harvard, there would be no doubt that film, not the novel, would be his circuit of expression.

We talk about self-destructiveness, not just in terms of murder (or attempted murder) and getting caught, but also in terms of gambling. Milos says flatly that all gamblers are self-destructive. Having made an entire movie which defies that notion, I stay quiet. Norman, passionately and a bit impatiently, jumps in with the idea that addictions conventionally perceived as self-destructive are often just the opposite, that (these are my words, not his) one descends precisely in order to protect one's capacity to ascend. We embrace when we say good-bye – first time ever.

I'm supposed to meet Don Simpson and Jerry Bruckheimer for a late dinner, but wires get crossed. Just as well. I want to write tonight, but I miss seeing Simpson. No one's sense of humour makes me laugh more.

Warren calls at 2 a.m. He's back from Rome with an even greater love for Morricone, the great Italian film composer who wrote the magnificent, haunting score for *Bugsy*. More talk about O.J. (How much greater his impact in gaol than it was outside!) Warren thinks he'll walk, but that a backlash will ensue. I avoid the subject of *Shrink*. I'm not ready to go out to LA for another three or four days. ('Could you repeat that, please?')

23 June

Is it possible that this journal will enter the bloodstream of delay, lateness, evasion; that it will become part of the psychodrama of delivery? Both David and Tom are apparently concerned that the paucity of entries they have received is an indication that deadlines may end up being violated. They would like to see more. This is an entirely realistic and not unexpected request. But I have yet to go over most of what I've written, and since I write in longhand with endless asterisks, arrows and notes to myself, I need time to copy, organize, transcribe and present. The brutal truth is that much of my best work over the years has been written in the margins of the *New York Post*, on the backs of scraps of paper and business cards, on the sides of laundry lists and receipts. It is all very well to be lectured (by example) by Hemingway and Eliot, Mailer and Stevens, Bellow and Vidal, about the job-like working mode of the writer. Pick a time every day, go to your office and perform. Who will question the method of the pro? Surely I would have been far more productive, completed a much thicker body of work if I had found a way of producing – something – *anything* – every day. But the closest I have ever come to such fertility is in this journal, and even it has tended to be written – albeit daily – in fits of inspiration. There is something faithful to the ultimate evanescence of all work in creating it on the run; and something effectively provocative, for me at least, in the recklessness of doing it in places where it may get lost. I need more time. When? Is this David speaking now? Or Tom? (Or is it still Warren and Jeff Berg?) When one is late, one is suggesting one's own importance. If they're waiting for me, I must be important or else they would have already left. The risk is that they *will* have left and not waited at all, in which case lateness reveals not significance but its absence. If this can be seen as a convoluted and ultimately sterile psychological exercise, an exercise doomed to try the patience of one's friends and often turn them into enemies, it is still no less difficult to discontinue than any other unconscious process. (Not an excuse; rather, a stab at an explanation.)

4 July

A sad, barren day. The entire American movie community is in either the Hamptons or LA. Everyone must be part of a couple and every couple must have a child or two. Fireworks for the family! No bad news, please. Movies that make us laugh or smile or, two or three times a year, frown. But no shocks, no nightmare, no catastrophe. *Schindler's List* is about as far as 'Hollywood' can go. It is done with forceful technical skill and ferocious emotional impact. Nothing in Spielberg's career would have prepared me, at any rate, for a film of such complexity, seriousness and historical ambition. In an era in which mass American views on the Holocaust are coterminous with views on evolution, UFOs and the Deity (which is to say that all rational faculties are suspended), any skilful effort at making people see what took place is welcome. But I am seized by a point made by Karel Reisz (both of whose parents perished in the Holocaust): how is one to respond to a movie which addresses the subject of the incineration of 6 million Jews and yet ends with a feeling of resolution and even celebration that a couple of thousand were saved, as if that slender anomaly were cause for some sense of triumph?

I walk the streets – nearly empty – talking to myself, talking to my dead father, my dead grandfather, my dead former nurse, all the people who made the Fourth of July a real holiday forty-five years ago, when I was just beginning to be formed. I flash back to the Polo Grounds where, from the age of six until twelve, my father, mother, cousin and I would watch the New York Giants – before their treacherous move to San Francisco – play either the Phillies or the Cardinals, Fourth of July double headers. Stern effort and an overwhelming sense of embarrassment do not stop me from breaking down in tears. I force myself to think of my unfinished work and the crying stops. Nothing like pressure to interrupt an emotional indulgence.

10 July

I try something I haven't tried in years. I take the rough draft of *Harvard Man* and gather a few strangers in Central Park, seven men and women ranging in age from twenty to thirty, and, after identifying myself – showing identification to prove my validity and to dispel all doubts that a madman with nefarious intentions is before them – I suggest reading them the entire script. They are curious. Much to my relief, I seem to hold their attention. But why engage in false modesty in my own journal? They respond with effusions of enthusiasm! No interruptions, no apparent wandering. It takes me forty-five minutes to perform. A no piss-interrupted movie. If *I* can hold them , reading everybody's part, male and female, in my halting monotone, then what could a group of skilful actors with a visionary cameraman and music do? So what am I waiting for?

13 July

What I'm waiting for is full satisfaction. I still don't have an ending. And even when I get one, whether it is death, romantic communion or isolation (what other options are there?), there will still be the problem, the burden, the *debt* of *Shrink*. I have never before tried working on more than one script at the same time. As someone with a rather scattered sexual history, the analogy would not be to attempt to carry on simultaneous sexual connections but rather to be in love with two or more women at the same time. I have never felt the sense of professional performance in writing – or, for that matter, directing – a film. The idea has always been to write from some complex source of experience, fantasy, desire, excitement, yearning and truth. Such absorption – like romantic obsession – is clearly best handled, most cleanly managed, one item at a time.

20 July

I reread my most recent entry and find that I've been contradicting it. The last several days have been spent exclusively on *Vicky*. As a fanatic for history, particularly American, I am increasingly excited by the chance to write – i.e., reinvent the very identities of – such seminal figures as Cornelius Vanderbilt, Frederick Douglass and Henry Ward Beecher. It is, in its context, a portrait of mid-nineteenth-century America – before, during and after the Civil War – when the nation was forging a decisive claim to sustained existence and discovering the shape of its identity. It is also giving me the chance to write a female character – an utterly fascinating, hypnotic, boundlessly ambitious woman – at the centre of a cinematic world. I did this with Elizabeth Carlson (Nastassja Kinski) in *Exposed* and found it oddly more enticing than writing male leads. Since on some pathologically megalomaniacal level I presume to co-opt the entire male gender, it never feels as though I am going too far outside myself when a male character is at the centre of my film. But to create that world around a woman is always to partake of the quest to penetrate the mysterious Other. So no matter how much writing I do about and for Victoria Woodhull, no matter how much reading and research I've done, and from no matter what dimensions of imaginings, she will still remain just outside my grasp. This is a bracing and enticing state in which to invent.

23 July

I wake up in a state of near panic. I have knots in my stomach and my heart arrhythmia (PVCs) is going haywire. I'm suddenly certain that all three of my scripts are suffering from my diluted efforts. I'm almost afraid to read them. I remind myself of my recent *Harvard Man* performance in the park, which gives me at least momentary reassurance on that one film. I read *Shrink* to myself out loud from beginning to end. It will be a great role for Beatty if I can ever get it – not just get it done, but get it – and I haven't got it yet.

I walk around the streets in the spirit of *Shrink*, talking to myself, playing scenes of harassment, gambling mania, sexual jealousy, frenzy bordering on madness. Anybody watching me would assume that I had slipped illegally out of Bellevue and that in fact both society and I would be better off if I were returned to its confines.

I run into John Heard, who did a remarkably affecting job in a sadly neglected, beautiful film: Ivan Passer's *Cutter and Bone*. I had been friendly with Heard a decade ago when he was living with Margot Kidder. He greets me rather coldly. Since I am not planning to use him in any future films, and since I have no particular interest in or need for his friendship, it strikes me as absurd that I should be disturbed by this lack of enthusiasm. Yet such is my hunger for attention, acclaim, praise and recognition as a master creator that I am indeed disturbed by it. I think briefly of trying something dramatic, such as grabbing his ear and slamming him down on the street, but I quickly discard this impulse as more self-destructive than curative.

The event sours the rest of the day. I like to think that I am beyond caring about the opinions of anyone, let alone the opinions of those whom I have no plans for in my life. At bottom, I know that I gain the profoundest satisfaction from finishing films which I view as fulfilments of their most extravagant ambitions – *Fingers*, *The Big Bang*, *Bugsy* and *The Gambler*; I know that when I half-succeed, as in *The Pick-Up Artist* and *Exposed*, I feel both pleasure and remorse; and I know that when in some essential way I fail, as I did in *Love and Money*, I am consumed with a sense of worthlessness and despair. That is all acceptable and I can incorporate such thinking and feeling into a viable notion of myself, but to be bothered by a limp reaction from an actor who is of no use to my future and who is plagued by habits which I loathe, is an unnerving embarrassment. I enter it into my journal in the spirit of the Underground Man: *I am a sick man. I am a spiteful man. I think my liver is diseased.* I have always suspected that half my creative energy comes from what I like least about myself: maniacal insistence, Machiavellian deceit and helpless addiction. So when I am forced to confront those forces I wish were not inside me, I look to be actually excited. For to dodge them is the greatest mistake and to use them the most constructive revenge. This is perhaps a clue as to why I find it out of my range to construct characters who are, in the grotesque jargon of Hollywood studio politics, people the audience can 'root for', or people in a slightly less revolting phrase (but only slightly less), the audience can 'sympathize with'. When I am asked whom the audience can root for in a script I've written, I usually answer either Macbeth or Richard III. But there are no longer many people around from whom I am able to get a laugh or even a grunt on that.

I ride on the subway. It is mobbed, filthy and suffocatingly hot. (The air-conditioning has broken down.) As I am jostled, I take particular pleasure in feeling submerged in this unappetizing chaos. I am convinced that the insularity of limousine life (or even ordinary, pleasant, comfortable, upper-middle-class Hollywood life, or life in Manhattan removed from the rabble) is fundamentally antithetical to any growth as an artist, to any maintenance of one's keenness. If only I could finish something with all these great impulses, insights, revelations! Too much living, not enough writing. Too much talk, not enough directing. Go home and work.

2 August

Delmore Schwartz. From the first time I looked into his eyes in a faded photograph, I felt the kind of recognition I have only felt once before with an American Jew, and that was with Bugsy Siegel. Delmore never reached the age I am already (forty-nine), and his energies had abandoned him even earlier. Yet there is something in his sad and wasted and aborted artistic life that I understand innately and feel as frighteningly close to my own fate.

5 August

Dinner with Harvey Keitel. It is another step in the erasure of the line between art and life, role-player and role, mythology and reality, to see Harvey, my own Harv, recognized, acclaimed, adulated, genuflected before. It seems like only yesterday – as my grandfather would say – that I could go anywhere with Harvey and be utterly undisturbed. An occasionally aberrant spirit would approach with a cry of *'Fingers'*, or a comment about *Taxi Driver* or *Mean Streets*. If now he is not as accosted as Schwarzenegger or Stallone, he is regarded with a far more rarefied level of respect. Reverence would, indeed, not be too strong a word to describe the awe with which his idolaters – male and female – approach him. He has recently predicted in *Positif* that *Harvard Man* will be my great work; he has suggested that I am ready to fulfill all my promise. As I sit across the table from him, I wonder if this is his heartfelt and passionate conviction or, largely the result of my own oft-repeated indications.

'It's time, Jimmy. You've got to do *Harvard Man*.'

'I am. I will. I'm on the verge.'

'You can't keep saying it,' he says. 'You've got to do it.'

'It'll be next,' I say.

'It's been three years,' he says. 'If you need my help, you know you have it. In any way.'

I can't say anything. We finish the meal in silence.

Outside on the street we kiss good-bye. *Fingers!* (If we die tomorrow, that's why both of us were here.)

15 August

It now seems as though Warren is ready to go ahead with *Vicky*.

'You're never going to finish *Shrink*,' he says.

'I'm already finished,' I insist. 'It's just a question of refinement.'

'Well, while you're refining,' he says, 'maybe we'd better make a movie.'

The script as now conceived revolves entirely around Victoria Woodhull. There is no male role which would be suitable for a leading man. That imbalance is fine with me in theory. *Exposed* certainly was Nastassja's movie entirely – neither Keitel's nor Nureyev's role could have existed, except in relation to hers. But if there were a way of expanding one of the men into something like nearly equal prominence, it would be all to the good. I haven't figured how but I have a hunch that Warren has.

There are days when my sense of excitement at the prospect of imagining and writing is so highly charged that I feel cheated and deprived if I'm not able to put everything else aside and engage with it passionately. There are also days in which I have such lethargy, such torpid psychic sluggishness, that no matter what I think or write, I know in advance that it will appall me when I read it the following day. That is how I woke up this morning. Now this news – something practical is about to happen! – spurs me, clicks me into an infinitely sharper channel. I rewrite several scenes in *Vicky* with a cold, excited eye. Energy is the least talked-about and least understood element in successful film-making. When one is shooting, one simply does not have the luxury of phoning it in on a morning when one does not feel at one's peak and cancelling until one does. It is inconceivable that certain scenes can escape entirely unmarked by the condition of the director on that day. This phenomenon is, of course, enhanced exponentially when one speaks about actors. Forgetting the obvious question of how the actor looks, there is the critical element of mood. I have broached this question in an earlier entry, but my point seems clearer now. The idea that film-making is a profession, crafted by professionals who are paid a lot of money to do a job, while rationally valid, misses the point. There is no substitute for inspiration. Unchecked and without complex underpinnings, it can easily result in the most mawkish of discharges. But without it, nothing of passion or urgent drama is imaginable.

Beatty's call – the introduction of imminence – inspires me. I write and rewrite well. Another uninterrupted eighteen months of this and we'll all be fine.

17 August

The dirty little secret of putting movies together in Hollywood today – although it is hardly a secret within the industry; it is only a factor unknown to the 99.9 per cent of the world outside – is the agency gang war. With William Morris fading and United Talent rising, ICM and CAA still occupy the substantial majority of the terrain. For financial, psychological, social and perhaps even spiritual reasons, ICM wants its clients together on a movie as much as CAA wants a walled-in CAA world on its films. As surely as human life cannot be created without an erection, a film – unless it is *The Big Bang* – cannot be conceived without a script. So it is the script which starts the battle. Some writers and writer-directors slip easily into the channels which their agency opens to them. Others – like your noble, uncompromising and artistically pure diarist – look beyond agency allegiance, paying no more heed in making casting decisions to ICM/CAA affiliation than they would to membership in the Crips or Bloods. The concrete way of making this point would be to cite a short list of ICM's female clients: Michelle Pfeiffer, Julia Roberts, Sharon Stone, Jodie Foster and Meg Ryan. There would lie the conventional plan in the setting up of an original screenplay. (Sharon Stone is the closest in this group in look and personality to the historical Victoria.) But there is no real hesitation here, or doubt. It will go to Warren and Annette if they want it.

19 August

After the initial shock into the void – the sudden obliteration of the self I had been carefully cultivating my entire life, up until that fateful day in my nineteenth year when I blew out on acid, triggered by John Rich's statement in answer to my question, 'How long will it last?' 'Oh, it never ends' – what characterized my condition of madness, among other startling reversals from everything formerly known, was the sudden radical shift in attitude and point of view in decision-making overall from one extreme to another. For instance, I knew that I had to kill myself one second, and then the next that I had to go to an astronomy class which would clarify all the mysteries I was exploring. I knew that I was God, and one second later that I was the devil. I knew that I was just an ordinary human being with no special skills or talents or assets one second, then the next with absolute certainty that I was an inmate in the insane asylum that was the planet earth and the only inmate aware of the earth's cosmic function.

While the shift is surely less dramatic, the sudden emergence of *Vicky* as the movie most likely to be my next has strange reverberations of acid madness. I realize I have been counting on doing *Harvard Man* all along. And I will do it. But I have assumed I will do it next. Now, at least a year and a half lies ahead, a year and a half of immersion in *Vicky*, Warren and Annette. This odd fate I feel with Warren, this nearly surreal closeness, this awareness that he understands what is in my mind and will suggest what is best for me, certainly what is best for him from me – defies comparison to any other personal connection in my life. It would be remarkable enough if it happened with just any actor (with writer–producer–director tags to be added appropriately), but it is downright spooky that it has happened with the one screen presence who most deeply invaded my imagination when I was first forming intellectual as well as emotional judgements about film. There simply was no close second to him in my iconography when I saw *Splendor in the Grass, Mickey One, All Fall Down* and *Lilith*. A dark, moody, sensual, wanton consciousness; a physical grace and power, a natural elegance – what other actor or star embodied such a paradox? And who from that era, besides Beatty, remains? Only Newman and Brando, and they have moved on to different sorts of roles. I am understanding even as I write this that it was almost unnatural to have assumed that the professional separation (surely it has not been a personal separation with the ongoing close and constant degree of contact) would have continued indefinitely. I had my period in which to make *Harvard Man* and didn't. It will now (I feel this quite profoundly today) have to wait until after *Vicky* has been made. I also understand that it is entirely possible that I will read this entry a month from now and need to describe it in Nixonian terms as 'inoperative'. But I doubt it.

24 August

Suddenly, it's all *Vicky*. The plan is for me to go to LA, sit with Warren and Annette, and listen at length to their reactions, suggestions and plans. I am excited. I am also somewhat suspicious of myself. *Harvard Man*, by its very nature, cannot possibly become what, for want of a less vulgar way of describing it, I would call an Academy Award film. It is too dark, too impacted, too strange. It occurs to me that I've had these thoughts before. Have I already written them in a previous entry? Am I going senile at forty-nine? My grandfather waited until his nineties. Am I so precocious in every area of my life that this nasty destiny will also hit me well before its proper time? At any event, *Harvard Man* – even as a total fulfillment of its wild ambitions, while capable of acclaim, I hope, around the world – cannot achieve that mass mall penetration, that industry centrality, which *Vicky* can achieve if it comes even close to what it should be. Is this prospect part of the enticement? I don't think so. I'm getting hooked by her as I was when I wrote her originally, sixteen years ago, for Faye Dunaway. Indeed, my first conversion will have to be from Faye to Annette (the same Faye found and launched by Beatty in *Bonnie and Clyde*). I am lucky. Vicky was a master of sex and language – her power came from her dexterous manipulation of both – and one would be strained to count even a couple of actresses over the past two decades who integrate these qualities as harmoniously as Dunaway and Bening.

1 September

Back in LA. I'm staying at the Malibu Beach Inn, a turquoise and pink three-storey hotel, the only place with pretensions to California elegance in Malibu. I've chosen it to be close to Warren, who is living on the beach a half-mile north while his earthquake-fractured house is being reconstructed. It is an hedonic place, with the ocean right outside my room and miles of beach in either direction, but a fair amount of sewage is still pumped regularly into the Pacific near this apparently edenic spot, and one swims in it at one's peril. Right out of *Death in Venice*, a surfer tells me that two lifeguard friends of his received lengthy staph infections from cuts infected by the floating shit in which they swam last year.

'Then why are you swimming now?' I ask him.

He looks me in the eye and says, 'Because I'm crazy.' Then he cracks up.

I must be crazy, too – not in the acid sense, the real sense – at least superficially so, because I follow him in and swim out as far as I can with reckless abandon, until I wonder whether I can get back. When I do reach shore, it is with that same sense of mischievously defiant relief, which I feel whenever I return from a nearly fatal ocean swim.

2 September

I visit Warren and Annette at their rented beach house and am introduced to Ben, their newborn son. Ostensibly he is named after Annette's father, but I know better. He is named after Benjamin Siegel, the progenitor of Warren's inner self and the practical cause of Warren's meeting with Annette. What I want to know is, when he develops in his forming years, will this little creature – actually, he's quite huge for an infant – be taunted as 'Bugsy' by his schoolmates? And if he is, will he go berserk and flash the homicidal rage at them which his father has within him, but so decorously contains?

We speak about *Vicky* only in general terms, but I know Warren well enough to recognize that the evasion of specifics is the harbinger of a serious, if constructive, demolition. It won't come tonight. It is too late and the occasion is too social. Herb Ritts, the photographer who has just done a series of portraits of Warren and Annette for *Vanity Fair*, joins us. Maybe tomorrow. In the meantime, I call Leonardo. He seems ready for *Rimbaud*. Perhaps this timing will work out all for the best. Surely he will not be too old in a year. As it is, no one takes him for nineteen, his actual age. In *Harvard Man* he should really be twenty or even twenty-one. I always enjoy speaking to him. He has wild wit on his answering machine, which serves as stand-up comic routine. The messages never make much sense, but leave me reeling. All I have to do is talk to him for two minutes to be embarrassingly homesick for being nineteen.

3 September

In the prologue to this journal, I suggested that it was *ipso facto*, as I put it, impossible to be late on a diary. Give me credit. I have managed to be late in spades. My second thoughts, revisions and endless dickerings have resulted in obtrusively late delivery for David, Tom, John, Walter, and Faber and Faber. Everybody is up in arms. Deadlines are being flouted. Catastrophe is in the air. How can I say with a straight face that I don't relish this torture? Having met my unconscious during my eight-day acid blow out, I know that it exists and, therefore, I know that it is always possible to be up to something I don't know I am up to, but my oh my, how silly to put friends through such discomfort!

Barry Levinson calls to invite me to the first screening of *Disclosure* in San Francisco – at Lucas's place in Marin – on the evening of the 7th. I call David and tell him I will supply him with a large fund of journal entries on that afternoon. I don't think he believes me. I am compelled to play Prince Hal, wilfully to create circumstances in which redemption will be necessary so that I can then avail myself of the challenge and be redeemed.

5 September

The air is foul. The water is polluted. I still sense an earthquake of monumental dimensions threatening underneath. LA has truly gone to seed. And yet, there is still the surface loveliness which hypnotizes and lures.

I go to Warren and Annette's for dinner, fully expecting that this will be our night. Instead, Barry Diller, Warren's old buddy from Paramount days and Fox as well (he was its chairman when we did *The Pick-Up Artist* there), appears in casual attire and the four of us head out for a friendly Chinese dinner. Diller has a terse and savage wit. Like all interesting companions, he keeps one on one's toes, forever wary of a moment of dullness, a lapse of precision. We float across the spectrum of current topics: babies; O.J.; how much money *Quiz Show* is likely to make; and the rivalry between Murdoch, Diller's former employer, who owns, among thousands of other properties, the *New York Post*, and Mort Zuckerman, who owns, among hundreds of other properties, the *New York Daily News*. Diller retains an odd and rather moving affection for Murdoch, even though they parted with apparent roughness.

There are a few figures floating around the international entertainment world – Diller, David Geffen, Michael Eisner and Ron Perlman – most of them (like myself) Jews, many from New York or LA. These wanderers from the lost tribes have taken a path different from mine. More precisely, they have amassed money along lines that conjure up Everett Dirksen's famous quip, 'A billion dollars here, a billion dollars there; next thing you know, you're talking about real money.' This phenomenon was made possible in the Reagan 1980s.

I first met Diller in 1978 when I was sharing an office with Beatty while preparing *Love and Money*, a movie which, unfortunately, I went on to do without him. Diller was running Paramount at the time. Eisner, Don Simpson and Jeffrey Katzenberg were under him. Beatty went off to London to make *Reds*. I continued using his office. At the time I was drinking from morning until night. One could say without fear of correction that if I was awake, I was drinking. One morning, Diller walked into my office unannounced. I was sitting at my desk with my notebook in front of me, pen in my hand, a bottle of Moët et Chandon White Star next to the phone and a champagne glass half-filled next to the bottle. Diller stared at me, then at the bottle, then back at me. At that moment, I knew I would have to find another financer for my movie. And indeed, I did: Lorimar. (Note to all future financers of my work: my last sip of alcohol was imbibed on 31 January 1983.)

'I don't like Warren any more,' Diller said flatly.

'Of course you do,' I said.

'I do not,' he insisted.

'Why?' I asked.

'Because,' he said.

'Because what?' I pursued.

Diller thought for a moment. 'Because every time I get off the phone with him, I've told him everything I know about everything, and he has told me absolutely nothing.'

So here we are, sixteen years later, with the lovely addition of Annette, Warren having made five movies since, I having made five movies since and Diller having run two companies since, and all of us on the verge. (On the verge of what?)

6 September

Warren, Annette and I meet for dinner at an Italian restaurant in the Cross Creek Malibu mall. Great food, serious criticism. I have heard nothing but effusions of enthusiasm from everyone else who has read *Vicky*: Steve Rebello of *Movieline*, Virginia Campbell (*Movieline*'s editor), Jeff Berg, Joey Funicello, as well as various students at Columbia and NYU, and strollers in Central Park. However, it is Warren and Annette with whom I am to collaborate, not the aforementioned enthusiasts. Remarkably, there is hardly a suggestion blasted sharply at me the validity of which I find it difficult to grasp.

The most interesting and ambitious notion will also solve the problem of constructing a role for a leading man (i.e., WB). Warren suggests emphasizing the conflict between Victoria and Henry Ward Beecher. The potential has been there all the time, but in the course of thinking about the movie as an epic biography, a picaresque journey through nineteenth-century America on the back of an heroically complex and fascinating woman, I have not seen before how inviting it would be to play out this ambivalent romantic drama. Beecher was the leading liberal preacher of his day – liberal, that is, on social and economic matters. Sexually, he was a man of deep repression and guilt, harboring an impaction matched in degree only by the ferocity of his carnal appetite. Victoria, who rarely had a sexual thought or impulse she managed to avoid enacting, attacked Beecher's oppressive sexual rhetoric in her news-paper, even as Beecher assaulted her from his legendary pulpit as a brazen slut. The catch is that they were fucking passionately all the while. Fucking each other, that is. Since the money for Victoria's newspaper emanated from the large and deep pockets of Cornelius Vanderbilt, with whom she and her sister had carried out extravagant amorous escapades, there is a vast fund of riches during this brief period of Vicky's life.

No mention is made of *Shrink* during these Florentine deliberations. And certainly no reference is made to *Harvard Man*. It takes me two courses' worth of enthusiastic responsiveness to convince Warren that I am only too happy to pursue the journey in this new direction.

George Cukor's endlessly repeated admonition to me – 'Always give an actor a part that allows him to show what he can do. You will never get him at his best if he has anything less' – resonates in my exacerbated consciousness. Henry Ward Beecher may not be capable of taking charge of this entire movie as Ben Siegel of *Bugsy*, but if I write him as we are now talking about him, he will provide Beatty with a substantial pluck of stimulation.

Back at the Malibu Beach Inn at two in the morning, I stand on my balcony ... and think till love and fame to nothingness do sink. The phone rings. It is Leonardo. Both of us are vague. I tell him I may be doing 'this *Vicky* movie' with Warren and Annette. He refers to Rimbaud, James Dean and 'other projects!' We will do *Harvard Man*. It's just, as Brook Benton sings, a matter of time.

7 September

This diary is late and David Thomson is beside himself. He needs my edited pages so that he can make his own suggestions and contributions. Faber – in the form of John, Walter and Tom – join the chorus. Strangely, I feel this lateness as a more pressing obligation than I do my actual cinematic work, without which there would be no journal. And I haven't even received a penny in advance! Conveniently, I end up in San Francisco for the first screening of *Disclosure*. On my way I miss three flights and arrive five hours after I've told David I would be at his house. I finally present him with a batch of pages. Having known me for sixteen years, he seems to think I am in a state of crisis. He is probably right. His son is extraordinarily handsome. I can't get my mind off thinking how intriguing it would be to start over, be fresh at five. I leave David's house and head towards Lucas's screening facilities. In the taxi, I am flooded with memories of my fifth year.

Disclosure is fast, slick, witty and well done. It is also not *Jimmy Hollywood*, which means that on some serious plain of consciousness Barry must know, as I do, that this is hardly the reason he was born. It also means that it will clear a $100 million with no problem whatsoever and could well finish at $150 million. Good for Barry! In the cinematic realm in which he half-functions, that is no small matter of urgency, particularly after *Jimmy Hollywood* and *Toys*. And, for that matter, *Bugsy* never pushed much beyond $50 million domestically. So having a huge hit will re-establish him as a director to be listened to religiously by those gentlemen in suits running around with their fingers in the air to see which way the wind is blowing.

As a film, *Disclosure* is far superior to the novel. There was no wit or style to the first half of that book, and unless I missed something in my skimming of the second half, not much there either. But the film is tight. Michael Crichton owes a serious debt of gratitude to Barry.

It is strange, milling about the Lucas complex afterwards with the western suburbanites who have become part of Barry's world, speaking with cautious enthusiasm and optimism, a quiet, measured respect and hope. This is not the world of 84th Street and Broadway, but it is a function of the breadth of this movie's potential that it will clearly appeal as strongly in New York as in Palo Alto, or Duluth, or Albuquerque, or New Orleans.

I'm staying at the Clift Hotel, now called the Four Seasons Clift Hotel, and I'm struck by the wild and dark seediness of the streets surrounding it. Here is this old, elegant and quiet hotel, five yards away from a world of pervasive and racially mixed prostitution, drug addiction, madness, poverty, disease and despair. San Francisco as a Central American country.

8 September

On my way to pick up some residual cheques at the Writers' Guild and Directors' Guild (I am back in LA), I stop at the Chalet Gourmet, a stylish and high-tech supermarket across the street from the Château Marmont, and run into Bobby Lipton.

There are certain stars who become so because fate, luck, or simple career success thrust it upon them. Earlier in their lives they were not exceptional in any way, nor would they have become exceptional had it not been for the isolated, nearly disembodied reality of their stardom. Robert Redford talks about himself as a rather unattractive misfit in high school, someone who was heading for no particular distinction of any kind. Yet now, he has become this brand name 'Robert Redford'. Warren, on the other hand, was a star in his own world before he ever got to Hollywood. Then there are those who were stars before they came to Hollywood, but whose roles as actors never enabled them to become stars with the public.

Bobby Lipton – the older brother of Peggy Lipton, the *Mod Squad*, *Twin Peaks* blonde – was *the* star in my summer world on Long Island. Driving a white Triumph TR6, dressed in white pants with white shoes and richly colourful shirts, always with a tan, always with shades, hair styled, bones angular, features chiselled – he was the Guy. In the late 1950s, no one in the Five Towns on Long Island with pretensions to hipness or distinction was without due reverence for Bobby Lipton. We were, most of us, regulars on the *Alan Freed Rock 'n' Roll Party*, a daily TV show on Channel 5, hosted by the Godfather of Rock 'n' Roll himself, Alan Freed. The show was a precursor to MTV. Alan Freed would feature famous groups and then allow his guests to dance to their music and to the piped-in sounds of other groups and stars. I once won the cha-cha contest (Alan called it the 'choch'), dancing with Vicky Warwick to Robin Luke singing 'Suzie Darlin'' (a song I was to use in *The Pick-Up Artist*, with Dennis Hopper and Molly Ringwald in the kitchen). But all the contest wins in the world didn't come close to matching the natural cool of Bobby L. Over the years I had run into him several times, always greeting him and being greeted by him with great, perhaps overly effusive, affection. He had a shot at actual film stardom for a brief while. He played a second-lead role in *Bullitt* behind Steve McQueen and then had a co-lead with Terence Stamp in a movie called *Blue*. But he drifted into soap operas where he calcified for fifteen years, hoping all the while to find a role in a movie which would persuade the world see him as the star that the Five Towns had known him to be. I thought seriously of using him as the male lead in *Exposed*, but I went with Rudolph Nureyev instead. By the time *The Pick-Up Artist* came along, Bobby was far too old. Now, here in the Chalet, I am struck by the whiteness of stubble on his face. He is, like me, far closer to death than he is to birth. As always, he is with an attractive girl. We trade stories of recent and hoped-for future work. I tell him about *Harvard Man* and about the journal, and guarantee I will write about him as the star he always will be to me.

9 September

Warren, Annette and I get further into *Vicky*. The idea of featuring the conflict, the great ambivalent war, between Vicky and Henry Ward Beecher is becoming increasingly intriguing. If I can write it well, will he set up a deal? Where? I assume at Warners, but one never knows with Warren. All during the preparation for *The Pick-Up Artist*, everybody at Columbia assumed that Columbia was where the movie was going to be made. I was certain of it. Warren's cousin, David MacLeod, acting as the producer, was sure of it as well. Then one day, Warren called me from his car and said, 'Come on over to Fox. Meet me in Diller's office.'

'Why?' I asked. 'What's up?'

'We're making *The Pick-Up Artist* at Fox,' Warren said.

'I thought it was at Columbia,' I said.

'You were wrong,' Warren said.

'Does Columbia know?' I asked.

'They will as soon as we get off the phone,' Warren said.

I think this mercurial method of working, fast moves and sudden strikes, is immensely appealing to studio heads who themselves try to be startling and inventive. WB doesn't have to try. His innate style is to be a step and half ahead of the quickest consciousness around him. It is looking more and more as though at least a period of rewriting time will be sped up, so that *Vicky* will have first crack at becoming my next film. Is waiting another year for *Harvard Man* going to hurt? I don't believe so. But if I did, I wouldn't be able to admit it to myself now anyway.

10 September

I meet with Leonardo for dinner at a Thai restaurant on Sunset and Doheny. It is deserted. The waitress, an attractive Thai girl of nineteen, is completely smitten by him. Leonardo may well be in that category of stars off-camera as well as on. Each new time I see him, I am struck by how much further he has grown into himself. It is as though the physical filling out which he is working on is the embodiment of an internal, psychological, emotional, spiritual, intellectual development: the development of an actor. And he is ingenious. His quickness and sharpness, his ability to get the point of almost everything right away and to put you on the spot for an explanation when he doesn't, is bracing. If he avoids drugs – which he assures me he does – I see nothing that can stop him from becoming *the* young actor of the next decade.

He tells me more about his plans to do *Rimbaud* and his ongoing consideration of playing James Dean. But, unless he is simply trying to flatter me, which I like to think is not the case, his strongest excitement is for *Harvard*

Man. He seems to know, almost as well as I do, that it is the role he was born to play. He promises again to tell me of any commitment he makes: that is, he will let me know in advance so that I have a chance to strike if I am ready. I tell him the same. If this connection extends into trust, as it seems to be doing and if the sort of strange pleasure we take in each other's company continues to grow, this can become a great and long collaboration.

Permit me the use of an embarrassing word – a word I gave Axel Freed (Jimmy Caan) in *The Gambler* when dancing with his mother – but I have been 'blessed' with two great actor connections, Warren and Harvey, and I need both of them to continue if I am to develop in my work. But if I am to be able to write as well for people half my age (and I hope I will be), to stay in touch with that lost part of myself, the much-missed youth (how much deeper my understanding of Conrad, whom I've always loved, gets every year), I must have an actor to embody it. I must have a channel. As I sit with Leonardo, I am feeling more clearly than I ever have before the significance of connecting to the actor personally. If he is going to be not just a performer, not just an actor doing a job or acting a role, but a true expression of my own inner life and outer drama – which is, after all, what at my most ambitious I am aiming for – then I need this boy to be the one.

15 September

I am back in New York and at loose ends. My life and my work seem to be moving in every direction but ahead. There is an urgency to find a new apartment. Seeing twenty places the past two days, none of them alluring, pushes me to an edge of frustration and impatience of which I am afraid. I need to go up to Cambridge.

20 September

Being in Cambridge is not so exhilarating as it was when I knew that *Harvard Man* was next. If I am going to be doing *Vicky* before *Harvard Man*, what am I doing here? I feel like an undergraduate groupie as I sit in Bartley's Burger Cottage, eating health food now instead of the cheeseburgers I ingested in multiples of three twenty-seven years ago at the same table. It isn't that my enthusiasm is waning one iota. I could – I would love to – start shooting today. I am ready. Give me the money, Leonardo, Barry Markowitz (my cameraman from *The Big Bang*) and we'll go! But if I am going to do *Vicky* first, then it seems a kind of tease.

The groups are ferociously exclusive. African-American, Jewish, preppie, theatrical, academic, jocks – it isn't that they don't intersect, it's just that there has to be a primary identity within the Harvard identity for nearly everyone.

My Harvard Man will be of several identities (much like his creator): athlete, druggie, academic and sexual wild man.

I go over to the Carpenter Visual Arts Center (Le Corbusier's only American building) and hang around the theatre. The Harvard film world seems a bit self-consciously insular. Its highest esteem is for Bosnian documentary or Mongolian memoir. Not that one can't regard that as a huge leap forward from *Sleepless in Seattle*, but it would be nice to sense less of a self-congratulatory sentiment behind the arcane taste.

I am disturbed that my mind is wasting energy on such thoughts. My job is to write, to plan, to prepare. Let Nora Ephron – that Titan of American comedy – and the Mongolians do what they will.

2 October

Dinner with Tom Luddy, Ed Pressman, Barbet Schroeder, and Alison Maclean. Ed Pressman is close to my oldest friend. An independent producer of extraordinary success, he has initiated the careers of Brian De Palma and Oliver Stone and was responsible for Barbet's *Reversal of Fortune*. We grew up in the same apartment building (the Majestic, on Central Park West, where Frank Costello was shot in the lobby when we were ten) and we had summer houses a half-mile apart on the South Shore of Long Island. We also attended the same grammar school (the Ethical Culture School) and high school (the Fieldston School) where we were, in succeeding years, vice presidents of the student council. Ed played football (he was a remarkable quarterback, current physical stature notwithstanding), while I played basketball. He came close to producing *The Gambler* and also *Exposed*, but things didn't work out. Now we have talked about the possibility of his producing *Harvard Man*, but again it looks as if that will slip as well, sooner or later. I like him – as I've always liked him – and it gives my life a sense of symmetry to be sitting with him here tonight: two absorbed movie figures, forty-six years after first meeting in the lobby of our nursery school, when we were barely able to form sentences.

Barbet and I launch into a bracing exchange on the absurdity of giving away stories and plans to those who wish to hear them for free:

'Let me pick your brain for a moment.'

'I want to hire you – I'm going to make an offer – but what do you plan to do after our deal is set?'

Tom, spurred on by my boasting of Ed's football heroics, reveals his own history as a golf prodigy. Comedians want to be singers; singers want to be actors; actors want to be directors; directors want to be athletes.

Nothing concrete will come out of this evening, just camaraderie and fun. I enjoy myself immensely. But I am not doing what I am supposed to be doing.

3 October

Dinner with Madonna, Harvey Keitel and Ron Rotholtz (with his wife). Ron is vice-president of Madonna's company, Maverick, which will be producing the movie about Dean Martin which I know I am going to decline to write. We sit in the back of a sushi restaurant on Hudson Street owned by Bobby De Niro.

On the way down, we stop at a Miramax-sponsored rally for Mario Cuomo, who I am quite sure is going to lose the gubernatorial race to an upstater called George Pataki. Uma Thurman, Billy Baldwin, John Cusack – an abundance of film people – are gathered to say, 'We want you to continue, Mario.' Cuomo is most impressed with Madonna. Harvey Weinstein is almost tearful in his urgency to drum up support. He runs Miramax with expansive energy and enthusiasm, and although he made the unspeakable and unpardonable sin of declining to bid on *The Big Bang* when it was available for distribution, his instincts have been generally good.

In the restaurant I get engaged in a rapid-fire repartee with Madonna, who wants to know all about Warren and whose aggression, irony, wit and insecurity combine to make her an appealing and rather touching figure. When I first met her four or so years ago at dinner with Warren, Sean Penn and Jack Nicholson, she seemed like a tough, shrewd businesswoman more than anything else. Now she seems like a barely contained bundle of conflicting energies with a seasoned and ironic detachment. I liked her performance in *Dangerous Game* a great deal, with Harvey and Jimmy Russo. The movie, relentless, funny and entirely engaging, went largely unnoticed, and I get the feeling when I tell her about my appreciation of it that she is either extraordinarily shy and modest or a tad uninterested in being reminded, even flatteringly, of any kind of generally perceived failure. I tell her that I think she can be terrific on film, and realize later that what I mean is that she would be a natural at improvisation, since there is hardly a sentence that comes out of her mouth that isn't either fresh or witty. I tell her about *Harvard Man* and realize that I have not yet incorporated an idea I've had for a while into any of the versions of the script: to have several publicly known figures weave in and out of the movie as themselves. I'm not sure it will work, but I plan to try it, and I must be thinking of using her in that capacity. My own Harvard life was spiced pleasantly and oddly by random encounters with figures as diverse as Natalie Wood, William Styron, James Dickey, Nabokov, Joan Baez, Jack Kerouac and Muhammad Ali.

Charlie Rose, on whose show I have appeared a few times and to whom I like talking, is eating with Ed Kosner and his wife, Julie Baumgold. Kosner edits *Esquire* and Baumgold writes for it; they are two former *New York Magazine* figures, fixtures in the musical-chair game of Manhattan journalism, both sharp and likeable, and fascinated, as Charlie Rose is, with the movies and the people who make them. Politicians want to meet actors, actors want to meet politicians, and journalists want to meet, court, be courted by, hype and obliterate both of them. Charlie is with Amanda Burden, and the two couples together are harmonious and congenial. The atmosphere of this entire restaurant is, I'm suddenly aware, casually jovial in an almost perfectly pitched and orchestrated way. Twenty years ago, Bobby De Niro was riding up to City College with me in taxis almost daily so that he could watch me teach and pick up ideas for the role of Axel Freed (in *The Gambler*) which both he and I were sure he would be playing. When Karel Reisz decided to use Jimmy Caan instead, it certainly didn't end, or even weaken, my friendship with him, but it didn't intensify it or lead it to fulfilment either. Now here he is, having established himself as the actor of his generation and the entrepreneur of Tribeca. It seems like only yesterday, as my grandfather would say, that he was insisting on paying for the taxi and asking for a receipt.

I stop at Quentin Tarantino's table with Harvey on the way out. Everybody is excited for Quentin. *Pulp Fiction* is clearly going to be the *succès d'estime* of the season. He looks at me as if ready to fire a quote from *Exposed*, but surprises me. It's from *Fingers*: 'Any motherfucker tell you that in certain situations his dick ain't worth a shit is *lyin'*.'

Harvey looks bewildered.

'It's from *Fingers*,' I say.

'Jim Brown's line to you.'

Harvey turns to Quentin and back to me, shakes his head as if in tribute to Quentin's mnemonic capacity.

'But tell him the whole story!' Quentin insists.

Now I go blank. What story? Quentin waits. When I don't respond, he supplies the answer to his own request.

'You told me what that came from. It was such a great story. Don't you remember? You told me that the line came from him, from Jim Brown. You were in his living room, in some wild scene with all kinds of people, and he said that line. Then you used it for his part in *Fingers*, and when he read it in the script the first time he said to you, "That's a good line. That's true."'

'Right!' I say, as if stirred up from a senile haze.

4 October

Before a showing of *Red*, Kieślowski's self-proclaimed last film, I sit in the vestibule of the Sony screening room, thirty yards from the office in which I held my first movie-related job (as reader at Columbia Pictures the summer after my high-school senior year). I am on the phone on a three-way hook with Ron Rotholtz and Billy Gerber. Gerber is a junior executive at Warner Bros, attractive, funny, a rising studio celeb. I'm not sure exactly how much he actually knows about movies. I do know that the purpose of this call – which is that I am to 'pitch' a presentation of how I would write this Dean Martin movie to Gerber so that he will ask his superiors at Warner Bros to give me a lot of money to write it – is one that I cannot play straight. I certainly am not going (*qua* Barbet Schroeder) to give away my structural ideas for free on a casual fibre-optic preview. So I hum and haw when asked what I would do, and finally ask Billy what he would do. He comes up with some idea which I can't remember, but I tell him that I think it's just terrific. I assume that he will think after he has hung up the phone, 'If my idea is so terrific then why the fuck am *I* not getting more than a million dollars to write this fucking movie?'

6 October

Ron Rotholtz calls to tell me that Billy Gerber feels I have not given a sufficiently clear and inspiring idea of how I would do the Dean Martin story, and wishes to proceed at the invigorating figures I demand only if I would be working with a film-maker. I know I should not take such amusement from this sort of idiocy, but the alternative is to take it seriously, which is absolutely out of the question. That these eventually become significant matters in my cinematic life would suggest that, from a practical point of view, I would be well-advised to adopt an earnest air, but two or three panderings and who would be left to do the work? It is as if by behaving in some sort of freshly personal and surprising way, one keeps one's energies honed. No one needs to know what is going on except the doer (and in this case, the reader of the doer's journal).

7 October

I have breakfast with Pierre Rissient and Jerry Schatzberg at a coffee shop on Seventy-fifth and Amsterdam. Pierre is the most passionate lover of movies I have ever known. He has seen nearly everything worth seeing and has an opinion bordering on religious conviction about every moment of each film. He has directed a couple of intriguing movies himself, written a fair body of criticism and served as the most famous and effective promoter and publicist of serious new cinematic work around the world. He has also invented Clint Eastwood as a film artist, having made Eastwood's reputation as a director in France from which it has spread around the rest of the planet. There is hardly a helpful connection which Pierre does not assist his friends in making. To be a friend of Pierre's, it is essential that he like your work. If he doesn't, he will tell you so and tell you in a way that will make ongoing civility a near impossibility. Fortunately, he has been generous enough to my work to enable our friendship to flourish for sixteen years.

I tell him about this journal, and he immediately reminds me of Jean Domarchi, a great French film critic from the 1950s, through to the 1970s, and a literary and spiritual fixture of the French New Wave. Pierre introduced me to him when *Fingers* opened in Paris in 1978 and he subsequently wrote a beautiful essay on *Fingers* in a book called *Cinéma d'Aujourd'hui*, entitled 'Une beauté moderne ou le cinéma selon Baudelaire.' Since Baudelaire was at the time – and still remains – my favourite poet, I was overwhelmed with excitement to be compared in print to my *semblable*, my *frère*. Now Pierre suggests I return the favour.

'Domarchi has been dead for several years,' he says, 'and people have all but forgotten him. There is no serious film criticism being written anywhere, and so there is no writing about serious film critics. You owe it to him to refer to him in your journal. You must keep his memory alive.'

There is something riveting and altogether mad about this ferocious insistence over greasy scrambled eggs in a fluorescent coffee shop. But, of course, he is right.

And so I say, 'Remember Jean Domarchi. And better yet, read him.'

Jerry Schatzberg, a gentle and personable friend, with a penchant for films as dark and irregular as *Panic in Needle Park* and *Street Smart*, isn't a filmmaker of heat at the moment. In France he is still revered (a cult built around him largely through the efforts of the peerless French critic Michel Ciment started with the Cannes prize for *Scarecrow*), but in Hollywood today most executives would sooner finance a movie directed by their fitness trainer. Jerry maintains a plaintive but stoic good humour about his endless and often frustrating struggles to get film after film under way. There is a diminishing, not to say vanishing, openness to serious films in which naturalistically rendered human drama is the central concern. Jerry looks to sing in his own key against all odds. At various times, Jerry, originally one of the top fashion photographers in the world, has lived with this or that international star-beauty of the moment: Deneuve, Dunaway, Dyan Cannon. He also owned clubs in New York in the 60s (among them Salvation), in which every one of the night world sought to be noticed.

Three middle-aged gentlemen with aberrational tendencies and fortunate doses of self-mockery looking at each other and into themselves in anticipation of their next move.

9 October

In LA for a day, keeping fresh with Leonardo. A quick dinner renews the rush. I'm not ready to read him my 'final' draft of *Harvard Man*. I need to see through the options with Warren. I don't want to make my move on *Harvard Man* until it can be done as a unit: read it to Leo, read it to the studio execs, set it up. Twenty-four hours. No lingering, humiliating wait-and-see bullshit where the reader writes coverage which he/she summarizes in a paragraph for a junior hotshot, who summarizes it once again, this time in a single sentence, for the guy who can say Go or No. Fuck that. Come in with the script, Jeff Berg, a defendable and tight budget, the actor attached, read it to a group of suits with the Authority present to consolidate, and then close. That's the way, the only way, for me.

12 October

I'm back in New York. So is Warren, doing press for *Love Affair*. Nothing connected to him is going to get resolved in the next ten days. It is too unnerving and depleting after two years of preparation, shooting and editing, to get the response in one quick pop. 'Opening Friday afternoon' is all you need to know if money is the queston – and, of course, for most people it is. *You* know what you've done (or haven't done), but there *is* a wicked temptation to think of one's work reaching beyond one's living room – personal satisfaction or despair aside.

16 October

WB tapes *David Letterman*. Robert Morton, Letterman's producer, and an old friend, a funny and likeable *Landsmann*, entertains us in his office. The interview, which I watch on a monitor, begins with Letterman's announcing to Beatty that he has seen *Bugsy* five times and that he considers it a great film, a masterpiece. I have two responses: I don't remember anything else about the interview; and DL is without comparison the smartest and best TV personality in the history of the medium.

21 October

Love Affair opens. The response to the movie is tame. Unlike the frenzied enthusiasm from David Letterman and his audience, Oprah Winfrey and hers, Larry King and an array of other small-screen stars, the movie audience isn't showing up. The reviews are mixed, with a general acknowledgment that tears are induced at the end, but without a corresponding sense that the movie must be seen. 'It's become a one-week business,' Warren says on the phone. 'You open and you stay, or you don't and you close.'

I take this failure personally. I feel, as if I myself were the object of the attacks, that horrible sense of gloating from his acquaintances and fair-weather friends. (Elaine May once referred to Warren as 'The best of foul-weather friends', as apt a description of him as I can imagine.) I feel paranoid on his behalf. Warren will not whine or even complain. He will not only refuse self-pity but will refuse to acknowledge that there is a problem for which pity, or even concern, would be called for. But he knows. And they know. He is still Hollywood, a star's star, as David Letterman said. But there will be reverberations, if not repercussions, including some with impact on the writer of this journal.

22 October

Warren suggests coming out to LA for a meeting at Fox with Laura Ziskind, who has set up a production unit. As a vice president, she is able to sponsor a certain kind of 'popular adult' film. She has read the *Vicky* script and is, according to both Warren and Jeff Berg, excited and eager. She does have a caveat. The script reads like a $40 million movie. With a 'soft' film, a period piece with a female lead and no physical violence, she is looking to spend $20 million. With the revised emphasis on Vicky and Beecher at the centre of the film, this change should be no problem. I speak to her on the phone. That she wants a meeting in person this week doesn't augur well, as far as I am concerned. Jeff Berg and Warren say all will be fine, but I am suspicious. Everything that needs to be said can be said on the phone. But I'll go out for it. This isn't *Das Boot*.

3 November

Warren and I show up at Laura Ziskind's office on the Fox lot. It is late afternoon and dark. The last time we were together here was during post-production on *The Pick-Up Artist*. It seems like only yesterday. Ziskind is a producer by background, having established herself primarily through *Pretty Woman* and its multi-millions. She is new at her executive job – a single, solitary woman among a squadron of male executives. I make a proposal that I be hired to rewrite my own script, to see if the resculpting we have talked about will work and to discover if the cost can be cut radically. The idea would be that in a few weeks we would all decide whether to go ahead and make the movie, in which case it would start at some point in the not-too-distant future – although it emerges that Annette has just taken on *American President* with Michael Douglas, a film Rob Reiner is about to direct. I sense myself to be oddly detached from the proceedings. Is it jet lag or *Harvard Man* haunting me? Warren plays the role of encouraging observer. Ziskind, likeable and bright, continues to profess enthusiasm, undercut by financial fear. I leave the meeting with a sense that nothing will come of it. Is *Vicky* destined to wait another sixteen years?

4 November

Ziskind calls as I am staring out into the Hollywood hills from my roof terrace at the Beverly Wilshire (the same room Warren lived in for twenty years, and Elvis Presley and Irving Berlin before him). She is, in her own words, 'wimping out'. 'I'm too nervous about the potential cost,' she says. 'I just don't see the point in advocating a movie, much as I love it, and would love to see it made, which I know down the road will be rejected because of expense.' In former years with former films I would have bent her to my will, by persuasion or by threat. Either I am getting more civilized, or it is really *Harvard Man* that I know I must do, and I am using her reluctance as an out. I meet with Warren in his office and we discuss the possibility of working together on his political film. I tell him about *Harvard Man* and my readiness to go ahead. He has his Moon movie and his Howard Hughes film to think about as well. I feel I am sitting with my brother at a turning point in a family crisis, perhaps after the death of an uncle. We may part temporarily, but we will come back together.

I meet Leonardo for dinner. He is filled with energy, excitement and anticipation. If we can stay at this pitch of connection, something astonishing can happen in *Harvard Man*. I am more and more startled at how shrewd he is about all aspects of the business. He is not just a great natural actor. He is very smart and wittily self-critical.

6 November

Back in New York, Harvey and I pace around his loft discussing our respective, immediate futures. *Harvard Man* now seems inevitable. Everything else has faded. He introduces me again to Embeth Davidtz from *Schindler's List*, his now intensely connected girlfriend. 'You must use her, Jimmy,' he says when she leaves the room for a moment. 'She is the best actress of any age or nationality anywhere in the world today. You can't go wrong.' It doesn't take me long to agree. She is bright and articulate and has that indispensable emanation – which no actor can buy, rent or steal – of random openness. Anything you might be told about this person would be believable. She is both in demand and eager to work, frustrated with the roles she is being offered. She would be – will be – ideal as the philosophy teacher and lover of Alan Jensen (Leonardo).

8 November

I speak today, as I do every day, with the firm of Beatty, Berg and Levinson. Warren is still unsure about where he will go next. Berg is expanding. His time is now shared equally with former Defense Secretaries, the Governor of California, the Rand Corporation, international bankers, Clinton and nearly everybody else around the world who is manipulating global destiny. This last group, of course, includes his clients, for it is finally they – we – who, I continue megalomaniacally to believe, are the real shakers of consciousness and therefore the future.

Barry's youngest son, Jack, has been in and out of the hospital with pancreatic problems – this coming only two years after the removal of a tumor next to the brain. At the same time, Barry is being pumped daily by the Warner Bros crowd. They are convinced – and are almost certainly right – that he and they are about to enjoy the hugest of scores with *Disclosure*. I promise to see Barry in San Francisco within a week to get him the budget on *Harvard Man* and the 'final' draft in preparation for his moving on Warner Bros to set the movie up. I still have Simpson and – if her parenthetical enthusiasm is to be taken seriously – Laura Ziskind at Fox as alternatives. But I am looking to Barry with near certainty.

Dinner at eight. Norman Mailer, Michael and Norris, Tom Luddy and I meet at Elaine's. Norman and Tom are still where they were the last time we ate and talked about Norman's nineteenth-century political mystery with Milos – unresolved. They are still looking for an actor. A table in limbo. I tell the group about an episode with Jack Kerouac in my senior year at Harvard that is long and wild and odd, with Kerouac and me as the butt of the jokes. Norman loves the story and says, 'Write it. You'll be able to get it published anywhere.'

The idea appeals to me and at two in the morning I start in on it. Suddenly, in my second paragraph, I stop. Have I slowly but completely slipped out of my box? In panic I rip out my *Harvard Man* script and read scenes aloud, revising.

11 November

With so much possibility and so little realized it strikes me as a suitably ironic gesture to introduce each of the three films I've been carrying in my mind and writing during the year of this journal. So I set down the opening few minutes of *Shrink*, *Vicky* and *Harvard Man*.

Shrink

INT. DR ALAN MANNING'S – DAY
Fall, New York. The Present.
Opening lines start over black and white titles.
        CUT TO:
Helga, twenty-five, dressed in a short, tight skirt, lies on a couch. At first we see just her

lower half as she strokes her bare legs, speaking seductively. Then we pan up and reveal her face. Only upon cutting to Alan, who is seated out of her view at the head of the couch, do we learn that we are witnessing a psychoanalytic session.

HELGA: What are you thinking? I feel your mind at work. Fantasizing. Why don't you make it real? What do you want to do with me right now? Tell me, Alan. What do you want?

ALAN: I want to know what you think your intention is in talking to me the way you're talking to me.

HELGA: My intention is to seduce you.

Alan seems calm only on the surface. There is a definite hint of erotic desire contained.

ALAN: Well you know that isn't going to happen. I am your doctor, Helga, not your lover. So, let's try again. Why do you think you're trying to arouse me?

HELGA: I'm not trying to arouse you, Alan. I *am* arousing you.

ALAN: Forget Alan. It's Dr Manning.

HELGA: Whatever excites you – as long as you don't deny that you *are* excited. As long as you don't deny that you have a huge, swollen, reddish, purplish –

ALAN: I think we would make more progress if we could get through one session in which we avoided all speculation on my phallic condition.

CUT TO:

Second group of black and white titles as Helga speaks:

HELGA (*voiceover*): Do you? Is that really what you think? Because I think something else entirely. Let's have some fun in here, OK?

CUT TO:

INT. ALAN'S OFFICE – DAY

Helga sits up, faces Alan.

HELGA: What would you do if I just jumped you? What would you do if I ripped off your shirt and tore down your pants?

ALAN: I would resist. And if you persisted, I would have to stop treating you.

HELGA: Great. Then we could just fuck each other to death with no professional complications.

ALAN: Based upon four months of your own stories and confessions on this couch, do you really think that finding a new man to fuck is the answer to your anxiety, your depression and your two attempts at suicide?

HELGA: One and a half.

ALAN: Or do you think that finding a doctor that can help you might be more to the point?

HELGA: You *have* helped me. That's why I want to thank you, Alan, in my own way.

ALAN: Dr Manning.

HELGA: 'Doctor' Manning. It's so formal. What if I just call you fuck-face?
> CUT TO:

Third group of black and white titles over which we hear:

ALAN (*voiceover*): See if you can get through the next twenty-four hours
without any sexual activity. You'd be surprised how many new channels it
might open up.
> CUT TO:

INT. ALAN'S OFFICE – DAY

HELGA: If sublimation is so hot, then why don't you try it sometime?

ALAN: What do you mean by that?

HELGA: You know what I mean.

ALAN: No. I don't know what you mean.

HELGA: Think about it. It'll come to you.
> CUT TO:

*Fourth group of black and white title cards over which we hear the clicking on and off of
an answering machine and the start of Doakie's message which will continue with Alan
on camera when we:*
> CUT TO:

INT. BATHROOM, ALAN'S OFFICE – DAY

*Alan's bathroom is like a hidden, second personal office. Phone, answering machine,
TV, sports gambling paraphernalia. He clicks on his messages. As he listens he checks a
racing form and a football betting sheet, circling his selections. He also opens a small
safe and examines the cash in it – $15,000 in hundred-dollar bills.*

DOAKIE'S VOICE: Hi, darling. Great news. David Cort is giving me a full room
instead of just a wall in his gallery for my paintings. So there'll be space
for at least twenty. And the *Times* is doing a profile to coincide, which
means they'll want a few quotes from my brilliant and industrious
boyfriend. So start thinking up some wonderful lies.

ALAN (*addressing the machine as if it were Doakie*): Lies or lines?

DOAKIE'S VOICE (*from the machine as if hearing him*): That's l-i-e-s as in
fabrications; it's lousy to admit it but since we both know that we live in an
age of marketing hype, and you're the absolute best at that sort of thing,
we may as well take advantage of it –

ALAN (*again addressing the machine, overlapping Doakie*): Thank you. Just what I
always wanted to think of myself as – a huckster.

DOAKIE'S VOICE: I didn't mean that last remark as an insult, but you *are* the
glibbest talker on Earth so why not put it to use on behalf of your
betrothed – whoops! Was that a Freudian slip or what? I meant *beloved* not
betrothed. I'm running out now to do some errands and I won't be back
until tenish, so if you want to have a bite with Andrew, or arrange

something else on your own, feel free. Love you. Bye.

A click. The next message comes on over the next set of black and white title cards.

DR BROMBERG'S VOICE: Dr Manning this is Dr Bromberg from the American Psychoanalytic Association. Just a reminder that you are lecturing on obsessive, compulsive disorders at 3 p.m. Saturday. If you need a car to pick you up, we'll be happy to provide one. Please advise. You can leave word on my machine or fax me. Looking forward. Ciao.

CUT TO:

INT. ALAN'S OFFICE – DAY

Next series of black and white titles over which we hear:

RALPHIE (*voiceover*): So I said to him, listen to me very carefully, buster: I'm here. I'm queer. Get used to it!

CUT TO:

Ralphie, thirty, clearly gay, is laying on Alan's couch doing scissor-kick leg exercises.

ALAN: And how did he respond?

RALPHIE: He fired me.

ALAN: So do you regret it now?

RALPHIE: Not one smidge. My personal dignity is far more important to me than a crummy paycheck from some pathetic homophobic asshole.

ALAN: Did he remind you of anyone?

RALPHIE: I *know* what you're thinking. You're thinking he was my father.

ALAN: Was he?

RALPHIE: Figure of authority, mustache, loud voice, hyper-critical, heavy-drinker, bulging gut – I guess you could say there are a few similarities.

CUT TO:

Next set of black and white titles over which we hear:

MELISSA (*voiceover*): *Definitely.* My father. I'm sure of it. Who *else* could it have been?

CUT TO:

INT. ALAN'S OFFICE – DAY

Melissa, thirty, lies on the couch. Alan takes notes.

MELISSA: Everything sexual in my dreams goes back to him. The bastard. The dictatorial son of a bitch. Lording it over everyone as if he were God just because he has some bony piece of flesh sticking out between his legs. Big deal! I wouldn't take one if you gave it to me for Christmas. I know I shouldn't hold it against him. He was born with it. But that doesn't mean you should be *proud* to have one. I would be *disgusted* . . . and *ashamed*! Wouldn't you?

CUT TO:

Alan's look.
> CUT TO:

Next set of black and white titles over which we hear the voice of Henry (who speaks with a Jamaican accent). Henry is twenty-five and nattily attired.

HENRY (*voiceover*): She's a *woman*! What else can I *say*? She may be my mother, God bless her, but she's still a woman which means she has no penis and therefore wants to hang on to mine. Isn't that what Freud says?
> CUT TO:

INT. ALAN'S OFFICE – DAY

ALAN: Don't worry about Freud. What do *you* say?

HENRY: I say that *all* women – black or white, young or old, tall or short, fat or thin, rich or poor, smart or dumb – want to cut your precious dick right off your body . . .

At this image, Alan winces.

. . . and stash it away permanently in their private vault for their own selfish purposes. Am I crazy or am I right?
> CUT TO:

Alan, who seems to ponder the question.
> CUT TO:

Next group of black and white title cards over which we hear Alan's answering machine click on with the first line of Lois's voice before continuing on camera as we:
> CUT TO:

INT. ALAN'S BATHROOM – DAY

Alan massages his head, as if to assuage a headache.

LOIS'S VOICE (*as if in a post-orgasmic haze*): Hi, Alan, it's Lois – in case you don't recognize my voice. I just wanted to tell you how wonderful I've felt all day just replaying everything in my mind. Maybe we'll be able to spend a whole night together sometime. Wouldn't that be nice!

A click. Alan dials her number and gets a busy signal. He dials again. Another busy.
> CUT TO:

Next title cards start over Steve's dialogue
> CUT TO:

INT. ALAN'S OFFICE – DAY

Steve, thirty-five, in a Nike jogging suit, lies on the couch.

STEVE: My wife thinks I'm a bad husband, my mother thinks I'm a bad son, my daughter thinks I'm a bad father and my secretary thinks I'm a bad boss.

ALAN: And so what conclusion do you draw from that?

STEVE: The only conclusion anyone with half a brain could possibly draw. I'm a magnet for women who have a problem with men.

CUT TO:
Next title cards – the sound of push-ups and heavy breathing.
CUT TO:

INT. ALAN'S BATHROOM – DAY
Alan is doing push-ups on the floor of his bathroom. The phone is ringing from a call Alan has made on his speaker phone. A voice answers gruffly.
RUSS'S VOICE: Yeah.
ALAN: Hey, Russ.
RUSS'S VOICE: Big Al! What can I do for you?
ALAN: I need a thousand dollars to win on Revellie Hanover in the eighth race at Yonkers tonight. And what do you have on the Cowboy – Lion game and the Eagle – Jet game?
RUSS'S VOICE: Cowboys are four and a half, Eagles are up to three.
ALAN: I'll take the Cowboys for six thousand and the Eagles for eight thousand.
RUSS'S VOICE: Whoa, whoa, whoa, whoa! Let's get a handle on ourselves here. You're already down thirty-eight thousand dollars and change for the week and we got a settle-up figure of forty. You want to meet tonight and pay up the thirty-eight to give yourself some breathing room?
ALAN: Tonight's not good. I'll meet you Monday. If I still owe you, whatever it is, you'll have it. I just need to do a little juggling.
RUSS'S VOICE: You're always juggling. You should be in the circus. What are you panting about?
ALAN: Push-ups. Are we on for the football and horses or not?
RUSS'S VOICE: I'll take your action. But listen good, Big Al, don't come up short on me. You hear what I'm saying?
ALAN: I never have.
RUSS'S VOICE: Yeah, but you *almost* have. And the amounts are getting larger and larger. You don't want to get yourself in a situation where you're going to be needing a doctor, Doctor – do you?
ALAN (*adding the clap of marine push-ups, doesn't answer*): I'll see you Monday.
Russ hangs up, Alan finishes his push-ups, splashes water on his face, dries off, combs his hair and dials another number twice – both times busy. He takes the $15,000 from the safe and puts it in his pocket.

Harvard Man

Title sequence: Multi-colored titles over black – fifteen cards in all – separate each of the first fourteen shots.
The first title card reads:

HARVARD COLLEGE – CAMBRIDGE, MASS. – 1994

INT. ALAN JENSEN'S DORM ROOM – LEVERETT TOWERS – NIGHT
Alan, twenty, lithe and handsome, moves in smooth, rhythmic harmony with Cindy Baldolini, nineteen, tightly built and cute. A Jamaican sound blasts from one box while Bach's 'St Matthew Passion' blasts from another, two warring pieces from two black Sony CD portables, one on either side of the pair of fuckers, each within reach of Alan. A small color TV plays CNN with the sound off.
    CUT TO:
Second title card
    CUT TO:

INT. BRIGGS ATHLETIC CENTER – HARVARD BASKETBALL COURT –
NIGHT
Harvard and Boston College basketball players run through pre-game warm ups. The crowd files in.
    CUT TO:
Third title card
    CUT TO:

INT. ALAN'S ROOM – NIGHT
Continuing in rhythm, Alan modulates the volume of the respective boxes, first raising the level of the Jamaican sound and lowering the Bach, then reversing them. The phone rings incessantly as CNN still flickers mutely.
    CUT TO:
Fourth title card
    CUT TO:

INT. BRIGGS ATHLETIC CENTER – NIGHT
At the Harvard bench, Cain Preston, the coach, black, forty and dressed with conservative elegance, checks his watch as he surveys his players' lay-up drill. He turns to Dave Fox, his preppy, late twenties assistant coach.
CAIN: Any news?
DAVE: Nothing.
CAIN: You tried his room?
DAVE: Twenty rings.
CAIN: We'll go with Kenner.
DAVE: At point guard?
CAIN: Markham's sick. You got a better idea?
DAVE: Andrews.
CAIN: Andrews can't dribble his way out of his own asshole.
    CUT TO:
Fifth title card
    CUT TO:

INT. ALAN'S ROOM – NIGHT
Alan, continuing in his rhythm with Cindy, lights a joint and after inhaling deeply himself, sticks it in her mouth. She inhales as well. He turns up the Jamaican sound, turns down the Bach. They move to the music.

Throughout, unnoticed by either Andy or Cindy, a CNN bulletin special report has interrupted regular programming. With the sound still off, taped images reveal the devastation wreaked by a tornado on the town of Merryville, Kansas.
    CUT TO:
Sixth title card
    CUT TO:

INT. BRIGGS ATHLETIC CENTER – NIGHT
The Boston College cheerleaders, male and female, practice their routine. Butch, twenty-one, the leading male, speaks to Connie, twenty.
BUTCH: I wonder where Cindy is.
CONNIE (*shrugs*): Cindy's kinky.
    CUT TO:
Seventh title card
    CUT TO:

INT. ALAN'S ROOM – NIGHT
The rhythm is getting hard. They still move to the Jamaican beat.
ALAN: You ready?
CINDY: Uh-huh.
ALAN: You going to get out?
CINDY: Oh, God!
ALAN (*exploding*): Bang!
As they come together, Alan quickly lowers the Jamaican and raises the Bach.
    Tran-*scendent*! Wow!
CINDY: Whooo!
ALAN: Yeah! . . . you're the girl, Cindy. You know that.
CINDY: And you're the guy, fuck-face. You know that.
ALAN: What time is it?
He checks the clock.
    Seven twenty-five?! The alarm didn't go off. How could it not have gone off?
Frantically, he starts to dress.
CINDY: It went off. You just had the music blasting so loud you didn't hear it.
ALAN: It's supposed to buzz for half an hour.
CINDY (*dressing quickly as well*):
    It would have. I clicked it off with my toe.

ALAN: Where was I?
CINDY: Down below.
ALAN: Why did you do that?
CINDY: Do what?
ALAN: Turn it off?
CINDY: What's more important, a great fuck or a basketball game?
ALAN: You're trouble, you know that? You *know* that, don't you.
She does.
    CUT TO:
Eighth card
    CUT TO:

INT. BRIGGS ATHLETIC CENTER – NIGHT
The warm-ups are ending. Cain approaches Kenner.
CAIN: Kenner. You're starting at point guard.
KENNER: Really? What happened to Alan?
CAIN: Do you see him?
KENNER: No.
CAIN: Can you handle the position?
KENNER: I hope so.
CAIN: You *hope* so.
KENNER: I'll handle it. I was a point guard in Junior High.
    CUT TO:
Ninth card
    CUT TO:

EXT. CAMBRIDGE STREETS – NIGHT
Alan and Cindy run full-speed across the bridge to Briggs Athletic Center.
    CUT TO:
Tenth card
    CUT TO:

INT. BRIGGS ATHLETIC CENTER – NIGHT
The players are at center court. The referee tosses the ball up. The game begins.
    CUT TO:
Eleventh card
    CUT TO:

INT. BRIGGS ATHLETIC CENTER – NIGHT
Alan and Cindy rush into the building – he to the Harvard locker room, she to the Boston College cheerleaders' dressing room.
    CUT TO:

Twelfth card
 CUT TO:

INT. COURT – NIGHT
Radway, the Boston College point guard, guarding Kenner, steals the ball from Kenner just as he is looking over to Cain for a sign of what play to call. Kenner passes Radway and fouls him just as Radway is laying the ball in.
 CUT TO:
Thirteenth card
 CUT TO:

INT. HARVARD LOCKER ROOM – NIGHT
Alan gets into his uniform with wild speed.
 CUT TO:
Fourteenth card
 CUT TO:
Cindy, dressing quickly, finishes putting her cheerleader's costume on.
 CUT TO:

INT. COURT –NIGHT
Kenner throws a cross-court pass which is intercepted by Martin, a Boston College guard who drives and scores.
 CUT TO:
Fifteenth card
 CUT TO:
Alan rushes into the court area and approaches Cain at the Harvard bench.
ALAN: My alarm didn't go off!
CAIN: Sit down at the other end of the bench.
Kenner dribbles the ball off his foot. Cain calls Alan back.
 Jensen! Get in there for Kenner!

Vicky

EXT. HIRAM, OHIO FIELD – 1844 – DAY
The sun is rising through a spring haze in a large field at the outskirts of a village. We move in on a colorful wagon on whose immense canvas cover is painted the words:
THE INCOMPARABLE CLAFLINS – SPIRITUALISTS,
HEALERS, MEDIUMS – Cures for Headache, Depression, Cancer – Life
Elixir for Beautifying the Complexion and Cleansing the Blood – Trances,
Transcendence – Numerology – Moderate Rates – Satisfaction Guaranteed.

 The family consists of four members: Buck, with a black patch over one eye, ostensibly buffoonish, with an occasional English accent which shifts back and forth into various American dialects in the middle of sentences. He wears a dark suit meant to make him look like a gentleman, but it is too large, even as his overall appearance and manner are always gruffer than his pretensions. Roxy, forty-five, his German wife, alternately a virago and a sentimentalist, yells with a Bavarian inflection one moment, weeps inexplicably the next. Vicky, in this scene six years old, is a ravishing, intelligent, mischievous girl. Where Buck's commonness is obvious through his gentleman's veneer, Vicky, dressed shabbily in calico, has a natural, aristocratic air. Tennessee, the fourth family member, is the infant daughter. Buck is studying a one-hundred-dollar bill, fingering it for texture, holding it up to the sunlight for inspection. Roxy nurses Tennessee. Vicky is cooking corn meal and salt pork over a fire.

BUCK: Brilliant! The man who made this is an artist.

ROXY: Then why did he sell them to you, five dollars for every hundred?

BUCK: Because he's a rotten businessman. Look how green it is! Feel it.

Roxy touches it, unconvinced. In the distance a man on horseback riding towards them becomes visible.

Hurry up! Get inside!

Instinctively Vicky drops her cooking and heads into the wagon, following Roxy who has rushed in with Tennessee.

CUT TO:

INT./EXT. WAGON – DAY

Vicky, Roxy and Tennessee huddle inside the wagon, listening to the rider coming closer, finally stopping and dismounting outside. Vicky, clearly acting out a familiar pattern, sheds her work clothes and slips on a clean white dress. Roxy puts Tennessee aside and combs Vicky's hair hastily. Tennessee, her nursing interrupted, starts crying.

ROXY: Shhh! Tennie, don't cry!

As this preparation is taking place we cut back and forth to the conversation outside between the dismounted rider, Fogle, a man of twenty-five, who speaks with a casual, mid-western accent, and Buck.

BUCK: Consumption, fever, scrofula, piles, asthma, amnesia – we can cure them all.

FOGLE: What about dandruff?

BUCK: Forty-eight hours and it will never return.

FOGLE: It's in my eyebrows, too. I'm headed for Cincinnati to marry my cousin. She's the Mayor's daugher and I don't want a lot of flaking.

BUCK: Of course not. Flaking is the death of love. A woman of means, I imagine.

FOGLE: My cousin? Well, yes, I –

BUCK (*examining Fogle's scalp – interrupts*): Ugly looking crust.

There are two roads to the recovery from all disease. One is through the mind, the other's through the body. Now, I have a liquid here containing the same ingredient Queen Victoria of England used to destroy the dandruff that almost ruined *her*.

FOGLE: Queen Victoria had dandruff?

BUCK: When she was eighteen. All you have to do is rub a little of it into your scalp and eyebrows twice a day.

FOGLE: How long will it take to work?

BUCK: A week. No more – especially if you supplement the physical treatment with the other kind.

FOGLE: What other kind?

BUCK: The *spiritual*! What else?

FOGLE: You provide that too?

BUCK: Do I look like a fool? Inside this wagon is the only true spiritual healer in the world, Miss Victoria Claflin.

At the sound of her name Roxy shoves Vicky out of the wagon and down, where her eyes meet Fogle's.

FOGLE: She's a bit young for a healer, isn't she?

BUCK: So was Jesus Christ when God sent him down into Egypt. Sit yourself down over there.

Fogle sits on a bench near the wagon. Vicky looks to Buck who motions her (with his eyes and facial expression) to go and stand behind Fogle.

BUCK: My daughter's powers – which the Greek philosopher Demosthenes has provided – can only pass from *her* hands into *your* skull if you loosen all resistance. Believe and you will be healed.

This last sentence is delivered in a musical, incantatory, semi-hypnotic tone, and as he says it, Vicky slowly raises her hands and moves them around and forward so that each hand is directly in front of Fogle's eyes, both of which are closed. Vicky seems transported as well, with an intense, distant, beatific expression. Her hands tremble slightly as she speaks (and Fogle obeys).

VICKY: Breathe in. Hold it. Now breathe out. Your body is light. Your pores are open. You're floating in air. Your blood is rushing to your scalp. You're warm . . . you tingle. Breathe in. Hold it. Breathe and keep your eyes closed. Again. Your spirit is reawakening. Keep your eyes closed. Now snort.

FOGLE: Snort?

VICKY: Like you were blowing your nose.

Fogle snorts.

Again.

Fogle snorts again.

Now breathe normal.

Fogle relaxes. Vicky comes out of her trance.

You can open your eyes now.

Fogle opens his eyes.

BUCK: That's twenty dollars.

FOGLE: Twenty dollars!

BUCK: Ten for the liquid, ten for the transformation.

FOGLE: The best doctor in Ohio dosn't cost twenty dollars.

BUCK: The best doctor in Ohio would feel honored to shine my shoes.
Alexander the Great and Napoleon Bonaparte live on in the body of my
Victoria.

VICKY: Let's make it eighteen. He seems like a nice man.

BUCK: All right. But only this once – considering he's getting married.

Fogle pays.

Come back whenever you need us, Mr Fellows –

FOGLE: Fogle.

BUCK: Fogle. Cancer, consumption, gout – whatever you get, whenever you
get it.

FOGLE: You're always here?

BUCK: Here or somewhere else. Just ask around. We're famous.

CUT TO:

EXT./INT. MONTAGE

Titles with music are intercut with:

*– The Claflin wagon parked in front of a barn which has a large 'For Sale' sign
prominently displayed. Buck is bargaining with the Barnowner. They shake hands.
Buck gives him four of the counterfeit hundred-dollar bills. The man counts them, puts
them in his pocket, looks pleased. He gives Buck a document.*

*– Buck, Vicky (now eleven) Tennessee (now six) and Roxy (seven months pregnant)
enter a general store in Homer. They mill around, examining food and cloth. Buck slips
a cigar into his pocket and each of the three women secretes an item or two. The
Proprietors and other Customers are oblivious.*

*– Vicky draws a man into a trance. She massages one hand while Tennessee massages
the other. Meanwhile, Buck removes two bills from the man's jacket hanging behind
him.*

*– Outside the Claflin barn. The caravan is parked in front. Buck is shaving in the
background. Roxy, pregnant, paces around militaristically, observing carefully, first
sniffing and testing the food, then hanging over Vicky. Tennessee is cooking corn meal
and salt pork. Vicky seems uninterested in her work, moves slowly, with a pained
expression.*

ROXY: Why're you so slow today?

VICKY (*reluctant; not looking at Roxy as she says it*): I have cramps.

ROXY (*whispering*): That's the devil inside you.

VICKY: You won't tell papa, will you?

Roxy doesn't answer but as Buck moves within hearing range, she steps towards him.

ROXY: Vicky has the curse.

Vicky winces in anger.

BUCK: (*to Roxy*): Well, everything changes. And don't give me any devil talk, I'm too worked up as it is.

ROXY: What are you worked up about?

BUCK: The food. I'm getting tired of corn meal. Before I got married, I was eating pheasant and beef and cakes and drinking French wines at lunch and dinner.

Roxy rolls her eyes sarcastically as Buck speaks. It's obviously a tale she has heard many times before.

But I'll be back. Sooner or later a man gets his due rewards.

Buck turns away and we follow him into the barn. He takes a cigar from a box and lights it; then, casually, drops the lighted match onto some hay on the floor in a corner which ignites immediately.

When he turns to go out, he is startled to find that Vicky has followed him in and seen him light the fire. She says nothing, just looks Buck in the eye. He starts to speak, doesn't, then suppresses a smile of complicity which she shares. He then strolls out of the barn puffing on his cigar, Vicky by his side. They join Roxy and Tennessee. As the barn starts to go up in flames, Roxy shrieks.

ROXY: My God! What are we going to do?

BUCK: Nothing. Stay calm. Tragedy builds character. We'll survive.

He winks secretly at Vicky.

23 November

I am fifty today. Goodbye.

Postscript

24 December

Leonardo comes to Warren's former home on the roof of the Beverly Wilshire. I read him most of *Harvard Man*. We plan, for the moment, to shoot in the spring. The studio set-up move will have to wait until after the New Year, when Hollywood returns from the ocean and the snow. Months ago I had given Leonardo cassettes of five of my movies. His only references to them have been casual – as if the actual response to them had already been registered – which it hadn't been. Now, just as he is leaving, he suddenly flops down on the couch in fetal position, feigning sleep, fingers flicking pianistically on his thigh. Then he jumps up, apparently startled by a loud noise. It is a perfect imitation of Harvey's behaviour in a scene near the end of *Fingers*. I laugh. This is one brilliant motherfucker. I play out the remainder of the scene, the brutal Oedipal exchange between Harvey and Michael

Gazzo. Leonardo laughs. We embrace soon.

Later in the afternoon Warren visits. He is astonished at how small his old living quarters seem. You *can* go home again. Just don't expect it to be the same.

THE END

The Career

*Each year we feature a study of a director's career,
rendered in his own words. This year we chose not one but
two film-makers whose work reflects the diverging paths
the moving image took after its birth – towards actuality
and towards fiction: Ken Burns, whose documentary epic*
The Civil War *redeemed national history and entered the
mind and nervous system of America; and Arthur Penn,
the celebrated director of* Bonnie and Clyde, *whose
feature films have a vividness, physicality and depth of
tragedy rare in contemporary cinema.*

Arthur Penn

5   Penn on Penn
Interview with Tom Luddy and David Thomson

Introduction

If only today's young generation of film-goers had an Arthur Penn to follow. From *The Miracle Worker* (1962) to *The Missouri Breaks* (1977), he made riveting, unexpected pictures, drawing upon hit stage plays, novels, folklore and folk song, moments from American history, and dark nights in the nation's nightmare. Whatever the ostensible subject, Penn's rapt eye for human detail – what Robin Wood called his 'aliveness' – led into metaphors for the American experience. Custer's disaster in *Little Big Man* (1970) and America's handling of its natives, could not be seen or felt without reference to Vietnam. *Bonnie and Clyde* (1967) were the actual Texas desperadoes of 1930, but they were spokespeople for the anguished liberation of the late 1960s. In *Night Moves* (1975), a private-eye story drew us into the fears and anxieties that followed Watergate and an era of assassinations.

Time and again, Arthur Penn told a gripping story and let us know that the movies were a way of uncovering our deepest feelings about our world. His narratives were so grave, so beautiful and so tragic. It is so long since we have had an inescapable tragedian among major American directors. Succeeding generations have been too cool for that depth of expression. Yet it has to be added that Penn's pictures were also full of humour, anarchy, passion and hope. No one has ever shown outlaws so full of life, or a teacher (in *The Miracle Worker*) so filled with foreboding about what she does. No one has ever made violence so natural, necessary or liberating – and remember that, for Penn, Helen Keller is arguably more violent than Bonnie Parker. To this day, *Bonnie and Clyde* is a gangster picture, a comedy, a road movie, a tragedy, a modern Western, a love story ... and that's a lot to cram into 111 minutes. It is also characteristic of Penn in that every person and actor – not just Beatty and Dunaway, but Estelle Parsons, Denver Pyle and Dub Taylor – is attended to with an immediacy that bypasses judgement. The eroticism in Penn's films is his rapport with actors, all actors.

He was already thirty-four when he made his movie debut, *The Left-Handed Gun* (1957), but he had had a rich training in TV drama (usually live) and he was in the process of becoming a leading stage director (*Blue Denim, Two for the*

Seesaw, The Miracle Worker, Toys in the Attic).

Born in Philadelphia in 1922, he is the younger brother of the still photographer, Irving Penn. He went to Olney High School and then into the Army, where he served in the infantry. After the war, he attended Black Mountain College in North Carolina, as well as the universities of Perugia and Florence. From an early age, he was a student at the Actors' Studio, an involvement that continues to this day.

At seventy-three, Penn has been active in devising a new programme at the Studio. His career did not flourish in the 1980s, but that says as much about the American film industry as it does about Penn. We talked to him in San Francisco as he explored new projects. But he lives now, as ever, in the East – in New York and in Stockbridge, Massachusetts, the site of *Alice's Restaurant.*

TL/DT: *You came to movies, by today's standards, a little later than people do. You'd been in the Army. You'd been to college and then you directed for television and for theatre. Had movie directing always been your goal?*

AP: Not at all. Theatre directing was my goal. I had done a little bit of theatre, but not Broadway until after my first movie. But my interest had been the theatre. I didn't really consider movies much, because I'd had a frightening experience as a child in a movie and hadn't really gone to them very often at all. Practically not at all until middle adolescence. It was a horror film that my brother took me to that just sent me under the seat, when I was probably five or six.

TL/DT: *In Philadelphia?*

AP: New York by then.

TL/DT: *Would that have been a silent film?*

AP: It could well have been. I just remember being absolutely terrified. I didn't go back. The movies almost never interested me at all, even as just an audience member, until a time later. I was more interested in vaudeville, for instance. I went to see vaudeville in Philadelphia. But it wasn't until around *Citizen Kane* that I really got the click of what that medium was about.

TL/DT: *So when it came to* Bonnie and Clyde, *you did not know the American gangster film that well.*

AP: I did know a couple of them, Edward G. Robinson, *G-Man* and a couple of Cagney films. That was only because I saw a few films in the Army.

TL/DT: *Presumably, then, there was a moment in time where you said to yourself, 'Well, it looks as if I'm going to be a movie director'?*

AP: That happened quite late. Because I did *The Left-Handed Gun* first, and then had a traumatic experience of Warners editing it without my involvement. At that point, I went to Broadway and did a bunch of plays, and they all hit. And so I thought of myself still as a theatre director.

TL/DT: *Of course, you'd done* The Miracle Worker *by then, you were in your third medium. Can you itemize what it was that said, 'This is working for me better in film than it's ever done before'?*

AP: The last scene of the play is that marvellous scene where Annie drags Helen out of the house to the pump with a pitcher and pumps water. As habit would have it she spells w-a-t-e-r into the child's hands, and as the water hits, so. Now, on Broadway it worked absolutely perfectly. The audience just sat there and started to weep, and in the theatre there was a sense of this breath-taking event. So when I came to shoot it in the movies, I thought, 'Well, this is something I'm not going to mess with.' No coverage, no cutting, nothing. I'm just going to set the camera up and watch this happen. We did it. I looked at the dailies and I thought I was going to die. It was terrible, because it was just theatre. It had no cinema in it. My stomach went into a knot. Then I decided, about two days later, that we were going to go back and do it again and we were going to cover it. I wanted every event. I wanted the water hitting that child's hands, I wanted that expression on her face, I wanted Annie suddenly to sense that there's something happening in those hands, I wanted to be able to control the time of this. That was the intoxicating experience of cinema. I suddenly realized that, boy, this is some medium. It's not theatre, it's not anything like theatre, it's another whole experience. And it really belongs to the editor and to the director, to make time over so that you can control it.

TL/DT: *So when you began to shoot it in that much more fragmented way, did you know in advance how you'd cut it, or was it more the excitement of knowing that there would be so many ways you could cut it?*

AP: I knew the sequence of it. I just didn't know how long each one would endure and what the rhythm would be. Because there has to be a slowly escalating rhythm to that, you know, so it's a few frames off here and there. But I was certain once I'd made the decision to shoot it that way, it was so obvious to me, even while I was shooting it, that it was going to be electrifying.

TL/DT: *Did it make you wish you could go back and shoot some of the earlier scenes?*

AP: Oh, exactly! If I had one complaint about having made *The Miracle Worker*, it was that I left it too theatre-based. To give you an example: in the theatre, Victor Jory, as the father, has to keep saying, 'Well, leave the child alone. That's how she is. Well, if you're going to take her to the summer house, two weeks and that's it. No more.' That was all theatre, to give Annie something to fight against. In the cinema, we didn't need that. You simply show this child as an unassailable phenomenon – you know, that mind shrinking, there's no way to reach it and time is passing, and you watch her stumble and fall. Laundry hanging on the line becomes something absolutely life-threatening, that she gets entangled in it and suffocates. A Christmas tree ball, in the titles, is suddenly something with which she could cut her vein.

TL/DT: *Let's go back and talk a little bit about your TV work. For most people today,*

The Miracle Worker

The water pump: Anne Bancroft and Patty Duke

that is an era that's almost as romantic as silent movies, and harder to see. Let's take
The Miracle Worker, *which you did, I think, as a* Philco.

AP: No, it was *Playhouse 90*. My memory is that by the time of *Playhouse 90*, that had become the Cadillac of the Golden Age. Back on *Philco*, we were on the Ford Model A era, where we would rehearse about eight or nine days, and then have two days on camera and go on the air. On *Playhouse 90*, we were up to about three weeks of rehearsal, and then some four days or so with cameras, and more than three cameras by that time. We were able to have four, five, six, seven cameras, which made things easier. Just pure traffic, you know? You could have cameras set up in another set where the actors were going to. Previously, you had to stay on one camera, release the other two cameras to get over to the other set so they were able to pick it up as this one finished, and that was constantly in one's mind. The dominant force was: can 3 get under 1's cable and get over? All that had to be plotted out at home. And the cameras had turret lenses. They didn't have zooms yet, so if one camera was on a loose shot and next I wanted a close-up on that, I had to go to another camera in between to some other shot, while this guy flipped lenses. It was an extraordinary body of training.

TL/DT: *Where were you when all the cameras were rolling, physically?*

AP: In the control room, calling them. You literally called them. You said, 'Three will be next on a 75mm medium, up here, second button. Hold it, hold it, hold it. Take.' Boom. And we were just talking. Each of us – the technical director was talking to the cameraman; I was talking to the stage floor managers. It was an extraordinary event.

TL/DT: *Was the writer next to you all that time, during the rehearsals and everything?*

AP: Particularly on *Philco*, where the writers were so involved with the whole entity of the *Philco* show, with Fred Coe as producer. The respect for the writer was so great on *Philco*; that was its distinguishing factor. So, yes, the writer would be with us. Paddy Chayefsky and . . .

TL/DT: *Overhauling the script and changing it?*

AP: Sometimes. Sure. When you've got a terrific actor going in some part it suddenly became very clear that you had to make a certain change to accommodate that. And they would. Bill Gibson was there for *The Miracle Worker*. That's about it, I think, on *Playhouse 90*. I did four of them. No, Rod Serling was there for one. One was *Charley's Aunt*.

TL/DT: *And most of these haven't survived, is that right?*

AP: No, they haven't survived. The reason, I believe, that has always been given to me, was that they were unable to decide a union jurisdiction. Because it was direct broadcast, it was to be AFTRA, which is the American Federation of Radio and Television Actors, but the Screen Actors' Guild made the very strong point that once it was kinescope, it was now on film. So they decided that the solution was to destroy them. They couldn't resolve it. They simply could not resolve the jurisdiction.

TL/DT: *You studied at the Actors' Studio, at least you were a part of the Actors' Studio. Let me be devil's advocate for a moment. In the last few years, there has been talk that maybe, for all the glories it produced, the Actors' Studio led American acting into too introspective and narcissistic a direction. I'm saying this just to provoke you.*

AP: You're succeeding.

TL/DT: *What is it about the Actors' Studio that's been so important for you?*

AP: Well, it is that introspection, if you will. It's the availability of personal emotion in a situation that's not – how should I say? – an agreed-upon attitude, but it's something that comes out of each individual actor. Consequently, it comes out differently from each one, so one can stimulate actors like Newman and Brando to do stuff that would be very hard to come by otherwise. At least it would be for me. If they weren't trained that way. Because it's a way in which they come to be comfortable with their own associations with those situations. It's a great 'as if' – 'As if I were genuinely Billy the Kid in this situation, this fills me in this strange way.' So you get that funny behaviour from Newman in *The Left-Handed Gun*, that seemed to me so appropriate and original.

TL/DT: *But do you not think that in some cases the Method has meshed with star status and has produced some excesses and even, in some cases – and Brando's the obvious case – a kind of reluctance even to work?*

AP: I wouldn't lay that at the feet of the Method. Brando's not working is very complicated. The product of so many things. No, I do think that an awful lot of people became sort of soi-disant Methodists, because they hadn't really studied this stuff. They saw: 'That's how actors act on a set, so that's how I'll scratch myself.' What the hell. You see it in all of its gradations, from people who really know what to do or how to do it, or at least how to trust what we were searching for, to those who are imitating them. But that's true of any acting style. You look at the British theatre, you can see the great stars, the great actors who can get through that declamatory style to something that is so personally moving. I mean, you watch Gielgud and there's nothing in the world that that man can't do. On the other hand, you watch those who are not Gielgud, many of them are terrible! Just a beautiful voice and all of those gestures.

TL/DT: *Let's talk about* The Left-Handed Gun *a bit. As a studio film, that must have got a lot of opposition. You said earlier that the film was really taken away from you at the end. Could you talk about it in terms of the battle you had with that film?*

AP: We didn't have a battle; we were so negligible on the Warners lot at that moment, nobody paid attention to us. We were a $700,000 film, or something like that, and Paul was not a big star, you know? He'd been under contract at Warners and they had dropped him. Then they picked him back up after *Silver Chalice* and made him do a few more films, and this was one of

Paul Newman in *The Silver Chalice* . . .

. . . and in *The Left-Handed Gun*

those films. But he wasn't greatly significant. At that time, there were big pictures. Spencer Tracy was making *Old Man and the Sea* for Zinnemann, Billy Wilder was making *Spirit of St Louis* with James Stewart, and I think Wellman was shooting *Lafayette Escadrille*. So we were this tiny little picture. Indeed, I had a cameraman assigned to me named Pev Marley, who was one of the solid old-timers, and at one point, very early in the shoot, we were lining up a shot, Pev was practising his golf stroke, and some guys came by and said, 'How's it going, Pev?' And he said, 'Got one of these television guys.'

TL/DT: *By that he meant what?*

AP: He meant, not one of the solid old guys who were going to do it in many takes and stuff. We had twenty-three days to make that picture and so I brought over all of the knowledge I had, which was considerable, from live television. What I did was go round on the sets and nail Dixie cups into the ground with the lens designation. That didn't set well, as you can imagine. 'What the fuck is this? It says 35 down here. Hell, oh, you want a 35 here? You know, the 35 in movies is not the same as 35 in television.' 'No, I didn't know that.' 'Well, you God-damn well better know it now.' That kind of dialogue. They were resentful of us, because television had come along and just bit them.

TL/DT: *Was there anxiety over the material, too?*

AP: Fortunately, nobody read the material. Except me, Leslie Stevens and Fred Coe, and Paul and the cast.

TL/DT: *Jack Warner didn't read it?*

AP: To my knowledge, nobody read it. Nobody even asked about it. The only thing was, we asked if we could rehearse and they said no.

TL/DT: *Had you directed the television play?*

AP: No. Robert Mulligan had directed it from a Gore Vidal play, which was quite different from this one. Stevens and I really wrote this.

TL/DT: *Did the day come when they had a sense that there were still echoes of Gore Vidal's kind of homoerotic ideas?*

AP: No. They cut the film and it was a kooky Western, that's all they ever thought of it as, and they released it on the bottom half of a double bill. That was the end of it in the States. It was not until it got to Paris and André Bazin and those fellows picked it up, but here, I don't think they perceived it as anything. The kind of memos I got were, I was shooting a scene one day, 'Too many wide shots'. Then I would go in and cover that scene the next day and the memo would be 'Too many close-ups'.

When Fred Coe and I arrived at Warners, we went up and were introduced to Jack Warner. Jack Warner took us on a walk around the studio, wanted to show it off, and in the middle of that walk – here we were planning to come and make a movie – he said, 'You guys are from television, right?' Mostly meaning Fred. 'Big stuff, huh?' Then he said, 'You want to take over our

The Left-Handed Gun: homoerotic overtones

The Left-Handed Gun: Arthur Penn with
the actors

television department?' We both said no, that what we came out here for was to make a movie. That was it for him. He didn't know what this television beast was. He knew there was money in it, he knew it was having an enormous success and thought, 'Better join it than fight it.'

TL/DT: *Did you have a sense, though, when you were making* The Left-Handed Gun, *of how very, very different it was from the Westerns of 1957–8?*

AP: Oh yes. Yes, I did. We both did. Leslie Stevens and I both knew that we were treading on sacred ground, peeing on sacred ground.

TL/DT: *What was it about* The Left-Handed Gun *that excited you?*

AP: Well, a couple of things. One, the whole theme of somebody writing about someone else and creating a figure that that person then cannot match, that would be a kind of tragic turn in the course of the film. Second, I would at last be able to shoot with just one camera, instead of worrying constantly about photographing the other cameras. Because that's the nightmare of live television, you know, that you can't move into places. Everything is on 180,* or less actually, and around the curve here. I could do things like where Paul decides what's going to happen and then flash-forward. I thought that this is just the most fun medium that ever has been. So the shock of having it taken away from me to be edited by somebody else was enormous.

TL/DT: *Was that a shock because you simply hadn't realized how the studio worked, or did they break their word?*

AP: No. They never broke their word. It never occurred to me until this guy came up to me and said, 'Hello, I want to introduce myself. I'm the most creative editor in Hollywood. My name is Folmar Blangsted and I'm going to edit your film.' I said that I was very delighted, as I thought we were going to do it together. It didn't dawn on me for a few more days that it was not to be that way.

TL/DT: *Were you actually barred from the process?*

AP: Yes. Warners said, 'You're finished. Your parking place is gone, your gate pass is gone.'

TL/DT: *When you saw the film, was it very different from what you'd intended?*

AP: No, no. It's tonal. It was just fortunate, because having come from television, I really didn't shoot very much extra stuff. I didn't, as they say, cover. I was on such a tight schedule that I had to come lined up with every shot in my script book to make the day. It was just move, shoot, take, move. So there wasn't a lot for Folmar to play with, but it's those six frames off here that would make it better, or twelve more frames there that would make it different. It's rhythm, I guess, just plain rhythm. They did cut one scene which was the culminating scene where Hurd Hatfield goes into the bar, after Billy has dumped the stuff on his back from the satchel, and he's weeping. He says, 'He

*180: the area in which everything is in front of you.

must be stopped.' It was a real portent of the closure. To my knowledge, that's the only scene that they cut.

TL/DT: *Did that editing experience ever happen again, or were you in charge by the time you did* Miracle Worker?

AP: Yes, we were in charge. It didn't happen again until *The Chase*, but there it was malicious. Sam Spiegel broke his word. We were supposed to cut it in New York and then when we finished, he said, 'All right, Arthur, where do you want to do your cut? Hollywood or London?' I said, 'You know, Sam, I'm committed to do *Wait Until Dark* on Broadway,' which I was. And he said, 'Well, darling, I can't bring the picture to New York.' That was it. I didn't see that picture until I finished the play and flew to London. They had already edited about eight reels, fully scored, everything. Mixed.

With *The Miracle Worker*, since it was a United Artists' picture, there was a clear presumption that the director would have final cut, and that was the practice of UA at that point – Arthur Krim, Bob Benjamin, David Picker. Sam, on *The Chase*, was attempting to evade that, but it was becoming more and more the dominant form of movies, because there was a new generation of people who came in with a distinctly different vision. But probably it was also associated in large part with TV, and there began to be more and more studios that were giving final cut to the directors. It was a presumption from there on. I did *Mickey One, Bonnie and Clyde, Little Big Man, Alice's Restaurant* – all of those were with the director having final cut. It was not just me, it was the practice with directors of a certain status. And it's relatively recently that studios have taken it back into their industrial vision. I think it's crazy, because you're turning over to an audience of people who have been witnessing films the option to voice their opinion that this film doesn't resemble what they've seen. They regard that as a liability or a detriment, where I would regard it as a significant difference, a leap forward or a leap in a different direction. Consequently, originality gets filtered out by that process.

I had one of those previews where they put the film on one of those great big dishes, a flat platter, and just as they started the film – this was *Target*, I think – bing! The film flew off the platter. Stopped the projection. Now, there's a big delay. Sam Cohn, who was there, said, 'Let's at least help the audience to feel that we want them to stay.' So they opened the candy concession free and these people came out and gorged themselves on huge amounts of popcorn, candies, soda and stuff, then they went back in. About forty minutes or so later, we started the film again. By this time they were on such a sugar high, I don't know who the hell they were! If you hire somebody to make a movie over a year's preparation and shooting, and so forth, then trust that person with that expenditure, why take away the very final essence of what that person brings to the film? But it satisfies their corporate egos and their belief that we're making products rather than art.

TL/DT: *If you had absolute power, would you never preview a film to an audience? Would you always believe in trusting your judgement and the judgement of the few people who had been on a film all the way?*

AP: Yes. It sounds terribly narcissistic, but yes, I would. That doesn't mean that I wouldn't preview for a different kind of information for myself, but I wouldn't have cards, I wouldn't ask for opinions. I would just see whether or not the rhythm of a given scene worked. You feel it. You absolutely feel it. I did a play in New York, *Two for the Seesaw*, and we then took it to London. The habit in New York was for us to stand in the back. So opening night, or preview night, or whatever it was, Fred Coe and I were standing in the back and Binky Beaumont came up to us right before the curtain and said, 'Oh no, dear boys. Oh no, no, no, no. There are two seats down there. You're going to be right in the middle of this.' His whole idea was that you've got to sit there, there's a lot of wisdom behind that. Absolutely. Certainly in a little preview, that's what I would do. It would be more meaningful to me that way, to feel the energy and the heat in the room if something was happening. But the worst thing in the world, it seems to me, is turning in little cards, because at that point each audience member becomes a quantifier, a person who says, 'Wait a minute. In my history, have I seen a film like this? Is *this* what I want to see?'

TL/DT: *That's when the marketing people take the power away from the production people?*

AP: Marketing people. I'll give you a perfect example of the marketing people's perspicacity. Benny Kalmanson – the man at Warner Bros, head of distribution – after looking at *Bonnie and Clyde* turned and said, 'This is a piece of shit.' Then he marketed it as if it were a terrible film and that was the decision. Then suddenly the film got away from everybody, but it was intended to go in a given path. It was booked and rented on split weeks. *The Graduate*, which had come out at the same time, had a five-week guarantee. You couldn't get that picture unless you guaranteed it five weeks in your theatre. We were guaranteed split weeks. It was terrible.

TL/DT: *Now,* The Miracle Worker *was a hit.*

AP: It was a big hit, but there was a certain peculiar residual tension, because when it was announced it was to be made into a movie, Audrey Hepburn wanted to make it and Elizabeth Taylor wanted to make it, and UA, for all of their great *laissez-faire* views, thought that they had really hit the jackpot. Then they were dealing with this group of crazy people who said, 'No, it's Anne Bancroft or nobody.' They were furious with us. So that even a year or two later, when I was speaking to Bob Benjamin about something else and this came up, I said, 'Yeah but Bob, both people won the Academy Award.' He said, 'Anybody would have won the Academy Award in those parts.'

TL/DT: *On the face of it,* Mickey One *is about the least likely film anyone made in the 1960s. Where did it come from?*

AP: Well, there was a play by Alan Surgal that I read with great interest, because it was about a comic and I'd had those two years on the *Colgate Comedy Hour* working with all those folks. What seemed to me to be really interesting – and this is layering it with so much baggage, but I'll risk it – what I was particularly concerned about in that period, which was in the early 1960s, was that the McCarthy period had ended ignominiously for the McCarthyites and yet nothing had really changed politically. People were still quite frightened and there was still the sense of being in somebody's thrall for your past. Whatever you did in your past – even if unknown to you – was somehow held against you and known to somebody. So I asked Surgal if this had any meaning for him and he allowed as how it did. So we then tailored that portion of the play to that idea and it was meant to be a political metaphor. I don't think it was seen as such and maybe that's partly my fault. I think a good deal of the obscurity of it could have been diminished and anchored a little bit better.

TL/DT: *It's also a movie about a certain kind of stage fright, a performer who loses the confidence to perform. Beatty is an actor with a curious reluctance to act. I wonder how that evolved in your working with him.*

AP: Well, on Beatty's behalf I have to say he sought me out and said he wanted to work with me. I said, 'I've got this film.' Beatty didn't like the film, he didn't like the script. He thought it was much too obscure, but he was willing. Beatty's very smart in that regard. So we made this film and I said, 'I'm going to push you. I'm going to push you.' There were days of tension, there was no question about that, but on the whole, he really was a committed actor. He hated the material, saying, 'Nobody's going to understand this fucking scene. Why don't we just say what it's about then?' And I'd say, 'No, Beatty, we're not going to say what it's about.' That was it. But I did push him. There were a number of sequences there where I kept saying, 'Come on, come on, you can do it better than that. Let's get out here and do it.'

TL/DT: *He was being reticent?*

AP: Yes. He's personally reticent about emotion. He doesn't like strong displays of emotion and he knew that he had been getting along very nicely on his good looks and his persona. He'd been very attractive in *Splendor in the Grass*. I thought he wanted to go over that barrier, over that line. So we did.

TL/DT: *Can I ask one more question about* Mickey One? *I can see the American political allegory there, but it also seems to me that after* The Miracle Worker, *there's something in the film that suggests a European influence, too. Were you thinking of making a film further from Hollywood in the Bergman/European sense?*

AP: Oh yes, because also between *The Left-Handed Gun* and *The Miracle Worker* in combination, I had had a chance to meet all the guys in the *Nouvelle Vague*. Godard and Truffaut and those people. We'd developed a little bit of an intimacy, of let's talk to each other through our movies, you know. And so both of them showed up on the set of *Mickey One*. They both came. Truffaut to

Mickey One: a performer who loses the confidence to perform

Mickey One: Warren Beatty

Mickey One: Arthur Penn on set with Warren Beatty . . .

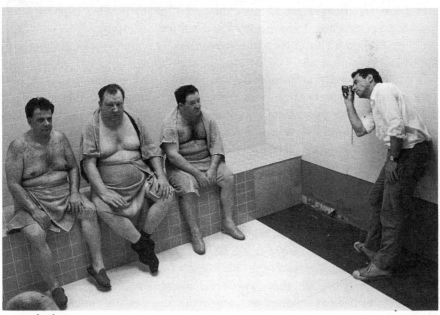

. . . and others

spend time with Alexandra Stewart, and Godard dropped by for a while and hung out. So it was not exactly a *Nouvelle Vague* as if the water were just flowing on to these shores. There was a riptide, too, going in the other direction.

TL/DT: *And you probably felt that your best audience for* The Left-Handed Gun *was already in Europe.*

AP: Exactly. I thought I had definitely made a picture that Europeans were going to respond to.

TL/DT: *Was it predictable, at the time of* Mickey One, *that Beatty was going to become a producer? Could you see that emerging?*

AP: Unquestionably. That was the dominant characteristic: his clear knowledge of the hierarchical structure of the business and how to conduct it! He was dynamite and it was clear then. Charlie Feldman was already one of his best friends and he was learning the business from him.

TL/DT: *Charlie Feldman can't have encouraged him to do* Mickey One.

AP: Can't have, no. But I don't think Charlie encouraged him at that level at all. It was entirely: 'What's the deal? How do you do it?'

TL/DT: *Was there ever any pressure on you from the studio to do it in colour?*

AP: No, no. I made the deal with them. After *The Miracle Worker* I said, 'I want to make two films, a million dollars each, and the only stipulation is that you guys can't read the script, and I just do the film and that would be it.' No requirement to have stars. So Beatty did that for a relatively nominal sum. But no, there was no pressure.

TL/DT: *The success of* The Miracle Worker *and the Oscars gave you the clout?*

AP: Yeah. But I never got to make the second picture. What happened was peculiar, because then I was making *The Chase* for Columbia.

TL/DT: *That wasn't the second picture in your deal?*

AP: No, no, no.

TL/DT: *What would that second picture have been?*

AP: I don't recall, because I thought I'd do *Mickey One*, then I'd do a commercial picture and then I'd come back and do something else by that point, but that would be several years down the line. They called me one day on the set of *The Chase* having seen *Mickey One* finally, and a more strangled conversation you have never heard in your life. 'Hi. We saw *Mickey One*. It's . . . it's good, its very . . . well.' Just these voices. It was Frankovich and Leo Jaffe and those guys. They didn't like it one bit.

TL/DT: *Now,* The Chase *seems historically remarkable in that within the space of a few years, it was possible for you to make what was evidently a big picture, with a lot of stars, a picture that is driven by fear and loathing of American society. Was there never any kind of caution about that?*

AP: Interestingly enough, there wasn't. I'm not sure that on reading the script it would have been as apparent as it was in the film. I mean, certainly there are those pure Lillian Hellman scenes of Henry Hull and those people carousing and that stuff, which was readable. But Lillian's dialogue is very hard to read for its undertone, you know? Fortunately, I'd had the pleasure of doing her play *Toys in the Attic* prior to this, so, by then I had developed a real understanding of her language, and what was in the script became more apparent. Things like the big beating of Brando was Brando's idea. He suggested how to do it. I didn't know how to do it. I was going to do it rather conventionally with a double and he said, 'No, I can do this. If we do it, we act it in slow motion and we shoot it in fast motion.' And that's how we did it and then the blood would come out. It was an astonishing idea and it worked brilliantly.

TL/DT: *You said that you thought that the full resonance was maybe not apparent in the script. This is a good moment to talk about something that is certainly apparent in the film, but I think is a keynote to your work. It's a very physical thing. You're one of the directors who does it better than anyone. Do you ever really instruct and indicate meanings?*

AP: No, I don't indicate meaning. I will sometimes demonstrate a physical move, but almost a travesty of a physical move, so that they invent it themselves. It's clear that they're not to imitate me. I don't know where it comes from or what it is, but I have a strong sense, both in the theatre and in film, of the physicality of the idea. That there's a physical correlative to an idea, to a meaning. Theatre is such a verbal medium and so I was always pressing myself to ask, 'If somebody didn't understand the language, what would they understand in this scene?' In *The Miracle Worker*, that was literally the case and that taught me a great deal. So I've always opted for that sense, that there is a physical correlative to the meaning of a scene, to the subtextual meaning of the scene.

TL/DT: *And you cast it freely? Or did your producer?*

AP: We cast it jointly, but I was dazzled by what Sam could do. I knew we had Brando right off the bat when I first signed on. But I was dazzled that he could get Jane Fonda and Redford. Then he said, 'Who do you want for these bank clerks?' and I said, 'Well, I know a wonderful actor I've seen in New York named Robert Duvall.' And Janice Rule was from the Studio. Jane Fonda was from the Studio. Dick Bradford was from the Studio. It was great fun to work with that cast. What troubles me in the editing is not that the film is badly cut. On the contrary, it's very well made, but has a certain stolid orthodoxy that troubles me when I watch it. I long for aberrations, and they existed. Brando did some improvisatory moments with the other players that were just breathtaking, scenes with Angie Dickinson and others, and they are not there. I think Sam feared those moments as being 'outside' the film when, in fact, they *are* the film. It's a nutty place, that town, and America sure was a nutty place when we were making that film. I wanted the film to be more dangerous and sadly I view it now as compromised.

TL/DT: *Is the scene with the horses going by one of them?*

The Chase: the beating (Angie Dickinson and Marlon Brando)

The Chase: Brando and Penn

The Chase: 'It was great fun to work with that cast'

The Chase: shooting . . .

. . . Robert Redford

AP: Yes. There were moments where he would do the damnedest things. That line about, 'You don't need another gun, you got all the . . .' That was pure Brando. Then, fortunately, I didn't even go to the line in the script. I said, 'That's great. Let's leave that.' But that's the part that dismayed me about the cutting. I mean, it's the movie I shot, there's no question about it. It just doesn't have the rhythms. And consistent with what you were talking about in terms of the physicality, the rhythmic cutting is such a part of that. That's what I was able, with Dede Allen, to do so well on subsequent films. We'd just nip a frame here, nip six frames there. It picked up the rhythm. Then let's cut here and it energized so. She had the same kind of physicality that I had.

TL/DT: *Let me ask you a more personal question. You are, to my eyes, a gentle person. You're articulate. You're slight in frame. Your films are some of the greatest treatments of violence in American film. Is there a violent side in you that we can't see?*

AP: Probably. I'm fairly certain there is.

TL/DT: *Were you in combat in the war?*

AP: A little bit, yes. In the Battle of the Bulge. I saw enough of it certainly for it to make an enormous mark on me. Probably I have avoided violence, physical violence, because I'm not big enough to take on most of the people.

TL/DT: *But with a tremendous feeling for it.*

AP: I don't know where or how it came into being, other than the way I've described, which is to try to make meaning in the theatre more apparent through body language than through verbal language.

TL/DT: *It's also often not just destructive violence in your films. One of the things that's remarkable about* Bonnie and Clyde *is that people almost discover themselves through violence. Do you believe that?*

AP: I do. I think they do. I think that people don't know what they will do in extreme circumstances. That's why I take such great pleasure in the sequence in *Bonnie and Clyde* where they rob the bank and C. W. Moss sees the parking place, parks the car and they come out of the bank. And that's what a comic scene turns into the first time that Warren shoots somebody and kills him. I thought, it must have all of the shock that's then going to dictate the rest of his life. It's an existential turn, here, that is incontrovertible. There's no going back from this moment and so it must knock you out of your chair. I couldn't get anybody to do it, to do the stunt, which was to come running out of the bank, get on the running board while the car's running – because we were doing it all right there, it was one shot – and I got my AD, Russ Saunders, who's a former All-American from, I think, USC, and he said, 'I'll do it. Just drag a mattress behind so that when I fall off I can hit the mattress.' And he did it. That face smeared against the glass. It's meant to be the most startling moment we have, until the end. We don't have killings, as such, between those two, really. So I thought, this one has to sear its way into us to know that their destinies are forever changed by this instant.

TL/DT: *And does that change free them?*

AP: Exactly. They thought: 'We can be ourselves and we can be important. And if nobody is writing about us, I'll damn well write about us,' as Faye did. That liberates the sexuality and it liberates the attitude, which is: 'OK, it's going to be a short burn, but it's going to be an intense one. That's joined with a kind of bucolic innocence, which is: 'If the banks are foreclosing on the farms and the houses, that's the object that we'd better attack.' It's as simple-minded as that, but as I remember that period of the Depression, it was extremely simple-minded.

TL/DT: *You just said that you harked back to the Depression. Obviously, it's a film set in 1930, 1931, whatever the dates are. I know when I saw it I said, 'This is a film about 1967.'*

AP: Yes, yes. When we were offered the opportunity by Warners to shoot it in black and white, which was sort of unheard of for them to regress in that way, we both distinctly turned it down. There was just no question about it.

TL/DT: *It had to be colour.*

AP: Had to be colour. Had to be *now*. The costumes had to be not what they really were, authentically, but with a kind of stylishness ... There's a wonderful quote from Bergman who said, 'It's a great film. The only trouble is it's not in black and white.'

TL/DT: *How important is the cameraman?*

AP: On *The Chase*, here I was in the midst of the great beast, you know? Run by Sam Spiegel. I was dealing with a cameraman and I remember Marlon coming to me and saying, 'Why? What's this about not getting our first shot at night until one o'clock in the morning?' And I said, 'That's this guy.' He looked at me in a leery fashion. He was implying: 'Get rid of him.' It never occurred to me. It just simply never occured to me. I bought into the whole system when I bought into that picture. I made a big mistake, a terrible mistake. Unfortunately I carried it over to *Bonnie and Clyde*, where I had an old-time cameraman. I said to Bernie Guffy, 'This is going to be my way, Bernie. When I want available light, that's the way it's going to be.' He didn't like that at all. I dragged him kicking and screaming through one scene after another. That scene where Estelle is blinded and she's in the headlights of the cars, I said, 'I don't want any lights. I don't want anything but the headlights.' He said, 'Nothing will come out.' I said, 'OK, we'll come back and shoot it tomorrow. But we'll get ...' And of course it came out. The trouble was, it put him in the hospital with a bleeding ulcer for three or four days.

TL/DT: *How had Beatty changed by the time of* Bonnie and Clyde?

AP: He was a freer actor, by a long shot. Also, he was the producer, so he had a kind of proprietorship over it, where I think he felt that he had to set a good example, too. So he was not the actor personality of *Mickey One*. He was much more in charge.

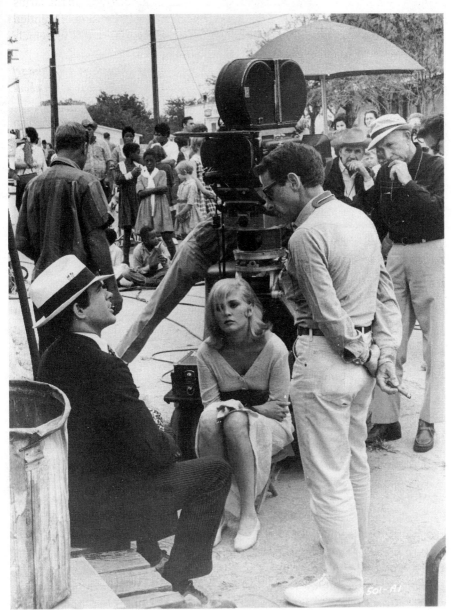

Bonnie and Clyde: on set with Warren Beatty and Faye Dunaway

Bonnie and Clyde: Clyde (Beatty) and Bonnie (Dunaway) . . .

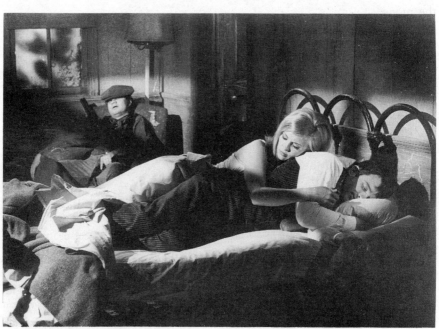

. . . and their mascot (Michael J. Pollard)

TL/DT: *I don't think he's ever acted as openly.*

AP: He was wonderful. And he got the physicality. I mean, once that line about the chopped-off toes was in the script, it helped him. It did. Gave him that walk. He's so forthcoming. He's the one who bumped his head when he was talking about not wanting to sleep, to not have sex . . . bumped his head. That was pure Beatty. I had nothing to do with that. We worked in a different way on that picture. We were down in Dallas and because it was such a tight, closed company, we'd rehearse the night before. After the day's shooting, we would just rehearse for an hour or so. That gave us the jump on the next day.

TL/DT: *Were the screenwriters down there?*

AP: No. Bob Towne was there.

TL/DT: *At your request or at Beatty's?*

AP: Beatty's request, although mine, too. I think probably also Benton and Newman. I think that they had exhausted themselves in the various permutations and reincarnations of the script they were doing for Truffaut, and then Godard, and then me.

TL/DT: *So there was a process of Americanizing in a major way. That was you working with Benton and Newman?*

AP: Yes. For instance, there was a very complicated relationship with C. W. Moss – a sexual triangle. I said, 'No, we've got to be dealing with more bucolic folk. They can't be that sophisticated.' If they're that sophisticated, then all the rest of their perception of 'Well, the banks foreclosed on us, so that's where the money is, so that's where we're gonna go' – which had to be a kind of ordinariness – could not survive in the face of that kind of sexual sophistication. They quite agreed once I made my point as strongly as I could, then they did it. But C.W. was supposed to be like a six-foot-two football player. More like the guy in *Petrified Forest.* I said, 'Oh, no. No, no, no. He's got to be a kind of mascot. He's got to be impressed.' When they say, 'We rob banks,' that's just got to take him right out of his life and into another life.

TL/DT: *One of the many remarkable things about that movie is that it is so funny and the laughs come so close to the awful moments. They're jammed up against each other in the most disturbing way.*

AP: A great deal of the credit for that goes to Benton and Newman. A good deal of that is in the script from the very beginning. Then fortuitous casting made moments like that much funnier. Seeing Michael J. Pollard try to park the car, it's funnier than a six-foot-two guy. It was just a series of happy choices. Beatty suggested Gene Hackman, having worked with him in *Lilith.*

TL/DT: *There's an entire subtext or plot element in* Bonnie and Clyde *which involves them becoming their own story-tellers. Was it chance or was it a link that you made between the situation in* The Left-Handed Gun, *where the Hurd Hatfield character is the chronicler?*

AP: It was pure chance. It was chance based on fact, that Bonnie did send this

The Shoot-Out: Bonnie . . .

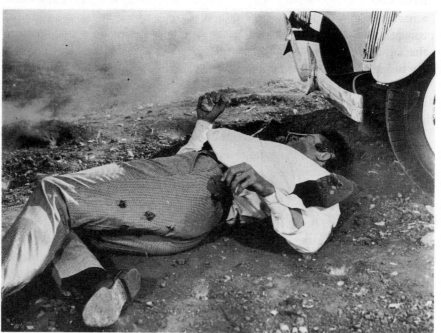

. . . and Clyde

ballad to the newspaper. Benton and Newman used it, and then I said, 'This is a pivotal turn. We've got to make this,' because I had had the idea in *The Left-Handed Gun*. So it was a combination of just raising it to prominence, to that kind of prominence, rather than just seeing it on a desk somewhere, you know?

TL/DT: *When the film opened, it didn't take immediately. There was a delayed response and I think it's fair to say that Beatty did some of his greatest work as a producer in that time.*

AP: Beatty was terrific, and so were Benton and Newman. They had both been on *Esquire* and in advertising, and they knew what they were doing. They just took it. Every once in a while they would express something to me, but I didn't have a feel for that, unfortunately. When they came up with that slogan, 'They're young, they're in love, they kill people', I was a little taken aback by that and I don't think I would have given it a vote of confidence. Beatty got it like that.

TL/DT: *Looking back, what does* Bonnie and Clyde *mean to you?*

AP: Well, not least a kind of 'clout' in the movie business. Second, the fact we were able just to go off and make it. Jack Warner was selling the studio at that point, so there was no real supervision. So we went off as a tight, autonomous little unit down to Dallas – just Warren, me and the actors and the production crew – and made a movie, and the movie we wanted to make. Third, and I think most profound, it was the first time I felt I was able to put the medium to work as a narrative device. The film medium became a part of the play. That's most conspicuous, of course, in the last scene, the slow-motion shoot-out. By now, that's a hopeless cliché; but at its time, and still even now I will claim that it has not been used as appropriately, or with such visual interest. As I said at the time, it's a spastic ballet. I had one of those epiphanies where I saw that scene as it was going to come out. We were making a legendary leap – this is William Tell, Robin Hood – from what probably took place. They were a couple of fairly squalid types, but we took the assumption that their story would *resonate* for the 1960s. We weren't that deliberate or prescient, but I did feel there was something anti-establishment about them as figures that really did matter at the time. That was an extraordinarily irreverent time – defying the draft! So I had a sense of it, but not to the degree the film registered on audiences.

TL/DT: *Had you foreseen the kind of reaction the film would generate?*

AP: None in the world, not in the world. Actually, I remember when we showed it to Bob Towne. He sat in a screening room by himself at Warners and we were both nervous, because Bob is a close friend and a very bright guy and a guy whose opinion we both cherished. He came out and he said, 'This is going to do $30 million.' And we said, 'Come on now. Come on now.' He said, 'No, I mean it. This is going to go through the roof.' I don't think either of us had even the intimation of that.

Little Big Man: The Narrator (Dustin Hoffman): 'History is a stew cooked up by a bunch of liars'

Little Big Man: Dustin Hoffman and Faye Dunaway

Little Big Man: The Little Big Horn attack

TL/DT: *I would assume that when* Bonnie and Clyde *came out you were besieged with offers, because it was a dynamic film and it was dynamite at the box office.*

AP: Yes. I had *Little Big Man* as a script for six years. It was something I couldn't get a studio to make, and then finally CBS Films agreed to make it.

TL/DT: *Because of* Bonnie and Clyde *do you think?*

AP: Undoubtedly, because they didn't get it as a film from reading the script. They couldn't feel it. You know, it was filled with the same kind of alternations that *Bonnie and Clyde* was filled with. Also, there was a good deal of prejudice, quite frankly, from the studio, old studio fellows, who didn't want a movie that was sympathetic to the Indians. The guy who was head of MGM said he would do it, and so he budgeted it and it came in over $12 million, which in those days was an astronomical figure. I said that it wouldn't cost anything like that. He said, 'I can't go to my board with that, and this is budgeted by my basic department.' Well, we made the picture about four years after that for $9 million, with nothing changed. But it was just that they were overbudgeted. And they wouldn't talk to me. I said, 'Let me talk to them and tell them how I want to shoot some of this stuff.' There was a period out there where the production department would budget it based on how *they saw* the movie. It had nothing to do with the particular point of view of the director. It was something left over from the old industrial days. Now, directors with final cut were having much more specific visions of how to make their films and they were consequently cheaper. Nobody will convince me to this day that failure to give the final cut isn't an enormously expensive event, because it throws it open and money goes down the drain.

TL/DT: *I wonder what you think about the treatment of the Indians in it, in hindsight.*

AP: I think it's a little bit romantic, you know? Chief Dan George is a romantic figure. It was fun having the homosexual Indian, and a contrary Indian in it – those are all from Berger's book. That part of it interested me, just developing a sociology. Dan George didn't find anything to object to about those events, although it was a very disturbing event in terms of our present-day sociology. At the time, when we were working on the Crow reservation, it did trigger an awful lot of fantasy phenomena in the Indians who were just supernumeraries, but Dan George didn't object.

So about the treatment of the 'Indians'. Well, it's funny. The tone of the whole piece is misanthropic. 'Whites', 'Indians' – history is a stew cooked up by a bunch of liars. Look at our own times. Christ! We had J. Edgar Hoover, a cross-dresser blackmailing a government of scoundrels, to use Lillian's perfect word. I mean, McCarthy, Nixon, Roy Cohn, G. David Shine – what a poisonous stew they were cooking out of Democracy. Watergate – a Laurel and Hardy three-reeler if ever there was one. And we aren't making films about that! That's absurd! It's the funniest, most terrible stuff and would make delicious movies, but we won't face it. Not in corporate movies. Hell, no. We'd rather have Merchant-Ivory bubbles blown at us than our very own truth.

Anyway, back to the Crow population. We were working on the Crow Reservation, and a movie about Little Big Horn and the chance to revisit the battle with Custer triggered an awful lot of fantasy phenomena in the Indians who were working on the picture.

TL/DT: *What kind of things?*

AP: Well, we discovered very quickly that if we wanted ten people, ten Indians, we needed to ask twenty; for a variety of reasons, ten would not show. There was one guy named 'Pie', who was a very dependable guy, so we moved Pie from being just one of the actors to our contact person with the Crow. Then he would sit around the set and read *Daily Variety*, and there he discovered that somebody was going to make Chief Joseph's story. So he thought, 'Well, I wonder.' He asked the make-up guy if they would make him up as Chief Joseph, then he asked Harry Stradling if he would photograph him doing the speech. Harry said, 'Sure, Pie, why not.' And he did it. Pie said, 'How much are you getting, Harry?' Harry said, 'I don't know, thirty-five hundred a week.' He said, 'In my picture, it's five thousand.' By that point, the hallucination had so progressed that, as I remember it now, we had to let Pie go finally. He was not functional any more. Dick Mulligan ran into him in a restaurant and he said something to Dick like, 'When you die and are ascended you will sit on my left hand.' He was into a Christ delusional state. Extraordinary. And the young man who played the homosexual Indian attempted suicide the night he finished. He said, 'I've never been so happy being who I am. Now I have to go back to Oklahoma and deny my whole identity.' So we were just messing with people's heads. It was terrible. It's the power of movies, you know?

TL/DT: *The period from* Bonnie and Clyde *on into the 1970s now looks like a golden age of American film. There were such great works – both parts of* The Godfather – *and overall, there was a willingness in the studios, or in the system, to make dark films, films that said uncomfortable things about America in many cases; a lot of the films do not end well, do not end happily. From today's standpoint, it looks like a lost, wonderful age. It must be chastening to look back and see the way things have turned.*

AP: I think the industry regressed, the movie world regressed into multinational corporations with divisions, and the divisions had to have a good, proper balance sheet, preferably one with a big, world-class $300 million film or $100 million film, depending upon when we're talking about. That forced it into a committee concept. And that swept into the studios all the kids who were coming out of film school, who now were film literate but didn't know anything about film. And they were made the readers and the editors and so forth at the studios. And they had the same people then look at the film with the executives. And it was madness to show a film to them. And naturally it has washed down to us who are making the films now. Having lost final cut. It's a very regrettable thing, because now you're a part of the committee, whether you want to be or not. It's an existential phenomenon, and it stinks. It doesn't make any sense. I mean, some of them are very nice people, and they view the dailies, but they don't know what the film is about or where you figure this will fit.

TL/DT: *Do you think it's going to turn back again?*

AP: Yes, some day, I think, through the independent film world. That's the only hope. Small films will do it, because there will be no room for that kind of intervention – there's no financial room. Now, you have to factor in all of your Disney executives and it's certainly non-creative. But I submit that it's certainly non-economic and non-productive.

TL/DT: *And the films are much less interesting.*

AP: They're terrible.

TL/DT: *So your next film was a gentler film than you had been making and a film without big stars; not a big Hollywood film – a sort of gentler, East Coast film.*

AP: I don't know why. For instance, I was offered *Butch Cassidy* and I said no, because I didn't want to do another shoot-out film. I didn't have an idea at that point, when I was saying no to these films, that I was going to do *Alice's*. I just thought I don't want to now do that same kind of movie again and I was being inundated with *Bonnie and Clyde* rip-offs. I didn't want to go into guns and that sort of thing. I was also very curious about the culture and the society at that point. And bang, some kids came over to the house in Stockbridge and said, 'Have you heard Arlo's new . . . ?' I said no, and they played it, and the next night we went to a dinner party and somebody said, 'Have you heard Arlo's thing?' And we said yeah, but they played it anyway, and by that time I could see the movie. I just said, 'That's it, I'm going to make that.'

TL/DT: *And you were back with UA.*

AP: I was back with UA. Again, very interesting little moment. Arlo had recorded it for Warner records, so when I called David Picker and said I wanted to make this as a film, he said, 'Unfortunately, you got to clear it with Warner records,' and added, 'They'll never let you do it here.' Well, they went to Kenny Hyman who was in charge of Warner Bros. and he said, 'Who the fuck's going to make a movie out of a record? Yeah, go anywhere you want.' So I called David again and said, 'Hey, believe it or not, it's free.' He said, 'We got a deal.' That was it. It was done that easily and quickly.

TL/DT: *There's a bit of a gap then. I wonder, on the face of it, I would have thought you would have been in great demand in the early 1970s, but there's a gap until 1975 and* Night Moves?

AP: Yes. There were some projects that didn't come together and some that I didn't really want to do that were interesting. Also there were my kids, who were at a certain age at that point. I'd been away such a great deal, you know, in Texas doing *Bonnie and Clyde*, and I thought that I've got to spend some time at home. I'd been invited to teach at Yale, so I taught a graduate film course

Alice's Restaurant: Arlo Guthrie and friend

Alice's Restaurant: Penn and the draftees

at Yale, but that was just a day's drive up to New Haven. The rest of the time I was at home for a few years. I just thought that these were delicate years for the kids.

TL/DT: *It never crossed your mind to move to Los Angeles like a lot of people?*

AP: No. Never. Peggy and I were out there when we were doing *The Left-Handed Gun* and we just didn't enjoy it.

TL/DT: *Now* Night Moves *is maybe the darkest of your films. Tell us a little bit about what it means to you.*

AP: It came into being through Alan Sharpe and Bob Sherman. They had been working together on it. It had previously been called *A Dark Tower*. It was the period after all those assassinations, you know? That depleted one's optimism: the ability to feel that tomorrow is going to be better was definitely gone. I thought that that's what this movie is about. Then also, I thought, gee, detective movies have always been so clever, the detective always figured it out at the end. What happens if he himself is psychologically blocked in an area that keeps him from being able to perceive what the central event is all about? I kept raising the stakes and then the ending had to be non-verbal. I didn't want somebody assembling everybody in the drawing room, you know, and saying, 'On that night you were so-and-so and so-and-so.' It should be revealed through images. That was the task we set ourselves. We didn't succeed in the most elegant fashion, but I think it's a good movie.

TL/DT: *No question. It's filled with a kind of paranoia. What are your feelings about that sort of wave of conspiracy or conspiracy-mindedness that overtook America and where do you stand on it?*

AP: Well, I'm terminally in the Oswald-alone camp and for this reason: I think the conspiracy theory is far too sophisticated. What is not recalled very accurately is the degree of anger toward JFK, by the Texans in particular, about the post-Cuban event, and I have more faith in psychosis than I do in conspiracy. Conspiracy has too many participants in it. Psychosis is entirely a self-contained system. That seems to me what Oswald thought, oddly: 'I will be a hero. I will have accomplished what everybody . . . ' And that's what it was. All these reaches for other figures who were involved in it? You can't keep secrets. You just can't keep secrets that long. They don't last. Nobody lasts.

I think it's that. I think it was that with Sirhan Sirhan. I mean . . . I had been working with the Kennedys, with JFK on the debates, as an adviser to their people. Then, consequently, Dick Goodwin asked me to start working with Bobby Kennedy and so I did. I worked with him once in Washington on his way to California, and then we were going to really resume and start a whole, full campaign and, of course, that was it. So no, I think that with these people, the time creates the trigger finger, you know? Interesting. Yeah, my darkest film.

TL/DT: *I wonder if you would talk about the relationship with Tom McGuane and how it came into being.*

Night Moves: Penn and Gene Hackman

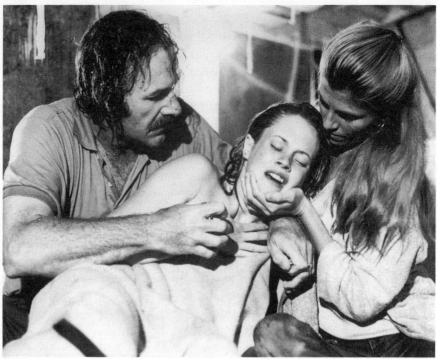

Night Moves: 'The ability to feel that tomorrow is going to be better was definitely gone'

Night Moves: Penn with Melanie Griffith

AP: Well, this is ironic. There was virtually no relationship with McGuane. I had had a relationship with him prior to it, while he was preparing to shoot *92 in the Shade*. Then he shot it. For the same producer mind you, Elliott Kastner, both *92 in the Shade* and *The Missouri Breaks*. He shot *92* ... and Elliott somehow took it away from him and had it edited by somebody else. In the meantime, *The Missouri Breaks* had gone out to each of us individually. Nicholson, Brando and I had said no. Elliott then said, 'Hey, how about if I can get Penn and Nicholson' – he said this to Brando – 'would you come in?' And Brando probably said yes. He said the same to Nicholson: 'If I can get Penn and Brando ... ' Then he came to me and said, 'I've got Brando and ... ' I said, 'I'm in.' Boom. Like that. There was just no question. At that point – I don't know how to explain this perversity – Elliott then invited McGuane to go to London to recut *92 in the Shade*. Now, there was a very lengthy period of deal-making. Nothing could be done on the script until the deals were set. Then the deals were set and it was go. We were off: six weeks later we were shooting.

TL/DT: *So you had no time.*

AP: We had no time and McGuane was still in London. We were confronted with a script which had marvellous intimations in it, but which we all saw as being somewhat more fragmentary. So we decided to convert that to an asset, to give it a much less formal structure. Now, people talk about it as having been a chaotic set. If it was, I was not there. That's all I can say to you. Marlon had some ideas, I had some ideas, Jack had some ideas and we discussed them. Not in public. What happened was that Marlon and I had developed this bizarre character of such great variability, unpredictability, that it even threw people on the set. Other actors didn't know that Marlon was now going to do something, be somebody else, and the whole idea of it was, Marlon was this *regulator*, and who the hell was a regulator if he was not this kind of chimerical creature who switched, who was here and there? And they would be startled. They'd say, 'But that doesn't match.' Then Marlon, who was a wonderfully inventive guy, came into that scene where Dick Bradford's laid out on the ice and says, you know, 'I have a toothache ... ' I didn't know he was going to do that. Then he spotted the coffin and walked over and got a piece of ice. That was perfect. He got a piece of ice out from under the dead body. It was just dynamite. That was the sort of stuff that we decided we would go with. So we had that scene out where Jack was irrigating his garden. That's a largely improvised scene, from a McGuane scene. Now, ordinarily, I don't like improvisation, improvised words that go in as pseudo-dialogue, but in this script, on a few occasions, they were done that way.

TL/DT: *And was the improvisation the result of your relationship with Brando or the fact that you'd had to start shooting with such a short preparation?*

AP: The improvisation was just Brando and I knowing each other, and the

The Missouri Breaks: Brando and the coffin of ice

The Missouri Breaks: Brando and Nicholson

sense that we didn't really have a strong, completed script under us. There were certain wonderful scenes that were completely scripted, like the scene with Jack and the girl, where she asks him to lay her. It's a wonderful, pure McGuane scene. But there were a number of others that weren't, and so Marlon and I just started on the idea of, well, if you're going to do all these killings, each one has to be at some point of ignominy. You've got to do it when somebody is on the crapper, or somebody is making love – 'you' being a kind of eunuch-like, non-sexual creature. That's the stuff that we invented. I said to Marlon, 'Hey, I need a scene in here before you get your throat cut.' He said, 'Give me a horse and a mule. I'll just play around with it.' And that's what we did. We spent a day with cameras rolling and he was just playing. He said, 'You're bad,' and all this, to the horse and the mule; he developed them as real characters and allowed himself a certain infantile play world.

TL/DT: *The way you talk about Brando, clearly there's great rapport. I think of this as his last great performance. Isn't it a tragedy that this prodigious actor left us?*

AP: It's a tragedy to the degree that his talent has been shut down – his sensibility and his genius – but I don't think it has disappeared. I just don't think he's had all that many opportunities. Even in *Apocalypse Now*. It's such a confined role, there's no room for the things that Brando does that nobody else does, you know? When Rod Steiger pulls the gun on Brando (his brother in *On the Waterfront*), one might expect fear or counter-violence or outrage. No. Brando is grief-stricken that his brother feels he has to do this, that he has descended to this level of desperation . . . of potential violence to his own brother. And Brando is pained for him! That's pure Brando. There's Brando on set: 'Give me a plate of carrots.' OK. And he just went. That's to what people ascribed, I believe, the so-called chaotic nature of the set. There was not a harsh word spoken on that set. Brando was in the picture under contract for twenty days. The last day he was there, I was forced to shoot a day-for-night scene, something I hate, and we were setting it up when Brando came to the set and said, 'What the fuck are you doing?' I said, 'I'm shooting a day-for-night scene.' He said, 'Why?' I said, 'On account of you. You're gonna finish today. It's your twentieth day and that's the deal.' 'Forget it. Everybody go home, come back tonight and we'll shoot it night for night.' We shot three or four more days than his contract ever called for. He volunteered. He was living in a trailer with his son Christian on the set.

TL/DT: *In hindsight, do you think that what he was doing was so interesting that it would have been good to know more about that character?*

AP: Oh, undoubtedly. Sure, sure. We were filling gaps, and we were filling gaps with the best actor around. It was a pleasure to watch him, because each one of those turns was like a high-wire act, you know, that he could pull off. Part of the problem in that film is that there isn't parity with Nicholson.

TL/DT: *Because sometimes he looks like a bit of a stooge.*

AP: That's right. And he's every bit as good. Jack's a brilliant actor and he should have been up there, but we didn't have the material and I didn't have the invention to raise that character level to parity with what Marlon was doing. I think Jack felt it – I know he felt it – and I think he was hurt by it.

TL/DT: *Do you think there was any way in which Brando was doing what he did as a kind of challenge to Nicholson, to say, 'Can you keep up with this?'*

AP: Quite possibly. The only trouble was that Nicholson was confined to the circumstances of the script and Brando was a free-range chicken, you know? He was out there going wherever his fancy took him, because there was no character. So it was no contest, because Jack was having to fight with one hand tied behind his back. He was holding the script and narrative line in place.

TL/DT: *We need to move on, but just in passing, I'd like to say that I think that it's one of those movies that has a superb sense of landscape. You're talking to two people who love driving in the West, that kind of thing, and there are landscape scenes in that film that are beautiful just in themselves.*

AP: I love the look that we succeeded in getting. I had a good young camera-man, Michael Butler, who got the sense of the colour of the light and then did that cabin scene with striated light. I thought that it had come from a photograph, an old black and white photograph I'd seen where that streaked light was there, and I said, 'That's what we want. That's what we want in the interiors and then for the exteriors, let's just go wide. Wide shots!'

TL/DT: *How was it perceived by the industry when it was released?*

AP: Not well. They wanted a final shoot-out. That was what UA kept saying: 'Give us a shoot-out.' And I said, 'It's not in this story. It's just not in this story. This man is not going to reveal himself walking through a Western town. He's not a quick draw gun. He needs to have a precise rifle that's perfectly honed and targeted. It's just not right.' They didn't like that.

TL/DT: *But it is one of the great death scenes at the end.*

AP: Yeah.

TL/DT: *But so quick you need to see the film again.*

AP: Unfortunately. That was one of those moments where I kept saying, 'Come on, Marlon, a little more, a little more, a little more active and longer. This can't go like that.' Finally, he said, 'What the hell do you want, you want this?' We weren't rolling and it was exactly what I wanted.

TL/DT: *He wouldn't do it again?*

AP: No. It was paroxysms of life surprised by death. It was just absolutely wonderful. Naturally, it went too far, but I would have been able to cut away from it. It was just perfect, but we weren't anywhere near rolling.

TL/DT: *Did you feel, during that film, that what Brando was doing was in part prompted by his feeling that movie-making is ridiculous? Because there is an absurdism there.*

Four Friends: Jim Metzler, Craig Wasson, Michael Huddleston and Jodi Thelen

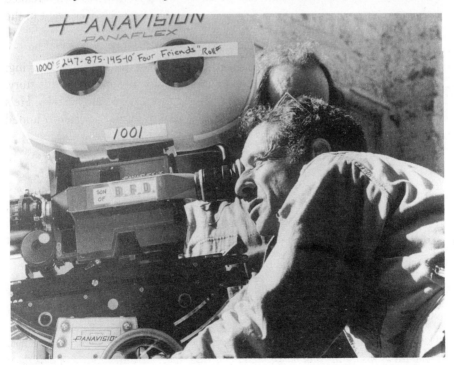

Shooting *Four Friends*

Four Friends: Arthur Penn with writer Steve Tesich

Four Friends: the open-air party scene

AP: I think that Brando brings that to every role. There's a part of acting that he feels is not a worthy endeavour. He doesn't like it and yet he does it brilliantly, but he doesn't enjoy thinking of himself as an actor. What a great figure he is, though.

TL/DT: *Do you feel that* Four Friends *is a misunderstood film?*

AP: No, I think it's a good film. I didn't know many trained actors of that age group, unfortunately. Very few. And every time we would audition a girl who was older, it just didn't seem to me to play. So I took a chance on a very young girl and I think she's very talented. I happen to like her very much.

It's peculiar, because that film is so warmly admired by the French and I've never quite understood why, what it was that was revealed in the film. It was a hard film to make, because it was sort of playing back on to the naïvety of the 1960s, you know? It was in that sense a romantic film on Steve's part, writer Steve Tesich. And I thought that we should make it more romantic rather than less. I wanted to call it *Georgia*. We ended up calling it *Georgia* in Europe. He didn't want to do that. I was, in that sense, following his lead, because I don't know that culture. I just simply didn't know it. So I was sort of inventing it, but I had no personal, really strong reference to it.

TL/DT: *We talked the other day about the extraordinary open-air party scene where James Leo Herlihy explodes. That is one of the most frightening scenes you've ever done. It always seemed to me that there was something in Herlihy that was vital to that scene. Could you talk about that?*

AP: I had known Herlihy at Black Mountain College. One of the things that happened at Black Mountain where I was a student was there were so many people interested in theatre that they asked me to teach a course in acting. I said, 'I don't know anything about acting.' I'd only had a brief experience with it in the Army. I said, 'What we'll do is we'll get Stanislavsky and we'll read it together.' Herlihy was one of the people in the class and he was very able, but he thought of himself then and always, I think, as a writer. Years later, he and a partner wrote a play called *Blue Denim*, which I directed in its first incarnation. Then when they were going to bring it to Broadway, his collaborator said, 'I don't want Penn at all.' So I was dropped from the project. Then I was in Paris and I saw a placard announcing *The Zoo Story* performed by James Leo Herlihy. I'd seen, I think, the first public presentation of *The Zoo Story* at the Actors' Studio, just in the Playwrights' Unit. Edward Albee had brought it there first, I think. So I wanted to see it again in a fully mounted production. I was struck by Herlihy's performance. It was so wired and he knew so much about that sort of homosexual pick-up with a sense of desperation in it that was just absolutely wonderful. And I thought, gee, if I could only get that sense of desperation in this character when I came to casting *Four Friends*. My associate, Gene Lasko, said, 'What about James Leo Herlihy?' The words weren't out of his mouth before I said, 'That's exactly the right man for this.' So we did it.

Target: Matt Dillon and Gene Hackman

Now, look, when I read the shooting of his daughter and Danilo, I thought, there are perhaps two ways of doing this. Have it happen rather surreptitiously, or flagrantly, and naturally what you said about me is true: given the choice, I'm going to go for the flagrant. So I just did. I picked the most wild moment, because I associate those crazy acting outs with no preparation.

TL/DT: *Target's next, I think. Now your head sinks. Were you trying to get projects on with some of the big actors that you had? I was always surprised that in the 1980s we didn't see you and Newman again, or you and Beatty again.*

AP: No. Warren had a few things that he asked me about, yeah, but I didn't want to, couldn't do them. They, the executives, didn't seem to want to do the pictures I wanted to do. It was very peculiar.

I had a wonderful script about Attica, a beautiful script written for UA. And the view was: it's going to cost more than $13 million and no black picture has ever grossed more than $13 million, so we can't do it.

TL/DT: *So you started meeting those people who came to the fore in the 1980s.*

AP: Like a wall.

TL/DT: *The issue was about how much it would cost, what was the marketing, the audience, not trusting you as a director to do something personal and strong.*

AP: Right. Exactly. A black picture hadn't made more than $13 million because there had been certain kinds of black pictures, but that didn't mean that this would not break through. It was very strong, from Tom Wicker's book, you know? It was a very strong social statement and a terrific script. Couldn't do it. Had a script based on an article that Jane Kramer wrote for the *New Yorker* called 'The Last Cowboy', on the nature of agribusiness taking over the ranches of these independent guys. Got a full script. Warners wouldn't go. So there were many, many such projects. I was asked to do a picture by Disney that I thought was not good at all and I declined. Then *Target* came along, bang, like that. Finished. Ostensibly a full script ready to go. I said yes, hell, I want to go to work. And Paris – and why not? So I did it. I went to Gene Hackman and said, 'Do you want to come in with me?' and he said, 'Sure, what the hell.' Then we talked to Matt Dillon and that was it. But it was its own kind of picture. Now, the interesting thing, beginning with *Four Friends* – at least the interesting thing for me – is that *Four Friends, Target, Dead of Winter* and *Penn and Teller Get Killed* were all started by one studio which gave up in the middle of the picture – that is, gave up the picture business. They all ended up at another studio to be distributed by that studio. In this case, Warner Bros. It was part of the buccaneer kind of guys who were coming into movies trying to make a killing, got into it, got a little scared, and got out of it. We were in the middle of *Four Friends* when Filmways . . . I don't even think it was Filmways then, I think we were sold to Filmways . . . Jerry Parentio and that company. We ended up being sold to Warner Bros, who distributed it with no sense of proprietorship at all. And there it was again with *Target*, a CBS film, you know? It was all go, and we were into it, we were way ahead of budget. We came in $1 million under on that picture, but CBS closed the division, the film division, right in the middle of it.

TL/DT: *With* Dead of Winter, *weren't you an executive who took over?*

AP: I was helping two kids who had been to school with my son. To get it launched, that was all. They wanted to go independent and I said, 'OK, go ahead, try.' They couldn't raise the money, so they came to me and said, 'Can you help us?' I said, 'I can only help you through a studio.' Well, the studio exacted a price which was 'you be the executive producer and godfather', and the unspoken part of that clause was 'if it gets into trouble and can't go, you've got to take it over'. And that's exactly what happened, two weeks into the picture.

TL/DT: *So you had no time to do any rewriting or anything?*

AP: No. I just left New York. They called me Friday night, said, 'We're shutting down the picture if you don't take it over.' I was shooting Monday morning in Toronto. It was fun, actually. It's not a bad picture.

TL/DT: *Going back to you and the horror film when you were a kid,* Dead of Winter *has got some very frightening things in it, in a sort of conventional, genre-like way.*

AP: Yeah. There wasn't a lot I could do with it, because the circumstances were all set. But I think it's pretty well done for that kind of flick.

TL/DT: *And around this time, weren't you going to do* Nostromo?

AP: It was later than that. I was going to be available as a stand-by for David Lean. He was sick and somebody had misdiagnosed it. Somebody had given him a bad cortisone series. He had been planning *Nostromo*, had a faithfully good script by Robert Bolt and he was going to do it. But he was showing signs of real illness. The money was apparently there. They came to me at that point and said, 'Look, David is having trouble getting insurance. They will insure him if you will back him.' I was his choice, apparently. So I said, 'Of course I will.' But I was supposed to stay in New York to be able to continue doing my work, which was preparing some other films. Slowly, as David's health didn't really improve, the insurance company kept raising the stakes: 'No, you can't be in New York, you should be in London doing some of the preparation on the film, just so that you're acquainted with it during that stage.' I said, 'Well, I don't really want to do that, but if that's necessary.' Before I knew it, they came back and said, 'No, as a matter of fact, you have to be on the set every day.' I said, 'You mean in a death watch? This is absolutely ghoulish.' I wouldn't be associated with it. So I said no. At that point, also, David's health was getting so bad that it was clear it was not going to happen. He could never in a million years have done that picture physically. It's just incredible. The march over the mountains was just unbelievable and it's the centrepiece of the film. It's never going to happen. My agents wanted me to get paid and I said no, I wouldn't . . .

TL/DT: *Let's come to* Penn and Teller. *I enjoyed* Penn and Teller, *but there's*

something about it, it seemed to me, that could have been more experimental. It didn't
seem like it should be made for a Warners, or whoever made it.

AP: It wasn't. It was made for Lorimar. I just plain blew. I had a conceit about
it, which was to do an absolutely pop movie. You know, that Godard idea of
'film is the truth twenty-four frames a second'. And I thought that it's also a lie
twenty-four times a second. Why not do a movie where we show blood galore,
the illusionist tricks of Penn and Teller, and even people going out the window
and it all being crazed? But I didn't get it up high enough. I just never got the
pitch. I couldn't, I just was not skilled enough. I had a funny, cartoonish
movie in mind and I didn't do it. I should have done it in 16mm. I should
have done it way outside of unions and all that stuff. It should have been
much wilder. What had interested me was to try to get to gallons of phoney
blood and crazy tricks. Just plain didn't do it. Sometimes the magic works,
sometimes it doesn't.

TL/DT: *When did you last direct on stage? It may have been more recently than I can*
remember.

AP: About four years ago. I directed a play by Janusz Glowacki called *Hunting*
Cockroaches. It had Dianne Wiest and Ron Silver in the cast. It was done at the
Manhattan Theatre Club and it was quite a success.

I'm going to be assuming the presidency of the Actors' Studio, and in the
past few years we have been slowly but meticulously formulating a Master of
Fine Arts programme which we're going to conduct at the New School for
Social Research – they have a long history of being available to slightly unusual
things in philosophy and the arts. It was a place where many of the first
intellectual refugees from the Nazis were housed; including Hannah Arendt
and Erwin Piscator. In effect, what we're doing is returning to the intellectual
nature of the Stanislavsky method of acting as a unified system. We're taking
the tangential elements of the Stella Adler approach, the Lee Strasberg
approach and the Sandy Meisner approach, and putting them back together
again into a comprehensive Stanislavskian method. That programme commences in September 1994 and I have been working hard on it, along with
James Lipton, who is really the innovator and sponsor of it. I'll be teaching
occasionally, as a guest, but our most distinguished members of the studio –
Pacino, De Niro, Dustin Hoffman, Paul Newman, Ellen Burstyn, Estelle
Parsons, Anne Bancroft, etc. – have all agreed to conduct seminars on craft,
open to the public, but free to the students. They'll be on 'how we did it' – for
example, we're planning to have Marty Scorsese, De Niro and Harvey Keitel
talking together about *Mean Streets*, and so forth. The craft will be stressed,
because so much of this has become glamorized.

TL/DT: *And film?*

AP: I think it's not a serious medium for the moment. The product is not
serious. I believe that the ground has been swept by multinational companies –

the Disney guys, you know? – whether literally at Disney or at other studios. The same cookie-cutter stamped them out. They do the same things at all the studios, which is, essentially, to ignore the content of the film and deal entirely with its results. In acting terms, that means very bad acting – result acting instead of process acting. I don't despair, because I've seen it happen before, but I think it's in direct relation to the idea of who has final cut. It happens when final cut belongs to a committee, and to a committee of rather startled deer, who don't have strong opinions and dare not venture until they hear what their bosses have to say.

TL/DT: *Why are you optimistic?*

AP: I don't think the medium can be trashed. It's an exquisite medium and one way or another it's going to sprout new plants. The basic narrative is something for which humankind hungers and it can't be trivialized totally. The triviality of the narrative we're telling now is a reflection of the triviality of our time. Film has always shown us how we behave. It's an exquisite record of how people dealt with their difficulties. This state we're in is not going to endure. Something will crash in the world – it begs it. We can't stay in this superficial state and survive, because we're turning a blind eye to the world.

6   Raising the Dead
Ken Burns in conversation with David Thomson

Introduction

Kenneth Lauren Burns was born in Brooklyn in 1953, and educated at Hampshire College in Massachusetts. He lives now in the small, idyllic town of Walpole, New Hampshire, which becomes a thriving base for post-production as his enormous and ambitious projects come to a head. For this, arguably, is the most productive and inspiring American film career of the 1990s.

As a documentarian, Burns worked steadily, emerging from student-like poverty to win awards and become a well-known figure at festivals: *Brooklyn Bridge* (1981); *The Shakers* (1984); *Huey Long* (1985); *The Statue of Liberty* (1985); *Thomas Hart Benton* (1988); *The Congress* (1988); *The Empire of the Air* (1991). But his work took a giant step forward as he made the eleven-hour *The Civil War* (1990), a PBS project that found vast audiences and which helped to alter American attitudes to its own history.

This interview was conducted in Walpole, in May 1994, as Burns completed the eighteen-hour *Baseball*, which played in September.

These are the bare facts. For the rest, let the interview reveal the bracing sensibility of Ken Burns and his sense of America and what it might be.

DAVID THOMSON: *You told me something Ted Williams said about what he'd always wanted.*
KEN BURNS: He said that when he was thirteen or so he had seen a shooting star, and he looked up and he wished: 'I want money, money, money, money, and to be the best hitter there ever was.'
DT: *Pick an age for yourself and what was your wish?*
KB: When I was seventeen years old I wanted to be John Ford. I knew as clear as anything, I wanted to make films about America, about the soul of America, that were filled with music, remembering, music that you would hum; stories that were dramatic narratives, that had heroics, but a complicated heroics; films that parsed the social life of the country at the same time: that is to say, approached the subject with a willingness to extend to the past a life as rich as ours today. So there are dances in Ford films, things that drive the plot along

Ken Burns with Babe Ruth (photo by Jerome Liebling)

but they mainly give you a sense of how people lived, or at least how Ford thought they lived. That's what I wanted more than anything else. To be a famous movie director.

I ran into Jerome Liebling and Elaine Mayes – social-documentary still photographers who dabbled in documentary – at Hampshire College when I started there in 1971, and they disenthralled me of this and reminded me of the power of what is true. This set me on a course that was both documentary, but steeped in a rich tradition of still photographic imagery and a humanistic sense of obligation to the subject, combined with a latent interest in history I had all my life. I started making films that used diaries and journals, tried to look at old still photographs, and tried to see from the evidence of the past – whether it was a photograph, or a diary excerpt, or a piece of music, or a building extant, or a landscape – something about the ghosts that were there.

DT: *I know that a number of professional historians have said that your movie of* The Civil War *ignores or neglects approaches that they prefer. That makes me think that one of your special qualities is to do history, but to do it with a great respect for a sense of history relevant to the period you're working in. You sometimes feel like a nineteenth-century historian. What are the differences between that approach and the more structural history prevalent today?*

KB: For most of the life of our republic, we have formally told our history from the top down: this is the story of great men doing great deeds. There was a tyranny to that, which ignored the myriad contributions of many different forces and groups in our society. So there has been, gratefully, a reaction in the last thirty years to that hegemony. What we have replaced it with is a new kind of tyranny of social relevance, of polemics, of history from the bottom up, which finds in the reading of the telephone book something more complete about how a people are. And that new tyranny is terrifically stifling, it seems to me.

I wish to suggest a synthesis of the two. That it is possible to engage the best of the top-down version – because great men often did do great things – with the most heroic aspects of the bottom-up version – minorities, women, labour, ordinary people and ordinary gestures, which in their aggregate set those great men, and women, in relief. I'm afraid, though, that those who have grasped the new history can see in my work only vestiges of an old nineteenth-century tradition. I would like to suggest that I'm rooted in an absolute desire to include as many of these points of view as possible, but without throwing out the old version. I believe that the word 'history' is mostly made up of the word 'story'. We are obligated as human beings to tell each other narrative stories about other human beings, and the best kind of story is unusual behaviour, heroic behaviour, villainous behaviour.

I also believe that, for the last 100 years, the Academy has kidnapped history from the people and set up a very special, almost sterile, environment where

The Civil War: History from the top down . . .

. . . and from the bottom up.

historians of one school speak to their colleagues who share their beliefs, do not insist that they know how to write or communicate history well, even to another school, let alone to a general public. I believe that history is, in fact, a public exercise. For the 5,000 years before that, we sang, we shouted, we excerpted, we serialized our history, and it was consumed at a level which the Academy has prevented. In the last 100 years we've seen a decline in historical awareness among the general population. So I would like to suggest a return to a Homeric mode.

DT: *You were telling me yesterday the story of how a neighbour, someone living in this very town, when they heard that you were making* The Civil War *said, 'Oh, maybe you'd like to look at this family journal.'*

KB: I am at a neighbour's house in Walpole, New Hampshire. He has a little flea-market antique shop and there on the desk is the almost vanity publication of his great-grandfather's Civil War diary. I am a year into the project. I've read dozens of diaries. I do not need another Union narrative – there are literally thousands of them – but I buy it out of a sense of loyalty to a fellow townsman. And I get introduced to a man named Elisha Hunt Rhodes, who fought from Manassas to Appomattox with the Second Rhode Island Volunteers, managed to survive, and left one of the best diaries the world has ever come across. I was able to get the book republished for Robert Rhodes, his great-grandson, and it's become a best-seller.

I go back and visit many of the people I've met while making other films. I go back to New Orleans a lot and to the bayous to meet the old Cajuns that were such ardent, long supporters including a ninety-year-old-plus judge named Cecil Morgan, who was eloquently opposed to Huey Long in my film. I told him I was working on *The Civil War* and he said, 'Oh, my grandfather wrote a book.' He pulled out *Recollections of a Rebel Reefer* by James Morris Morgan. He was a Navy man for the Confederacy and, as I was putting the book down, a piece of paper slipped out. On it was a note from James Morris Morgan to his great-niece Louise. He said, 'Dear Louise, When the incidents in this volume seem strange and distant to you, just remember my grandfather's grandmother Morgan and her tales of how she danced with George Washington. The past to the aged does not seem as far as does the dim future. And the only thing that abides with us always is the love of those who are close to us. Affectionately, Your great-uncle, James Morris Morgan.' That was like a gift of opportunity!

DT: *When you first came to this town you came as a virtually impoverished film student and in the most remarkable way, you have made a small, intimate, picnic-going film studio here. And you've been working steadily at your work and art for fifteen, twenty years. Clearly,* The Civil War *changed your place, in the film-making community, but it also changed your place in this country.* The Civil War *had an extraordinary success. You told me yesterday that the book sold 1 million copies.*

KB: If it had sold 100,000 it would have been considered a mammoth best-seller.

DT: *I'm reminded of a quote from* Baseball. *Bob Gibson, is asked after a great game, 'Did that surprise you?' And he says, 'Nothing I do surprises me.' Were you surprised?*

KB: I don't know, to be absolutely truthful about it. Because I do feel that I am possessed by American history; that I have – and it sounds so corny and maybe nineteenth-century-ish – some sort of mission or a clear destiny to sing, in a Homeric way, the epic verses of our country. Not to sugar-coat them or to paint a pretty picture, but to reveal who we are. To ask the question that has animated everyone in my films: Who are we as a people? But having said that, there was a sense that I knew what I was talking about and how I could connect. So I was flabbergasted by the response. I mean, documentary film-makers take a vow of poverty and obscurity, and I was perfectly comfortable in that. At the time of *The Civil War*, I was quite well known within the documentary community and had in a way helped to reinvest historical films since my film on the Brooklyn Bridge. But it was not a general celebrity of the kind that I've enjoyed since.

I remember that two days after the Gulf War started, it was just terrifically cold. I was up in Brunswick, Maine – the home of Joshua Lawrence Chamberlain, one of the heroes of the Civil War – speaking at Bowdoin College. I was petrified that, in the combination of cold and the Gulf War, everyone should rightfully be back home in front of their TV sets, watching what was going on. The man who had planned to introduce me was George Mitchell, the Senate Majority leader, and he could not leave Washington for all of these reasons. I had driven pretty far, alone and away from my family. I arrived there in a field house and there must have been 1,200 people – they couldn't fit enough people into this place – who had come to talk about the Civil War. In fact Mitchell had recorded a piece, which was piped into a loudspeaker, and he spoke exactly about what I was going to talk about. So it was ghostly when I finally got around to speaking. The president of Bowdoin College introduced me. He said, 'We are all here, we are all surprised that we're here, because we wish to complete a conversation with Ken that we already feel we've been having.' And that is the highest compliment. That is what it is: a kind of conversation.

Now, there's intensely personal reasons for why I get up in the morning and what animates what I do, that has to do with family history. But one of the by-products of this sort of inner war is this conversation that's going on, and it happens all the time. Because if you don't know where you've been, you can't possibly know where you're going.

DT: *You spoke about deep, personal family spurs. Can you elaborate?*

KB: My mother died when I was nearly twelve years old, of a cancer that was eating away at her. There was never a moment in my life I wasn't aware that my mother was dying. So I am animated by some sense of trying to communicate with the past. The thing that I do well – if I strip away all the theoretical, drifting snow that attends to what I do – is very simply that I take evidence of the past and make it come alive. You have now seen the *Baseball* film, with twenty-five sound-effects tracks making a simple still photograph sound like you're there. For a moment you think that the umpire's raised his hand, instead of it being frozen in the 'out' signal. Even though there is not one single photograph of a battle in *The Civil War* (in the million photographs that were exposed, there's not one shot of actual fighting in the Civil War), there are moments where you feel like you are there. That is some attempt to touch people that are gone in my life, particularly my mother.

DT: *Your mother was always sick, but I don't yet understand the particular pressure that put upon you in terms of what you're doing now.*

KB: For a little boy, I think it required me to keep her alive. To engage in the magical thinking that children do. So that when she did die, she really didn't die. One of the things that I have is the single-mindedness of purpose to try to resurrect the past, which I think is a gesture towards waking the dead. I mean, I was an adult from the very beginning. I was involved in the survival of my family. But I remember that, as a little boy, the thing that used to give me terrific anxiety was watching the treatment of blacks, watching the fire hoses and the dogs in Selma, and just writhing in pain at the injustice of it, not realizing that I was tying the cancer that was eating away at my mother to the cancer that was eating away at my country. And that the two were so prevalent – I didn't understand until I had arrived in LA, quite accidentally, on the afternoon that Rodney King was released from the hospital from his beating. The existence of the videotape had been made known about an hour before I turned on the TV set, and he was at a news conference in a wheelchair. I had the same reaction that I had watching the dogs in Selma. I suddenly began to have some way of sorting through emotions that overtake me. So finally, it doesn't really become a question of 'Who are we as a people' but 'Who am I?'

DT: *When your mother died, did you feel you'd failed? Did you feel there was a sort of duty to keep her alive?*

KB: I didn't feel that on the surface, but that's clearly what happened. I remember that for years afterwards, every time I blew out a candle on a birthday cake, I would wish that she was alive. I was convinced, even two or three years later, that this might be a quite elaborate dream and that therefore I might wake up. While those things fell away, like dead skin, somewhere I had internalized a sense that she wasn't dead. I was completely unaware of the anniversary of her death, and I've only just in the last few years begun to recapture a sense of 'Yes, she did die', that she is someplace. Yeah, I think I discovered a sense of responsibility, of failure for not having kept her alive. Which may be the great animating principle of what I do – of trying to find, particularly because I'm so drawn to heroic example. Today, we've been failed by our contemporary media on what we know about heroes. We have a puritan attitude towards people in public life. The Greeks have known – therefore we have all known – for thousands of years, that heroes are complicated and tragic and have dark sides. That's what makes a hero and that's what's most interesting. Whereas we assume a purity that has never existed in any human being, delight in elevating that person and then take perverse delight in uncovering a bad side, painting a gigantic scarlet letter A. But actually a hero is a constant and is a beacon, so that I can look at Jackie Robinson or Abraham Lincoln – who I am unabashed in suggesting to you are heroes for all time, not just for Americans, but for humankind – and find a kind of blasé attitude that has to be worked through.

DT: *You've not mentioned a father.*

KB: There was a father. My father was and is an anthropologist. He's now retired and I think he was equally devastated by my mother's illness and death. It paralysed him in a way. I think that made it all the more important for me and my brother to go out in the world and slay dragons. My brother Ric* is making documentary films as well. He's found expression in some of the darkest moments. He's done a magnificent film on the Donner Party, possibly the single bleakest moment of our past, and taken Coney Island and seen in its superficial gaiety a kind of netherworld lurking underneath the surface. It's a very interesting way in which both he and I have exorcized this terrific pain.

DT: *In that period of eleven or twelve years, when you were doing what you could to sustain your mother, were you and your father collaborators in that?*

KB: That's interesting. I don't think so. I knew that I adored him terrifically, but he was distant. He was troubled, I think, by the death that was overtaking his family. I couldn't say that we connected or collaborated in this. I think that we – all three of us, the three survivors, the two boys and the father – found different ways to abolish this demon.

DT: *Is it possible that he could have even regarded you as a rival? I can see a way in which you might have been an awesome child to whom to be a father.*

KB: Yes. I feel that in some ways I was aware that I might have been the most powerful male there, which is an incredibly Oedipal dynamic; that combined with the death of my mother is a kind of punishment for those sorts of awarenesses. I think I'm still fully the victim of that. I mean, there's a great deal of self-limitation that I impose upon myself as a result of that now thirty-five-year-old dynamic. Because somewhere along the line I must have perceived that, even as a little boy of five. I don't have any direct memory of that, but I know that that dynamic is true.

DT: *How does your father respond to your films?*

KB: He is terrifically proud. I think he has found a great deal of solace in the

---

*Ric Burns, co-writer and co-producer of *The Civil War*, has since made his own films, *The Donner Party* and *Coney Island*, and is working on a history of the American West.

success of his sons, and particularly me. I mean, Ric has also had terrific success with what he's doing, but, you know, I think my success is a source of great pride and we talk about it. There're times where all he wants to hear about is where I've gone and what I've done; and he clips articles. I think he has a kind of life in that. I think there's a bitter-sweet aspect to it for him, too: there, but for the grace of the terrible jokes that the universe plays on us all, it might have been him. He's still the most brilliant man I have ever met.

DT: *I would think, therefore, that there are ways, albeit background ways, in which you can detect his influence on your films.*

KB: It seemed to me, growing up, that he knew everything. Absolutely everything. I come from a family of scientists. My mother was a biologist. His father and my grandmother were biologists. My uncle is a biologist. So there was this vast scientific world that my father seemed to know everything about: the Latin genus and species of certain butterflies and bugs, he knew every rock, he knew trees – he knew everything. But then he was a social scientist, so he had a fine political mind. For the last half of my childhood we were in Ann Arbor, Michigan, in the midst of just the most exciting political foment that you could ever imagine. Like Berkeley, but in a nicer community. We went to riots together. We put on football helmets and got tear-gassed protesting the war in Vietnam, or just making an active statement about the counter-culture. Terrific. I think that the way of approaching things intellectually which both Ric and I have, that's a great gift. I've said this over and over again, that I'm an emotional archaeologist. The dates and facts and dry events of the past have little meaning unless there's some glue that binds them together, and then binds this collective experience to us now. That glue is a kind of emotional truth about what happened, or an emotional vibration that comes out of the collision of these events.

DT: *I've been in this town not quite a day, but someone has said to me of you that in the last few years, 'Oh, he's changed a lot.' What do you think they mean?*

KB: I don't know. I know that there was a sense of settling in – very comfortably – to a sense of celebrity. But I'm guarded against the love that comes at me all the time, so that it is possible for me to move through this celebration of what I've done cleanly. There's no danger of arrogantly asking for the best table at the restaurant. I live in a town where all of my celebrity plus fifty cents gets me a cup of coffee and that's the way I want it. The people here respect me for what I do, but I respect everybody for what they do in equal proportions. It's a true home. I've lived here now twice as long as I've lived any place in my life. My children were born in my bed. This is where my roots are and I hope that I'm buried here.

DT: *You must also have been very good for the town in the sense that when you're intensely in post-production, you bring a lot of people here. It's a town of a size that can feel a difference like that.*

KB: I'm sure that there has been a quantifiable economic advantage and I'm sure as we've just closed down the production, business has fallen off at the lunch counter. But I think that's what's happened in *Baseball* – we came in and brought an energy to the town, young people that they wouldn't normally see, creative people that they wouldn't necessarily have seen, who were all wonderful human beings. There wasn't a bad apple in the bunch. The town took to them and they to the town in spectacular ways. There's been a grieving process over the last month at the loss. We had a party, we were celebrating the end of the film and there were tears. There was this sense that we had created an immense family. This is definitely not an industry here. This is essentially one man's art in which, for some strange reason, in this case thirty-four other people at the height of production, from unpaid interns to higher paid union editors, served that man's art. But did so in a sense of community and family that was, I believe, as sustaining to them as it was to me. I know that I could not have made it through the trials and tribulations of my life without the sort of sustaining love that came from these people. So that I'm bereft right now. My children are sad at the number of friends who have departed.

DT: *I think you edited* The Civil War *in New York?*

KB: I had made all of my films up here, with the exception of *The Statue of Liberty*, because I was editing *Huey Long* simultaneously, so I spent a week up here editing *Huey Long* and then I'd race to New York and edit *Statue of Liberty* there. I did that with Paul Barnes, and he was the best editing experience I had. When I started *The Civil War* I knew I would hire Paul. At that point, he wasn't going anywhere, so Mohammed came to the mountain and I spent almost three years living in a tiny one-room apartment, Monday through Friday, and having this joyous family life up here. It was terrifically hard to do. I used to drink a lot. I gave up drinking to add three or four more hours to my daily working schedule so I could do *The Civil War*. I came back and after that, we'd invited Paul up to work on what seemed a short film, *Empire of the Air*, and he fell in love with Walpole and moved up. I think the combination of both of us here allowed me to say, on *Baseball*, 'OK, you're coming to us.' I bought a house in the centre of town that became our editing centre. We really made it a community. We brought up several people from New York. We trained several people from Dartmouth and Keene State College as interns and graduated them into things. People who just walked through the door. One fellow simply got sick of LA, left, moved here and ended up working for free. Then, he became so invaluable that we hired him. He's one of the great gifts to our production, Greg Longi. And other people. When we made *The Statue of Liberty*, Paul's assistant was a guy named Bruce Shaw and the unpaid intern was a woman named Tricia Reidy. Bruce and Tricia became editors on *The Civil War* – Tricia more an assistant editor – and then on *Baseball*, Tricia became a fully fledged editor with Paul. Bruce has stayed in New York, but we

The Editing House, Walpole, New Hampshire (photo by the Prudential Brown & Tent, Realtors)

'We really made it a community' (photo by Maureen Keleher)

pulled in another assistant and made her, Yatta Lerea, fully fledged, so there's a sense of a self-perpetuating family. There are several of these editors who are still in town. They've been out of work for a month, and they're going to spend the summer here. I've been talking to some of the editors about trying to keep this house as a production centre, so that we can say to someone, 'You may live in New York, but wouldn't you like to enjoy the isolation, the quiet that would be represented by coming here?'

DT: *When did you know you were going to do something on baseball?*

KB: I was sitting in a bar in Washington, DC, in 1985. I had just said I was going to swallow *The Civil War*, sitting with Mike Hill, who was a co-ordinating producer on both of the films, and he said, 'What about baseball? Wouldn't that be great to do next?' I went 'Yes!' so loudly that I've known every inch of *The Civil War* way that I would do a story of baseball. In fact, when the radio thing fell in my lap, kind of accidentally at the end of *The Civil War*, as I was already doing *Baseball*, I put in some Morse code at the end of the credits that says 'Baseball next'. And I still get letters from ham guys all the time saying, 'I heard that. When's your baseball thing coming out?' Somebody could get a Ph.D. doing the intersections of my films, because *The Brooklyn Bridge* is in five of my films. There are sentences that are exactly the same in *The Shakers* and *The Civil War*, *The Congress* and *The Civil War*, *Huey Long* and *Baseball* – there's a sense of history as a weave.

DT: *So baseball has been there in your mind. Talk me through that nine years.*

KB: The first four years I was on other films, but these have a way of incubating. You know, sitting in my backyard right now is an exact duplicate of Jefferson's garden pavilion in Monticello, which I've had built for nearly a year now, because the film that I'm beginning to gear up on is *Thomas Jefferson*. I've built this folly in my backyard, out of the same bricks that Monticello uses, the same mortar that Jefferson insisted be used, the Flemish bond.

So all the while I was making *The Civil War*, I was thinking about baseball and beginning to realize how baseball was the secret to the Civil War. We think our history is wars and generals and presidents, but why? The narrative of this game, our national pastime, is a more precise mirror, a clearer mirror of how we've been as a people, than anything that we find in our political mirror. I realized that it was possible to abandon the political mirror, which had just liberated 4 million Americans from ownership by other Americans, that had settled once and for all this notion that you could take your ball and go home if you didn't like what the national government was doing, and then abandon these things. So if you can gather up the threads, by the time I'd locked the picture in September 1989 on *The Civil War*, I began working on *Baseball*, writing things. By the time we had finished prints out on *The Civil War* in April of 1990, I was filming Red Barber, the first interview. Just as Shelby Foote was the first interview on *The Civil War*, we filmed Red Barber. And I had done several interviews by the time *The Civil War* came out. I was already immersed in not only *Baseball*, but also this *Empire of the Air* radio project.

DT: *When you first take a project like that, when you really begin grappling with it, you obviously make very practical decisions like: 'A few people I'm almost certain to need could die any day, therefore I'll go interview them.'*

KB: Yes. Exactly.

DT: *But does major conceptual thinking or decision-making occur then, or do you know in advance that it is in the editing that they will really –*

KB: I know everything and I know nothing. The concept is understood, but I want to hold it at arm's length, because I know everything is in the editing. So I set off writing my script completely oblivious of whether there are images to illustrate whatever that script might contain. Conversely, I go out and film what I feel like filming, what my heart tells me to film, without worrying about whether I am illustrating something. In fact, I have a shoe illustration, what I call equivalence, where you're not talking about Lincoln and showing Lincoln, but showing something else. It has an effect where one and one equals three. That's what I want: the more that's produced, that's given off by the collision of stuff. I know that's going to come in the editing, so I go off and I collect, don't talk about too much, I don't do too much reading, I let others do a lot of the reading. I want to be the audience's representative.

OK. Where does it begin? How do you start? I like this quote by Walt Whitman: 'In our sundown perambulations of late, through the outer reaches of Brooklyn, we have observed several parties of youngsters playing base, a certain game of ball. Let us leave our close rooms, let us fill our lungs with air. The game of ball is glorious.' Walt Whitman. What do we show? Well, we have an aerial view of downtown Brooklyn, *circa* mid-nineteenth century. Let's do that and move in on a church. OK, then we have another shot of a Brooklyn neighbourhood, pull out from the shadow of a church – you're in the steeple looking down, there's a shadow of a church. You pull out. And as you do, you begin to hear boys playing. The third shot isn't Brooklyn, it's Glens Falls, New York, but it's kids who look like they're in the backyard of the neighbourhood in the second shot, so we zoom in on the kid on the bat crack, and these three, OK, how do we parse? Over the course of three years, that sequence gets refined, and that's what I do all the way to the last eighteen hours and thirty-one minutes and eighteen seconds down the line, and I just go over it and over it and over it again. I suffer tremendously, but I do two things well in my life. First, I raise my chldren well. I have a kind of distance and closeness to them. I let them go and I know what to do. Second, I have a trust and faith in the process of what I do. There are times when the Merkel Boner, which is maybe forty or fifty still images, is dead. It's 1908, you wish there was a newsreel. And yet look at it now. I found some newsreel of the Polo Grounds of that time, stuff I could have with poetic licence easily put in there, and I left it out, because I knew that the still images were moving. We got it to that place, but it's long and arduous. A lot of my colleagues say, 'It's so easy, what Ken does, because he works in little segments.' These things are not there in the beginning, and they emerge so torturously. But I wished it to be so seamless that the audience reaction is to get into this world and then to pull out.

DT: *Because* The Civil War *had an immense chronological drive, when I watched it I felt little sense of the chapters getting out of line, if you know what I mean. They followed in a way that seemed inevitable. One of the things that I find particularly interesting and exciting about the baseball film – which is chronological – is that some of the ties are much more unexpected. There are moments where one feels the film is taking a curve, and then suddenly you'll go away to something that no one else would have foreseen. Would you talk about that a bit?*

KB: The immense drive of *The Civil War* was not inevitable. It is because it is a compact chronology and such an important moment in our history. If my mother's death is the traumatic event in my childhood that has informed every moment of my future from that death, then the Civil War is the traumatic event in the childhood of our country that has informed every moment and every aspect of who we have become. It was easier to have a narrative drive right through *The Civil War*, but it was not easy to find what it was and to say, 'At this moment, we can drop the Battle of Murfreesboro in favour of talking about eating worms and what the soldiers ate.' There was a huge fight and I said we had to get rid of Murfreesboro because we couldn't do it. We had to move Sherman's march from here to there. We did stuff like that. It was very hard. And at the end, it's wonderful, and I have every artist's fury at having created a seamless piece, yet still wanting people to appreciate the art. I spend more time on the editing than any other film-maker that I know. I have worked in experimental cinema and cinéma-vérité, and this historical stuff is absolutely the hardest work I have ever come across. Which is why I like it.

  Baseball presents an opportunity. Where do you grow? How do you push these things? You take a subject that isn't four years. You take a subject that's 200 years. That has as its beginning a mythology which the entire country believes, the Abner Doubleday* story, and the attendant acquisitions of mythology about it that attended the game. How do you do it? It's like jazz. You need to have a way in which you establish a theme, and then you can go off in riffs and variations. There is a moment in jazz when you feel as an audience, as a listener, that the instrumentalist has gone off too far and they've lost something. Then all of a sudden he or she has brought it back and the theme is restated, and there is a kind of joyous epiphany at that moment. That's what I've been looking for in *Baseball*. I've been saying that this is so complicated. In *The Civil War*, you got to know three-dozen characters, maybe a dozen

---

*According to legend (widely adopted officially by baseball), Abner Doubleday invented the game.

intensely, and you got to know two-dozen events intensely. Well, here you get to know maybe three-dozen events intensely. Maybe fifty people and twenty of them are like members of your family. But these occur over 200 years and are not necessarily related. So we have to plant seeds. We introduce Branch Rickey in inning 1, and you have no idea who this guy's going to be. In inning 2 he comes along and he fails. In inning 3, he gets a job in baseball and he starts inventing the farm system. In inning 4 the farm system is growing new product and he's having success. In inning 5, you meet the Gashouse Gang, the product of this farm system. In inning 6, he leaves, aged sixty-three, to take over the hapless Brooklyn Dodgers, where in 1945 he announces to the world he's going to implement the most important change in the history of the game. This is the guy who in the opening of the film, in the overture of the film, we say is a tight-fisted Methodist; a cross, one sportswriter said, between a statistician and an evangelist, who profoundly changed the game, twice. And now by inning 6, you realize what the word 'twice' meant. In inning 7, he loses control of the Dodgers. In inning 8, he dies. And in inning 9, you miss him.

DT: *You talk about the progression of Rickey's life and career, and that is a progression. Obviously you're taking great chances in that in one episode – you're dropping a loose end. "Twice." And you're not answering it. You're straightaway doing something that television tells all its practitioners you can't do.*

KB: Right.

DT: *And in terms of how this is going to play, you're asking the public to wait a week, let's say, to get the answer.*

KB: Exactly. It will be a week before you find out the true meaning of the word 'twice', if you've never heard of him.

DT: *You're giving yourself an extraordinary challenge, but I think there's a momentum in the show that will succeed. I was referring, though, to something a little different. There are moments – I can't give you an exact example, but you can obviously furnish them – where there is a line being pursued and several chapters will develop the same situation, more or less. They'll be the development of one World Series, one post-season. Very dramatic, maybe. Then you will really whip away . . .*

KB: Right.

DT: *. . . to some tiny, local, provincial aspect of the game.*

KB: This is music, you see. Every metaphor and analogy that I use in editing, when I'm talking to the editors, is about music. It's about intervals between the notes. It's about intervals between the measures and the movements. It's about breathing in and out. So that what happens as I've learned over twenty years, is what is going on in *Baseball*. This is simply Aristotelian poetics, if you want to put it on a literary scale. But I prefer the musical analogy, because you have something ordered in time. You're regulating the amount of time that someone can hear a note or see a shot. You can think of all the elements that I bring in as an orchestra: that the still photographs are the strings; that the music itself is the brass; that the sound effects are the percussion; that the narration is the woodwinds; that the first-person voices are the bassoon – however you want to do it. So you conduct this stuff. That's one thing going on.

However, what you have to do if you're going to tell a story – and this is literally Aristotelian poetics – is that you have to breathe, you have to let information go, so you can have a big [sound effect] crash of timpani, the World Series that you talk about, fade to black, and then pick up with a kid in some corner lot in Jamaica, Queens. And there's something. You're repeating the theme, but you're repeating it with a single instrument, and that builds up to something else, and the next chapter you join something else to it.

So if you were into semiotics, for example, you could take all of my films – and particularly *The Civil War* and *Baseball* – and say that I give a chapter title and that chapter title will either pay off right away, at the end of this chapter, or at the end of the next untitled chapter. The chapter does a couple of things. It releases you from all the information you've just had. It says, 'OK, let it go. We're starting again.' And it's a restatement of the theme. At the same time, it's also a punchline that will eventually pay off or might pay off right now. When we begin the Jackie Robinson story, a title comes on: 'This I know', and then you hear a voice: 'This I know.' It's Red Barber and he tells you about the moment Branch Rickey told him he was bringing a black man up. Or another time, it doesn't pay off until the last moment of the whole chapter. We have a chapter in *The Civil War* called 'The Kingdom of Jones', and you say, 'What?' Then you go through the South, the home front in the South, and you find out how the war effort's going and how the women are contributing their urine for nitre, and they're taking their hair and weaving something and the Spanish moss for something else, and that these people are doing something else. But then some people are escaping from the draft. In fact, some areas are pro-Union and there are 10,000 North Carolinians who go north to fight for the Union, and in Jones Calley County, Alabama, they've run off the tax collector and set up their own little pro-Union state, and newspapermen call it the Kingdom of Jones. Then we fade out. That's fifteen minutes from the title, but it brings everything together.

DT: *You've referred to Aristotle. You've talked about music. I would have brought in maybe people like Dos Passos even. We're not talking about films. Am I right in thinking that you do not feel strongly the influence of any particular tradition of movie editing?*

KB: Yeah, I have to be truthful about that. If I'm going to be a good interview subject and honour my forebears and stand on the shoulders of giants, which I do, I would tell you that when I met Jerome Liebling, who's a superb still photographer, and Elaine Mayes, who's a great still photographer, they showed me a lot of films. It started with Flaherty, who I feel kind of blasé about, but John Grierson – *Night Mail* and *Song of Ceylon* – I really loved. I liked a lot of the experimental films of the 1960s, like Bruce Conner, Peter Kubelka. They got me excited. I liked a lot of what Pennebaker and Leacock were doing, if Pennebaker and Leacock would stay home. I liked Wiseman when he hadn't invented a religion around what he had done. It's really hypocritical of me to say that, because I've built a huge religion around what I've done. And I like Fred's work. It's just that I think he thinks it's truth twenty-four times a second, as Godard said. As a high-school student, when I read Godard had said that, I thought, well, cinema's also lying twenty-four times a second. I saw a film called *City of Gold* by Wolf Koenig. I loved that film. Haven't seen it in twenty-five years. And Perry Miller Adato made a film on Gertrude Stein called *When This You See Remember Me*. Those films really influenced me. Since that time, I love documentaries. I'm always impressed when anybody ever finishes any film, particularly documentaries, because they're so hard to make.

But really, I'm just doing my own thing, and it owes as much to history and to something completely new, and to dramatic films. I mean, I knew everything about American cinema, French cinema and Japanese cinema. I owned every book, I read everything. In referring to Nicholas Ray, who directed *Johnny Guitar* and Philip Yordan, who wrote it, Andrew Sarris said, 'Yordan set out to attack McCarthyism, but Ray was too delirious to pay any heed as Freudian feminism prevailed over Marxist masochism and Pirandello transcended polemics.' *The American Cinema*, page 73.* You know? Now, I was in high school and I was saying, 'I want to know what that means.' So I found out what that meant, but I found out at the moment I started making films. I've never bought a film book since then. I've simply been; I've realized this thing about American history that was in me, in my breast, this sympathy for the Republic.

DT: *You come out of a very New England documentary tradition. You've talked about many of the people who are its father and mother figures. You are unlike most of the practitioners of that form, not just in your vision and the literary, philosophical dimension of that vision, but also in your fundraising.*

KB: [Laughs] Yeah.

DT: Baseball *is eighteen hours long, and cost $8 million to make. Which, of course, by the standards of the West Coast these days would be unthinkable. They would be ashamed of you for that. By the standards of the group of documentary film-makers from which you come, I'm confident that just the numbers alone, let alone the success you have had with the numbers in the past, must amount to betrayal.*

KB: My other big complaint about my colleagues is the sense that I must have some unfair advantage. My only answer is, I work really hard. My proposal to the National Endowment for the Humanities for *Baseball* is twice as long as my proposal for *The Civil War*. I ended up getting a total of $600,000 more out of

---

*In fact, this quote is exactly correct, but it comes on p. 108 of Andrew Sarris's *The American Cinema* (New York, 1968).

them over several years – not because of that. The single-mindedness of what
I've done has been often criticized as arrogance. I usually know what I want in
the editing room, or I know how to be patient with my process to get it, and I
also know how to get the money for what I'm going to do. It's never, ever been
easy. I've never snapped my fingers and received it. I've crossed the 't's and
I've dotted the 'i's. I knew my stuff going in, I used the scholars that they say to
use. They're not window-dressing. I bring them in. They help us out. Because
I've had success and because I touch the nerve, I can go to the places where
the money is easier and it will be forthcoming now. But it isn't easy. You still
have to sell it. There's never an arrogant assumption on my part that because
it's my idea, it therefore desires funding, which is often the case with people
who've done lesser work. There are a million good ideas. I've rarely heard a
bad idea for a documentary film. I can't even think of one. It's really about
whether they have confidence in a film-maker's ability to do it. And have they
assembled the resources necessary to do it? These are the only criteria for
funding these days. There's so little money. It's not so much that I'm eating it
up. I just think there's an envy. I get paid about one-fifth what I could get paid
if I went out and did what so many of my colleagues do – industrial stuff, or get
paid at union scale. I could easily make more than the modest salary that I take
on these PBS things.

   I work with public television for two reasons. One, the money is there.
There's more money to make films. Public television and its related agencies,
the National Endowment for the Humanities, the National Endowment for the
Arts, the corporations – such as General Motors, who have underwritten
magnificently not only my films, but the promotion of those films and the
educational outreach – the attendant corporations and the private foundations
are where you can get the budgets necessary to do what I do. I spend two and a
half, three years in the editing room. I'm still a million and a half short, as we
speak, before the release of *Baseball*. I'm still raising money for that. It wakes
me up at four o'clock in the morning. That's when I got up this morning. I
asked Shelby Foote about U. S. Grant, he said, 'He had four o'clock in the
morning courage.' That meant you could wake him up at four o'clock and tell
him that the enemy had turned his right flank and he'd be cool as a cucumber.
I've learned four o'clock in the morning courage. It's still present, even when
people think I must be sitting poolside in Walpole, New Hampshire.

   The other reason to be with public television is that I own my film. I
determine where it is distributed. And if it does well (in which I choose my
subjects not with a cynical eye towards the bottom line, which I've also been
accused of, I pick subjects that are in sympathy with America, but most of my
films never made anything), then I stand to benefit. I have friends who have
written films in Hollywood that have made $250 million, and they've never
gotten more than their screenwriting fee. I say, 'You've never done it? This is a

crime.' But they are now making $100,000 a week doctoring scripts, and that is the perverse, almost prostituting way that the system pays them for their earlier success. That doesn't happen in my world. I've controlled it. It means I'm willing to take a vow of poverty to control it, and have, and each one of my films says 'Copyright, Kenneth Lauren Burns'.

DT: *But the vow of poverty you talk about has paid off.*

KB: Yes, it has. But I've also paid off these grants, too. The National Endowment for the Humanities gave me $1.35 million for *The Civil War* and just three months ago, in the late winter of early 1994, I finally, three and half years afterwards, paid back that grant.

DT: *The deal on your grant money is that because you own the film –*

KB: I am required to pay back those agencies that wish repayment, like the Corporation for Public Broadcasting or the National Endowment for the Humanities, on 50 per cent of their percentage contribution. So, if the National Endowment for the Humanities gives me 40 per cent of my budget, I pay them 20 per cent of the money that comes to me, which is often itself 9 per cent of gross, if it's a home video distributor. I'm more than willing to do that, I have made money on this, but I also gave away half a million dollars to the people who work for me. You know, I'm not obligated to send the editors a cheque every quarter, just to tell them that I love them, and I'm sure if *Baseball* makes some money that same thing will happen. I live inexpensively and modestly in Walpole, New Hampshire.

DT: *But now this means that the deals in foreign countries and the videotape deals and any other deals, book deals, you do those. You make those deals.*

KB: Yes. I have an attorney, but I negotiate on those things. I choose the distributor that I want to do it, I argue over terms. I'm a good businessman, I'm an independent.

DT: *That must take a lot of your time.*

KB: Yeah.

DT: *I get the feeling – when you say 'I'm a good businessman' – that that is not time you resent. It's time you enjoy.*

KB: Yes. There's satisfaction in convincing someone to distribute my film and to give me terms that are commensurate with other people, the best people in that industry; or to play two people off against one another to get a better price for it. I think it's what it's about. I won't take money from T-shirts and caps, and stuff like that. I'm putting that into non-profit. But I am happy if my films, my books and my soundtracks make money to enjoy that.

DT: *I would guess at this stage on* The Civil War, *you probably made more money on the book than on the film, is that right?*

KB: That's right, yeah. Because there's so many more people involved that the equation payback was more extensive on film-related deals. Not everybody wanted a piece of the book, or were smart enough to ask for a piece of the book, or demand, I should say, a piece of the book.

DT: *How early in* The Civil War *project did you say, 'There must be a book in it'?*

KB: Right away, and I knew exactly what it was going to look like. In fact, I insisted with Alfred Knopf that I control the design. It was something that they were loathe to give up, but I insisted on it and I chose them because they were willing to extend that. They were significantly low on the advance, but I asked my agent what a modest success would be, and he said that 100,000 copies would be a blockbuster. And I said, 'Well, where would we be with all the offers?' One of them, which was the highest money, we would have just paid back the advance. But with Knopf we would have paid back their advance and then some, so I said, 'Let's go with Knopf. They're the best in the business.' As it turned out, we sold a million copies.

DT: *What are the parts of the process of making a film where you are more open to suggestion and collaboration? And what are the parts where you know to trust yourself in any –*

KB: All of them. And actually, if you go into the editing room, people will tell you that I'm absolutely sure and I'm sometimes rigid when I am sure. I won't tolerate going off on a tangent if I don't think we should do that, but if I hear from anyone else in the room – and it can be the cleaning lady – that something's not working, we'll go off and fix it. The classic example is what I told you about the piece about Bob Costas, in which the editors wanted this piece out as being too much, over the top. Every time we'd take it out, I could hear the fact that I missed it. I put it back in for a final screening, and the people that we talked to were so poignant on how they'd been drawn to what Costas said that we left it in. Now, I've had a couple of screenings of moments from the film, and when I've screened that segment, it's been the single thing that people have been talking about. But I'm willing to do it. I take a writing credit on my films, because not only do I contribute to the original drafts – the opening piece about Ebbets Field is mostly mine – but every sentence or every paragraph is rewritten or rearranged, and I'm constantly writing, all the time. We have a computer terminal and Mike Hill sits there and we do it. Some people can give me a word or some people can write a sentence, and it goes into it. I think I'm very, very open. You'd have to talk to Lynn, Paul and Mike, the people who are there in the cockpit of the editing, to get an objective opinion. I feel like I honour the contributions of other people. But at the same time, it isn't a democracy in there. I have to tell you that.

DT: *Let's talk about* Baseball *particularly. Let me phrase the question in this way, because I'm sure it's a question you've had many times. 'I'm not interested in baseball. I understand that some people like baseball, but I've never understood it, I've never followed it. It just seems a kind of man's world.' Why should those people watch the film?*

KB: It's the story of who we are. It happens to be about a particular subject that is so identified with men that, in our degenerating polity, people would perhaps find it something they wouldn't want to be in. Arthur Schlesinger said, 'There's too much *pluribus* and not enough *unum* in this country.' I'm looking for ways in which I can illustrate the joy of union, from which all of our blessings flow: as individuals, as communities, as states, as a country. Baseball to me is the clearest way to take us from the Civil War to the present. People would come up to me while I was working on *The Civil War*, women mostly, and say, 'I love all your other films, particularly *The Shakers* and *Brooklyn Bridge* and *Statue of Liberty*. But the Civil War, I'm not interested in that.' And to each one of them I'd say, 'I'm making it for you.' Now those very same people, or people like them, mostly women, come up to me and say, 'I loved *The Civil War*, but baseball, my husband's into that.' I'd say, 'I'm making it for you. Do you remember, were you into military history?' And they say, 'No, not at all.' I'd say, 'Well, why did you like *The Civil War*? It's all military history.' They said, 'But it's about people. It's about emotions. It's about the stories. It's about the tensions. It's about America. It's about us.' This is the story of the national pastime of our republic. I think that baseball happens to be like the canary that the miners would take down into the mines, to let them know about the quality of the air. As long as that canary is alive, our republic will be alive.

This is the story of race. What the Civil War started was left unfinished and made manifest in the treatment of African-Americans in our national pastime. It had its new beginning on 14 April 1947, when Jackie Robinson arrived, and the history since then has been the history of the same old stuff. This occurred not at a lunch counter, not on a city bus in Montgomery, Alabama, not in a school in Topeka, Kansas, but in our national pastime. So what was it about this game, in which the racial drama which is the central tension of our republic, this glorious republic, founded as it was on the noblest idea yet advanced in humankind that all men were created equal, that could tolerate in its initial encoding the existence of chattel slavery, that could four score and five years later begin to fight a war that would supposedly end, at least in a statutory sense, that institution, that peculiar institution, and could then ignore all of that and keep it woven into the fabric of our society? Race is obviously the central tension of our narrative.

This is the story of the age-old struggle between management and labour, between the owners and the players. When labour is organizing at the end of the nineteenth century, so are the baseball players. When anti-trust is breaking up large corporations in the first two decades of this century, baseball is there, attempting to drive a wedge between management and capital and trying to bring something down to labour. The most outrageous contractual arrangement in the history of American labour is the reserve clause. It says that if I have a one-year contract with you, I can control your future for ever. No one ever tested it. The Supreme Court wouldn't touch it. Justice Oliver Wendell

Holmes, whose quote begins *The Civil War*, ruled that baseball was not interstate commerce in the commonly accepted sense, and that the government basically would not interfere in what is obviously – a first-year law student would tell you in Contracts – the most egregious contractual arrangement ever invented, besides chattel slavery.

This is the story of immigration and assimilation, as wave after wave of English, of Irish, of German, of Polish, of Central European, of Southern European, of African-American, of Hispanic, of Asian groups come and adopt the national pastime of their country, and find in it, in the acceptance and the understanding of it, a much better badge of citizenship than anything that can be conferred by a piece of paper.

This is the story of popular culture and advertising. Of mythology. How we like to see ourselves. How we really are and the lies we tell to mitigate that tension.

DT: *One reason why I think* The Civil War *did so well was that you taught people – or retaught them – about what had happened. You made them feel that they had been there. But you also took that lesson and carried it forward to where we are now, and gave us hope and confidence that, in going through the Civil War, we had progressed and improved. From what I sense from* Baseball *as a whole, there is a similar feeling at the end that, whatever the woes of the game, whatever the abandoning of Brooklyn –*

KB: And greed, the TV –

DT: *– all those things, on all sides, on labour's side sometimes, as much as on management's – this is a play, a pursuit of happiness that is vital to our future.*

KB: It's medicine. Baseball is medicine.

DT: *But let me say, the Civil War brought about the emancipation of the slaves. In the years and decades since, much legislation has been passed, and where it had always been passed, it has been enacted to make equality of opportunity a reality. However, more blacks are unhappier than they've ever been and whites still fear blacks, and at the level of baseball, Brooklyn has never been the same. It is very striking that the players once enjoyed themselves more than they do now. Therefore, let me say to you, how are you so sure things have improved?*

KB: I'm not sure that they have improved. I think that everything you've said is true, and I think the series painfully points that out. I mean, when Jackie dies it hurts, because of the suffering he's gone through, but also because of how little progress has been made. His autobiography, that we quote from at the end, is called *I Never Had It Made*. That's really hard for me to accept. Then a chapter or two later, we meet Hank Aaron and the chapter title is called 'Dear Hank Aaron'. You think it's sweet, and you meet this sweet story and this incredibly sweet man. Then you realize that the title comes from the 3,000 unsigned letters a day that he's getting that begin, 'Dear Hank Aaron, with all that fortune and all that fame, you're a stinking nigger, just the same.'

But I don't think Kirby Puckett would agree with you, as he goes up against the board at the Metrodome and slams in and robs somebody of a home run, or I don't think Ozzie Smith would agree with you. I don't think that Bo Jackson would agree with you. I know my daughters would be horrified to hear what you said. And, in fact, as you were looking and nostalgically breathing in the third inning – where someone said, 'I won't pick shit with the chickens unless I get what I deserve' back in 1915 – my daughters were playing a baseball game that was as exciting to me (well, my daughter won last night) as anything I've seen. They love Mo Vaughn, who we've met, who wears the number 42 in memory of Jackie Robinson, whose father played in the Negro Leagues, and who offers a kind of continuum.

Yeah, I think that you could have turned from *The Civil War* and said, 'Yes, we emancipated the slaves. Yes, we ended this threat of secession. But look what happened. Nothing was done in race relations for seventy years.' I think more to the point is that *The Civil War* was a conversation about something that we really didn't know. It was reminding us of a birth right, and we grabbed it. *Baseball* is rekindling memories that we'd forgotten that we had. That's actually a more powerful thing. I can't go anywhere and talk about *Baseball* without somebody saying 'My father' or 'I remember'. What I found, in the collision of all the social themes that we talked about, were four immensely powerful emotions of time, memory, family and home that this game summons up and animates in people.

So you can say that baseball's never been better. More people are watching it on TV. More people are going to see it. The stadiums are getting more beautiful. The play is remarkable. I don't know whether I would take Bob Gibson over Roger Clemens if my life depended on it. Right? Roger Clemens at his peak, Bob Gibson at his peak. Or Carl Hubbell. Red Barber tells us, we asked this. Or Walter Johnson, Shirley Povich tells us. Or Cy Young, someone else tells us.

DT: *I remember talking to you, I think the first time we ever talked, about* The Civil War, *and I asked you then, would you ever be drawn into feature film-making? I'm pretty certain you said no.*

KB: Right. I did.

DT: *No matter that to be John Ford had been that great dream. I know now that you have at least begun talking to the classic house of fame and ill-repute, Disney, about what might be a new movie about the Jackie Robinson story. Now, I think you know that'll never work.*

KB: I think you're right. I feel like I owe it to my past and to a sense of fluidity in my present to offer my future the possibility of seeing what a feature film is like, but because I understand the truth of what you said, I have designed my situation with parachutes and, I think, a clear eye that will keep me in good stead no matter what happens. I was approached by many studios after *The Civil War* which assumed that I wanted to trade up to the real world. I insisted, I hope politely, in every instance that I considered where I lived to be the real world. In fact, I have funding for the next six years for documentary films, through the courtesy of General Motors and the Pugh Charitable Trust. I can make small documentary films to the end of the millennium.

However, I had this curiosity about narrative film. It had been what had animated me from the very beginning. I knew that the strength of my documentary films lay in the editing room, being able to fix things at the very last moment, and to see it new. To have a kind of naïvety, almost an emptiness at the beginning of a project, and to be filled not only with my curiosity and interests and learning, but also by my being. I am the audience's best representative as I am making my film. Feature films seem to be the opposite of that. When you and I spoke four years ago, I was absolutely adamant – as I think I still am – but I was approached, finally, by a friend at Disney, at Hollywood Pictures, who said, 'Are you interested in the life of Jackie Robinson?' Now, Jackie Robinson is the animating spirit of the baseball film. I said, 'Yes. I would like to see that, but I will not direct this film. I do not want to be the author of this film. I would like to be a co-producer who would watch the process, to see whether it's something that I would be interested in.'

Fortunately, I stalled the conversations with them for about a year and a half while I was making my film. In the meantime, Disney had made a deal with Merchant Ivory, so I suggested to my friends at Disney that this might be a suitable project for Merchant Ivory to be involved in. Merchant Ivory leapt at it and have agreed to serve as executive producers if this film gets made. We added a third co-producer from Merchant Ivory, which I felt set an appropriate pick against potentially meddlesome studio involvement – even though this was not my film – and we've set about hiring a screenwriter and talking about who might direct it.

That's as far, in the late spring of 1994, that the discussions have gone. I've had several instances of sitting with the writer and been as happy as I am in the editing room, talking about what would be in this film, and that excited me. I spent two hours on the script conversation, just pacing up and down through my office in a conference call to Los Angeles, and was a pig in shit. It was exciting as hell. Now, this is a mercantile process. It's quite unlike mine, in which I have grant money, my investors have no control over my subject, and I have a public television agency that puts it out free of commercial interruption. I don't know how much this feature-film process will corrupt, but I've designed a system in which I can walk away from it, because I am producing it and not directing it – it is not an authorship. I am willing to extend authorship to someone else. I have yet to decide who would be able to do it. I think the end of the process will be the most interesting conversation that we'll have about this subject, if this film gets made.* At the end of the process I will know a

*In the event, Jackie Robinson's widow sold the rights to the story not to Burns but to Spike Lee.

lot more about what a feature film is about, creatively, and whether this fits in with me. I suspect that it does not. I suspect, as you do, that what I do in documentary is kind of unique, and that it's what I know best.

DT: *But you are driven – I think driven's the word – by an idealism that, if they ever understand it properly, will shock some of those people. But – and here's the thing that I think is frightening – you have an idealism which I'm confident you've had all your life and which, therefore, you may feel confident in knowing and holding. But it can escape. You describe the situation as one in which you have parachutes. There are ways of falling that the parachute does not understand.*

KB: Yes. I understand that. You're talking about seduction.

DT: *Absolutely. And no one's above that.*

KB: That's why I live in Walpole, New Hampshire.

DT: *Well, long may you live in Walpole, New Hampshire, and don't let anyone make a theme park of Walpole. You must know, you must sense that in a country where there is as great a song of success as there is in America, there is also such dire envy. And there must be many people, many of whom I'm sure once upon a time were good friends of yours, who are praying for your fall, not to put it too dramatically.*

KB: Oh sure! It happens all the time. Praying is probably the word.

DT: *Because it will excuse them.*

KB: Of course it will. I see that. Let me go back and tell you a little bit about my films. My films are like my children. My children are the most important thing to me. My films are the next most important thing to me. Each one of them is like a child. Someone asked me, 'Which is your favourite film?' and I said, 'Which is your favourite child?' That was my instant answer. In that, in a way, I can't fail. I've already failed. I've already made films that I've been harder on myself about, but only inside. I would never reveal that to that film. I love my Shaker film as much as I love *The Civil War*. It does things that *The Civil War* doesn't. *The Civil War* grew up and became a famous and rich child. *The Shakers* did not, but it's no less my child and no less a part of me. Therefore, anything that isn't in that relationship is not my work. It's some other activity. I give speeches a lot. Sometimes I get paid an ungodly amount of money to give a speech. Tens of thousands of dollars. I give a really good speech. I'm a great public speaker. I only do one or two of them a year, because I know that it's like chocolate cake: if you eat too much of it, it will make you sick. One of the curses of this whole, gigantic thing that you describe is their inability to do this. I am so driven that I will sabotage anything that's actually comfortable. Making documentary films is not comfortable. There's no reason why Ken Burns should spend fifteen hours a day in an editing room for two and a half years. Every day. I should be able to come in every two weeks and say, 'It's not working. Fix it.'

So I don't know if seduction will be a problem, or whether it might do me good to be subject to a little bit of seduction, to stop and enjoy the process. But I can't imagine that the Hollywood model . . . I love the city of Los Angeles, by the way, because I read Raymond Chandler novels as a boy, so when I arrived there, I knew how to get around.

DT: *When you say, 'I love all my films in the way I love all my children,' I have heard monsters in Hollywood say the same thing.*

KB: Uh-huh.

DT: *It's a little bit of a cliché.*

KB: Yes, it is. Just like idealism spouts clichés.

DT: *You said earlier that you were funded up until the end of the century on what I think you called smaller documentaries.*

KB: Yes. I proposed an idea called 'American Lives'. I don't know whether I can use that title or not. It's just the working organization. I had been drawn to it in *Huey Long* and *Thomas Hart Benton*, and indeed in all of my films that have an element of biography as one of the formal structures – that is, getting to know complicated people as a way to progress the narrative. Particularly in *Huey*, which was all about one person, or *Benton*, all about one person, I realized that I wanted to work on biographies. And I felt that we had become a country in which some of the most important people had fallen into disuse. So how do you go back and recapture people? I thought of doing Thomas Jefferson, Lewis and Clark, Jack Johnson, perhaps, Mark Twain, other people who have been done before, but to see them in a new way, particularly in the pre-photographic era with Lewis and Clark, and Jefferson. I wanted to try to tell stories using live cinematography and paintings, which is much harder than still photographs, and present it as a series of five films. General Motors, the Pugh Charitable Trust and Arthur Vining Davis Foundation said yes about a year ago and funded modestly five documentaries, so I'm pursuing those. We've already begun shooting on *Jefferson*.

DT: *Having done two enormous series, do you think a return to the reduced scale such as you've outlined will satisfy you?*

KB: I don't know. I'm really curious about it. When I was making *The Civil War*, I made two ninety-minute films ... I was an idiot. *The Civil War* was bigger than any one person should have been handling. I made a ninety-minute film on the history of Congress and the biography of Thomas Hart Benton. And while I was doing the early work on *Baseball*, I did a two-hour film on the men who made radio, called *Empire of the Air*.

So I think I'll work in a more manageable way. It's so hard. Henry Adams said, in the middle of the nineteenth century, 'There are grave doubts at the hugeness of the land and whether one government can comprehend the whole.' And it was this magnificent expression of the great anxiety of the nineteenth century: whether this fragile, seaboard collection of former colonies could encompass the entire continent; whether the government that they had devised of, by and for the people, could in some ways expand, tolerate, to take in that continent, particularly with the question of slavery hanging over it. And it did. And it did so – with the exception of the extermination of native populations and the rape of the land – rather magnificently. It did comprehend it, but we struggle today to comprehend these things and that's a major theme in our films.

But in making these films, I have to know everything. It isn't just those eighteen and a half hours. It's the 600 hours. And that is unbelievable. It wakes you up in the middle of the night in a cold sweat, thinking. In *The Civil War* it used to take me down to the editing room two hours before the editors came in. I'd come in at seven, and they'd come in at nine, and I would just reel through footage.

DT: *In* Baseball, *Gerald Early says, 'There are only a few things this country's produced that' – I forget exactly what he says, but . . .*

KB: That 2,000 years from now, when they study this civilization, there are only three things it'll be remembered for: the Constitution, jazz music and baseball. They're the three most beautifully designed things this civilization's ever produced.

DT: *And you've now dealt with two of them. Obviously jazz would be a very intriguing subject for a film. A very difficult subject because it is so much a thing to be heard, without speech, and your films are so devoted to speech. It occurred to me afterwards that there's a fourth that many people might put in that list – although it's a far more ambivalent achievement – but it's certainly one that most societies outside America would immediately put there, which is the movies.*

KB: Yes. I knew you were going to say that.

DT: *I wondered whether that has ever interested you as a big subject, too.*

KB: Yes, it has. Barry Diller, who I've become close to as a result of the initial wooing at the studios. He was the only person who didn't woo; he just said, 'I wanted to meet the person who made this film.' At that time he was at Fox. I sat down with him and we became pretty close friends. We still are. He really wanted to make a film about the men who made Hollywood, and that intrigues me a lot. I have a feeling that there's tons of stuff that's been done really well, particularly by the Brits, about us.

I think the most interesting thing is that these Eastern European Jews came to our country, ran into typical Protestant, WASP racism, and took and built an industry from the men who seemed destined to control that industry. They took it from them and invented an America more true to its ideals than those men who were the direct descendants of the men who are our founding fathers. To me, that is the most interesting story. The Rockefellers and the Edisons were anti-democratic, and the Eastern Europeans fleeing the tyranny of their history came and invented an America that we are closer to today, because of their intervention. A classic example is their son, Frank Capra, and *Mr Smith Goes to Washington*. (It's not my favourite film. I like *It's a Wonderful Life* for Capra, because of the dark side. That's *Blue Velvet* thirty years before

Blue Velvet.) That to me is the phenomenal story of who we are.

DT: *There's a difference, I think, in that the Rockefeller types in the most part had a literal sense of what happiness was, but not much ability to enjoy it. The immigrants – essentially Jews, but not only Jews – I don't think they ever spelled it out, but in their bones they knew that happiness was a fantasy. Once you know that, it's the most democratic happiness of all.*

KB: Exactly.

DT: *Because it's unlimited.*

KB: The pursuit of happiness is not that. It's a kind of evolutionary progression. It is about educating. This is a body that is not going to evolve physically, but it has certain spiritual possibilites. I think what Mr Jefferson understood was that we could create, by extending to every individual his life and his political freedom, a climate in which the irony of superficial, hedonistic happiness could be made manifest, and that we could, in some people, create the conditions in which a more important spiritual development could take place. I believe that's the promise of our republic.

DT: *Last question, but it's a big one. Earlier on in this interview you said that you never really had a childhood. I looked at you as you said it and I thought, 'Why is that statement so remarkable?' Please don't be offended. I'm sure you know this. You have a wonderful child's look. But, of course, that doesn't mean you've ever had a childhood.*

KB: In fact, it may be the reason why I have a child's look.

DT: *Well, it coincides with someone I'm now working on, because Orson Welles was exactly the same. Because he had brilliance, he was treated as an adult from the word go until the day he died. Despite the great bulk, he had a child's look. But one of the things that interests me about Welles particularly was that, at a very early age, by the age of twenty-five, he had conquered theatre, radio and film. He was, in a way that I don't think you are, very vulnerable to boredom, and whenever he did stupid things it was usually because boredom had taken over. He said later in life that he learned so much about making films on* Citizen Kane, *that no film ever interested him quite as much again.*

KB: That's like saying that you could make love once and it was so great that you would never make love again.

DT: *Well, a certain idealism. Crazy, but –*

KB: Oh, I know, and the reason why, I could say, is because I know what that is about.

DT: *Welles had a serious flirtation with politics in the years after* Ambersons. *Long afterwards he would tell stories – and he turned them into jokes – that he might have been the senator from Wisconsin instead of Joseph McCarthy, because there was an attempt to promote him for that, he was friendly with Roosevelt and he did write speeches for Roosevelt. Now I think that enough people knew enough even then to know that Welles was so chronically devious a person that it would never have worked. However, you seem to me to have just about every attribute I would want to see in*

politics in this country. You are a good speaker, a great speaker. You have an unforced
idealism that is beautifully expressed when you speak. You have a concern for the
deepest issues. You have reached a point in your life, obviously, where you meet or can
meet many of the people who are power brokers.
KB: I know them all, in politics.
DT: *Am I dreaming?*
KB: No. I have wanted to be President of the United States. That has been my
lifelong dream.
DT: *How old are you now?*
KB: I am forty. I'll be forty-one when this comes out. I will not do it. I was
serious enough that my wife used to say, 'You're insane. Why do you keep
talking about this? You're absolutely insane.' I've known in my bones that
that's what I've wanted to do. All along. I've met Reagan and can speak with
utter calm in front of him, and Bush, and Clinton, and I move among the
United States Senate. I know half the people; I would feel no qualms about
calling them by their first names. Politics is about one thing: it's either the yes
or the no. To be involved in politics is to be sounding the yes or sounding the
no. My whole life – and the reason why I am potentially seduced by it – is that I
am interested in the last sentence of Lincoln's first inaugural address, in which
this man, who understands what I'm about to say better than anyone else,
looked out at a Southern audience and said, 'We must not be enemies. We
must be friends. Though passion we may have strained, it must not break our
bonds of affection.' Then he gave the last line, in which he was trying to stir
the common past of those who were different and were about to fight him,
though it hadn't happened yet. This is 4 March, right, and it's going to be 12
April. He said, 'The mystic chords of memory' – he used a musical term,
c-h-o-r-d-s – 'stretching from every battlefield and patriot grave to every living
heart and hearthstone all over this broad land will yet swell the chorus of the
union when again touched, as surely they will be, by the better angels of our
nature.' That is the declaration of principles tacked up with Joseph Cotten to
the window of my heart. My strength is in both, in trying to combine both, and
to be involved in politics is to have to be one or the other. What I remind
people of is how you can come together. That's the important thing that I do.
So that even as I take a stand against Disney,* the first thing I do is that I reach
back out to Michael Eisner and say, 'How may I facilitate communication with
you and the historians so that they may hear that in you, which is real, and that
you might hear in them the sincerity of their positions?' Now that may be trying
to bring my parents back together again.
    I believe sincerely what I'm trying to find is a place of trust, where I can

---

*Burns was one of many people who spoke out against the proposal, by Disney, to create a Civil War
theme park in the area of the battlefields. In the end the project was abandoned.

actually take in love and love in a personal way, rather than in a giant way. I love nothing more than standing in front of 5,000 people Saturday before last and giving a commencement address, and this morning as I put my daughters on the bus, this man drove up, slammed on the brakes, got out of his car while it was running and came over to me and said, 'That was the finest speech I've heard.'

DT: *You mustn't shrug it off. They would not say it if they did not mean it. I'm sure, in every case, it's a considered judgement and it's exactly what I'm asking you in this question. You cannot be like this without having people turn to you. You have extraordinary character.*

KB: People turn to me all the time, and people have asked me to run for office all the time, particularly since I come from a small state that has adopted me to its bosom. When I gave a speech and showed clips from *Baseball* three weeks ago, it was the lead story on the New Hampshire news that night, and they did live breakaways as the Governor was talking with me. And when I gave the commencement address, it was on the front page. My message is about multiculturalism and its dangers. The great gift is to have somebody around there reminding them, the partisans, of the possibility that when you sound notes together, which is called a chord, when you do so with the highest possible intentions, they are mystic chords of memory. That when you act in concert – another musical term – you have the possibility of calling forth the best in us. What Lincoln called 'the better angels of our nature'. So I am interested in the better angels of our nature. And you do that through waking the dead, I guess. So it's not unlike a horror film either.

The Process

This section, which focuses on the creative processes involved with the craft of film-making, contains the following:

Sidney Howard
We pay special tribute to this gifted screenwriter with two pieces: his letters home while he was writing the screenplay for Gone with the Wind, *the irrational whims of D. Selznick proving more intractable than adapting the novel; then in a more reflective mood, he analyses the role of the screenwriter in Hollywood in the 1930s.*

Chekhov's Children – In their own words
Louis Malle filmed André Gregory's production of Uncle Vanya *in a translation by David Mamet. Oren Moverman infiltrated the set and got the participants to describe their roles in a play that was conceived as a spectator-free never ending rehearsal and how they finally surrendered to a camera.*

Sound Design – The dancing shadow
Movie sound tracks are becoming not just louder, but generally more assertive, the technology now allows them to challenge the primacy of the image. Walter Murch, the distinguished film editor and inventor of the appelation, Sound Designer, describes its rise and rise, decibel by decibel.

Playing Cowboys and Indians
Eddie Fowlie, prop master and much more, divulges some of his secrets and describes his symbiotic relationship with David Lean.

Lunch and a book – Observations on Director/Cameraman relationships
*John Seale, the Australian Cinematographer (*Rain Man, The Firm, Witness, Gallipoli, Year of Living Dangerously*) describes his methods of connecting with directors, divining their intentions and serving their visions.*

7

Letters Home 1937–1939
Sidney Howard

Introduction

Sidney Howard was first and foremost a playwright. At the age of thirty-four, he won the Pulitzer Prize for *They Knew What They Wanted* (which would be filmed several times). He also wrote *Half Gods*, *The Silver Cord* and *The Late Christopher Bean*. Several of these plays drew the attention of Hollywood, and so by 1930 Howard's services were being sought as a screenwriter. Against his better instincts, he yielded. He needed the money to give him time for the theatre and to help support his farm, in Tyringham, Massachusetts, so he wrote the scripts for *Bulldog Drummond*, *Condemned*, *Raffles*, *Arrowsmith* and *Dodsworth*, among others.

It was a worthwhile compromise and one he enjoyed, despite the necessity for trips to California. But then, in 1936, David O. Selznick asked him to do a screenplay from Margaret Mitchell's *Gone With the Wind*. It was an offer the writer could not refuse, but it made for hell as well as glory. Howard wrote letters home, from California, most of which are now at the Bancroft Library at the University of California. This selection from those papers is reprinted by the kind permission of Sidney Howard's heirs.

As far as the story of *Gone With the Wind* is concerned, the letters home (generally to his wife, but sometimes to his agent or others) tell a story of mounting frustration and disillusion. Howard never lost his liking for DOS, or his feeling that it was going to be an absolutely remarkable picture. But his observations amount to an indictment of DOS as producer and manager.

8 January 1937 to Margaret Mitchell

There are several letters to her, and they seem to have had a shared attitude towards the film – hopeful, but inclined to cynicism.

Cukor is here having belladonna put in his eyes and gold put in his teeth. He is on his way to Europe for two or three months. Shooting has been postponed [i.e., the very early hope of starting in March 1937]. The picture will be released about next Christmas . . . I expect to have the script mailed in about ten days.

Two things emerge from this: that Cukor was physically present during the script-writing, and surely the first source of advice; and that Howard did the script in the two months that followed delivery of the treatment (14 December 1936). Cukor's role is spelled out in this next letter.

11 January 1937 to DOS

Thank you for mailing me your reactions to the treatment. It was a good idea

Sidney Howard (in suit) with George Cukor

for you to do so because, believe it or not, Cukor has lost his. I don't think that there is much of any value in any treatment, beyond that of forcing a writer to do some initial planning and discover for himself where the most obvious snags are going to come.

George and I are spending every afternoon together. He has already had script on the first two sequences and I can come pretty close to giving him most, if not all, of the first draft before he sails on Saturday.

You don't have to worry about actual changes. There is ample material in this book without adding anything new of our own. The tough nut is the arrangement of the material. The book is written in a series of islands: good enough novel technique, but you have to produce a picture, not an archipelago.

The script done, in January 1937, he went out to Los Angeles in the spring, although DOS tried to send him back – but the word only reached SH *en route* in Phoenix, Arizona.

29 March 1937, to Harold Freedman (agent)

Selznick has wired me that I shall be unwelcome on the 1st of April but that he has stalled me long enough and is prepared to receive me. I hunch that he may send me straight back East to work with Cukor . . .

DOS did talk of them both going East to see Cukor, but:

14 April 1937, to his wife

Last night Selznick told me that he is afraid the trip East is out due to his story troubles on another picture. I am disappointed, but not as much so as if I had really believed in it at any given point. The change will shorten the job. The trip East would have lengthened it.

The best of recent Hollywood stories happened to me last night. They asked me, some days ago, to write a ballroom love scene for the *Zenda* script and I wrote one. Last night Selznick said to me: 'Could you let me see a rewrite on that ballroom scene?' 'Sure,' says I, 'how do you want it rewritten?' 'I don't know,' says he. 'I haven't read it yet.'

17 April 1937

No one has yet mentioned *GWTW* to me but I have cut 35 pp. from the first four sequences and am beginning to hope I shall have the script down to length without omitting anything of importance for the story . . .

Selznick hates color but has commitments. I am to see the best of all color films to date on Tuesday. It is called *A Star is Born*. I also hear that it is a terrible story.

I was to discuss love interest with Selznick at ten this morning, and here it is five and he hasn't got here yet.

21 April 1937, to his wife
Yesterday we were treated to an all-day discussion of love in *Zenda* at
Selznick's house . . .

I dined with Selznick for our first and not at all satisfactory conference on
GWTW. In the course of which he said that he didn't mind my spending five
months on the script and I had better count on staying here with him until
September [SH's contract was up on 5 May]. So I had to take a stand and the
upshot is that my trip East is off and that Cukor comes out here and we finish
up in my time . . . If only they would forget about *Zenda* I could finish *GWTW*
in no time.

22 April 1937, to his wife
My future is confused as usual. This *GWTW* job will be cleared up by or
about May 15th but only to a point. Cukor is to come West to work with me
but I cannot be certain that Selznick will get round to the detailed participation
on which, it appears, he insists. Selznick, a very nice and polite gent, has still to
learn that there are several equally good ways to skin a cat. He has the same
failing Thalberg had of seeing only his way and failing to realize that his way,
filtered through author and director, may, eventually prove less effective than
the author's or the director's way accepted by him.

29 April 1937, to DOS
I am unhappy about the present because the purpose of my trip West was to
complete a shooting script for you and Cukor and, since neither one of you has
been able to take this job on with me, you don't have much to show for my five
weeks' salary . . . I have, after all, been standing by since the middle of
February, when I shipped the rough draft out here. I postponed the production
of my play from February to September, turned down Metro's offer to shine
up *Walewska* and abandoned a trip to Mexico, one after the other, to conform
to *GWTW* dates, which have, through no fault of your own, changed pretty
frequently.

29 April 1937, to his wife
This madness here continues and goes, even, from bad to worse. Yesterday,
Selznick's secretary was given a farewell party to celebrate their departure for
New York. I called this morning to ask when they are going, to learn, if
possible, what is expected of me . . . The only explanation I can find for the
keeping of Cukor in New York is that Selznick cannot bear to let him and me
work without interference. If I succeed in seeing Selznick before he leaves (if
he does, indeed, leave) I shall tell him that if he can guarantee giving me every
chance to finish the job before June 1st I shall see it through . . . if not I leave
next Wednesday.

29 April 1937, to Harold Freedman

This fellow Selznick – very nice, very polite and very able – was born with no sense of how to organize his time. His troubles with *Zenda* which prevented my coming West after Christmas are still continuing unabated. He has had no time to read my script of *GWTW* and has read the book only very hastily. In the five weeks that I have been here I have pretty much wasted my time completely.

1 May 1937, to his wife

I had so much rather be eaten by a shark than by Selznick.

2 May 1937, to his wife

This fellow Selznick cannot believe that any one has anything else to do but work for him . . . Selznick has been going East himself every day for two weeks and keeping his entire organization in a turmoil.

DOS changed the plan again: Howard was to go home and return on 15 June for a month's work – not long thereafter, it was postponed to 15 July. At last, in July, real work does start.

20 July 1937, to his wife

We are hard at work now on *GWTW* but I cannot discover that any one is any nearer than before to casting. Cukor talks as though his mind were made up but I doubt if Selznick ever makes up his. It is to be in one picture after all and the cutting problems are, as I knew they would be, appalling. I go to Cukor's every day at noon, Selznick joins us in the afternoon . . . Cukor's house is like nothing I have ever seen. Never has anything been so done by decorators. It is, I think, as beautiful as any interior I have ever seen but each room is, in the most nance sense, a perfect show window rather than a room; so much that when I saw Cukor himself in his own library, he seemed to belong there no more than a shop saleslady belongs in a perfectly dressed shop window.

22 July 1937, to his wife

Day before yesterday, with *GWTW* swimming along, Selznick decided to retake the final scene of *Zenda* and there seemed no way to get back to the main issue other than for me to write him a new scene and for Cukor to shoot it. Thus I am high and dry because Selznick has taken advantage to disappear into God knows what type of limbo and Cukor is on the stage or in the cutting room and my job has stopped dead at the bazaar. Due, I gather, to the fact that they have again postponed shooting until January or February and again don't care whether I am here or not. I sent in a message yesterday to call Selznick's attention to the fact that my departure happens, in spite of all, three weeks from this coming Sunday and he sent for me post-haste and protested wildly that nothing could be done by then and I said that was just too bad and there we are.

On 5 August he handed in the script, much swollen by Cukor's additions. It was fifteen pages longer than first draft.

In October, DOS and Cukor came East to work with Howard as he rehearsed a play.

26 November 1937, to Margaret Mitchell
Selznick left New York with the script still uncompleted and is now urging me to come back to Hollywood for another two weeks in January, which I hope to be able to do, not only because I should hate like the devil to turn the job over to some other writer but also because I am interested to see how much money a picture producer is willing to spend to pay men for not being allowed to earn their pay.

Hollywood, 16 January 1938, to his wife
I have had three good sessions with Selznick. Color is now on the wane. Bill Menzies is making the most exciting color sketches for the picture, but there is little likelihood of its being made in Technicolor. The talk, according to Selznick, is to lay off all further pictures in Technicolor and to wait for the perfection of the Eastman process.

20 January 1938, to his wife
Yesterday, in the midst of a conference at Selznick's, the bell was rung and the butler appeared. 'Oh, Farr,' says David, 'remind me to go back on thyroid in the morning.'*
Howard hung on until March, and then quit – leaving DOS bitter.

A year passed, but late in March (as shooting went on) Howard was called back: 'I dread it.'

5 April 1939, to his wife
I was shown the cut film up to the scene they were just shooting when I walked on the set. Namely, the scene in which Rhett leaves Scarlett at the crossroads. I thought the stuff beautiful in color, dull and cold in action. Leigh quite extraordinarily fine as Scarlett, though not really an actress of much accomplishment. Gable simply terrible as Rhett, awkward, hick, unconvincing. Melanie virtually cut out of the picture along with any scenes of heart interest. They have done nothing much to my script except put in a lot of unnecessary movie construction in the matter of connecting scenes which has required them to cut down the good playing scenes of the book . . . Vic Fleming† says: 'The screen is no place for trivial characters.'

*Selznick took many medications and drugs, including thyroid extract.
†Victor Fleming took over as director of the film when George Cukor was fired.

8 April 1939, to his wife

My job was to lay out the end and put it back into shape for shooting. Selznick is the same. He is still obdurately refusing to cut the story material or to condense and combine, and I have already seen a full-length picture up to the return to Tara. Moreover, it is a full-length picture, incompetently written and shot and directed without either charm or atmosphere. How really astonishing that a man can spend the time and money he has spent and find himself so unready at the end. And he is as completely unready as though he had barely started.

(In the evening) Selznick calls me, having traced me through my secretary, to come to his house at once. I refused and made the engagement for eight yesterday morning. 'Here is a scene we are shooting at ten this morning,' says Selznick. 'Rewrite it for me.' I pointed out that it was a scene which could never be included in the final picture because, through an oversight, all the dialogue and incident had been used in another scene. 'That's it,' says David. 'I want new dialogue and incident.' Not so easy. I studied the situation still further and declared that the scene was not needed. He insisted that it was. I dashed over to the studio and wrote a scene. They shot the first page. Then Selznick decided to agree with me. The scene was, indeed, not needed. But something was needed. Extras and camera crews waited while I beat out an alternative. Then they shot the original scene in spite of the fact that the dialogue and incident had already been used elsewhere . . . The whole thing because Selznick had written the scene himself some weeks ago and just found it and because Gable said he couldn't learn the lines. I shall be finished early next week. The problem arises then: when will he read what I have written and clear me? Then he will put still another writer on my new script which he will not have read and the new man will spend another two weeks redoing what has already been done so often.

12 April 1939, to his wife

I give Selznick a scene to shoot on which I work with care. I see it on the screen and he has rewritten every trace of dramatic style out of it, every bit of character, and, to my mind, every bit of illusion.

18 April 1939, to his wife

Darling

Back at the studio after dinner solo at the Brown Derby to horsewhip myself through a bit more of this chore the end of which cannot, now, be far distant. A letter from you this morning written on Saturday after I had wired you that I could not get away Saturday night. The ribbon reverse on my Remington is a little half-submerged steel button on either side just below the carrier. You push in the side that sticks out, repeating the operation when the ribbon has run through and requires reversing.

I can now, for the first time in my life, say with confidence that I know what the word 'tired' means. My own private weariness, apart from nausea whenever I look at a page of this script, is less my trouble than the miasma of fatigue which surrounds me. Fleming takes four shots of something a day to keep him going and another shot or so to fix him so he can sleep after the day's stimulants. Selznick is bent double with permanent and, I should think, chronic indigestion. Half the staff look, talk and behave as though they were on the verge of breakdowns. When I have anything to say I have to phrase it with exaggerated tact and clarity. Then I wait and wait for the reaction which may or may not come. It is impossible to get a decision on anything. That in itself is really backbreaking. I say, 'What do you want, David?' and David has not the faintest idea. My difficulty in breaking away is not going to be leaving the script unfinished because I can finish it easily and may even get it OKed. The jam I see ahead is the hypersensitive state of everybody connected with the picture. I have never been placed in quite this position of having everybody come to me to take their troubles to David because I am the only person around who doesn't upset him. And he feels that and calls me in to listen to all manner of problems with which, as writer, I have nothing whatever to do. And I want to get home. I look at those pictures stuck in my hotel mirror. I think about you. I wish to great God you were here, though what you would be doing with yourself even I cannot imagine. $500 per diem is not enough. It is something to know, however, that yesterday and today of my extension is $900 nearer solvency. Tomorrow and day after doubles that sum. I may not be able to do better at leaving than to get enough scenes ahead to persuade David that he will save money by taking me off payroll even if he has to call me back for a day or so. I just lack the finance courage to make a break that is too brutal. With all his drawbacks, he is a great deal easier and a great deal more agreeable to work with than Goldwyn or any of the big studios, and *The Constant Nymph* can take all my worries off my neck for this summer and leave me with comparative peace and even a few dollars over to do a thing or so that might be fun on the farm or in the form of a holiday. You will have to trust me, my darling, to make the best deal towards the reestablishment of practicable family life which I need a much as, if not more than, you do.

The sensation of yesterday, at which I hinted over the phone this morning, was Miss Leigh's announcement that she was pregnant. It was whispered to me with the news that she would have to suspend shooting for five days and what did I have ready to shoot which would not require her. I had plenty ready but the sets had not been OKed by David and were not yet built and could not be finished for another ten days and that meant five days wasted at $20,000 per diem. The little mouse saved the lion. But the terror now is lest the story should leak into the press. As David says, the South is laying for him – because he has put an English girl in the part, the women's clubs might easily get the picture banned in whole areas.*

. . .

Don't commit yourself too far about your scheme for coming West with your father† and mother. That's a good deal of effort and expense just to show them how to get to the Brown Derby. When your father has stood around a studio from eight in the morning, when he may well be called, to six or seven at night, he will not be much interested in evening entertainment. Also, if I get clear of here, I don't want you pulling out a week after I get home. That's too tough. They can roll their own. He has a professional engagement. Let him feel lonely during his off hours. He has his wife with him. You don't give a hoot about my feeling lonely. I am a little disturbed to hear about the orchestration of the Waltz. It was undoubtedly made by Al Newman on whom I was counting to make things agreeable for your father at the studio. He can certainly make them disagreeable if he wants to.

Reports from the Playwrights about *No Time for Comedy* are encouraging. Line out to the street all day. I met Stanton Griffiths at the Brown Derby tonight and Kit‡ had telephoned him that she has a hit or what looks like one. Your report sounds as though Guthrie had elaborated and slowed matters, rather than giving them the pace they needed. Kit's method is slow and he keys her productions to her. He is no good for comedy anyway. I can't think what else would have made that play seem tedious. Maugham is after me to dramatize his new book for the stage. I have the galleys but have not yet read them. It doesn't look like my street. Marquand's book is my idea of a complete delight and a damn distinguished job into the bargain. Mind, I don't say that it's as good as George Apley, but the study of the Hale family is really astonishing in its wit and observation. I am a bit resentful of his rechristening Bob Sidney. Did I write you that? Marquand is an interesting and inspiring character. All these years of S.E.P.§ pot-boiling and suddenly he emerges as our most distinguihsed satiric novelist. I used to believe so hard, got so disheartened about him, am now so bucked up. Even for myself. Ego aside, he is one of the brilliant men of our time.

When, in your letter, you mentioned your plan for three days at Tyringham, I wept literal, real, salt tears. Not long postponed. I shall really be wiring you when to expect me tomorrow. I love you, my darling, and need you in my business badly.

---

*Leigh and Olivier were then lovers, but she had a husband and a child. Selznick took great pains to keep them in separate residences in Hollywood, and he was always fearful of the risk of scandal.
†The composer, Walter Damrosch, who was eager to work in Hollywood.
‡Katherine Cornell.
§Saturday Evening Post.

Epilogue

Gone With the Wind was finished; it did open. And Sidney Howard won an Oscar for its screenplay. But he was not there to receive it, for he died in August 1939 in a tractor accident on his beloved farm. So he never saw that *Gone With the Wind* did play.

8

The Story Gets a Treatment

Sidney Howard

If one goes to the root of the matter, motion pictures are neither written nor acted, but made. It is the combination of director with cameraman which, more than the writer, more even than the beloved screen personality, gives the finished picture its life. Apart from the original story material, the writer's function in the making of pictures is a secondary one. Since the screen as we know it draws the vast bulk of its story material from books, periodicals and the stage – with a few imaginative excursions into biography – the screenwriter's task is really a job of adaptation hack writing, cut to the dimensions of the director's demands. The screen does not yet ask of its writers much more than technical ingenuity. The present purpose is to describe and to discuss the screenwriter's share in picture-making, but it seems as well to admit forthwith that there is no immediate likelihood of literature on celluloid.

The process by which the screen adapter goes to work is in itself designed to cancel out inspiration. Let us suppose that Mr Sinclair Lewis has written a novel in which the picture studios see possibilities. The supposition is a reasonable one, because Mr Lewis frequently does write novels and the studios are apt to covet them. The selection of Mr Lewis's works to illustrate this chapter makes its writing the easier for me, moreover, because it has been my good fortune that I have on three occasions served Mr Lewis as a screen adapter, and much of my motion-picture experience derives from my work on *Arrowsmith*, *Dodsworth* and *It Can't Happen Here*. For our purpose, however, Mr Lewis has written a new novel and his agent has sent it to the New York offices of each of the different studios.

Immediately on its receipt by each office, the book, manuscript or slather of galley proof will be turned over to an exceedingly overworked employee known as the reader, who will personally conduct its first faltering leaps towards the screen. Mindful of the fact that most picture executives are busy, busy men who would not be given to reading under any conditions, the reader proceeds to reduce Mr Lewis's work to a brief and inevitably inadequate synopsis, embodying the highlights of the story, any morals pointed, remarks on the likelihood of its popularity, and adding his own critique in which, the book being Mr Lewis's, he almost certainly recommends buying the picture rights. Then ensues a period, of intense interest to any man of Mr Lewis's literary attainments, during which the different studios compete with each other in offering large sums of money for the motion-picture rights to the preceding six months of the novelist's life.

The period of competitive bidding terminated, Mr Lewis disappears from the arena. Economically he is better off than when he entered it. Artistically he is much the same. A book is a book and a picture is a picture, and Mr Lewis will not again be given a moment's thought by anyone until, three days preceding the picture's release, the studio publicity office remembers that he won the Nobel Prize and invites him to a private showing of the picture in exchange for an endorsement to the effect that the picture is ever so much better than the original novel. I may remark in passing (and from experience) that Mr Lewis is afflicted with a kindliness towards his stage and screen adapters which amounts to an aberration as yet unnamed by psychiatrists. The screen hack (or adapter, as we prefer to be called) begins his labours immediately after Mr Lewis's first payment has been handed over.

He may begin in a variety of ways according to his position in Hollywood's slant on the writing craft. If he is what is known as a New York writer – that is a term employed to cover all writers who are not residents of Hollywood – he will be summoned to interview an important metropolitan executive who has not read the book, may have glanced through the reader's brief synopsis, but is expert at conveying-the-impression with just the suitable amount of literary enthusiasm. Arrangements being concluded between the executive on the one hand and the writer's financial obligations on the other, the first discussion of the screen version of Mr Lewis's latest terminates in an argument over whether the writer shall fly to Hollywood or take the train. The New York executives of studios almost invariably, I have found, advocate flying for writers, though very few of them would think of flying themselves. They are all husbands and fathers. So are a good many writers, and poor sailors to boot. The major consideration, however, is always the pressure of time. The picture – so the writer is told – must be ready for production in virtually no time at all. Wherefore, and not knowing that he has a year and a half to spare, he boards the overnight plane to Los Angeles, there to report to a producer who probably is too busy with golf or the races or his favourite endocrinologist to see him during the interval between his arrival and his first two or three weekly salary checks. This interval the writer will employ in thinking how he will spend his salary and making sure that his studio office is equipped with all the supplies he would never dream of buying for himself. He may even reread Mr Lewis's novel.

All screenwriters, however, are not New York writers, nor even high-salaried members of the Hollywood studios' literary staff. It is just possible that the studio which has bought Mr Lewis's novel may have no immediate plans for it. Every studio has on its pay roll a group of so-called 'younger writers', ranging in age from eighteen to sixty, who draw very small salaries, sit in very small offices and, because they have not acquired a thing known in Hollywood as 'prestige', waste their lives in the process of being 'broken in'. It is not impossible that Mr Lewis's novel may pause for a time to further the 'breaking in' of one of these mute, inglorious Miltons. Here it will be developed into a full-length motion-picture script which no one will ever read. Inasmuch as this step in our story is almost invariably a dead end, we may, as the studios do, proceed, as though it had never been, to the day on which our New York writer has been called to his first story conference.

I am aware that a great deal of fun has been poked at Hollywood story conferences and that most of it has now grown stale. It must be obvious, however, that the first story conference is an essential milepost in the screen-writer's contribution to the making of the picture. It is then that he tells the producer and the director the story of the picture which the one is to produce and the other to direct. I have often thought that this constitutes the most important function that he has to perform, because directors and producers are notably reluctant readers.

Our hypothetical story being the work of Mr Lewis, neither director nor producer has any fault to find with it – yet. In fact the first story conference is almost certain to end on a note of amiable optimism. The writer has a great angle on the material, the director is going to do a great job of direction, the star is going to be great in his or her role, a great picture is going to be made. The writer retires to his office and office supplies to write what is known as the treatment.

Now the treatment is a description on paper of just how the screenwriter plans to make Mr Lewis's novel into a picture. He will by this time have made himself so familiar with the book that he knows it better even than Mr Lewis, who forgets his own books with a happy alacrity. The writer may employ two or three styles in the writing of the treatment. Many, I have noticed, go in for highly coloured expression and become, so to speak, barkers for the job they are about to do. This style went well with producers of the old school, but its effect is not guaranteed on the more recent models. Some writers, in what I consider a mistaken honesty, adopt an aseptic attitude in the writing of their treatments: that is to say, they tell the producer exactly what he is going to get. This I do not recommend. To begin with, it is impossible in summary to say clearly what any picture is going to be like. One cannot, for example, sum up characterizations. The producer, furthermore, at least in the early stages, always wants more than he is going to get and the style I have employed and found most successful is the informal but reassuring approach, the kind of thing the late Henry Van Dyke would have done as a preface to a young poet's first volume of poems. The main object, after all, is to tell the producer that everything is going to be all right, which, at this early point, he is only too willing to believe.

Once the treatment has been accepted with slight modifications at a second story conference, the writer proceeds to write his first draft of the script itself. It is not well to put too much of one's heart into this first draft. There was once a writer who explained his failure with an adaptation by claiming that he made the mistake of writing his fifth draft first. This somewhat enigmatic remark will become clearer as our discussion proceeds.

For myself, whenever I start writing my first draft of a screen adaptation, I find fault with the whole process up to this point. I discover that long before I have had opportunity to develop any convictions of my own, I am seriously confused by the unconsidered opinions which have been thrust at me and which have distorted any intention I may have had when I wrote my treatment. I proceed therefore on the theory that the sooner the first draft is on paper the sooner the real work will begin. My single object is to put the book roughly into picture form, sequence by sequence and scene by scene, including in it as many picture ideas as may occur to me, but making no particular effort towards a finished script.

The process of reducing a novel to picture form is really much the same as that of dramatizing it for the stage. Plays, however, have in great measure to be redramatized in order satisfactorily to fulfill the screen's demands. A novel is a story which its author tells without any help from the outside. A play is a story so written that it is incomplete without the services of a company of actors. A picture is a story written to be photographed, and so keyed in its writing that the camera will never be called upon to photograph anything not visually interesting. Narrative, which is of great value to the novelist, is impracticable on the screen until it is dramatized into those conflicts between characters which produce dramatic situations in photographable action. The play scene in which two actors may sit on a sofa and discuss matters of engrossing interest to the theatre audience is impracticable on the screen because it is dull to photograph. Two illustrations occur to me.

It will be remembered that the crucial situation of Mr Lewis's *Arrowsmith* has to do with an experiment performable only upon human beings, the purpose of which is to test an inoculation against the bubonic plague. Martin Arrowsmith goes to the scene of a West Indian epidemic committed to dividing the possible victims into two lots. One lot is to be inoculated, the other to be left without inoculation. The observed results are to constitute the substantiation or discrediting of the inoculation. Mr Lewis spends a considerable portion of his book on making this clear in scenes which, though fascinating to read, would have been deadly to photograph. After Arrowsmith has worked out an entire series of preliminary experiments, he and his chief, Gottlieb, discuss the problem in long passages of scientific dialogue.

When we came to making all this clear and interesting in the screen version, Mr John Ford, the director, and I had to devise an entirely new episode for the early part of our picture, basing it upon an incident which Mr Lewis had mentioned only in passing. We took a moment, in that portion of the novel which deals with Arrowsmith's early career as a country doctor, to develop a local cattle epidemic in the course of which Arrowsmith divided the cows in a single barn into two lots, inoculating one lot and leaving the other unprotected. We made this interesting by building it up into a fist fight between Arrowsmith and the state veterinarian. Its real value, however, lay in the single shot in which Arrowsmith was able to point to the healthy condition of the inoculated cows and to the empty stalls of the uninoculated. Then, when we came to our climax, Arrowsmith required only one reference to those cows in Dakota and the picture could move on without delay to its climax.

My other illustration has to do with the transferring of a play scene to the screen. In the third act of the play I made from Mr Lewis's *Dodsworth*, which I subsequently redramatized for the screen, there occurs a scene in the American Express office in Naples. In this scene Dodsworth, abandoned by his wife, now a lonely traveller through Italy, re-encounters Mrs Cortright, the second woman of the story. The thing on the stage was simple enough. Mr Huston as Dodsworth and Miss Sunderland as Mrs Cortright sat down on a bench and said the things which had to be said in order to advance the story. In Mr Goldwyn's screen version, if the two actors sat down at all it was only for a moment. Then, still speaking the lines of the play, they moved out of the office and got into an automobile to drive through the streets of Naples. For this ride the conscientious Mr Goldwyn had, through his foreign photographers, provided actual Neapolitan backgrounds. Thus, by a simple screen device, a play scene which would have been photographically uninteresting became one of the more notable moments of the picture.

In my opinion, novels make better pictures than plays. The playwright selects for his material a story which is most effectively told within the scenic limitations of the stage and is likely to suffer from over-elaboration on the screen. The screening of a play requires expansion, which is bad for a work of art. The screening of a novel, by contrast, requires contraction, which is apt to be good.

The motion-picture form lies somewhere between the novel and the play. It rejoices in at least the geographic freedom of the novel because it can move easily from place to place as a play cannot. However, the motion picture must do without the repose of either novel or play, and therefore without the reflective expansion of either idea or emotion. It has its own and most rigorous technique, which is best described by saying that a moving photograph must move and keep moving. In other words, its story, to be well told, must be told continuously in action. What the characters think or feel on the screen must be expressed by doing, and only strong and clear thoughts and emotions can be expected to pierce through a medium which, even in colour, lacks the reality of the flesh and blood of the stage on the one hand and of the novelist's personal spell on the other.

The talking picture should if possible never pause to talk about itself. This is a lesson which many directors and writers of Hollywood have still to learn. One still sees too many picture scenes which are no more than photographed play scenes. By this I mean scenes in which the director has deluded himself into the belief that he is satisfying the action demands of the picture medium by moving his camera round and about a theatre stage and cutting from close-up of A to close-up of B.

It has been said that the dialogue scenes of talking pictures should be written as though each were a full-rate cable for every word of which the writer has to pay out of his own pocket. Length hangs like doom over any picture. Wonderful as the motion-picture camera is, it is still a piece of machinery, and photographs of actors and actresses are not living actors and actresses. It is probably this removal from reality – or, if you like, from contact with a living imitation of life – that so sharply restricts the time accorded a picture for the telling of its story. Audiences will sit in the theatre and watch living actors with complete contentment for two hours and a half and, when they are remarkable actors in a remarkable play, for close on three hours. It does not matter how excellent a picture may be, it is, in my opinion, too long if it runs beyond an hour and a half. Even as fine a thing as the screen version of *Mutiny on the Bounty* – and that is a fine thing, judged by any artistic standards – seems too long to me. Thus the impression of the freedom of the motion-picture medium is largely an illusion. I have more than once struggled with the writing of sequences which were technically as difficult and as limited as the sonnet.

Furthermore, each new mechanical development of the screen seems to increase the exigencies of screenwriting. Some ten years ago, the invention of sound altered the entire approach for director and writer as well as for actor. The difficulties of writing for colour pictures are still to be explored. Colour is far more than a technical addition. It will, in my opinion, alter the approach to picture-making quite as profoundly as did the introduction of sound ten years ago. I do not know how many directors and writers will at this time be prepared to agree with me when I say that I find the problems of colour far more baffling than those of sound. They seem to require me to develop a painter's imagination to a degree of which I am incapable. Black and white photography has its own visual continuity. It can move from walnut library to summer garden or from Greenland to the Sudan without any sudden shock to the eye. The colour picture cannot take such liberties. In black and white, for example, we can send our hero to his library window, cut without shock to a brief flash of what he sees out of doors and return again to the library. That cut will, in colour, be both unsightly and distracting, because it is not a shift from darker to lighter gradations of black and white, but from dark brown to pink, yellow and green. We shall be required now to work out a new and more subtle method of moving from place to place. We shall also, I believe, have to invent a way of

writing and directing our scenes so that the relative values of their compositions will maintain some degree of visual balance. I remember very clearly my
dismay as I first watched Mr Robert Edmond Jones's production of *Becky
Sharp*, a picture produced in colour but directed according to the usages of
black and white. In that picture, scene after scene began with the most
beautifully composed arrangement of colour, only to disintegrate immediately
the action started into such confusion that I found it difficult even to follow the
story.

But I am again digressing from my account of the screenwriter's job. I adopt
my system of being generous with myself on my first draft of a picture script
because I know that no one is going to pay much, if any, attention to it except
the director, who, under ideal conditions, now becomes my dominant collaborator. The opening sentence of this chapter states that pictures are made,
not written, and the director has to make them. When, therefore, the director
and the writer sit down together, it becomes the writer's duty to say to the
director: 'How do you propose using your camera? How do you propose
handling the action in the best photographic interests of the story you are going
to tell?'

The director now proceeds to contribute his ideas and the script begins to
take the form of a motion picture. There are still directors who like their
manuscripts divided into many hundreds of little scenes; close-up, medium
shot, long shot. The more modern director, however, prefers a manuscript
which reads as simply as a play. He will wait, even beyond the actual shooting,
until the assembling of the film before he makes up his mind concerning the
more technical details.

I have found it valuable to include the studio's art director in this collaboration, because even the most gifted of directors can, if he is willing, make good
use of the art director's exclusively visual type of mind. The larger studios of
Hollywood divide their picture-making into various departments which have
little contact with one another. Smaller production units, notably Mr Samuel
Goldwyn's, are too clever for this. It is Mr Goldwyn's custom to keep his
highly gifted art director, Mr Richard Day, in constant touch with the progress
of the script. The result of this triple collaboration is a completely illustrated
edition de luxe of the script which contains literally dozens upon dozens of
thumbnail sketches both of photographic compositions and of camera angles.
This method of working not only provides the director with invaluable mem-
oranda when, finally, the cameras begin turning, but tends to keep the script
itself a thing to be looked at rather than to be spoken. That, it cannot too often
be repeated, is the all-important quality for any picture script to achieve.

I do not know how Mr John Ford and Mr Dudley Nichols worked together
in preparing the screen version of Liam O'Flaherty's novel *The Informer*, but I
have always felt all possible admiration for Mr Nichols's work on that picture. It

is a piece of screenwriting which any man interested in the medium should study for its truly beautiful economy, its photographical eloquence, its faithful translation of the material from one medium to another and the selfless professionalism with which the writer has served his director.

At the end of a fortnight or three weeks spent on this second draft collaboration, the script returns to the producer and the real fun begins. All producers seem to be divided into two types. For myself, I prefer the type which undertakes to produce, more or less, the picture the director and screenwriter have given him. That type of producer, though he may impose criticisms and amendments of his own, keeps in the track which has been laid down, spares director and writer no end of headaches and usually turns out fully as good a product as the other type. The other type, of which there are too many examples, seems to be a kind of kiwi, as the British Royal Air Force used to call its ground officers after the Australian bird which has wings but cannot fly. By this I mean the producer who is neither director nor writer and would like to be both.

This type of producer operates without the wisdom to see that another man's way of telling a story may be as good as his own. His determination to get his picture script written and rewritten until it coincides exactly with his own conception is more than likely to choke out the last germs of spontaneity and life. It frequently leads him to engage a whole series of writers, both in collaboration and in sequence. This not only wastes untold quantities of money – such producers have more than once spent close on half a million dollars in screenwriters' salaries – but deprives the finished picture of any homogeneity of style. Producers of this type are to be avoided by the wise director and screenwriter.

All producers and directors seem to have one weakness in common. They are unwilling to face the fact that their scripts are too long, and proceed in the delusion that they will not need cutting after the film has been shot and put together. The picture which is cut to length in script can be smoothly cut and the cuts blended over so that they will not afterwards be apparent. The picture which is shot from an overlength script and cut after it has been put together will always show the bad joints of crude carpentry.

The script from which the picture is made – it may be the second or the fifteenth, according to the type of producer – is called the shooting script. Before it can be made, however, it has to be submitted to the censorship experts of the Hays office and these gentlemen scrutinize it in their knowledge of what is permitted by the Censorship Boards of varying states. Their function is to warn the producer against the deletions which he may expect in any given state, if he violates any of that state's regulations. I am always sorry if I am not present at one of these censorship sessions because nothing gives me more pleasure than anger at censorship. Censorship is so inaccessible. It operates in its methodically remote way and one never gets at it. One never meets the censors. One never knows what type of fanatic or racketeer the censor may be. I find it comforting to sit in the same office with Mr Hays' experts and to scream at them as though they were themselves the censors, and they are accustomed to being screamed at and seem not to mind.

It is healthfully infuriating to be told that storks bring the babies in certain states, that the word 'Communist' cannot be mentioned in the Dominion of Canada, that Hitler, Mussolini and the Republican party may be offended by Mr Lewis's *It Can't Happen Here*, which must therefore be banned on the eve of its first day of shooting. In that connection I remember one of the most charming, I think, of all censorship observations. One episode in that unproduced script showed how Mr Lewis's editor-hero escaped from the American dictator's concentration camp. Jessup, the editor, reaches a farmhouse in the Green Mountains of Vermont, where the women of his family are waiting to welcome and to secrete him. Among other things he is given a bath, in the course of which his wife has to scrub his back for him. No camera ever looked at the scene, because, as I have said, the whole enterprise of the picture had to be abandoned out of deference to Hitler, Mussolini and the Republicans. The censors, however, warned us that the business of the back-scrubbing was permissible only if the actress who was to play the wife was cautioned never to look down. The couple were past fifty and had been married long enough to be grandparents, but the wife must not look down, for fear, presumably, of making some startling anatomical discovery.

Once the criticisms of censorship have been made, the script proceeds to what is called the *breakdown*. In this stage of its development it is taken over by technicians who estimate with astounding exactitude how many days will be consumed in the shooting. These technicians transform the script from some 120-odd typewritten pages to a vast board covered with tiny tickets, each ticket representing a scene or *set-up*, and the total number of days' shooting produces still another crisis in the picture's progress, because it is the length of the shooting schedule which most determines the ultimate cost of the picture. The technicians work on this breakdown day and night until the total of days and dollars is ready. Then comes that final painful conference in which art perforce gives way to business and the writer–director collaboration has to face the music of subtracting a hundred thousand dollars from the budget. Once this is done – and it has to be done in spite of the screams of writer and director – the writer's contribution has been made. He is very seldom on hand while the picture is shot. If he is one of the regular Hollywood writers, his agent has shipped him on to pastures new. Our New York writer is free to return to New York or whatever part of the country he calls his home. He may take the train or walk if he likes. There is no longer any pressure on him to fly.

There has existed among authors, and for many years, a great snobbery against writing for pictures. The New York author has been ashamed to engage himself in it and the screenwriters have been hypersensitively defiant about it. There is no longer justification for either snobbery or defiance. The mechanical improvements in picture-making have been paralleled by an equal aesthetic advance and closely followed by an astonishing growth in the taste of the picture public. With each year the best product of Hollywood has become increasingly beautiful to look upon and increasingly mature in its choice of subject matter until, in the pictures of René Clair and in such Hollywood offerings as *Pasteur* and *Zola*, the taste and intelligence of the screen public has outstripped that of the New York theatre audience.

However secondary the writer's function in the making of pictures may be, two facts should at once be conceded: that as long as writers earn their living by writing they are economic nitwits not to earn at least some of it where the pay is both high and certain, and that to the very vast majority of the international public, the screen has superseded both plays and novels. In view of these facts, it is always amazing to me that more writers have not realistically turned their minds to studying the technical aspects of screenwriting. A leading Hollywood producer recently told me that of all the droves of writers in and out of Hollywood, he knows less than fifteen capable of seeing a script through from treatment to production. This statement may well have been coloured by unfortunate experience. It is, however, a custom in Hollywood to provide a screenwriter, who finds plenty of time to learn golf and contract bridge, with a continuity writer. A continuity writer is a gentleman who shakes his head gravely over any idea the screenwriter may have to offer and remarks: 'That may be all right but it isn't pictures.' His function is to relieve the writer of the obligation to learn his job and to complicate the already complex collaboration with his director. I have never myself had to contend with continuity writers, but it is undoubtedly true that the studios could not operate without them. Frequently the New York writer-hero of this chapter is, upon his arrival in Hollywood, given a neatly typed outline of the picture as it is to be made, with orders to conform to it. Though the producers may with some justice explain this condition as a result of literary laziness, I believe that the whole system of the employee-writer is basically an unsound one.

The creative instincts do not thrive on salary. When a screenwriter boasts that he has managed to get twenty or thirty weeks of employment out of a single picture, he is, in my opinion, indicting the system which makes him an employee. The average screen adaptation of book or play should be ready to shoot after six or eight weeks of normally intensive work. If more time is needed, there has been waste somewhere. The producer will claim that the writer has wasted it and the writer will counter with his total of the days he has spent waiting for the producer to read what he has written.

I cannot, in justice to the producer, refrain from one observation calculated to endear me to my Hollywood colleagues. The more fortunate of screen adapters – in which number I am happy to include myself – are probably the most preposterously overpaid men on the face of the earth: at least, we are paid as much for doing as little as anyone now visible to my naked eye. The producers, on the other hand, pay far too little for original story material. Novelists and their publishers have not even begun to claim their share of the Hollywood loot. This chapter is designed as a compendium of practical, rather than artistic, hints. Within the last year, one of the most illustrious of all publishing houses sold the picture rights to one of the outstanding successes of modern fiction for exactly one-fifth of the value placed on it when a second studio tried to repurchase it from the original buyer. It is time for the fraternities of novelists and publishers to wake up to the state of the world in which they are operating.

This is not to say that there are not many screenwriters capable of the most excellent work. The writer–director collaborations of Hollywood produce a round dozen of first-class picture scripts every year. I have already paid my respects to Dudley Nichols's version of *The Informer*. I can scarcely say less of Mr Robert Riskin as Frank Capra's collaborator in those two most enchanting film comedies, *It Happened One Night* and *Mr Deeds Goes to Town*. Talbot Jennings, once an original author of distinguished accomplishment, did remarkably by *Mutiny on the Bounty*.

The fact remains that the hundreds of screenplays turned out each year by the Hollywood studios contain few if any more items of real excellence than are to be found among the few dozen stage plays of the New York or London theatrical season. The obvious moral of this is that the money which builds and equips studio plants and motion-picture theatres can neither build nor equip a talent for writing. The more fundamental explanation of it is that literary talents seem to derive most satisfaction from being left to their own independent devices between the bindings of books and in the dingy and dusty reaches of backstage.

The screen will get most from its writers, and the writers most from the screen, when motion-picture bookkeeping and business methods have been so revised that the author of a picture is paid a royalty on its gross receipts and not a salary while he is writing it. Why I should be paid a salary while I am adapting a novel to the screen and a royalty when I dramatize the same novel for the stage I do not understand. I do know, however, that in the studio I am through on receipt of my last salary cheque, whereas in the theatre I am at work up to the last moment before the opening night, because, being human, I know that my reward is still to come and depends upon my doing my very utmost. Art, like a great deal else, is made more interesting by financial returns. The screen will presently have to revise its method of dealing with its writers, just as writers will have to revalue their attitude towards the screen.

This is all the more true because the screen is rapidly running short of material. Contemporary literature no longer supplies the demand. A Hollywood story editor has complained to me that authors these days are falling down on their job. Screen material used to be easily found. Now he must read hundreds of plays, novels and short stories in search of one worth making into a picture. For this shortage the screen itself is in large measure responsible. Too many authors, of talents both rising and matured, are delegated by the studios to rewrite the works of other men and are thus kept from writing on their own account. Hollywood would do well to confine the purely technical business of screen adaptation to writers who are adaptors and technicians by temperament and to leave every man capable of original creation free to work on that. The enormous number of pictures made every year has driven the studios back to revivals of former successes and to refuge in the classics. Neither revivals nor classics will fill the gap for ever and the need for original screenplays is already pressing.

A considerable amount of original screen material is constantly in course of concoction. This may be an unkind, but is not, I think, an unfair way of stating the case. The original screenplay presents a knotty problem to both studio executive and film distributor. A successful stage play or a best-seller novel is each a known quantity and bears a thoroughly advertised title. The unknown work written directly for the screen is a mystery to the public except as a vehicle for a popular star. 'I need a picture for March and Gaynor,' says Mr Selznick, and Director Wellman and Author Carson join with him to concoct an assembly of safe and sane formulae known as *A Star is Born*. The venture proves a profitable one, but is unlikely to crown with fresh laurels the brow of the producer of *David Copperfield*. The original screenplay has not yet grown beyond the synthetic vehicular phase. Until it does so, we shall not have to take it more seriously than it deserves, and that is a good deal less seriously than we take the adaptation of established novels and plays.

But the day of important original screenplays is near, when our O'Neills and Kaufmans will be writing for the screen as independently as they now write for the stage and arranging for their productions, not out of deference to the higher weekly salary, but with the same greed for the best artistic conditions of cast and direction which they now impose upon the theatre. This is inevitable because the best talents for producing, directing and acting have already been drawn to the screen and because the stage's bitter complaints against the screen will very presently be silenced in virtual extinction and the thing called drama, of which stage and screen are both passing manifestations, will continue indefinitely to entertain mankind. In the screen drama that is to come the director will continue his domination, at least until the screen has welded director and screenwriter into a single individual. But the writer's side of this superman will still play second fiddle and screen drama will not be literature but something else, something new. It is always a sound idea in art, as in life, to welcome anything new when it is good, and motion pictures seem bent on growing better and better.

9   Chekhov's Children –
in their Own Words
Edited by Oren Moverman

Cast

Film Director	LOUIS MALLE
Theatre Director	ANDRÉ GREGORY
Film Producer	FRED BERNER
Vanya	WALLACE SHAWN
Yelena	JULIANNE MOORE
Dr Astrov	LARRY PINE

Prologue

In the spring of 1994, I put aside a script I'd been working on for the longest time and proceeded to infiltrate the closed set of Louis Malle's *Vanya on 42nd Street*. I had heard that Malle and his old *My Dinner with André* accomplices, André Gregory and Wallace Shawn, were shooting David Mamet's adaptation of the Chekhov classic, *Uncle Vanya*, in the long-defunct New Amsterdam Theater, and was quite curious to see what their unique form of collaboration was all about. After some moments of uncertainty and careful improvisation, I was able to find a position of sorts in the small, low-budget production. Upon walking on the set I realized that something extraordinary was going on – that this was no routine filming of a play, but rather an event that was only one part of a long artistic journey that had started years ago with Gregory, and culminated with Malle's personalized documentation of the work.

Curious to define that journey and understand its significance – cinematic or otherwise – I began conducting separate interviews and casual conversations with a few of the key contributors to the project. I soon discovered a complex and somewhat abstract narrative about theatre, film, life, death, acting, rehearsing, technology, finance, performance, reality, love, spirit and the search for the truth – themes that pour out of this *Vanya*, and yet are relevant to all film-makers at the close of the first century of cinema.

The following is a composite of words and thoughts collected during the summer of 1994, just before *Vanya on 42nd Street* was due for release. This verbal collage is about one Anton Chekhov, performed and lived by his artistic children.

Act I

ANDRÉ: In a certain way, I've been working on this Chekhov canvas these last twenty years because, before I stopped directing in 1975, I was working on *The Seagull* which was presented in New York and got devastating reviews. Like Treplev in *The Seagull*, I became angry and hurt since I was trying to go in a new direction that was very delicate – much like the way Chaplin was going in a new direction with *A Woman of Paris*. So, like Treplev, in a certain way, I just burned my manuscript, committed suicide and left the theatre, even though, without my knowing it, the manuscript just got put away for many years and was taken up again with *Uncle Vanya*.

The thing that brought me back to directing – and I don't know why exactly – was Chiquita, my wife, getting ill.

LARRY: I think he needed to have some sort of other thing, because he had given his life over to supporting Chiquita, in a wonderful way. So he had in *Vanya* his own little world that he could go to. Actually we all did.

ANDRÉ: I was appearing in an all-alcoholic production of *The Tempest* in Massachusetts – a horrible, horrible production where I was making a fool of myself as Prospero – when my daughter and a young Japanese actress suggested that I direct them in scenes from *Uncle Vanya*. So I reread the play, which I'd done I think for the first time when I was thirty-two years old, and suddenly I was directing again. I knew Wally Shawn should play Vanya, and I went out to a memorial service for George Gaynes's son, who had been killed in a freak accident in India, and when I saw George really destroyed at the memorial service I thought, 'If George would do Serebryakov, and if Wally would do Vanya, I'll do *Vanya*.'

WALLY: He just asked me to be in it; that was it. He said he was only interested in working on it for a summer, rehearsing it. He reassured me that we were not going to perform it. Well, I mean, I had no interest in theatre and didn't really want to become involved in a theatrical project. But he assured me that it wasn't going to be that, and that we were not aiming to show up on Broadway, put on our funny noses and actually perform the play. I guess it was very tempting to me and I said yes.

ANDRÉ: I think I cast in a way almost no director does – I don't hear of any director doing it this way – because I never audition, ever! I usually go on the combination of either knowing the actor, having worked with the actor, or, if I don't know the actor, I have extensive talks, hours and hours and hours of just talks, and meetings – having dinner, or having lunch and seeing if we're really on the same wavelength. Now, some of these actors I worked with before many times: Jerry Mayer, George Gaynes, Wally and Larry Pine.

LARRY: We have a huge history together. We go back to 1967: NYU, Jerzy Grotowski, the Manhattan Project and *Alice in Wonderland*. Nowadays, I do lots of leads in regional theatres. I do functionary roles in inconsequential movies. I did a lot of day-time soap-opera work which is the equivalent of working in a factory. Every day I would leave the studio and think, 'Oh God, that was so awful!' It's work, but you can't rise above that medium. There's no truth or art in it.

So when André calls, and he's interested in doing something, I always want to work with him. I know it's going to be fun and it's going to be a huge challenge, and I have no idea what will happen.

ANDRÉ: Brooke Smith, who plays Sonya, had almost no experience in the theatre. She was a friend of my son's; he'd seen her work and recommended her. Lynn Cohen was suggested for the role of Maman. Somebody else told me about Julianne Moore's work and I got together with her.

JULIANNE: He asked me what I was planning on doing with my summer, and I said, 'Oh, I don't know. I should probably go out to Hollywood and try to make some money,' because I was doing a lot of theatre and I was broke. And he said, 'Well, I would rather you spend the summer doing this workshop with us.'

ANDRÉ: Of course, when I was talking with Julianne, what I didn't realize then, and do now, is that she looks exactly like my mother when she was young; she's the kind of woman who's archetypal in my own relationships. I myself am always attracted to the Yelenas: the hopeless, lost, introverted woman with a lot of potential who may not achieve it.

JULIANNE: I guess we just hit it off, and so I thought that I could always go to Hollywood, but the chance to work on *Uncle Vanya*, let alone the chance to work with this company of people, and with this director, wouldn't come up ever again. Like when I did *Hamlet*, I did it because you don't do *Hamlet* that often. Maybe there are people who specialize in it and do it a million times, but for somebody like me, chances are I'll play Ophelia once. Just like I'd play Yelena once. But I'll always have the opportunity to make money, or at least I hope so. I mean, I can wait on tables. But *Uncle Vanya* won't happen again. And so I told André I'd do it. I think that André had cast us not for our strengths, but for our weaknesses; each of the actors has something to do with the weaknesses in the character they play. It was really interesting and kind of scary to work that way – to keep coming back to a character, thinking that you're so different than she is and then finding out that you're not. That was rough!

ANDRÉ: I think one of the questions the play asks is: Is there anything beyond hope? This became a question for all of us: Ruth Nelson, who I cast as Marina, the old nanny, was dying; one of the actors was having an identity crisis; another was thinking of leaving the theatre; Chiquita was fighting cancer; George was dealing with the death of his son. So *Uncle Vanya* became a little island of light where we could be together, and explore our hopelessness.

LARRY: Nobody knew what we were getting into. André always sets up a world that is artistically safe, so that you're able to do anything. And the same people kept meeting year after year to do this exploration. You'd go off into the world to shoot a movie, or do a play, do a commercial, or whatever, and come back and meet, and all of a sudden we would look at each other and say, 'Gee, we're all back doing this again. Isn't that amazing!' And this happened over a period of *four* years.

ANDRÉ: The reason that I started to rehearse for long periods of time was that when you do it in five weeks, what you do is you figure out what you want to say ahead of time and then you find the best way to say it. But what I kept getting frustrated by as I saw these productions was that what wasn't in it was what I didn't want to say. See, that's the interesting thing – to find out what you don't know. What you do know is not very interesting.

So I just let the actors go on their own. And if they get lost, and want help, I'm there to help them. Now, this is also more like the process of good therapy. A good therapist doesn't know where you should go in your life; they're like Virgil in the *Inferno* – they're by your side to support you on the journey. If you need some advice they're there to comment, but they're not telling you where to go. *You* go! You go on your individual journey. The director's job is to bring all these long journeys together into some unity.

JULIANNE: It's liberating and absolutely maddening at different stages. Basically, he lets you go and go and go, until you run out of steam with one particular choice or a certain idea. It's intoxicating. And then you get to a dead-end, and you turn to André and say, 'Well, now what?' And he asks, 'Well, what do you feel like?' And you want to knock him to the ground, because you can't get out of it. He forces you to find the way through it yourself. The result is you end up with a production and characterization that are intensely personal, where you really have created every little drop of it. Every bead of it belongs to you, to your history with that character, and to your past with those particular actors.

WALLY: André doesn't seem to do much, while actually he's guiding everybody through his particular taste and interpretation of the play. There seem to be clear interpretations, certain choices that are made. Somehow, in some mysterious way, those are André's choices, although he never tells us to do those things. He never says, 'Well, this is how I interpret the play.'

ANDRÉ: For me, rehearsing is like fishing. You put a lure on the line, you throw it out and you wait. You don't know what kind of fish is going to come up. Most directors know what they want; I have no idea what I want.

LARRY: It's the truth of the world that is created in the rehearsal process that intrigues André. You go into a scene with somebody and you don't think of objectives, where you came from, where you're going – it doesn't matter. What's going on at the time is what matters.

WALLY: The goal of the whole project was to reach a point where you didn't think about it, where the lines popped out of your mouth as the most natural thing to say in the circumstances.

ANDRÉ: It's not normal rehearsing; it's much closer to life. It's not acting; it's more confessional. In acting, because you generally do it within a certain economically prescribed period, you have to achieve a result. So any result that gives you the impression that it will affect the audience is fine. But it may not be the truth! So we literally had to live the questions. There's an area in this where working on a role and the spiritual journey become one. The work process is not just about doing the play; it's about creating an environment in which people can enjoy celebrating their full potential. So it's also not quite theatre.

Act II

ANDRÉ: In the beginning, we thought nobody would ever see our work; we weren't going to do it for anybody. Then we found we could show it to some people, but only fifteen or twenty. That was the only way we could do it and maintain the integrity of the work.

LARRY: I would have invited as many people as possible, and more. I always hated that we only did it for thirty, thirty-five people. And they wanted to do it for twelve!

WALLY: When we were rehearsing, we were not rehearsing with the intention of doing it in the big theatre, or in any theatre. Consequently, we rehearsed in a normal tone of voice without projecting our performances, you might say. The way that we were acting it was as if we were in a movie. Eventually many of us felt that it would be enjoyable to have some people watch. But it was obvious that it couldn't be more than about twenty-five, because we would have been inaudible.

JULIANNE: I always disliked having an audience. It was very difficult for me. The way we worked on it was so personal. When I'm working on a character, I'm working on it for me. I don't have a performance goal when I've gone into something that's an open-ended workshop. Nobody said anything about performing it. André refused to call it 'performance', even though we did it in front of people. He'd refer to it as a 'rehearsal', which I thought was rather hypocritical because it wasn't. It was neither fish nor fowl: it was never really a performance; it was never really a rehearsal at that point.

LARRY: We showed the rehearsals at the Victory, a decaying old hulk of a theatre on 42nd Street, and André would say to the audience, 'We don't know what is going to happen this evening. We hope it turns out to be something that you like.' They'd sit there, only a few inches from us, and we'd start. After about fifteen minutes, they'd realize nobody was trying to create anything beyond what they were looking at. We were not trying to make people think we were in Russia or anything. We were trying to explore the text of Chekhov in the simplest, most truthful fashion. So people let down their guard. A lot of people said, 'You ought to make a movie out of this.' And of course since Wally and André worked with Louis Malle on *My Dinner with André*, they wanted Louis to come and see it.

WALLY: We had a great time doing *My Dinner with André* with Louis, and so the thought of doing something with him again was very appealing.

ANDRÉ: Louis came to see *Vanya* in its second manifestation and was deeply moved by it. He'd never seen my work as a director, so for him I was a weird character in *My Dinner with André*. I think *Vanya* may also be one of his favourite plays. Wally and I approached him sometime after that about making a film, and he was a little hesitant, but open to it. He was going to come back and see it again.

But then Ruth Nelson got very ill, just before he could have seen it again. Louis had to have open-heart surgery. Chiquita died. Ruth died. And we gave it up.

LARRY: André went into mourning for a year, and we thought it was over.

ANDRÉ: Then Wally and I were working on another project, and he said, 'God, I miss *Vanya*, how much I'd love to play Vanya again.' I started talking to the actors about the possibility of getting them together *again*, and when I was talking to Julianne I think she said, 'What about it being done as a movie?'

JULIANNE: I said, 'Listen, there's no way I would do it again as a play. We've exhausted it! If we do it again, it's got to be different.' I think all of us felt that it needed to be finalized. We never had a final performance, we never wrapped it up. Film is a way to finish something. It freezes it. You capture the performance and you walk away. Theatre never ends, it's never over. The technology of film allows it to be over.

ANDRÉ: But the problem with technology, I think, is that it closes down the imagination rather than opens it. *My Dinner with André* is a radio play. Most films tend to feed you the visuals, so they leave nothing to the imagination, to your own creativity. The question was still: why do a film?

WALLY: Quite simply, if *Uncle Vanya* was ever going to be seen by more people, it had to be a movie.

ANDRÉ: So it was a cast decision to make *Vanya* a film.

WALLY: Everybody in the company is a movie actor. Everybody loves movies, and the idea of working with Louis Malle was a thrilling one for all the actors. It was a privilege to do such a thing.

ANDRÉ: Part of the problem of doing *Vanya* again was: who in the world would ever replace Ruth Nelson? In a certain sense she was irreplaceable. She was also central to the nature of the way our work grew because she was fighting illness for almost the whole time that we worked. She couldn't walk our first summer, she just sat. She was the lodestar for all of our work. She forced us constantly towards simplicity and authenticity.

JULIANNE: In acting one always has a tendency to go too far: to cry too much, to be too angry, to do too much stuff. In life something happens, someone dies, or someone gets hurt, and you realize you're just standing there. You're not doing anything! You're not crying! So Ruth's health added a levelness to it all, a sense of what it is just to live with life and death – that it's not histrionics.

ANDRÉ: The last time we did *Vanya* she was literally dying on stage, so you were seeing the essence of what the work is about. She'd come in very ill and I would say to her, 'Ruth, we don't need to do this. It's not like we've got a contract or are charging money.' And she said, 'But this is my life.' She had a bed set up, a cot in the dressing room, and she would say, 'Wake me always about ten minutes before I'm supposed to go on.' She was very weak. And when we would wake her, she'd come on with more pith, vinegar, anger and energy than she'd ever had.

And in the last scene where Sonya is doing her last monologue, there would be gentle tears that would be coming down Ruth's cheeks, because one eye was already in another world. So, in a sense, that couldn't be replaced. You couldn't just get an actress, and also for this group you needed a very special kind of actress.

Sitting at my desk one night, I suddenly thought, maybe Ruth has a friend. So I called her son and he said there are three still alive, and one of them is Phoebe Brand, who of course is a legend now, because she originated many of the Clifford Odets women in the Group Theatre. She stands for the committed, engaged person. She's passionate about the theatre. Well, she *is* the theatre!

WALLY: So finally, it seemed as if the work had reached the stage when everybody was ready to do it as a film – including André.

ANDRÉ: Wally and I got together and went to Louis again.

Act III

LOUIS: They came back to me in December 1993. I remember they were sitting right here, and they said, 'We would like to do it!' I wasn't sure, but I said, 'OK, then we must do it quickly. Investigate if everybody could get together in the spring.' That's how it started.

FRED: Louis wanted to shoot it in New York City and knew that I lived here, and had done a lot of low-budget films based here. I told him years ago that I would always be happy to do anything with him, since I so much enjoyed the experience of working as his assistant director on *Alamo Bay*. We knew that in its conception it was a specialized movie, so we had to cast the financiers accordingly. It wasn't about how much money we could get, because we knew that it needed a modest approach to be successful. You couldn't spend a lot of money. It had no bona fide stars, and all the rest. So all the typical conventions of fundraising were out the window.

We ended up with an unorthodox funding scenario where we split the domestic and foreign rights, and then supplemented it, much the same way that you would for a legitimate theatre endeavour, with angels – private investors who, in a limited partnership with the creative members of the company, became profit participants.

LOUIS: My preoccupation was to try to keep as close as possible to the way they had worked; although it was obvious that the moment we transported it to another medium, a certain number of things had to change. It was my role to make it into something that would look like a film, but I was constantly preoccupied with trying to keep it close to what they had been doing all along.

FRED: The intention was to preserve the intimacy of André's staged version. We talked about the film maintaining the integrity of the open-rehearsal concept, and doing it in an unpretentious, energetic fashion.

Now, the Victory theatre was slated for renovations as part of the 42nd Street Renewal Project. There was some major opening with the governor and it was not available. I think they were doing an asbestos removal, and they had suggested to André and Louis going across the street to the New Amsterdam Theater, which was scheduled for renovations by Disney to become a flagship theatre for family entertainment on 42nd Street. It had once been home to the Ziegfeld Follies, musical comedy, and in fact some great theatre, then ultimately porno. It had gone through its 42nd Street transitions. But it had been gloriously rain-damaged over a period of about four or five years, so it had the weirdest, most beautiful design that had been caused by this random neglect, which seemed a perfect backdrop for Chekhov.

JULIANNE: We started rehearsing with Louis to get back into it; it'd been months since we'd done it. So it was a time for us and for Louis to see, examine and look more closely at the play. It was pretty much our work, except that he would, as anybody would, have a different perspective every once in a while and say what he saw.

WALLY: There is no doubt that when we were in Louis's hands we were responding to his taste and to his preferences, although we were coming to it with a certain knowledge of the characters. So Louis questioned everything, and forced us to put into words what had been completely non-verbal, even to reveal secrets that we had kept for years. And, of course, that had a certain effect. But he never said, 'Well, your interpretation of Chekhov is wrong. This is what I think the character is doing in this scene.'

LARRY: Louis demanded that we know what we were doing. He demanded it as the movie director. He demanded that there wouldn't be anything left up in the air. We would tell people that every rehearsal is different because we don't know what we're doing. But here Louis would say, 'I don't understand what went on there.' So we had to make it crystal clear for Louis, so he could shoot it – we had to make it so he would accept it.

LOUIS: It's complicated to define those things because it's very subtle and there are no rules. I would think that certain actors need much more adjustment to be in front of the camera than others. I took it for granted that they came to me, having worked with André for four years, so I was not going to re-rehearse them – that would have been silly. But I knew that in front of the camera their performances would be different and on camera they would look different. So we had to make some adjustments and we did, but we had very little time to do it. For some of them it was hardly necessary and for others it was more work.

JULIANNE: For me it's easier as an actor to pretend that there's nobody else there. Film has the ability to be a very personal medium because at the time that you're working, the audience becomes an intimate thing – the camera! If you feel comfortable with the camera, feel safe with the camera, you can let the camera in, in a very personal way. The irony is that you reach your widest audience through film.

ANDRÉ: So then we who had spent years working, suddenly had to do it in two weeks.

LOUIS: Shooting a feature film in two weeks was like filming without any safety net. It's a very dangerous sort of film-making, because you make a decision about how you're going to shoot a scene and then you have to stick to it. What you usually do is give yourself the alternatives of having at least two or three versions of it for the editing room, but we didn't have time for that.

At the same time, there was so much concentration, and so much intensity, and so much energy that I cannot imagine it would have been as good if it had been shot in six weeks. Some flaws in the film would have been avoided if we had had more time. From time to time there was a weak moment because the actors were tired, or because we didn't have time to do it again and again. But I think what's going to strike people about this film is the quality of the acting. Acting in Hollywood movies these days is so horrendous that it doesn't stand comparison. But it has to do with the fact that it's very hard for actors to be good when you have a six-hour set up. As an actor, you have to wait and wait and wait, and do it again, and then wait, and do it again, and then you lose it. This production had the intensity and concentration of a theatrical performance, which is completely unique, and you can see it in the acting.

JULIANNE: I think *Vanya* travelled a shorter distance in becoming a film than it did being performed in front of an audience. We worked in such a quiet way originally that when people started coming, we were forced to open it up – certainly in terms of volume. When it became a film, we were able to revert back to our workshop habits and make it more intimate.

ANDRÉ: Because we had to do it in two weeks, we were forced to be truer to our process. It was so raw and fast and immediate, that it kept us within the framework of our own way of doing it.

LOUIS: There was an excitement, a completely new element in doing it for the camera. So they were scared, they were excited, they were incredibly concentrated. There was a real miracle happening. I also enjoyed the fast pace because, as I'm getting older, I'm getting impatient; there's something about the process of film-making that I find excruciatingly slow. When I started making films, it was much faster. We had less money and we had to go faster. But now, the way they make movies – big commercial movies – takes so much time, and so many people that I get bored. I didn't get bored on *Vanya*; it was a treat for me. I've been able to work like that before. For instance, on *Au revoir les enfants* we were shooting very fast. We were shooting only six hours a day because of the children, but those six hours were very fast. When you work with children or stage actors, you must not tire them or let them lose their concentration. The difference with *Au revoir les enfants* was that I shot it for eleven weeks, but short days, six hours instead of fourteen or fifteen, and it was more precise because it was a period film. But that's the way I like to work.

FRED: We shot the film in super-16mm because we wanted to make sure that the mechanics of film-making didn't overpower the intimacy of the theatre. Also, Louis had much more specific creative reasons for wanting to do it in super-16, in addition to wanting to move quickly. It was all about the length of takes – because of the 16mm magazines and the ability to do good, long, ten-minute takes. In a piece like this, where the speeches are long and the page count is long, he didn't want to be interrupted. So the super-16 format was conducive to that.

Still, it's always a pain in the ass to do super-16 blow-ups at the end of the day because it's such a small negative, but I do think we captured the energy. I think the actors felt a little freer in front of the camera.

LOUIS: I needed a cinematographer who was a good camera operator, because we were going to do a lot of fast, hand-held shooting. I saw *Ballad of Little Jo*, which Declan Quinn shot and Fred produced, and I thought the photography was very, very good. Then about a year ago I had a drink with a friend of mine in England who had been the production manager on *Damage*, and she said she had just worked with a young Irish-American cameraman named Declan in Ireland. I saw the film they made and I thought it was quite brilliant.

FRED: Declan is a very sensitive and dynamic cameraman; he has an ability to find the intimacy of a piece. I know that one of the guiding principles of what Louis likes to film is the people themselves – his films are very much about human faces. And Declan is keyed into that. The faces he films look wonderful, but always in a naturalistic way.

LOUIS: We decided to hand-hold the camera suspended from a wooden crane on a bungee cord. It was an experiment really! We knew pretty much what the actors were going to do, but we wanted to give them freedom to move about. Stage actors are known never to respect their marks when they're in films. It's because on stage, if they move three feet off the mark, it doesn't matter. In films, the camera operator yells, 'Cut' – you cannot frame it.

Then at the beginning of the shooting I realized that they were all very much on their marks when it was necessary, but we were already using the bungee cord. It works in the first act because it is a little messy – an exposition with a lot of entrances and exits. In the second and third acts we replaced the bungee cord with a dolly and it actually turned out the same, except that the bungee gives you more freedom. I knew that Declan had worked with that technique before and was very good at it, so I was not worried about it being somewhat improvisational. The elastic cord gives a movement to the camera that is fine, but you cannot cut it with a shot where the camera is completely fixed. But, actually, our camera was never completely fixed; even when it was on the dolly, we kept it a little loose in order to keep that feel. The reason why I didn't use the bungee all the way through is that when the play becomes much more intimate, I felt the camera movement should be less noticeable on screen.

Since my early films, when I was showing off like all young directors do, I haven't liked the camera to be a character. I don't like: 'Oh, what a great movement! Oh beautiful!' I hate that! Especially on something as intimate as *Vanya*. So I think at some point during the first act you forget what it is – that it's a rehearsal in a theatre and the camera is hand-held – you're very much in the play. We still had to respect the intermissions, at least between Acts I and II and between II and III, because there's such a jump of time in the play – it's three months later. But an intermission between III and IV would have been detrimental. And, of course, I always felt we needed a prologue for the film.

WALLY: Well, it had to begin with the actors appearing, and showing that it's a film of a rehearsal. It's not a film of *Uncle Vanya* in that way. As an audience member, I would rather see something like this and I would get more from Chekhov than I might from seeing *Uncle Vanya* performed in costumes from 1900.

LOUIS: I felt there was an interesting contrast between this refined adventure of a group of people getting together for months and working on a Chekhov play, and their environment – the fact that they were doing it on 42nd Street.

ANDRÉ: That is why the prologue is so lovely. These people are tripping along the street in the middle of shit and transvestites and heroin. The prologue says: This is not a movie of a Russian play; this is a movie first of all. This is not *Vanya* – because you're prepared for a sort of PBS-style, filmed play, but this is a document of an event that's gone on before, that was about putting on a play. It says: what you're seeing is somehow about today.

LOUIS: A few months after I saw André's *Vanya* for the first time, I was supposed to come back when they did it again. I was passing through New York and I remembered they were starting at eight o'clock at the Victory theatre. I told them, 'I'm sorry, I might be late because I have something to do.' I was twenty minutes late and they started without me. I stayed outside because they locked the door, as we did in the film, but I was hoping the stage manager would peek out to see. So I stood a half-hour outside on 42nd Street and it was summer and just about the same light that we had when we shot the prologue – and what was going on!!! That's why we ended up calling it *Vanya on 42nd Street*. I think it's important to indicate that it's a quintessential New York project. That's why in the soundtrack we kept the presence of the police sirens and Wally drinks from an 'I LOVE NY' cup. We kept all that, so even when people forget where we are and just follow the play, I hope they'll never pretend we're somewhere else. It's like when somebody came up with a samovar and I said, 'Are you crazy? A samovar? If we have a samovar, we are finished! This is the end of us!'

FRED: In the end it always was and is a movie. So it wasn't only about everything being natural. The costumes, even though we began with people's own clothes, were slightly modified to give the palette a cohesion. And Eugene Lee, our designer, made sure that even though it was shot in this broken-down, gloriously disastrous environment, the theatre had touches and pieces to it – whether it was NYC police barricades or old theatre seats – so that there would be a look of spontaneity to it. You don't want the actors to feel made up; you don't want to sense that they're in costume; you don't want to feel that you're on a set. But there has to be a certain design to that. There are also artificial elements which we added to the movie that have to do with thunder and lightning, alluding to what the characters are going through in the play. So the line is a bit blurred between rehearsal, the play and the film, and the hope is that at some point the play completely takes over, and you're in it. We try to do that on every level.

ANDRÉ: What is wonderful in this kind of collaborative work is that, by the time it's finished, nobody knows who did what. A crucial moment in this whole concept is when the Nanny/Astrov scene begins and you don't know if you're still in the prologue or you're in the play. Louis thinks I made that suggestion!

WALLY: But it was really Larry who came up with the idea that the small talk of the actors should slowly slide into the play.

LARRY: I don't think that was my idea. The only thing I said was that I thought it would be fun if Phoebe and I would walk in and start saying the dialogue and Wally would be asleep on the bench. So we would walk down to the table and talk about how life sucks and all that kind of stuff, and by the time we got to the table the play would begin. That's all I said. I thought it could be seamless, that nobody would know when the play had started. It's important that we all stay who we are and that it is all one thing. We didn't change to play these roles; we're just people trying to do this play, trying to be incredibly real and yet truthful to Chekhov . . . I guess it was sort of my idea after all.

FRED: The earliest portion of the collaboration took place in the rehearsal weeks. Louis was sort of circulating around with his video camera and working with Declan, and then discussing with André the possibility of restaging something, or reblocking it so it was better for the camera, or to give it a different shape – not dramatically, but physically. There were different discussions at that point and André was always more than willing to find ways to accommodate what Louis was going to need.

ANDRÉ: What Louis and I have in common is that we don't feel all that comfortable articulating a lot. Maybe because it makes it too fixed, and maybe because articulation is so imprecise anyway, and both of us have a very strong sense of the depth of the unconscious. So we never had one creative discussion during the actual shooting – none that I remember.

LOUIS: It's difficult to explain. It was not like we said, 'Let's establish how we are going to work out our collaboration.' We were working so fast!

ANDRÉ: Before we began shooting, when Louis and I were talking about how the film should be credited and everything, I said to him, 'You know, if it's going to be mine, this work, it's really got to be yours.' If he hadn't made it very personal to him, I don't think it would have been what I'd done. But that means enormous trust. I never questioned when he was setting up the shots; I would look at every shot, but I never questioned it. There wasn't even time for that.

LOUIS: It was organic, in a way. I had to work out the shots and to run the set and make very fast decisions about the camera and the movements, so that was all mine, of course. But then when we got to the takes, I was very much aware of André's opinions and how he felt. Most of the time I think he was genuinely surprised by how good everybody was.

FRED: What really distinguishes this version, which I think was also true of *My Dinner with André*, is that it is Louis's directorial eye that takes you as an audience where he would like you to go. And so where a play typically, in a proscenium fashion, would be haphazard in terms of where you want to go, or fairly straightforward, given that you would usually watch the person who's speaking, or at least the people involved in direct conversation, here there's an additional sensibility that's been layered into the process which is that of a gifted film-maker. And you follow that lead.

But what the film was always about were the performances; what the film was always about were the words. So there needed to be an elegant way to bring those to the screen. It was never about production values, although they were solid. It was never about lighting, although I think it's exquisite. In other words, it was never about so many of the elements that have to do with making films: locations and getting there, dressing, etc. There was a lot of simplicity in the filming concept in order to make the performances accessible.

Act IV

LOUIS: When I first started editing *Vanya* with Nancy Baker, I said the same thing I said to Suzanne Baron, the editor I worked with for twenty years who did *My Dinner with André*, 'We're going to choose everyone's best moments and we're going to patch them together, and I don't give a shit if it doesn't match or if it doesn't cut. We'll make it work!' It worked brilliantly, actually. In *Vanya*, it's not quite the same because it's a little more diverse. But we always gave the actors their best performance on film – even if we had to get into some monkey business to manage it. That was the rule.

WALLY: There were a couple of times during the shooting that one felt, 'Oh, God, I can't decide; I'll do it two different ways and let Louis decide in the editing room.'

LOUIS: I was always trying to tighten the performances. I think the rhythm on the stage is completely different and I had in mind a different rhythm and I told them that. The fact that there was so much energy and so much intensity on set changed the rhythm as well. The presence of the camera, the culmination of a process, this moment of truth that everybody was aware of, gave something to the shooting that a run-through one Sunday afternoon couldn't.

ANDRÉ: Whenever we did the play on stage, it lasted from two hours and twenty minutes to two hours and forty minutes. This time it was under two hours.

LOUIS: When people ask me what editing is for, I say, 'Well, editing is for improving the performance of the actors.' I remember having a big fight with Sean Penn because he said, 'In the cutting room, you destroy our work, you chop it up!' I feel it's exactly the other way – it's just that I might judge an actor's performance differently from the actor himself. I think I'm more capable of judging it than they are. It's amazing how much coherence and focus you can give to a performance. A screen actor's performance is delivered by pieces twelve seconds long; it's completely impossible to keep it together. In the cutting room we give it that cohesion. This was not so much the case with *Vanya*, because we were shooting in long takes and in continuity.

We worked comfortably for three weeks editing *Vanya* on the AVID, then we had a screening, made some more adjustments for a week, and that was it. I must say I'm crazy about electronic editing; it's a great progress in film-making. It's not so much the speed, it's the incredible flexibility. It gives you the possibility to be more daring, to try more things. In conventional film-editing, when you cut the film, there's a point when you can go no further. Eventually you've cut the film into so many pieces that it doesn't hold together. So there is an almost physical limitation to what you can do. With electronic editing, there's no limitation; you can go back, change it, rechange it and try something else – it's so easy. It allows much more fine-tuning, you can experiment more. The one and only weakness of the AVID is the image definition on the monitor; because the image is digitalized, the pixels are so-so. So it's a good precaution to go back to the work-print once in a while and look at it on the big screen. We were not able to do that because it was a question of finance; but when I saw the first print of *Vanya*, I realized I would have made only a few changes – less than I expected – if I had had more time and the possibility of looking at it on the big screen instead of a computer monitor. I think it's absurd not to work on the AVID or on one of their competitors that are just as good. It took me a year and a half to cut those huge documentaries on *Phantom India*; I would have cut them in six months with the AVID.

When we were watching the film print in its entirety for the first time with the proper soundtrack, and under the best possible conditions, it became clear that the power of the film comes from a great text and great acting – anything in between is insignificant. To put it together is a vast amount of work, but that's what it comes down to. I keep being amazed by how good these actors are and how powerful Mamet's adaptation is.

WALLY: Of the translations that I've seen for Americans to perform, there is no comparison. What Mamet writes is a wonderful text. It doesn't call attention to itself, it doesn't use American slang, or it doesn't contain things that leap out at you as not being appropriate to the period. Everything in it is something that a human being could say. Well, it takes a real playwright to do that. We couldn't possibly have done what we did with any other translation that I've seen, because the whole idea was to do it very naturally, as if we were just regular people talking.

LOUIS: If you read the play, you're stunned because in so many ways it's such a contemporary play. At the same time, it's perfectly about its time, about a particular milieu of a decadent rural aristocracy that Chekhov had used in several plays and his short stories. So it's perfectly placed in time and in a certain culture, and yet when we watch the play we say, 'Well, this is about us!'

FRED: In purely commercial terms, I think there are very few films these days, particularly coming out of America, that deal with ideas and feelings, and take a scalpel to what makes us strange and interesting as human beings. I think the film-making community is always looking for rich material. And in the absence of really great writers, who have a strong philosophical voice, the classics are re-emerging as a diverse source of exploration.

JULIANNE: It's a play about the end of a century, about time passing and things changing. The horrible, sad, tragic thing about *Vanya* is the way it ends: these people's lives were filled with possibility, there was so much possibility, then it changes and it's over, and we're at the end. They'll never be those people again; they'll never be in that situation again; they'll never see each other ever again. That's the horrible thing about the end of the play. For me, it's all about endings – about change and death.

ANDRÉ: Of course, one way to deny death is the filmic way. It's a way to preserve life for ever, but it's an illusion, a lie. In fact in all the Chekhov plays there's the stripping away of illusion as a necessary process towards really living your life – the illusion of marriage, the illusion of love. And film is a real medium for illusion. So in a way you're taking *Vanya* into the lion's mouth by making a film.

Epilogue

FRED: It's an amazing thing that *Vanya on 42nd Street* works as a theatre experience, but at the same time it's completely cinematic. You're watching a play, but at the same time it's not like any recording of a play that you've ever seen – it's genuinely a movie.

ANDRÉ: *Vanya on 42nd Street* is not just a movie about my *Vanya*. It's a movie about the theatre, and this odd band of people who still care and are still struggling with the problems of an active culture in a space which is disintegrating; where the walls, because God has literally rained on them, look like Pollocks, De Koonings, Dubuffet, and soon it's all going to be slicked over and become a Disney thing.

FRED: *Vanya* was conceived, financed and shot in the time that it usually takes to pitch a film and get an answer.

LOUIS: *Vanya* made me think that I should do it again – I should make more films. I wasn't even sure about that. I didn't have any fun on *Damage* for various reasons that I don't want to get into, but basically I was feeling very bad and I stopped shooting in the middle for ten days because I had to go to the hospital. So I was dragging my feet to the set. I had problems with the actors. I mean, when you're weak you shouldn't direct; it's a job where you cannot expose your weakness, or else you're finished. So I was thinking back then, maybe it's time for me to move on to something else – writing. The conclusion is that in order for me to have the sort of fun that I've actually had on most of my films in the past, it has to be done as lightly as possible and without a crew of seventy-five people – and fast. That's the way I like to do it!

FRED: At the end of the day you had an incredibly rehearsed, wonderfully probed and psychologically rich version of *Vanya*. And when Louis brought his eye to it, he introduced a similarly elegant, interesting visual spin on that. So you get the best of both worlds.

ANDRÉ: The film ends in the theatre. There's no epilogue. You don't really go back out. The questions and issues are left in the theatre, and that's where we want the audience to take over.

Louis Malle

Wallace Shawn (seated), Larry Pine and Brooke Smith

Louis Malle, George Gaynes and Julianne Moore; Lynn Cohen

Fred Berner and André Gregory (seated)

Walter Murch

10   Sound Design:
The Dancing Shadow
Walter Murch

It disappeared long ago, but in 1972 The Window was still there, peering blindly through a veil of dust, thirty-five feet above the floor of Samuel Goldwyn's old Stage 7. I never would have noticed had not Richard pointed it out to me as we were taking a short cut on our way back from lunch.

'That was when Sound was King!' he said, gesturing dramatically into the darkness.

It took me a while, but I finally saw what he was pointing at: it looked like the observation window of a dirigible from the 1930s, nosing its way into the stage.

What is now Warner/Hollywood Studios had been built originally for Mary Pickford when she founded United Artists with Chaplin and Fairbanks. And it was there, on Stage 7, that Samuel Goldwyn produced one of the earliest of his many musicals: *Whoopee* (1930), starring Eddie Cantor and choreographed by Busby Berkeley. In 1972, Stage 7 was temporarily functioning as an attic, stuffed with the mysterious lumbering shapes of disused equipment, but forty-two years earlier Goldwyn's director of sound Gordon Sawyer had sat at the controls behind The Window, hands gliding across three Bakelite knobs, piloting his Dirigible of Sound into a new world . . . a world in which Sound was King!

Down on the brilliantly lit floor, Eddie Cantor and the All-Singing, All-Dancing Goldwyn Girls had lived in terror of the distinguished Man Behind The Window. And not just the actors; musicians, cameramen, director, producer, even Goldwyn himself – no one could contradict it when Mr Sawyer, dissatisfied with the quality of sound he was getting, would lean into his microphone and pronounce dispassionately, but irrevocably, the word 'Cut!'

As far as Richard was concerned it had all been downhill from there.

His father, Clem Portman, had been head of the sound department at rival RKO studios, just down the street from Goldwyn, and had helped to create the sound for such films as *King Kong*, *Gunga Din* and *Citizen Kane*. Richard had followed his father's pioneering footsteps and become a mixer himself, one of the best in the industry. On that day in 1972 we were on our way to finish the soundtrack for *The Godfather*.

The situation was not quite as bleak as he liked to imagine, but the late 1960s and early 1970s in Hollywood *were* a relatively quiet period in the evolution of film sound. The stereo magnetic soundtracks of the roadshow films of ten years

Whoopee

earlier were no longer being produced (the last one was made in 1971), along with the diminishing fortunes of the film industry in general. Dolby and Digitalization were yet to come. The release format for the sound of *The Godfather* would be virtually identical to the format used on *Gone With the Wind*, made thirty-three years earlier.

So forty-five years after his exhilarating coronation, King Sound seemed to be living in considerably reduced circumstances. No longer did The Man Behind The Window survey the scene from on high. Instead he was usually stuck in some dark corner of the stage with his little cart. The very idea of him demanding a 'Cut!' was inconceivable. Not only did no one fear his opinion; they hardly consulted him and were frequently impatient when he *did* voice an opinion. Forty-five years had turned him from King to footman . . .

At least that was how it seemed to Richard.

There is something feminine about sound's liquidity and all-encompassing embrace that might make it more accurate to speak of Sound as a Queen rather than a King. But still, was Richard's nostalgia misplaced? What had befallen The Window? And were Sound's misfortunes really what they appeared to be, or was she a Queen for whom the crown was a burden, and who preferred to slip on a handmaiden's bonnet and scurry around incognito through the back passageways of the palace?

A brief venture into our own biological histories might provide a clue.

Four and a half months after we are conceived, we begin to hear. It is the first of our senses to be connected up and functioning. And for the next four and a half months we luxuriate in a continuous bath of sounds: the song of our mother's voice, the swash of her breathing, the piping of her intestines, the timpani of her heart. All during the second half of pregnancy Sound reigns as a solitary Queen of the Senses: the close and liquid world of the womb makes Sight and Smell impossible, Taste monochromatic, and Touch a dim and generalized hint of what is to come. Whatever we think of our universe at that point – and there is no doubt that we *are* thinking – comes to us primarily through the graces of Sound.

Birth, however, brings with it the sudden and simultaneous ignition of the other four senses, and an intense jostling for the throne which Sound had claimed as hers alone. The most notable pretender is the darting and insistent Sight, who blithely dubs himself King and ascends the throne as if it had been standing vacant, waiting for him.

Surprisingly, Sound pulls a veil of oblivion across her reign and withdraws into the shadows.

So we all begin as hearing beings – our four-and-a-half month baptism in a sea of sound must have a profound and everlasting effect upon us – but from the moment of birth onwards, hearing seems to recede into the background of our consciousness and function more as an accompaniment to what we see. Why this should be, rather than the reverse, is a mystery. Why does not the first of our senses to be activated retain a lifelong dominance of all the others? The reasons, no doubt, go far back into our evolutionary past, but I suspect it has something to do with the child's discovery of causality. Sound, which had been absolute and *causeless* in the womb, becomes something understood to happen *as the result of*. The enjoyment a child takes in banging things together is the enjoyment of this discovery: first there is no sound, *and then – bang! – there is*.

Anything in our experience that first seems to be absolute and self-sufficient, and then is suddenly revealed to be only part of a new, larger context, must suffer an apparent reduction in importance, and this is what may have happened with hearing relative to the other senses.

Something of this same situation marks the relationship between what we see and what we hear in the cinema. Film sound is rarely appreciated for itself alone, but functions largely as an enhancement of the visual. By means of some mysterious perceptual alchemy, whatever virtues the sound brings to the film are largely perceived and appreciated by the audience in *visual* terms – the better the sound, the better the image.

At any rate, in our deepest secret biological histories there lingers an equivalent of The Window, relic of an age when sound's rule was absolute. The analogy is not precise, but may be close enough to help determine whether Richard's nostalgia was justified, or whether sound gains more by giving up her crown than by keeping it. It is enough for the moment to note that this is an open question, and that the issue of causality has something to do with it.

Just as Sound had been the Queen of the senses through lack of competition, what had given film sound its brief rule over the image was the fact that no one had yet figured out how to cut it, or mix it. As a result, everything had to be recorded simultaneously – music, dialogue, sound effects – and once recorded, it couldn't be changed. The old Mel Brooks joke about panning the camera to the right and revealing the orchestra in the middle of the desert was not far from the truth. There was a cumbersome six-disc system, operated by wooden pegs, that gave some ability to superimpose and dissolve, but for the most part Clem Portman, Gordon Sawyer and Murray Spivack had the responsibility for recording Eddie Cantor's voice *and* the orchestra accompanying him *and* his tap dancing, all at the same time, in as good a balance as they could manage. There was no possibility of fixing it later in the mix, because this *was* the mix. And there was no possibility of cutting out the bad bits, because there *was* no way to cut what was being chiselled into the whirling acetate of the Vitaphone discs. It had to be right the first time, or you called 'Cut!' and began again.

Power on a film tends to gravitate towards those who control a bottle-neck of some kind, around which manoeuvring is difficult. Stars wield this kind of power, extras do not; the director of photography usually has more of it than the production designer. For the technical reasons just mentioned, film sound in its earliest versions was one of these bottle-necks, and so The Man Behind The Window held sway with a kingly power he has never had since. And he could have remained enthroned for ever if there had been no further developments beyond the original Vitaphone technique.

But there is a symbiotic relationship between the techniques that we use to represent the world and the vision that we attempt to represent by means of those techniques: a change in one inevitably results in a change in the other. The sudden availability of cheap pigments in metal tubes around 1870, for instance, allowed the Impressionists to paint quickly, out of doors and in fleeting light; and face to face with nature they realized that shadows come in many other colours than black, which is what the paintings of the previous 'indoor' generation had taught us to see.

Similarly, humble sounds had always been considered the inevitable (and therefore mostly ignored) accompaniment of the visuals, stuck like an insubstantial, submissive shadow to the object that 'caused' them. And like a shadow, they appeared to be completely explained by reference to the objects that gave them birth: a metallic clang was always 'cast' by the hammer, just as the village steeple cast its shape upon the ground.

The idea that sounds could be captured, preserved and played back later was not only considered impossible; it was hardly considered at all. In fact, sound was the prime example *of* the impermanent: a rose that wilted and died as soon as it bloomed.

Magically, sound recording loosened the bonds of causality and lifted the shadow away from the object, standing it on its own and giving it a miraculous and sometimes frightening autonomy. King Ndombe of the Congo consented to have his voice recorded in 1904, but immediately regretted it when the cylinder was played back and the 'shadow' danced on its own, and he heard his people cry in dismay: 'The King sits still, his lips are sealed, while the white man forces his soul to sing!'

The true fluidity of sound was not fully realized until the perfection of the sprocketed 35mm optical soundtrack (1928), which could be edited and put in precise sync with the image, opening up the bottle-neck of the inflexible Vitaphone process. This opening was further enlarged by the innovation of rerecording (1929–30) whereby several tracks of sound could be separately controlled and then superimposed and recombined. Vitaphone itself had faded from the scene by 1931, but as with any rapidly developing technology, the reality was more chaotic than it seems at a distance of almost seventy years – in 1929 there were more than thirty-five competing systems (from Bell-o-tone to Vocafilm) of which only one, RCA Photophone, has survived more or less intact. In addition, these developments took some time to work their way into the creative bloodstream. As late as 1936, films were being produced that required only seventeen additional sound effects *for the whole film* (instead of the thousands that we might have today). But the possibilities were richly indicated by the imaginative sound work in Disney's animated film *Steamboat Willie* (1928) and De Mille's live-action prison film *Dynamite* (1929). Certainly they were fully established by the time of Murray Spivack and Clem Portman's ground-breaking work on *King Kong* (1933). The optical soundtrack was the equivalent of pigment in a tube; and sound's fluidity, the Impressionists' coloured shadow.

In fact, animation – both of the *Steamboat Willie* and the *King Kong* variety – probably played a more dominant role in the evolution of creative sound than it has been credited for. With live action, the documentary illusion of 'what you hear is what you get' could be maintained – for a while, anyway. In the beginning, it was so astonishing to hear people speak and move and sing and shoot each other in sync that almost any sound was more than acceptable. But with animated characters this did not work, since they are shadowy creatures who make no sound at all unless their creators create the illusion of it through

Steamboat Willie

King Kong

sound out of context: sound from one reality transposed on to another. The most famous of these is the thin falsetto that Walt Disney himself gave to Mickey Mouse, but a close second is the roar that Murray Spivack provided King Kong.

At any rate, the construction of a film's soundtrack began to be a much more elaborate, time-consuming process, one that involved more and more people in various departments, and began to extend over the length of the entire film-making process. The good old days of *do it right the first time* and The Man Behind The Window were gone. To Richard's regret, the days of *fix it in the mix* had begun.

But there was another innovation that was to accelerate and deepen the process even further; one that has a personal dimension for me – magnetic sound.

In the early 1950s, when inexpensive tape-recorders were first becoming available to the public, I heard a rumour that the father of a neighbourhood friend had actually acquired one. Over the next few months I made a pest of myself at that household, showing up with a variety of excuses just to be allowed to play with that miraculous machine: hanging the microphone out the window and capturing the back-alley reverberations of Manhattan, scotch-taping it to the shaft of a swing-arm lamp and rapping the bell-shaped shade with pencils, inserting it into one end of a vacuum cleaner tube and shouting into the other, and so forth.

Later on, I managed to convince my parents of all the money our family would save on records if we bought our own tape-recorder and used it to 'pirate' music off the radio. I now doubt that they believed this made any economic sense, but they could hear the passion in my voice, and a Revere recorder became that year's family Christmas present.

I swiftly appropriated the machine into my room and started banging on lamps again and resplicing my recordings in different, more exotic combinations. I was in heaven, but since no one else I knew shared this vision of paradise, a secret doubt about myself began to worm its way into my pre-adolescent thoughts.

One evening, though, I returned home from school, turned on the radio in the middle of a programme, and couldn't believe my ears: sounds were being broadcast which I had only heard in the secrecy of my own little laboratory. As quickly as possible, I connected the recorder to the radio and sat there listening, rapt, as the reels turned and the sounds became increasingly strange and wonderful.

It turned out to be the *First Panorama of Musique Concrète*, a record by the French composers Pierre Schaeffer and Pierre Henry, and the incomplete tape of it became a sort of Bible of Sound for me. Or rather a Rosetta Stone, because the vibrations chiselled into its iron oxide were the mysteriously significant and powerful hieroglyphs of a language which I did not yet understand, but whose voice none the less spoke to me compellingly. And above all told me that I was not alone in my passion.

What had conquered me in 1953, what had conquered Schaeffer and Henry some years earlier, was not just the considerable power of magnetic tape to capture ordinary sounds and reorganize them – optical film had already had this ability for decades – but the fact that the tape-recorder combined these qualities with full audio fidelity, low surface noise, operational simplicity, the ability to record over the same piece of tape again and again, and above all, low price and availability. The earlier forms of sound recording had been expensive, available to only a few people outside of laboratory or studio situations, noisy and deficient in their frequency range, and cumbersome and awkward to operate. And once recorded, you could not erase and start again.

The tape-recorder extended the magic of sound recording by an order of magnitude, and reduced the size and cost to the extent that a ten-year-old boy like myself could think of it as a wonderful toy: the tape-recorder encourages play and experimentation, and that was – and remains – its pre-eminent virtue.

By the 1960s, magnetic sound had completely replaced the optical process (except in the final theatrical release-print) and the tiny transistor was busy replacing the bulky and unreliable vacuum tube. The dismantling of these two old bottle-necks and the resultant 'democratizing' of the craft of film sound opened up more creative possibilities, but proportionately reduced sound's kingly power.

Yet at the same time, the studios were suffering one of their periodic financial troughs, and research and development budgets had been cut back or eliminated.

It was just around this time of simultaneous expansion and stagnation that I was hired to create the sound effects for and mix *The Rain People*, a film written, directed and produced by Francis Coppola. He and I were recent film-school graduates and were anxious to continue making films professionally the way we had made them at school. Francis had shot *The Rain People* using all his own miniaturized equipment and saw no reason to stop now when it came to post-production. He felt that his previous film (*Finian's Rainbow*) had become bogged down in the bureaucratic/technical swamp at the studios, and he didn't want to repeat the experience.

He also felt that if he stayed in Los Angeles he wouldn't be able to produce the inexpensive, independent films he had in mind. As a result he, fellow film student George Lucas and I, and our families, moved up to San Francisco to start American Zoetrope. The first item on the agenda was the mix of *The Rain People* in the unfinished basement of an old warehouse on Folsom Street.

Ten years earlier this would have been unthinkable, but magnetic sound and the transistor had opened things up to such an extent that it seemed natural for Francis to go to Germany to buy – almost off the shelf – mixing and editing equipment from KEM in Hamburg and hire a twenty-five-year-old ex-film student to use them.

Technically, the equipment was state of the art, and it cost a fourth of what comparable equipment would have cost five years earlier, if you could have found it at all. It was high-speed multi-track equipment with 'rock and roll' erase/rerecord and video playback. This halving of price and doubling of quality is familiar to everyone now, after twenty-five years of microchips, but at the time it was astonishing. The frontier between professional and consumer electronics began to fade away.

In fact, it faded to the extent that it now became economically and technically possible for one person to achieve what several had before, and the other frontier between sound-effects creation and mixing also began to disappear.

From the beginning, the Zoetrope idea was to try to avoid the 'departmentalism' that was sometimes the by-product of sound's technical complexity. That tended to pit mixers, who were brought up mainly through the engineering department – direct descendants of The Man Behind The Window – against the people who came up with the sounds, who were mostly from editorial backgrounds. It would be as if there were two directors of photography on a film – one who lit the scene and one who photographed it – and neither could do much about countermanding the other.

We felt that, given the equipment that was becoming available in 1968, there was now no reason for the person who came up with the sounds and prepared the tracks not to be able to mix them. The director would then be able to talk to one person about the sound of the film the way he was able to talk to the director of photography about the look of the film. Responsibility for success or failure would lie squarely with that one person, and because communication problems would be reduced or eliminated, the chances of success would be increased.

So the films *The Rain People*, *THX-1138*, *The Conversation*, *American Graffiti*, and *Godfather II* were all done in this manner, which has subsequently been followed on most of Francis Coppola's and George Lucas's films in the intervening years, as well as those of Saul Zaentz (*One Flew Over the Cuckoo's Nest*, *Amadeus*) and Phil Kaufman (*The Right Stuff*, *The Unbearable Lightness of Being*). In general, it has become the standard approach to film sound in the San Francisco area.

Originally, we had no name for this approach, although my credit on some of the early films was 'sound montage', which had mostly to do with the fact that I was working non-union at the time and didn't want to raise any unnecessary flags.

On *Apocalypse Now*, however, in addition to picture editing and rerecording, my other task was to develop a design for the use of the film's quadrophonic sound in the three dimensions of the theatre: when should the sound (for dramatic reasons) focus down to a single point; when should it expand across the front of the screen to stereo; and when and how should it use the full dimensionality of the entire theatre? No dramatic film had been released in this format before, so we were moving into uncharted waters. I thought I was doing a job similar to that of a production designer, except I was decorating the walls of the theatre with sound, so I called what I did sound design.

The name stuck, and has since been used by many others, not without controversy. One friend (a mixer) said, only half-jokingly, 'If someone on one of my films gets the credit sound designer, I call myself the sound redesigner.' Frequently, the name is used by people who simply *design sounds* (that is, create special sound effects that could not be found in libraries) rather than those who *design and execute the overall soundtrack*.

Short of restricting sound design to its original meaning on *Apocalypse Now*, it is this latter definition that I would encourage: someone who plans, creates the sound effects and mixes the final soundtrack, and thereby takes responsibility for the sound of a film the way a director of photography takes responsibility for the image. In other words, it is the original Zoetrope method that we started with in 1968, which was the direct descendant of the way we had done things in film school.

Actually, it sounds very close to reinventing, with modern techniques, The Man Behind The Window. But the name 'sound designer' does uniquely describe a role that has been made possible only by the more recent advances in sound-processing technology. And if present trends continue, this blurring between creating, editing and mixing will only increase – how far, it is hard to say. The sound editor using a digital work-station is now able, routinely, to combine sounds in ways that were formerly practical only in the mixing theatre. And vice versa: mixers can quite easily create and edit sounds with the tools that are increasingly at their disposal.

All of the techniques that early on liberated the shadow of sound to dance on its own also progressively increased the number of people involved and thus diminished the kingly power of The Man Behind The Window. But they repaid what was taken away ten times, a hundred times, in creative power – in the increased fluidity and malleability of sound. Now the digital and automated grandchildren of those same techniques have the potential to restore to one person the control that could only formerly be exercised by several, but not at the expense of the all-important fluidity and malleability of the sound.

Beyond the controversy, though, of who is called what, or who does what job, the important thing is the final soundtrack and its internal balance and clarity, its relationship to the picture, and the creative possibility of reassociating sounds with images that are different – sometimes astonishingly different – from the objects or situations that gave birth to the sounds in the first place.

It might have been otherwise – the human mind could have demanded absolute obedience to 'the truth', but for a range of practical and aesthetic reasons we are lucky that it didn't. The reassociation of image and sound is the fundamental pillar upon which the creative use of sound rests, and without which it would collapse.

This reassociation occurs for many reasons: sometimes simply for convenience – walking on cornstarch, for instance, happens to record as a better 'footstep in snow' than snow itself; or necessity – the window that Gary Cooper broke in *High Noon* was not made of real glass, the boulder that chased Indiana Jones was not made of real stone; or for moral reasons – crushing a watermelon is ethically preferable to crushing a human head. In each case, our multi-million-year reflex of thinking of sound as a submissive causal shadow now works in the film-maker's favour, and the audience is disposed to accept, within certain limits, these new juxtapositions as the truth.

But beyond all practical considerations, this reassociation should be done, I believe, to *stretch* the relationship of sound to image wherever possible; to create a purposeful and fruitful tension between what is on the screen and what is kindled in the mind of the audience. The danger of present-day cinema is that it can suffocate its subjects by its very ability to represent them: it doesn't possess the built-in escape valves of ambiguity that painting, music, literature, radio drama and black-and-white silent film automatically have, simply by virtue of their sensory incompleteness – an incompleteness that engages the imagination of the viewer as compensation for what is only evoked by the artist. By comparison, film seems to be 'all there' (it isn't, but it seems to be), and thus the responsibility of film-makers is to find ways within that completeness to refrain from achieving it. To that end, the metaphoric use of sound is one of the most fruitful, flexible and inexpensive means: by choosing carefully what to eliminate, and then adding sounds that at first hearing seem to be somewhat at odds with the accompanying image, the film-maker can open up a perceptual vacuum into which the mind of the audience must inevitably rush. As a result, the film becomes more 'dimensional'. The more dimensional it is, the more impact it has on the viewer, the more it seems to speak to each viewer individually, and the more the sound can become a representation of the states of mind of the central characters, approaching the pre-verbal 'song' that Stephen Spender called the base ground of poetry: 'a rhythm, a dance, a fury, a passion which is not yet filled with words.'

Every successful reassociation is a kind of metaphor – what Aristotle called 'naming a thing with that which is not its name' – and every metaphor is seen momentarily as a mistake, but then suddenly as a deeper truth about the thing named and our relationship to it. The greater the stretch between the 'thing' and the 'name', the deeper the potential truth.

The tension produced by the metaphoric distance between sound and image serves somewhat the same purpose, creatively, as the perceptual tension produced by the physical distance between our two eyes – a three-inch gap which yields two similar but slightly different images: one produced by the left eye, and the other by the right. The brain is not content with this close duality and searches for something that resolves and unifies those differences. And it finds it in the concept of *depth*. By adding its own purely mental version of three-dimensionality to the two flat images, the brain causes them to click together into one image *with depth added*. In other words, the brain resolves the differences between the two images by imagining a dimensionality which is not actually present in either image, but is added as the result of the mind trying to resolve the differences between them. The greater the differences, the greater the depth. (Within certain limits: cross your eyes – exaggerating the differences – and you will deliver images to the brain that are beyond its power to resolve, and so it passes on to you, by default, a confusing double image. Close one eye – eliminate the differences – and the brain will give you an image with no confusion, but also with no third dimension.)

There really is, of course, a third dimension out there in the world: the depth we perceive is not a hallucination. But the *way* we perceive it – its particular flavour – is uniquely our own; unique not only to us as a species but also in its finer details unique to each of us individually, because everyone's eyes are a different distance apart. And in that sense it *is* a kind of hallucination, because the brain does not alert us to what is actually going on. It does not announce: 'And now I am going to add a helpful dimensionality to synthesize these two flat images. Don't be alarmed.' Instead, the dimensionality is fused into the image and made to seem as if it is coming from 'out there' rather than 'in here'.

In much the same way, the mental effort of fusing image and sound in a film produces a 'dimensionality' that the mind projects back on to the image as if it had come from the image in the first place. The result is that we *actually see* something on the screen that exists only in our mind, and in its finer details is unique to each member of the audience. It reminds me of John Huston's observation that 'the real projectors are the eyes and ears of the audience'. We do not see *and* hear a film; we hear/see it. This metaphoric 'distance' between the images of a film and the accompanying sounds is – and should be – continuously changing and flexible, and it takes a fraction of a second (or sometimes even seconds) for the brain to make the right connections. The image of a light being turned on, for instance, accompanied by a simple *click* – this basic association is fused almost instantly and produces a relatively flat mental image.

Still fairly flat, but a level up in dimensionality: the image of a door closing accompanied by the right 'slam' can indicate not only the material of the door, but also the emotional state of the person closing it. The sound for the door at the end of *The Godfather*, for instance, needed to give the audience not only the correct physical cues about the door, but it was even more important to get a firm, irrevocable closure that resonated with and underscored Michael's final line: 'Never ask me about my business, Kay.'

That door close was still related to a specific image and, as a result, it was probably 'fused' by the audience fairly quickly, although it required a few more milliseconds than the simple click of the light switch. Sounds, however, that do not relate to the visuals in a direct way function at an even higher level of dimensionality and take proportionately longer to resolve. The rumbling and piercing metallic scream just before Michael Corleone kills Solozzo in *The Godfather* is not linked directly to anything seen on screen and so the audience is made to wonder at least momentarily, if perhaps only subconsciously, 'What is this?' The screech is from an elevated train rounding a sharp corner, so it is presumably coming from somewhere in the neighbourhood (the scene takes place in the Bronx). But precisely *because* it is so detached from the image, the metallic scream works as a clue to the state of Michael's mind at that moment – the critical moment before he commits his first murder and his life turns an irrevocable corner. It is all the more effective because Michael's face appears so calm and the sound is played so abnormally loud. This broadening tension between what we see and what we hear is brought to an abrupt end with the pistol shot that kills Solozzo: the distance between what we see and what we hear is suddenly collapsed at the moment that Michael's destiny is fixed.

(This moment is mirrored and inverted at the end of *Godfather III*. Instead of a calm face attended by a scream, we have a screaming face in silence. When Michael realizes that his daughter Mary has been shot, he tries several times to scream, but no sound comes out. His face is contorted by grief and anguish, but the scream that you would expect to hear with such a face is missing. In fact, Al Pacino was actually screaming when the film was shot, but the sound was removed in the editing. Even though we are dealing here with an *absence* of sound, a fertile tension is created between what we see and what we would expect to hear, given that image. Finally, the scream bursts through, the tension is released, and the film – and the trilogy – is over.)

The elevated train in *The Godfather* was at least somewhere in the vicinity of the restaurant, even though it could not be seen. In the opening reel of *Apocalypse Now*, however, the jungle sounds that fill Willard's hotel room come from nowhere on screen or in the 'neighbourhood', and the only way to resolve the great disparity between what we are seeing and hearing is to imagine that these sounds are in Willard's mind; that his body is in a hotel room in Saigon, but his mind is off in the jungle, to where he dreams of returning. If the audience can be brought to a point where they will bridge such an extreme distance between picture and sound with their own imagination, they will be rewarded with a correspondingly greater dimensionality of experience.

The risk, of course, is that the conceptual thread that connects image and sound can be stretched too far, and the dimensionality will collapse. The moment of greatest dimension is always the moment of greatest tension.

I might add that in my own experience the most successful sounds seem not only to alter what the audience sees, but to go further and trigger a kind of *conceptual resonance* between image and sound: the sound makes us see the image differently, and then this new image makes us hear the sound differently, which in turn makes us see something else in the image, which makes us hear different things in the sound, and so on. This happens rarely enough (I am thinking of certain electronic sounds at the beginning of *The Conversation*) to be specially prized when it does occur – often by lucky accident, dependent as it is on choosing exactly the right sound at exactly the right metaphoric distance from the image. It has something to do with the time it takes for the audience to 'get' the metaphors: not instantaneously, but not too long either – like a good joke.

In all of this the question remains: Why do we generally perceive the product of the fusion of image and sound in terms of the image? Why does sound usually enhance the image and not the other way around? In other words, why does King Sight still sit on his throne and Queen Sound haunt the corridors of the palace?

In his recent book *Audio Vision*, Michael Chion describes an effect – what he calls the 'Acousmêtre' – which depends on delaying the fusion of sound and image to the extreme by supplying only the sound (most frequently a voice) and withholding the image of the sound's true source until nearly the very end of the film. Only then, when the audience has used its imagination to the fullest, as in a radio play, is the real identity of the source revealed, almost always with an accompanying loss of imagined power of the source of the sound: the Wizard in *The Wizard of Oz* is one of a number of examples cited, along with the Mother in *Psycho* and Hal in *2001* (and although he didn't mention it, Colonel Kurtz in *Apocalypse Now*). The 'Acousmêtre' is, for various reasons to do with our perceptions – the disembodied voice seems to come from everywhere and therefore seems to have no clearly defined limits to its power – a uniquely cinematic device. And yet . . .

And yet there is an echo here of our earliest experience of the world: the revelation at birth that the song which sang to us from the very dawn of our consciousness in the womb – a song which seemed to come from everywhere and to be part of us before we had any conception of what 'us' meant – is the voice of another and that now she is separate from us and we from her. We regret the loss of former unity – some say that our lives are a ceaseless quest to retrieve it – and yet we delight in seeing the face of our mother: the one is the price to be paid for the other.

This earliest, most powerful fusion of sound and image sets the tone for all that is to come.

11   Playing Cowboys and Indians
Eddie Fowlie in conversation
with John Boorman

Introduction

I knew Eddie Fowlie, the legendary prop master, only by reputation. David Lean loved him, always kept him by his side.

When I was preparing *Beyond Rangoon*, the magnitude of the task of reproducing Burma in Malaysia became clear. Tony Pratt (production designer) said to me, 'Let's try to get Eddie.' And Eddie came, a long mane of white hair flowing behind him, fierce eyes glaring defiantly at a world that might dare resist his intentions. He hobbled a bit, because they had removed his foot recently and reattached it, as a ring of stitch marks on his ankle testified. But he was always barrelling along at a fast walk with his big belly thrust out before him like a battering ram.

We were on the Equator: jungle, fast-flowing rivers. There were villages, bridges and cities to build and dress. Already into his seventies, surviving on a diet of steak and beer, Eddie left us all gasping in his wake.

He insisted that he take on set dressing, as well as props, and was peeved that I wouldn't given him special effects also.

At the end of the day, over a beer, Eddie's stories would come rolling out. One day I turned on a tape-recorder. Here's a sample of what he told that day.

JOHN BOORMAN: *You used to work with David Lean. You were with him all the time, weren't you?*
EDDIE FOWLIE: Yeah, well, we were friends, John. We were like brothers.
JB: *He always talked about you.*
EF: As soon as David started a new idea, he'd ask me to do a recce to find a location where the picture could be shot. I'd get a map and look at the contours of the land, look at the prevailing winds. On the prevailing-wind side there are more trees than on the leeward side. For *Ryan's Daughter*, because the coast was so important, I studied the nautical charts. I did this in London, having already gone through Spain. First thing, when David sent me out from Rome – where he was writing with Robert Bolt – the first place I looked was the north of Spain, because you can usually keep to schedule in Spain, almost always keep to schedule. The weather's reliable. The technicians will work day and

night, it doesn't matter to them. That's the attitude of the Spaniard. But I found it too green. The North Galician coast was too green. While Ireland isn't as green as people say.

JB: *It's grey and brown, isn't it?*

EF: That's right, and I think the story required that greyness. So coming through London, I was doing this recce with the Rolls Royce . . .

JB: *The one David gave you?*

EF: Yeah, the one David gave me. I stopped at a hotel in Kensington, bought some maps and spread them out on the bed. After a little study, I put my finger on a spot: I bet it's there. And that was Dingle. We can do anything in film, but sometimes you need God's help. I always look first for what God needs to provide, and on this particular occasion it had to be a great long beach going into the distance, with a cliff that rose out of the sand, with a nice top on it where they picnicked and where the idiot boy could go into a cave down below. Now, that's not a set you can build, so I had to find that and then build the rest around it, but I couldn't find what I saw on the map.

I went all up and down the west coast of Ireland looking for it. I kept returning to Dingle. It's got to be here somewhere. Finally, I went across a private farm at one end and there it was! That beach at Tralee – Banner Beach – one of the most beautiful beaches you'll see anywhere. And from there on, I found all the other locations around it.

I phoned David and I said, 'You've gotta come. I've got everything.' He said, 'I can't come now, I'm writing.' I said, 'David, if you don't come now, we can't be ready, because the only thing I can't find is a decent-looking village. We've got to build the village, they all look wrong, but I've got a nice place to put one.' 'No, no, no. I can't come.' 'Well,' I said, 'David, you know in the Galway Great Southern Hotel? I've got you a lovely room and there's an open log fire in it.' 'Oh well, I'll come.'

I used to do all these recces on Kodachrome, John – none of these fancy pans, all stuck together. I just used to pick out what I thought was an attractive set-up. Mostly so the director didn't waste his bloody time looking at things he didn't need. Then I projected these pictures in the hotel bedroom on quite a big wall. David got a nice impression and in true colour. I knew the minute I put that one up – the one of Banner Beach – that was the winner. I'd saved that for a special position on the carousel. This location, you approach it up a little slope and all of a sudden you're on the top of the slope and it takes your breath away. So Dingle it was.

Then there were the Blasket Islands, where the bus comes in and the soldier gets out. David said, 'What a stage entrance for any actor.' That's how he used to talk. He always talked about the entrance or the exit from the scene.

JB: *He was very good at entrances, wasn't he? They were indelible. The character would be introduced in such a way that they were cut right into memory and you knew exactly who they were.*

EF: But, you know, he was a very ordinary man, in his own way. He was from Croydon – just a suburban boy like the rest of us – but he was a dreamer. Well, we're all dreamers, I suppose, but he had talent . . .

JB: *And an intensity . . .*

EF: A total perfectionist. *Total perfectionist*. Nothing was any good unless it was perfect.

JB: *There was one occasion when Kurosawa came to London to launch a film – I think it was Ran – so they organized a dinner for him and they invited a number of British directors. David was there, sitting opposite Kurosawa. The rumour about Kurosawa is that he does one set-up a day. Before he shoots, he gets it all ready and rehearses and rehearses, and then before he shoots they meditate for ten minues. And so, we're sitting there at dinner and I lean across to Kurosawa and say to his interpreter – because Kurosawa doesn't speak any English – 'How many set-ups a day does Kurosawa-san do when he's shooting a film?' So we wait while a long exchange occurs in Japanese and finally his translator said, 'How many set-ups a day does Mr Lean do?' So David said, 'He asked you first.'*

EF: That's him. He was quick off the mark.

JB: *So there's another big conference in Japanese, then the translator presented Kurosawa's Zen reply: 'As many as necessary.'*

EF: Actually, you bring something to mind when you say that, because very often we wouldn't shoot anything until near the middle of the day. Then during the afternoon we'd do the day's work, because he'd get the whole thing designed and he knew exactly what he wanted to shoot. Sometimes he wouldn't come to work until ten o'clock in the morning, and then we'd sit in the caravan and drink coffee and talk about it for a while.

JB: *What a luxury.*

EF: But then we'd go out and it would all be in the script – he knew exactly what he was going to do. The technicians would be putting things in all the right places and by the end of the day we'd have the day's work done.

JB: *How many days did you shoot Zhivago?*

EF: It was only about two years. I remember on *Lawrence of Arabia* we had a party down in Almereia for the anniversary of one year of shooting and we had yet to get to Morocco!

JB: *Did you do A Passage to India?*

EF: Yeah, I did.

JB: *That was done rather quickly; it was quite a short schedule by his standards.*

EF: Yeah, it was really. I'll tell you why. I went out and did the reconnaissance for many months. I drove all over India. North, south, east and west. It was wonderful. Then, again, I thought, 'What do I need God's help for?' On this one, it was the rock monolith which the elephant goes up, and the caves. Now you gotta find that. Once you've found that, everything's done. One day I was by a banyan tree. It was the biggest banyan tree I'd ever seen. Huge. It was like a village with everything inside, roads! And then, way in the distance, I saw this thing. I gotta get there! It was a long way off.

Well I got there, finally, and it was a monolith of rock. One enormous mountain made of one solid rock. Nothing else there. Red granite. Phenomenal thing to look at. I thought, 'That's it. I'm in. I'll find the rest of it.' That was near Bangalore. The rock was nearly forty-five minutes out of Bangalore – which was longer than I normally like. I set myself up in a hotel, run by an old English Colonel, Indian Army. Finally, we put the construction sheds in there, everything into that hotel. Everything was there. The whole fucking film studio. Ten minutes down the road I found an old maharaja's palace, with huge grounds with everything in it: streams, jungle, everything we needed. We shot the film there – ten minutes down the road! That's the reason why we were able to shoot so quickly. You could go back to the hotel for lunch!

JB: *You did that in Sri Lanka with* The Bridge on the River Kwai. *You shot that pretty quickly. Was it true that you used Sri Lankan extras for British soldiers?*

EF: Yeah, we got beggars and derelicts from Colombo. People without arms and legs, things like that, and we painted them white.

JB: *Painted their skin white?*

EF: We made booths for the make-up people to spray 'em as they came in. They were mostly Sri Lankans. There weren't too many Europeans in that prisoner-of-war camp. Percy Herbert and a few up the front.

JB: *There was a fifteen-year gap between* Ryan's Daughter *and* A Passage to India.

EF: Yeah, he wouldn't take criticism, David. He wouldn't take criticism.

JB: *Are you talking about that dinner with the New York critics, where he was vilified?*

EF: That's why he backed off. He just sulked. I tried for years to get him back.

JB: *He spent a good few of those years preparing* The Bounty. *Tony Pratt worked out in Bora Bora on that.*

EF: I asked Tony to come out.

JB: *Tony told me he went out there and sketched the whole film, every shot, which was really for the financiers. He said that David never came to look at the sketches. Tony showed me the script at the time. I thought it was magnificent. It would've been David's finest film.*

EF: He wanted to do two films. He always said to me, 'I'm gonna have two and I'm gonna have them running at the same time in the West End, so that you can come out of one theatre and then, the next night, you can see the continuation.' It was an innovation and it would have been marvellous.

JB: *The second part was the trial, wasn't it?*

EF: That's right. *The Lawbreakers*, he called it.

JB: *It was about what happened to Bligh when he got back.*

EF: Bligh was a good man. Bligh was one of the greatest seamen, ever.

JB: *Wouldn't you say that Bligh and Christian represented the two sides of David? One side was the disciplinarian, the perfectionist, which was Bligh. The other was the romantic dreamer, Christian.*

EF: I think you've hit the nail right on the head there. It was David, totally. You know, I read a book about Captain Bligh and I thought that this was a very new idea, because the Americans who wrote *Mutiny on the Bounty* got it all wrong. Some Americans wrote it.

JB: *Charles Nordhoff and James Norman Hall, Conrad Hall's father.*

EF: Bligh was Captain Cook's navigator. If you look at the charts of Dublin Bay when you go home, you'll see 'Lieutenant Bligh' on them. He charted all the home waters. He was one of the greatest navigators that ever lived and they did him a great injustice. And so, I scribbled off an idea, just about eight or ten pages of a draft idea. David was just going to leave the Berkeley Hotel and go to Los Angeles, so I said, 'David, look, have a read of that when you're on the *Queen Elizabeth* and chuck it over the side if it's no good. I went off to work on *The Greek Tycoon* and one night, in the middle of a shoot out at sea, David Rattery came out to me and said, 'You've got to go ashore, there's a call from Warner Bros.' They said, 'Where are you? We've been looking for you. David Lean wants you here.' I called him and he said, 'What are you doing there? I'm going to do your thing. Get over here, right away.' We never did it, but I had four bloody marvellous years. All over the Pacific I went. I know all the islands now. They're part of my life, part of my soul, the Pacific Islands.

JB: *Part of me, too. I made a picture out there. They're magnificent, aren't they?*

EF: Yeah, they're *the* part of my life.

JB: *So, with* The Bounty, *you spent four years, you went to the islands, to Bora Bora, but what happened? Why didn't he get it made?*

EF: Warner Bros were going to do the two pictures, and David asked me to go up and see Lee Katz, which I did in Los Angeles, and explain the situation to him, because at that time – now this is not generally known, but John Box, who was out there with us, wanted to go home for Christmas. David said, 'Are you with me on this picture, or not?' and John said, 'Well, I've got to go ask my wife.' David said, 'That's not good enough – you're with me, or with your wife.' 'Well, if that's the case, then I'm going back to my wife.'

So Lee Katz (he's a completion guarantor) and his girlfriend (who owns Citibank or something) came down and we entertained them on a beautiful yacht in Suba, and then went to the island of Fiji, and we're having a wonderful time. Then round the dinner table, Lee said, 'What do you think it's going to cost, David?' 'Well, so and so,' and Helen, Lee Katz's girlfriend, says, 'Oh no, it'll cost much more.' So David turned to her and said, 'You know nothing about making movies. You stay out of it.' The next morning

Lee said to him, 'You'll have to apologize to Helen, because you've upset her. Otherwise, I won't be able to continue with you.' So David said, 'If I say something, I don't apologize'. And that was the end of it.

JB: *The end?*

EF: As simple as that.

JB: *Really.*

EF: He pulled out. Then, David's agent, Phil Kellog, who was called the producer, was on an aeroplane with Dino de Laurentiis and talked to him about picking it up, which Dino did. Then, one day at the Beachcomber Hotel in Tahiti with Dino and his daughter Rafaella, Dino was going to call himself the 'producer'. David said, 'You're not the producer, Phil Kellog is my producer. You're the presenter. You just supply me with the money. Anyway, the money is all tainted money. You're a gangster and I'm an English gentleman, and I don't really want to work with gangsters.' And that was the end of that one, and they were both crying, Dino and Rafaella. David shot himself in the foot on two or three occasions. He desperately wanted to do it. He said, 'This would have been my best film.'

JB: *I'm sure it would have been. I vividly remember reading the opening and he somehow made you feel that this voyage was the equivalent of going into outer space.*

EF: That's it. That's exactly what it was meant to do. He leaned over backwards to make it sound like that. One of the times we were sitting together down in Spain, where I built my house, we were just sitting in one of the Rolls Royces, listening to the radio, to the first Apollo going up, and we were both almost in tears about it. He said 'Why is this so moving?' I said, 'It's human achievement, David. All humans associate themselves with other people's achievement.' And it stuck with him. One of the things he talked about once, he wanted to make a film to show how humans evolved, how they discovered fire and the wheel. What a dreamer.

JB: *The memorable thing he said to me at the end, when he was dying, was: 'I hope I'll be well enough to make this picture. I feel I'm just getting the hang of it.'*

EF: He was talking about *Nostromo*. It wasn't an easy thing to do. I didn't want him to do it.

JB: *When he was getting ready to make it, he sent me the script and asked me if I would be the stand-by for insurance purposes. I read it and I couldn't do it. I would love to have done it, for him, but I thought that if he died after the first day and I had to make this thing, I wouldn't know how to do it.*

EF: I hate to tell you this – and I've never told anyone – but the first time it was written Spielberg read it and went, 'Oh, oh oh . . . ' David wouldn't stand for it.

JB: *Spielberg was involved?*

EF: Oh yeah, Spielberg was gonna go all the way with it. I never wanted him to do it, that bloody thing, I wanted him to do *Victory*, which I think is a better melodrama. Of course, all Conrad's characters are people with some deep pain inside them, which isn't too easy to portray, is it?

JB: *All the interesting stuff is going on inside heads.*

EF: *Nostromo* should be a long television series – it was written as a serial. Conrad wrote it for a magazine over a long period of time, which is why, when you read the book, you've gotta keep referring back to find the continuity. But the characters are marvellous.

JB: *I remember going to David's house while he was working on the script of* Nostromo, *on his desk was his notepad and there was his tiny writing right to the end of the page, no margin. I said, 'What are you doing?' He said, 'Oh, I'm just going through the book and writing out scenes that I think are cinematic.'*

EF: That's right. Tiny, tiny writing right to the edge. And when he was typing, if he found that a word edged a bit into the margin, he'd cancel the whole fucking page and start again. If you'd got an envelope and were going to write an address on it, the first thing he'd want you to draw would be feint pencil lines so that you'd write the address correctly and then rub the pencil lines out. Everything, every fucking thing you ever did, had to be exactly perfect.

JB: *But you said a surprising thing to me once about David Lean. You said he wasn't a technician.*

EF: He wasn't a technician at all. He didn't understand the techniques of it like you do. No way. He needed his cameraman and people like that to guide him all the time. He knew nothing about the techniques. If you talked to him about mattes or anything like that, he wouldn't know what you were talking about. All he wanted to know was whether it would look beautiful on the screen and whether his dreams would come true. That was all.

JB: *He knew about editing, though?*

EF: Oh, editing. Christ, oh yes. That's why he wrote the scripts like that.

JB: *So they were already edited.*

EF: Yes, almost within a few frames.

JB: *He said to me once, 'I was lucky because I started editing during the silent period and when sound came in, you then had to put the soundtrack on one side and the picture on the other on the Moviola, and it was too cumbersome. I used to memorize the dialogue and then I would cut just with the picture.' So he was still free to work fast and catch the rhythm of editing.*

EF: I'm absolutely certain that's what he did, because once he had written the script he'd never refer to it again. He knew it off, absolutely off by heart, every word, every blink of an eyelid. All he ever required from everyone was total perfection. Total. I'd think he was wrong sometimes, but it always turned out there was a good reason. He always used to invite me to look through the camera. Always. Just before we'd start shooting, he'd say to Ernie Day, 'Now get down and let Eddie have the camera for a while.' And we'd do the final set dressing.

On *Doctor Zhivago*, the girl is a librarian and she's living in this apartment. He said, 'Have a look, what do you see?' 'I think it looks bloody good, David. I can't see anything we can improve on.' 'Too many daisies.' Too many daisies! Because I got a few daisies on the grassy background. Of course, when you think about it, there was a reason: we have a change of season and the next season is in snow. So, too many daisies – too much white. Spoils the transition. There was always a reason, but subtle.

JB: *Alec Guinness said to me that David was only interested in the externals of acting. He wasn't interested in the internal workings of an actor's process.*

EF: 'Just smile, or twitch your eye' – it was always like that. 'Your lip should tremble.' He would tell 'em to do that.

JB: *Rather than saying, 'Here you are experiencing fear.'*

EF: David always said to me, 'He's resisting me, he's not doing it . . . he thinks he knows . . .' things like that. He wanted only the way he felt it should be. Then from you, you were a different character and David would feel that character too and you would have to do it his way. That's what Alec means.

It didn't matter how you interpreted the part, it had to be the way David interpreted the part within his soul, right inside him. He'd dreamed that for two years and knew whether the man should blink twice, three times, or once. I remember one time with James Donald. Alec is in the oven in *The Bridge on the River Kwai*, and James Donald is supposed to be begging him: 'Please do as they say, you're gonna die in there, please come out.' David said, 'He resisted me, I'm going to crucify him.' He kept him kneeling there in the hot sun. Alec wasn't there. We were with the camera, pretending to be Alec. And we went on and on and on. Take after take. I don't think there was any film in the camera. But he just kept on, pretending to be shooting him, until finally James Donald *was* begging, really begging. James said to me once, 'Could I have something to kneel on?' because it was all hard stones and everything, and David said, 'No, you can't.' And the man was begging and crying at the end: 'Please, get me out of the sun!' David could be cruel to actors. David didn't like actors. As far as David was concerned, they were just a prop. They had to interpret *exactly* everything he said.

He was very smart in as much as we'd discuss carefully how we were gonna play the scene – the cameraman, Freddie Young, and so on – everything down to what lens is on the camera, was all discussed. Then he'd get the actors, for instance Johnny Mills, and he'd say, 'What do you think, if we played it like that? . . . ' and pretend that they were going to be involved so that they began to get a little enthusiasm about it.

It was a very dirty game, really, because he knew very well what he was going to do with them. A lot of them tumbled to it, I think.

JB: *Well, what about* Zhivago? *You did all that snow, didn't you?*

EF: All of it.

JB: *How did you make the snow?*

EF: Well, first, I've gotta tell you I did the special effects on the picture as well as the props. It was a Metro-Goldwyn-Mayer picture and they said, 'We can't give you two credits because of the syndicates . . .

JB: *The unions.*

EF: . . . in America.' I said, 'I don't give a shit about the credit, just put the money in the bank.' They said, 'We want you to have a special-effects credit because we think you'll get an Oscar nomination.' Well, of course, when special effects are real, they should look as if they're not special effects, shouldn't they? You've failed otherwise. So, all of that, the whole thing, is a special effect. Even when the horses come galloping across the lake and the machine-gun goes 'rrrr', it's all on a hot summer's day.

JB: *In Spain.*

EF: Yeah, in Spain. We were going to shoot it in a place called Soria, where it was supposed to snow. Old Johnny Box had got it all picked out for the snow. He was gonna build the ice house there, but it didn't snow.

There was a terrible panic about it, naturally. 'So, what'll we do?' 'Don't worry, John,' I said. I got on to a factory in Barcelona and got down two big trailer-loads of plastic sheeting and I stretched it all over as far as you could see into the distance, white plastic sheeting, and then threw marble dust all over it. But the palace itself, the ice palace, David often used to say to me, 'How did you do that bloody palace? The inside of the palace? Because everyone always asks me.' I never did tell him. What I did was very simple: old-fashioned Cellophane – which you don't see much of nowadays, but it's wonderful stuff – when you crush it and then flatten it out again, it's got a million facets on it. They'll stay there for ever, millions of facets. I just took it in bunches, rolls and rolls of it all over the place, and stapled it on to the walls. Then I got paraffin wax in a big cauldron, boiling on a stage with the door shut, in this hand I had a pressurized Hudson spray, and I threw cups of the paraffin up on to the walls and hit it with cold water. It not only shaped it immediately into icicles, but it secreted little beads of water within the paraffin.

JB: *This on top of the Cellophane?*

EF: Yeah, then after that I blew salicylic acid all over it, which doesn't hurt. It's what aspirins are made of, but it's got a lovely . . . not a glitter which is too glittery, it just glitters a little bit. And on the floor was soap flakes, just regular, ordinary Lux – you remember the old-fashioned Lux soap flakes – all over the floor, so that when people walked on it, it crunched. It was difficult for the actors to walk on and had just the right atmosphere.

JB: *How did you discover that? Did you just work it out for yourself?*

EF: You just figure it out as you go along.

JB: *What did you use for falling snow?*

Doctor Zhivago: the ice house

EF: In those days, for falling snow there was only polystyrene. That's all there was. But I didn't use it like people do now. I'd get it in billets, big billets, and put it through the planing machine and plane it. It floats differently, doesn't stick to people like beads. It falls off. I actually used a bit of paraffin wax on Omar's clothes and face (so that it stuck), but if you put it through the planing machine, an ordinary wood-working planing machine, it looks nicer. All over the roof-tops of the Moscow street I had, I suppose, about ten or twelve fans up there, with men operating them, and I blew the whistle once and they fed the fans with snow, and it all fell from a great height down below, and I blew the whistle twice and it stopped. The street became quite thick with it, when those Cossacks came galloping down the street. It worked very effectively on that red train. Remember that red train? It dashes through and has a whole cock's tail of snow flying behind it. These things aren't real. But nobody knows and it looks real, doesn't it?

JB: *What did you do with the horses slipping on the ice?*

EF: That was another thing about David: he hated stuntmen. He said he could always see what they were doing. 'I can see you pulling that horse down.' For this particular scene, I levelled a patch of ground with road graders, a huge, huge patch, until it was a flat surface, and spread it all with white atlas cement. White atlas cement is the stuff you rub in between the tiles after you're done doing the bathroom.

JB: *Grouting.*

EF: That's right. All over, except in certain places I put down sheet iron. Then on top of that I poured all the soap I had left over, boiled it all and poured it all over everything. Then I put marble dust on top of that, so you couldn't see where one thing started and one thing finished. Of course, when the horses hit that at full gallop, their legs just went up and they were on their backs. The stuntmen didn't even know it was going to happen. That's why it looked so good. Richard Lester said to me when we were doing *The Three Musketeers*, 'I want one of those lakes, like you made for David Lean.' I don't know if you ever saw the picture, but there was that sword fight on ice with Frank Finlay and people, but I used it a little bit different there, because they weren't galloping at speed. I put down the same base and then I went to the floor-polish factory – good old-fashioned sloppy stuff like we used to use in the Army, in big tins. There's no way they were going to stand up on it, you couldn't!

JB: *What did you think of working with Lester?*

EF: I'm very fond of Richard Lester. I think he's got a brilliant brain, brilliant. His great god is Buster Keaton.

JB: *That's what he did, didn't he? In a sense, he made talking silent comedies.*

EF: That's right. He used to write for the Goons.

JB: *I love your stories about* Land of the Pharaohs.

Doctor Zhivago: Cossacks gallop down the snow-covered streets

Doctor Zhivago: horsemen galloping on the snow-covered lake

EF: Howard Hawks, I liked him very much, he was a gentleman. A tall, stringy gentleman.

JB: *He knew his stuff, didn't he?*

EF: Yeah, a very cool customer. A very cool customer indeed. You know, we had 10,000 extras in that picture, a 10,000 crowd. We made them look like 20,000. We'd do an automatic pan in another place, having moved the 10,000 people and the piece of foreground. I think he was probably a good technician.

JB: *What was he like with actors? He got good performances from them.*

EF: I think he was probably more of a mechanic; of course, that film didn't require a lot of acting, really. The film hadn't started, but I'd been on it a long time. When I started on it, it was just Hawks and William Faulkner. Warner Bros put me on it. I'd worked for Warner Bros for many years. I didn't meet David Lean until *The Bridge on the River Kwai*. I had a good reputation with Warner Bros and Gerry Blackner (he was the head of Warner Bros for Europe) sent for me to come out to Rome. He said, 'Go down the corridor and you'll see a door with "Howard Hawks" on it. Go in, he's expecting you.' Now, the script wasn't even written. William Faulkner was writing it, but Hawks said, 'We're going to make this big Cinemascope picture about building the pyramids.' I immediately got cracking and I ordered twenty chariots to be built. When the script came out, there weren't any chariots in it, but I sold them to Robert Rossen, who was doing *Alexander the Great*. He bought the bloody things and I made a profit.

Then, when we were in Eygpt, one day in the bar of the Mina Hotel, Hawks said to me, 'This Frenchman's never gonna get this picture done.' It was Alexander Trauner. He was the production designer. 'Will you build me a set?' I said, 'Yeah, tell me what you want and I'll do it.' Just he and Faulkner were there. Faulkner was nearly always pissed, actually. Hawks took a bottle of beer and he poured it all over the counter and he said, 'That's the River Nile,' and he put the bottle down, 'and that's the sun.' He put the glass over there and said, 'There's the camera and that's about three miles long. And all down the side I want about 10,000 people pulling rocks down to the cranes. Can you do that?' I said, 'Yeah, I'll do that.'

I had a good operation going. I had quite a big department. I wouldn't go into the studio, you see. I refused to go into the studio because it was controlled by Trauner. So I set up my own in the stables of the Mina Hotel, like an independent company. Hawks said, 'How long's that gonna take?' I said, 'It'll take about ten days,' which was a bit of a wild guess. However, that night I moved everything, the whole lot, all the trucks. There's an interesting side to this because I rented a coach on the train to take all my men down south. *Valley of the Kings* was happening there about the same time and they'd got a load of slave girls on the same train. I have vivid memories of that. Anyway, to get this built, I went to the Aswan Dam immediately and got some

Land of the Pharaohs: the cranes

Land of the Pharaohs: the litter

barges loaded up with all the cement, all the wood and everything. It was very simple, really, because all you had to do was stand up the bloody palm tree trunks, shoot a fire hose at the bottom and they just went down in the ground like that. You put a top on them and you've got a crane! So, really, it wasn't all that difficult and in ten days it was done.

In the interim a man came out from Burbank called Chuck Hanson. Never left the studio in his life. I used to walk up and down that river bank in a white suit and a hat, to look the part, with a whip. Knowing full well those bastards hated me. They worked and we built it, and Hanson came and said, 'The only way I found out where you were (I'd had to find the location, because there's buildings all along the river Nile) was because I saw a launch back in Aswan loading up with beer.' I said, 'That's my beer.' He said, 'We don't drink beer on American outfits when we're working.' I said 'I don't give a fuck what you Yanks do. English drink beer, especially me.' So when Hawks came down he was absolutely over the moon about the whole fucking thing, and I told him the story and he said, 'Eddie, you shall have your beer. What would you like?' Without thinking about it – I didn't think anything would come of it – I just said, 'I'll have forty bottles of Stella every day.' Now forty bottles of Stella beer – they're in pint bottles – that's forty pints a day for the whole picture.

JB: *He set it up?*

EF: Yeah, I had to put on another prop truck to carry it! Well, while I was in Aswan, Trauner sent down a chap, Noël Howard, and he took photographs of all the things I'd done. When I got back to Cairo they'd got drawings done of all my sets, date stamped and in the plan chests. And worse was that, I wouldn't do anything he wanted. I did all my own things. I used to go to the museum – Tutankhamun, sarcophagi and handle all these things. It was wonderful. They didn't seem to give a shit about it and I copied them all, just copied those things: gold leaf and everything; the sarcophagus with Jack Hawkins's face on it. I also made thousands and thousands of weapons, spears and things, and in the scene where they're coming back from battle, I'd got all the tips in gold, which is the material they used. Where the things were tipped on top, I left little streamers to catch the sun. Trauner used to say to me, 'I want these dirtied down, dirtied down,' and I used to say, 'Sod off!' So when I got back from this episode down in Aswan, he'd taken all my stuff out of my prop room, taken it into the bloody film studio, painted it all and taken all the gold bits off. I went with my trucks, took it all and put it back my way.

JB: *What did Hawks say about all this?*

EF: What Hawks finally did say, much later on when we were in the rushes theatre, was 'Thank God you made the tips of those spears glint, and those little bits glisten, otherwise we'd have had a forest of sticks coming over the sand.' It looked wonderful, but he'd already put Trauner in his place. I shouldn't say this about Alex because he was a brilliant designer, but he wasn't *practical* in many ways. But designers are like that: they see it on a drawing, or they see the scale, but they don't see it from the camera lens; they don't see the subtleties the camera's going to find.

One day Trauner said to me, 'Will you build me a litter?' He never came near me, normally. They had an all-French art department, I was the only Englishman on it and not very well liked. 'Will you build me a litter?' Because they couldn't do it. It was a huge drawing, beautifully done, full colour and it was for a litter. The concept was good: fifty-two men were to carry it, and on top of that stood twelve more men with another litter, and on top of that litter sat the golden throne with Jack Hawkins on it, and behind him stood these people with ostrich-feather fans – Metro-Goldwyn-Mayer stuff, which I thought was phoney. I said, 'Yeah, I'll build that for you.'

At my gate I used to keep a man with a gun, a Lee Enfield 303, to keep Trauner out. Well, to keep everyone out, really. I looked at this drawing. I got a sample of material, put it under stress and strain, and found it was impractical, so I threw the drawing away and built my own. I copied stuff out of the museum, I got in woodcarvers, who carved wonderful lotus flowers along the edge, and did it all in gold leaf and blue enamel. It was really lovely and one day Trauner said to me, 'Could I come see the litter?' I said, 'Yeah, you can come and see the litter,' and we walked all round it. He always had a little dachshund dog on a string. He said, 'Ze litter, it's beautiful, no?' I said, 'Yeah, it's lovely.' Then he said, 'Is it like ze drawing?' I said, 'No, nothing like the drawing.' He said, 'Why is it not like ze drawing?' I said, 'Drawing wasn't any good.' 'Where is ze drawing?' I said, 'Over there in the wood shavings.'

JB: *What about the pyramids? What did you do about the pyramids?*

EF: Well, we cleared one side and repaired it to make it look as if it was new.

JB: *How did you do that?*

EF: With plaster. It was full of debris. Sand and stones and everything was on them. Not easy to walk up them, really. So we repaired it and cleaned it up. Of course, the pyramid was finished with what they call crushed strawberry granite – you know, the red granite you sometimes see on the floors in banks. It was smooth and polished, originally, to shine in the sunshine. That granite came from Aswan, which is where we went to do the crane thing. The granite quarries of Aswan faced the pyramids. You never stop learning, do you John? The vast knowledge you get in this business. I mean, I left school at thirteen and I've gained all this knowledge.

JB: *Joan Collins was in* Land of the Pharaohs, *wasn't she?*

EF: I knew Joan before. I met her first on a little picture directed by Noël Langley, who was a writer – a funny little picture with George Cole, who was a young man with black curly hair then, and Bunny Hare, Kenneth More and Joan Collins. They'd been shipwrecked on an island and it was called *Our Girl Friday*. We filmed it in Majorca before it became a tourist place. We built a beach with coral rocks, we planted palm trees and everything. Three times we planted palm trees and dug up a skeleton each time. The police stopped us for a while, but then they decided that it was a beach where pirates used to bury their people, because all these skeletons were standing upright. Later on, when I went to work on *Land of the Pharaohs*, I said to Howard, 'I know a girl who would play the part of a slave very well. It's a girl called Joan Collins.' Then when we got back to Rome to continue filming, I walked into the rushes theatre and there was Joan! 'Oh Christ, Joan! How nice to see you. You got the part of the slave?' She said, 'No, I'm the fucking Queen!' And she has been ever since.

I got arrested a couple of times. One time they locked me up in Spain because I said to the chap, 'I'm not going to answer any bloody questions.' So they locked me up in the dungeon for the night. And when they brought me out in the morning, they said to me, 'You know, this is life. You're not making a film. This is real.' And you know, we do feel like that. We treat people differently. It's all a game. It's like a dream. The whole fucking thing's a dream. I'm still playing Cowboys and Indians.

Lunch and a Book:
Observations on Director/
Cameraman Relations
John Seale

Relationships between the director and cameraman on any film differ as much as the film subjects themselves. Some associations are complex, some uncomplicated. The physics of filming remain the same, but personalities vary enormously. I have found some directors to be very easy-going on the set, some more distant and isolated, while others feel that tension brings out the best in people. When the going gets tough some directors need nurturing and understanding, whereas one director I recall could only see the funny side to disastrous situations.

Often the most difficult period is pre-production. Sometimes, after only the briefest of meetings, you must start to understand the director's visualization of the project. I believe that there is only one way this is possible – by listening, listening and more listening. Directors have commented that initially I don't say very much, but most of my potential queries are answered as they explain the look, the feel and the mood of the film, and what they generally aim to achieve. Some directors find this initial communication difficult and use various methods to explain their concept. Some directors use storyboards or shot lists; sometimes films are viewed or paintings used as reference. Other directors might not use as much visual material, relying on verbal examples – long discussions on visuals, colours, composition – all very specific information and, once again, a lot of listening takes place.

Surveys are most important. The location should be seen as soon as possible so any queries can be related to the visual area. As the director talks about the actors moving within the sets, you quickly try to visualize the position of the sun, windows, natural or practical light sources, etc. During these surveys I find it essential to lock into the director's thoughts on the choreography of the scene.

One director in pre-production was generally fairly quiet. We went to lunch and discussed the visuals. There wasn't any real reference to anything past or present, so by the end of the lunch we decided that, as it was a contemporary film, we would just go out and shoot, using whatever happened with the locations and light. Later that day the director, Barry Levinson, left me with a coffee-table book, *The Cafés of Europe*, which became the basis for the 'look' of *Rain Man*. Lunch and a book established the 'look' and style. The apparently

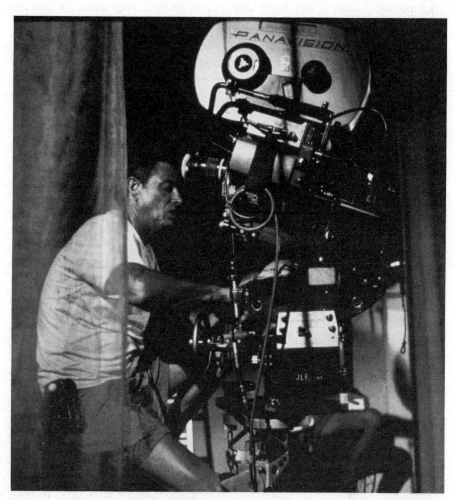

John Seale (photo by Bill Rubenstein)

simple style of this film was, in fact, just photographic reality. The available light was photographically balanced, raised or enhanced to record the scene on film. The two main characters were very real, so we tried to set them in a real world. I did try to make the desert exteriors visually beautiful for the audience, but they were generally ignored by the two characters who were blind to their surroundings.

On *Dead Poets Society*, Peter Weir's schedule in the last week of pre-production included closed-door discussions with me between 8 a.m. and noon every day. This was much to the chagrin of the rest of the crew as the director is a very popular person during that last week of pre-production. But the time was well spent and by the end of the film we had averaged twenty-one set-ups a day (including night shoots) on location! Most of that 'speed' could be directly related to the time I had spent with Peter, his ability to communicate and my interpretation of his ideas.

A full and comprehensive shot list issued on Sunday night for the coming week's schedule was the system used on another project. Pre-production came down to locations and logistics, some film references and not a lot else. Most of the colour information was gleaned from the production designer's still photographs. In fact, most of the photographic ideas came from those photos. Usually the production designer has been working on the film for months prior to the cameraman's arrival and already has a wealth of information from the director. The 'reference' photographs tend to be taken from viewpoints of the director's choice and by going through these stacks of still photographs you can start to interpret the director's train of thought.

Once the filming commences the cameraman is suddenly at the top of the creative wedge with the director, whereas during pre-production other department heads demand the majority of the director's time. When the camera rolls the relationship between the director and the cameraman is cemented. There is a mitring of thoughts and ideas, at times the most intimate of communications. The weeks of pre-production 'listening' broaden into a complete understanding and comprehension of the director's thoughts and ideas.

I had what I thought was a great idea on one project and said to the director, 'Hey, what if this shot did this and cut to that shot for this and then cut to that and . . .' The director agreed that it seemed a good way to go. We commenced lighting, but a short time after, the director sidled over and asked, 'How did it all go again?' Obviously the director was confused, so I back-pedalled to his original idea, we rehashed it and agreed that that was the way we would go. The director was back in the chair, confident and happy, and we continued with the schedule. I have found that to confuse a director with your own ideas can be very counter-productive. They must feel confident in the sequence of shots and their ultimate ability to edit it. Cameramen always seem to have a bundle of ideas, but they should be wary of changing the flow of the director's thoughts by presenting a different series of shots. Even so, I still enjoy offering the odd suggestion, but I am also more than willing to accept the rejection of an idea. The director may have a logistics problem, I may have misunderstood the point of the shot, or it may be simply a change of pace. Directors hold the flow of the entire film in their head and a cameraman's input must be able to be absorbed into that rhythm. Other directors take all the input they can get and actively seek suggestions. After a quick discussion a compromise of ideas is reached, but still on the director's line. There was a situation when I had an idea about a scene due to be shot in three days' time. I put it to the director whose immediate response was, 'But we're not shooting that tomorrow.' I realized that the director's homework was for the next day only and, once locked into that day, it was very difficult to get any ideas accepted. However, if I was to think two or three days ahead, it could give him the chance to think it through.

Before the advent of the video split, there was a very strong bond between camera and director. I think the camera then made a more important contribution towards the welfare of the actor. Now the video can play back the performance and the actors can, in many cases, call their own shots. Many years ago when I was working as a camera operator on a television series directed by Ken Hannam, he told me that he could always tell if he had a good take by the way I answered his 'Cut. How was it for you?' The answer was simple – I could always tell by the way he called 'cut' whether or not he felt he had the performance he wanted. As the operator I would quickly assess the visual operation and call out an answer which would correspond to his enthusiastic (or otherwise) 'cut'. We had some good laughs about that one year later.

There have been times when it just doesn't seem to come together at all. We were well into a shoot and we hit a small scene, about three shots, and we just couldn't get it together. For an hour we went: 'What about here? ... What about there? ... How about this? ... How about that? ...' but nothing seemed to cement. I had suggested everything I could. For almost two hours we were racked with indecision. The producer was irate, as he believed it was the cameraman's responsibility to keep up the pace. Eventually we got the scene, in retrospect with a simple solution, but it highlights how difficult it is for some producers to understand that film-making is not a production-line industry.

Some directors prefer to work very fast and loose. Apart from night shots, which require special treatment and are somewhat locked in to certain angles, the rest of the shooting can often be quite haphazard. We adopted this easy approach on *Witness*, where Peter Weir changed angles and ideas very fast. The light was dropping, we changed to high-speed stock, went to 200°. What we didn't realize was that a lot of the crew had walked off the set some time before, reasoning: 'We'll have to come back to reshoot this.' We didn't have to, of course, and there were some embarrassed looks from the crew as they were called back to the set. It gets frantic at times when you are working fast, but in a way I really love that style. There is an energy in fast film-making that is very exciting and most actors seem to respond to that energy level as well. Sometimes this fast shooting can create a photographic style of its own. By not having time to 'touch up' the lighting, the film can take on a look which is often assumed to be the predetermined style.

Another important factor is the interpretation of the script. For example, in *Children of a Lesser God* we had the choice of two swimming pools: one a photographically appealing pool with large glass-brick windows, quite magnificent; the other was uninteresting, bare and windowless. In making my decision I balanced the attractiveness of the two pools against what was required by the script, and the choice had to be the unattractive one. It matched the lead character's needs for seclusion and silence, and represented better the prison-like surroundings. Even though the selected pool was inferior photographically, many people commented on the sensuality of this scene.

Often I have difficulty ending one project and starting another. The main problem with such a change-over is ending the elevated level of communication with the director and the crew. Things are humming along and then suddenly it is all over. A short time later you are prepping for another film – a new script, new director, new crew, new style, new rhythm, new personalities. I have to clear out the 'feeling' of the last film completely before I can commence the next with a fresh approach.

When selecting a script I am much influenced by the writer, choice of director and casting, and, in retrospect, acknowledge that in the past I have been drawn towards films about human drama in contemporary settings.

Certainly, one of the most interesting aspects of film-making for me has been my relationships with directors. It is a challenge endeavouring to interpret their vision, which is made all the more absorbing by the variety of their approaches to the task. I have been privileged to have worked with many great film directors, each of whom, in their own way, has given me just that little bit more insight into the esoteric world of film-making and, specifically, cinematography.

Gotta Dance

Gene Kelly danced his way into cinema history with a step that was uniquely his own. Sally Potter immerses herself in the world of Tango, discovering in the process lessons for life – and for cinema, too.

13   An American in Paradise
Gene Kelly interviewed by
Graham Fuller

Introduction

Just as the following interview was going to press, I attended a screening of Luc Besson's first American feature, *The Professional* (1994), starring Jean Reno as a French hitman in New York and Natalie Portman as the orphaned adolescent he takes under his wing. Lugubrious and naïve except when he's killing, the Reno character escapes from himself by watching Gene Kelly movies. We see him in a Manhattan revival house watching Kelly on roller skates in *It's Always Fair Weather* (1955). And later, when the girl does a series of impersonations, the big lunk fails to recognize her Madonna, Marilyn and Charlie Chaplin, but immediately identifies the singer of 'Singin' in the Rain'.

It's a small homage, but a potent reminder of the impeccability of French taste in cinema. Kelly, of course, is a Francophile – a fact amply demonstrated in *An American in Paris* (1951), *Les Girls* (1957), *Gigot* (1962) and *The Young Girls of Rochefort* (1968) – as well as a chevalier of the Legion of Honour. I'd contend, though, that the French respond to something in the Kelly persona of the late 1940s and early 1950s that, emotionally and intellectually, reminds them of themselves: like Belmondo empathizing with Bogart in *Breathless*. As brashly American as he undoubtedly was, Kelly also had a common, metropolitan quality that was unique among Hollywood music men: his pushiness, his sexual vigour, and his nervous energy are redolent of the boulevardier or the testosterone-driven matelot. He could have easily played a Parisian in America.

A far more complex figure than Fred Astaire, who danced without effort but always seemed remote and amused by the experience, Kelly danced sensually, ecstatically, because the music seemed to pump through him like blood, or Beaujolais, and yet self-consciously, too. There is no other Hollywood song-and-dance man who took so much uninhibited physical pleasure in his performances while making us wary of the musical's Utopian promise. Against that, it was Kelly's streetwise, Everyman figure that did most to liberate the genre from its 'putting on a show' tradition. Kelly and Stanley Donen's masterpiece *On the Town* (1949), filmed *plein air* on the streets of New York, remains the supreme example of the fully integrated musical narrative in which fantasy and reality coexist.

Born in Philadelphia in 1912, Kelly became the most agile and virile performer in American films since Douglas Fairbanks – to whom he paid tribute in *The Pirate* (1948) – and a fine throaty crooner. In a white sailor suit or polo shirt and pre-Gap khakis, he was sometimes more at ease dancing with other males – Astaire, Frank Sinatra, Donald O'Connor, Jerry the Mouse – or himself, than with women, such were the fraught sexual politics of his films. An indefatigably macho romantic, he usually played the hyperathletic initiator of partners like Judy Garland, Vera-Ellen, Debbie Reynolds, or Leslie Caron. That Kelly's persona was essentially priapic is revealed amid the heady Impressionist artifice of the Gershwin ballet in *An American in Paris*, where he dances in a flesh-toned sheath before the splayed skirts of the Moulin Rouge cancan dancers. Only Cyd Charisse could bring Kelly to a standstill, as she did from a sitting position with one endless, imperious leg in *Singin' in the Rain* (1952). 'MGM didn't know what they had with Cyd, did they?' Kelly said to me when I interviewed him at his Beverly Hills home in March 1994.

For forty years, he danced and sang, choreographed, acted – memorably in *Christmas Holiday* (1944), *Marjorie Morningstar* (1958), and *Inherit the Wind* (1960) – and directed. In his prime, he reinvented the music man only six or seven years before the musical itself began to fade from view, with the advent of rock 'n' roll. As Kelly himself sang, in the 'I Got Rhythm' number in *An American in Paris*, 'Who could ask for anything more?'

GRAHAM FULLER: *What did you think of that Gap ad that implied that you were no longer with us?*

GENE KELLY: The Gap people knew I was alive, because they phoned me and asked my permission. But their office was flooded with calls from old fans who said, 'Is Gene Kelly not around any more?' because the ad said, 'Gene Kelly *wore* khakis.' They're doing another ad on a billboard in San Francisco and I was going to call them, out of sheer mischief, and say, 'Are you going to use the past tense or the present tense? Is it "wore" or "wears"?' As you can see, I still wear khakis.

GF: *Tell me about your early days in Pittsburgh. What comes to mind?*

GK: I'll be as concise as I can. I went to Penn State College as a freshman in 1929. And, as the world knows, the Wall Street Crash occurred. In the Kelly family there were five children – of which I was the middle one – and our folks said, 'Dad doesn't have a job, our money is running out and we're paying a mortgage on our new home. If you want to finish your education, you'll have to make your own way.' I had the usual jobs – ditch-digger, soda jerk, gas pumper, and so forth. My mother had a job as a receptionist at a dancing school and had the idea that we should open our own dancing school; we did and it prospered. Meanwhile, I enrolled as a sophomore at the University of Pittsburgh, because I could live at home, and all I had to do was earn my tuition. Four of us graduated from Pitt. Then I went into law school. I had been there a month when I realized that it wasn't about being Clarence Darrow – it was about learning about torts – so I quit that and continued to teach dance for another five, six years. Then I went to New York. I'd studied dance in Chicago every summer and taught it all winter, and I was well rounded. I wasn't worried about getting a job on Broadway. In fact, I got one the first week.

L. B. Mayer had seen me on stage in *Pal Joey* [1940–41] and asked me to come to meet him. He said, 'I hope to have you at MGM.' And I said, 'I'll wait until the show is through. Then I want to take a test out there, not here,' because MGM was famous for its bad screen tests. Mayer said, 'You don't need a screen test. I'll hire you when you're ready.' Well, when I got a notice from MGM, it said, 'You must take a screen test.' So they must have forgotten.

When David O. Selznick came to town I said, 'Your father-in-law is a son of a bitch because he lied to me.' He said, 'Do you want to sign a contract with me?' So I did and I came out here. That was supposed to be for one picture, then I could go back to Broadway. I was with Selznick for about six months, but he had nothing for me. He was still coasting on *Gone With the Wind*. So he just loaned me to MGM and they bought out my contract. We were all indentured servants then – I hate to use the word 'slaves', but it's true. I was at MGM for sixteen years.

GF: *Did you ever do a test for them?*

GK: At MGM? No. I made a couple of tests for Selznick because I wanted to look at the camera to see what it was about. They weren't very good; as a matter of fact, I think they were pretty bad. I never saw them. But I could see that there was some kind of cinema know-how. I quickly learned that with Judy [Garland] in my first picture, *For Me and My Gal* [1942]. She was so good. I sort of followed her around on those little vaudeville routines we did. Judy was not a highly advanced dancer, but she was a great little hoofer – she was marvellous, the quickest study I've ever known.

GF: *Did you know from the beginning that you wanted to incorporate different styles of dancing – tap, ballet and modern – into your routines?*

GK: Not from the beginning. But as I taught dancing and as I learned, I began to teach myself and to set my sights higher. I'd studied ballet in Chicago with a teacher [Bernice Holmes] who was a protégée of Adolph Bolm, the great Russian dancer, and I'd seen that I could work in all kinds of dance, but none of them alone satisfied me.

I had a few idols who were the pioneers of modern dance – Martha Graham and Humphrey Weidman – but their outlook was different to mine. I wanted to invent some kind of American dance that was danced to the music that I grew up with – Cole Porter, Rodgers and Hart, and Irving Berlin. So I evolved a style that certainly didn't catch on right away, but I had some good mentors in New York who encouraged me. I was very happy when I got to be friendly with Martha Graham because she approved of what I was trying to do. She went to see my movies and she told me which numbers she liked.

After *For Me and My Gal*, I was pushed around for a few years doing films where I didn't have dancing partners – little programme pictures, which I was glad to do because I liked to work. But then I did *Cover Girl* [1944] on loan to Columbia, with Rita Hayworth, and that's when I began to see you could make dances for cinema that weren't just photographed stage dancing. [Producer] Arthur Schwartz told Harry Cohn that I was perfect for the part. Cohn was desperate for a juvenile lead; he didn't have one. I did the choreography for a few numbers. That was my big insight into Hollywood and Hollywood's big insight into me. After I came out of the Navy [in 1946], I determined to stay out here and develop more dances specifically for films.

GF: *Had the Arthur Freed group already been thinking about experimenting with their musicals when you arrived at MGM?*

GK: No. As a matter of fact, the next musical I did with Arthur Freed after *For Me and My Gal* was *Du Barry Was a Lady* [1943], which was atrocious and I told him so. I said, 'Arthur, you know, you don't want to do this.' Meanwhile, he did try other things, like *The Clock* [1945] with Judy. And, finally, through the influence of a lot of ex-Broadway people like Vincente Minnelli, Roger Edens [composer/producer], Saul Chaplin [composer/producer] and Irene Sharaff [costume designer], we started to do a new kind of musical. Arthur encouraged that; when we'd ask him to bring out new people, he would bring them out. Some of them worked out, some of them didn't: I don't think I should name names. A few just couldn't get on with film. In those days, MGM musicals made the most money for the studio, so they could afford to splurge on new talent. We would say, 'You should try Michael Kidd,' so Arthur would get Michael Kidd. When I did *Du Barry Was a Lady*, Arthur said, 'Who'd be good for this?' I said, 'Well, there's a young fellow in New York who is working for RKO. His name is Charles Walters. Bring him over and let him do the choreography' – even though there wasn't much on that film. Charles was bright and knowledgeable and turned out to be the most underrated musical director MGM ever had. At any rate, Arthur gave us our heads, so to speak, collectively.

I worked with other musical producers. For instance, the fellow who first pushed me at MGM was Joe Pasternak, who made *Anchors Aweigh* [1945]. Joe was very helpful, but he was only interested in singing. I had to work opposite Kathryn Grayson but there was nothing I could do with a high C, so I had to make up dances with a little mouse, or dance with Sinatra, or do a dance on an empty stage.

GF: *Freed brought Minnelli to MGM in 1940, although he didn't direct anything*

'I had to make up dances with a little mouse'

until Cabin in the Sky *[1943]* . . .

GK: I knew Vincente for his work in New York. He had been a designer for
Radio City Music Hall and had directed Broadway revues. We approached the
MGM milieu at roughly the same time. I remember he designed a little
tableau for Mickey [Rooney] and Judy, which got Arthur and Roger Edens
excited. Vincente had such great taste; it was always a pleasure to work with
him. *Meet Me in St Louis* [1944] is still my favourite musical; it's one of those
films that's just about ordinary people. Charles Walters did the dance direction, by the way. It was probably the first all-round Freed Unit picture on
which Arthur found the level we should be working on.

GF: *How did you get together with Stanley Donen?*

GK: Stanley was a chorus boy in two of my Broadway shows and came out here
as a chorus boy for MGM. When they fired him, I said, 'Come on down to
Columbia and work as my assistant.' He was like a son to me. He, Hugh
Martin, Ralph Blane and all that New York gang practically lived at my house;
it wasn't *this* house – that burned down in 1983, but I rebuilt it on the same
spot. Sinatra, Judy, [Betty] Comden and [Adolph] Green were steady visitors,
and then people from Hollywood started to come. Pianists and composers like
Lenny Bernstein, Oscar Levant, Johnny Green, Roger Edens and Saul Chaplin would play the piano. There was Harold Arlen, Sammy Cahn, whomever.
It was a musical house, a fun house.

GF: *Did the things you did here find their way into the films?*

GK: A lot of Comden and Green stuff was tried out here for fun; we didn't do it purposely. Martin and Blane had come out here to do *Best Foot Forward* [1943] as a movie – I'd choreographed it for them on Broadway – and then they began to compose songs mainly for Judy in *Meet Me in St Louis*. So we would hear the songs here before they would do them at the studio. We were just a group of local entertainers amusing ourselves. We'd play charades and when the foreigners would come, like Noël Coward or Maurice Chevalier, we'd chat or talk politics. We were all, with a couple of exceptions, left-wingers, all Roosevelt people. But we – the Kellys – never got invited to the big soirées here. For example, Basil Rathbone and his wife gave huge parties for what was known here as the upper crust, but we were never asked to those. My parties? . . . well, we were the working stiffs. L. B. Mayer once had a party for *Gone With the Wind* and Vivien Leigh and Laurence Olivier asked for us to come. That's the only time I was ever in Mayer's house.

GF: *Did you get on with Mayer?*

GK: No. I can't use four-letter words because you might print them, but at that time – to give him as good a face as I can – he was more interested in his race horses than new talent.

GF: *Tell me how you would go about choreographing a dance, for example, George Balanchine's gangster ballet 'Slaughter on Tenth Avenue' in* Words and Music *[1948]*.

GK: That was an easy one, because the music was already written. In movies, you usually have thirty-two bars and you have to do arrangements *ad infinitum* on those same thirty-two bars. 'Slaughter on Tenth Avenue' was already an entire piece of music. All I did was write a new libretto. The libretto that Balanchine used in the Broadway show [*On Your Toes*] was comedic and had been hilariously performed by Ray Bolger, who always stayed perfectly attuned to the audience.

I wanted to do it as a tragic scene where I got shot and the girl got shot – more like grand opera, or tragic ballet. We started out doing a Bolshoi thing, with a lot of magnificent lifts. I had a great assistant, Alex Romero, and we took turns lifting Vera-Ellen – she was great at that. Finally, we saw that we had some high spots, but we had lost our story. So we threw practically all of them out and went into the story of the girl vamping the guy, then the bad guy coming in trying to get the girl and shooting her. It was interesting to do, but less trouble than doing a piece where you start with an idea in your head.

GF: *What about the Moulin Rouge sequence in* An American in Paris *[1951]?*

GK: That also started with a finished piece of music. I was guided by Impressionist painters. That Gershwin music spoke to me of Toulouse-Lautrec's *Chocolat*. So I dressed up as the jockey and took his first pose, then went on interpreting the music. Again, that wasn't as hard as, say, the dance in *Cover*

An American in Paris: dressed up as the jockey

Girl where I danced with myself. I also shot that myself. Harry Cohn and the director [Charles Vidor] didn't even come down to the set. They didn't think it was possible that you could pan and dolly in double exposure, because it had never been done. I just sat in an armchair and thought it all out, battling with myself like a writer.

GF: *And 'Singin' in the Rain'* [Singin' in the Rain, *1952]?*

GK: Arthur Freed put it in the picture after it had started. He came to me and said, 'What are you going to do with it?' I said, 'Well, Arthur, I don't know yet. But I do know I've gotta be singing and it's gotta be raining.' There was no rain in that picture up to then and this was a quirk of Arthur's – but lucky for us. So I got together with Betty and Adolph, who were just geniuses at this sort of thing, and they set that whole evening in the rain and wrote me a little good-bye love scene to do so I could go from that to the euphoric state of being in the rain. I had to sit down and say, 'Where do I start? How do I leave this girl, get out in the street and dance in the rain?' It had to work like a story. I kiss this girl good-night and I'm so in love I don't care if it's raining and send my car home, put my umbrella down and act like an eight-year-old kid, sloshing through puddles and being happy. The trouble I had was getting *into* the rain and I found that through Roger Edens, who gave me that vamp. He said, 'How about [sings opening eight bars of 'Singin' in the Rain'] dooda-do-do, dooda-doo-da-do-do?' That got me walking and feeling the rain. What is always the most difficult is the bridge from dialogue to music. In the old musicals, they just said 'I *lo-ve* you' and started singing. Finally, the public said, 'This isn't real.' That's something we changed a lot at MGM. You had to stay in character, or come out of that character in some kind of fantasy way, but you couldn't *lose* the character, otherwise you'd be constricted.

GF: *Were you a genuine admirer of Fred Astaire and Ginger Rogers?*

GK: I think of them as the last of the great dance teams. When I grew up in the 1920s and 1930s, there were a lot of dance teams in movies – some of them forgotten now. The amazing thing about Ginger and Fred was that they sang *and* danced *and* talked together beautifully. They deserved their reign out here. There were other dancers who were damn good, but Ginger and Fred were outstanding.

GF: *Your persona in your films was very different to what we'd seen in musicals before. You played a very pushy, abrasive, working-class guy.*

GK: Well, that's what I was – working class.

GF: *Very different to the Astaire persona.*

GK: Exactly the antithesis. When I grew up in the Depression, I hated the rich, because my father was out of a job and everyone in our family was working to try to get food on the table and literally pay the rent. I hated the kids who could drive a car to school and spend twenty-five cents on lunch; we had to spend a nickel or a dime. So I grew up with a dislike for that.

Singin' in the Rain: sloshing through puddles and being happy

When you saw a musical in the 1930s, all the floors were black and white and shiny, and the sets were art deco, and everybody was dressed up to the nines. They were musicals for the rich, but everybody adored them. People would spend twenty-five cents on a movie and go without lunch. But all my dancing came out of the idea of the common man. I started doing that when I did Bill Saroyan's *The Time of Your Life* [1939] on Broadway and played a guy who didn't have a job and was out in the street. I was influenced very much by my social and political thinking.

GF: *Your dancing had a particularly masculine quality, too.*

GK: Because I was raised as an athlete. Originally, I didn't want to dance – I wanted to be the shortstop for the Pittsburgh Pirates. I've said that so many times, it's a cliché, but it was true. It wasn't until I started working my way through college and teaching children that I began to feel that I loved dance. Then, when I was twenty or twenty-one, I saw a ballet for the first time, the Monte Carlo Ballet Russe, and I said, 'This is an amazing life.' That's why I decided to study ballet. But I never wanted to dance in a 'polished' film – and I didn't. I put on a top hat, white tie and tails with Astaire once as a gag in *That's Entertainment, Part II* [1976] and did it briefly in a stage number in *Summer Stock* [1950].

GF: *In fact, you had your own customized costume: loafers, white socks . . .*

GK: . . . T-shirt and jeans, or khakis. Even in the ballet in *An American in Paris*, I wear black pants and white socks and a polo shirt. That was my outfit. I wore handmade moccasins that were like dance slippers; they could bend so you could point your toe. All the other dancers before me danced in suits or shirts, which hid the body line, but I wanted you to see the line. The sailor suits I wore in *Anchors Aweigh* and *On the Town* [1949] – bellbottoms, tight waists, skimpy tops – were the greatest dance outfits ever conceived.

I made one picture, *Living in a Big Way* [1947], that nobody ever saw. The picture flopped in previews and an executive at MGM asked me to put in some dance numbers to see if we could beef it up. It was a terrible picture and nothing could save it, but I remember I did some dancing in a T-shirt and jeans with a Navy working cap – the kind they still wear on aircraft carriers. I tried Marine caps, but they weren't as effective.

GF: *Did you feel that the 'An American in Paris' ballet was the pinnacle of what you were attempting at MGM?*

GK: I guess it was at that time, because nobody had ever done that long a dance number – it was seventeen minutes long. Everybody said it couldn't be done, except Arthur Freed, Vincente Minnelli and myself. But then the executives at MGM had said we couldn't sing and dance through the streets of New York in *On the Town* and we'd said, 'Oh yes we can and we'll show you.'

GF: *In 1952, you came to England to make a very personal project,* Invitation to the Dance.

On the Town: 'bellbottoms . . . were the greatest dance outfits ever conceived' (Gene Kelly and Vera-Ellen)

GK: All the big studios had frozen funds in Europe and they would lure us out there with the promise of the tax-break we'd get if we stayed eighteen months. They said I could do three pictures and I agreed to do it if one of them was an experimental dance picture of my own, *Invitation to the Dance*. I set the production up in London. All the music was written. I had hired costume designers and was having the sets built when one of our actors dropped out because of the money. An agent had got hold of him and said, 'This is an MGM picture; you should be getting paid like Clark Gable.' I tried to persuade the actor to do it because it was an experimental film and that even our star, Igor Youskevitch, was only getting a little over scale, but it was no good. I cabled MGM and said, 'I'll have to hold off the picture.' They said, 'No, no, we can't stop now, or you'll have to come home. You'll have to step in and perform yourself.'

That meant I had to invent something that I could do. I couldn't dance beside Youskevitch – I hadn't done ballet for years. The only thing I could think of was to play the clown who's tragically in love with a young woman in the 'Circus' episode. Before that we had a different story about an older woman who's frozen out by two guys fighting over a younger woman. I had Jacques Ibert, the great French composer, working on the music. He was very flexible and was able to switch things around. So I did that role, although very begrudgingly. I'm not fond of it. I'm not fond of the whole picture, but I should have been firmer and told MGM, 'I'm not going to do it. I'll come home.' After that, I didn't trust anyone who said they would appear in a picture until they were on the job.

When I did come home, the publicity department got to work and said, 'This multi-million-dollar musical . . .' which it wasn't. It was done for literally what they would pay for half of a B-picture. Then they didn't release the picture until 1956. By that time, my dream of showing off these great ballet dancers was over, because television had shown them – so the bloom was off the rose. The picture had cost $665,000 and I got a consortium together and raised $1 million to buy it off the studio at a profit for them. But they wouldn't sell it; that's the way corporations work.

GF: *Which of your straight acting roles gave you the most satisfaction? You were excellent, for example, as the H. L. Mencken-like journalist alongside Spencer Tracy and Fredric March in* Inherit the Wind *[1960].*

GK: I guess *Inherit the Wind* was as good a job as I ever did, although maybe I acted better in *The Black Hand* [1950], which was a programme picture that made a lot of money. In some scenes in *Inherit the Wind*, I reverted to over-acting, which I'd never gotten over from my days on Broadway. But I think I held enough back beside Freddie and Spence to be plausible. There are scenes in *Christmas Holiday* [1944] and *Marjorie Morningstar* [1958] that I think are tip-top, and one in particular in *Marjorie Morningstar* that I'd be proud to look at with someone. Generally, I don't think that much of the picture, but people love it.

GF: *When the great period of the MGM musical began to come to an end, was it difficult to let it go?*

GK: No. After *Invitation to the Dance*, I did a few more pictures for MGM, including *Brigadoon* [1954], then, when the management changed, I got out of my contract with the proviso that I would owe them a picture as director. It wasn't such a hot deal. I did *Les Girls* [1957] and *The Tunnel of Love* [1958], but without much heart.

So those were my days at MGM. I went back to Broadway only once, directing *Flower Drum Song* for Dick Rodgers and Oscar Hammerstein. I'd worked with Dick before, but never with Oscar, so I enjoyed that. Then I did a lot of TV specials. Some of them were quite good.

GF: *You went on to direct films like* Gigot *[1963]*, Hello Dolly! *[1969], and* The Cheyenne Social Club *[1970], but after* The Young Girls of Rochefort *[1967], you seldom danced again. Did you know that it was time to quit?*

GK: A dancer with any intelligence has to start at sixteen and think, 'I'm going to have the shortest career in the world.' But most of them don't. Most great dancers go on creaking and outliving their time. I was ready to throw it in when my time came, when I couldn't jump on a table any more – the same as a boxer, or an athlete who can't run that extra hundred yards. So that's what I did – I quit dancing. But it had been a living.

[This interview originally appeared in *Interview* magazine in May 1994 and has been reprinted, with additional text, by kind permission of Brant Publications.]

Sally Potter and Gustavo Naveira (photo by Jose Mateos)

14   The Tango Lesson
Sally Potter

After a few days and nights in Buenos Aires, I realize that as a city it reminds me of Paris mixed with New York, Moscow-style.

It has some of the architectural beauty of Paris without any of its chic vanity: it has the cultural energy and long, straight, neon-lit avenues of New York without its egocentricity. It has the shabbiness of Moscow and the atmosphere of a city that has survived terrible political turmoil and repression; but this is not Eastern Europe – it is Latin America.

And bubbling away at the heart of the city is the beat of the tango. Every night of the week you can, if you wish to, dance until dawn.

Entering into the world of the tango – as a visitor, an outsider, a gringo tango tourist – I am welcomed and taken to its bosom like a long-lost friend or even family.

The music reaches into me – the lyrics express a kind of desperate extremity that has no voice in English culture – and the dancing lifts me to a state of rapturous joy.

Each day I take two or three lessons and each night go out to dance at two or three *milongas* (dance halls).

The lessons take in the full spectrum of the tango as it manifests now, from the original authentic *milongera* style – minimal, close-hold salon dancing, where the couple focuses exclusively on each other and enters into an entirely private world governed by subtle signals – to the theatrical, sometimes extravagant style designed to be seen, to show off both partners to maximum effect and to take the moves to their own extremities of speed, virtuosity and grace.

And somewhere in between lie the tango philosophers, epitomized by Gustavo Naveira, who understands both worlds, loves the history and feels the essence of the tango, and also shines brilliantly in the improvised vocabulary that at its most eloquent becomes astonishingly agile and continuously unexpected.

At night in the *milongas*, Jeff (my host and guide in Buenos Aires) and I watch riveted as couples in their fifties, sixties, seventies step on to the dance floor and start to move. A portly man in a grey suit with a grey bushy moustache and red swarthy face, accompanied by his elderly plump wife, her swollen legs packed into twinkly gold shoes, take the floor and astonish with their gazelle-like grace and lightness of touch. Turning, gliding, pausing, kicking, swivelling, in perfect unison, with perfect mutual understanding, and a visible respect and compassion for each other's qualities and frailties and strengths – *this* is how to grow older.

For the tango is a dance that matures with age. It's no respecter of youth and thinness – though those have their place too. The young dancers, limber and athletic, also twizzle their own way to heaven. But here in the *milongas* – the large, usually shabby dance halls, perhaps decorated with some balloons and tinsel – the mournful, joyful strains of the tangos burst out of the crackling sound systems. This is where the working people – bent, fat, balding, bewigged, poured into lycra mini-dresses, squeezed magnificently into pointy shoes, bosoms thrusting, pot-bellies grandly presiding – this is where the tango glows like a testament to survival and graceful hope in the face of the ravages of ageing, political repression and the apparent meaninglessness of daily life.

Here the ordinary becomes extraordinary and the kitsch becomes beautiful.
    Here the grotesque become adorable and the misfits find a place; here the has-beens become somebodies; here the humans become gods.

On Following

In the tango, as in most social dances for couples, one person leads and the other follows. It is the norm for the man to lead and for the woman to follow. In Europe and North America, where nothing is taken for granted when it comes to gender definition, this is seen either as problematic, or, usefully, as an opportunity for women to learn and experience both roles. In Argentina, it is an accepted division of labour and implies nothing derogatory for either sex.

As someone who leads for much of her working life (as a director), the opportunity to learn what it means to follow was a blessing.

Someone once said that Ginger Rogers did everything that Fred Astaire did, only backwards and wearing high heels.
    That is certainly true of following in the tango: far from being an expression of passivity, it is one of acutely skilful manoeuvring, at high speed, often backwards. But this is just the most obvious part of the form. And the form is based on a contract. One person (the leader, whether male or female) chooses and shapes the steps of the dance, the other (the follower) responds so

instantaneously that it is as if the two dancers move as one in an extraordinarily elaborate choreography.

The best leaders make their partners look and feel like creatures of consummate grace, beauty, strength and skill. The best followers make their partners look and feel the same. Each enhances the other's sense of self and feeling of freedom.

The joy of being a follower is that it demands a complex and sometimes paradoxical series of qualities. You must be both completely centred and balanced, yet able to move at a moment's notice in any direction; you must be completely in control of your body, yet surrender control of where you are going; you must be completely grounded, yet free enough to feel that you are flying; you must be toned enough to provide enough resistance to the leader so that he (or she) can direct you, yet be completely relaxed so that there is no obstruction; you must be completely mentally alert, yet your mind must be 'empty'. Above all, you must be completely in the present. Without the sheer now-ness, you cannot follow at the speed and with the precision that is required.

Entering into this state of alert receptivity, I find the energy coiling in my abdomen like a spring, every anxiety banished from my mind, my ears open to every nuance of the music, my body responsive to every tiny pressure and touch of my partner until I feel that I *am* his body and he is mine. In other words, I enter a state of pure libidinous energy which I have only ever experienced either in love-making, in meditation, or in the rapturous moments when, either writing or singing or directing, all seems to unify and become itself at once, effortlessly.

The tango is often caricatured as kitsch eroticism: a couple clasping each other in a parody of 1920s' togetherness. That's the Europeanized public image of the tango. On home ground the sexuality is there, but it is sublimated. The moves do not imitate the sexual act. But they are sometimes violently quick, or agile – wordless expressions of a life force when it connects two individuals. For above all, the tango is an expression of connectedness. You cannot dance tango alone.

Every time you take the dance floor with a stranger, you are entering an agreement to step over the precipice into the chasm between you – you negotiate the unsayable; you try to express the inexpressible; you give voice to the 'I and thou' that Buber wrote of; you use each opportunity, within the discipline and codes of the dance, to say, 'I hear you.'

*

So, pretence is out of the question. You feel immediately if the partner is sensing you or is oblivious to your rhythm, your body. You sense immediately when your partner opens himself to you or closes against you.

You communicate wordlessly: 'How far can I go with you? How deep can we reach into each other? Who are you? Can you feel who I am?' And together you can, in some glorious moments, soar away to heaven. Then you go back to your seats, your hearts pounding. A little bow, perhaps, a nod, a thank you. The social codes safely contain the adventure that is at once sensual, athletic, musical and spiritual.

Gustavo

Almost every day I cross Buenos Aires to Gustavo's small, mirrored first-floor studio in the fabric district. He's sometimes late – still asleep at five in the afternoon after a very late night – and must be woken by a phone call. Then he arrives, a little shamefaced, at the local café bar where we are waiting; but a few moments later in the studio, once the music is playing, he enters into his unique form of concentrated teaching.

In my case, he senses intuitively that I will learn best kinetically. We hardly talk at all. We just dance and dance and dance. He glides and turns, this way and that, gently removing my arms if I press too much on his shoulder, very occasionally stopping to explain a move; but mostly teaching wordlessly through doing, through repetition. If I miss a step the first time, he will present another opportunity to catch it soon after.

Heavy lidded with concentration, his moustached face becomes Buddha-like. And like a good-natured monk, he laughs easily.

Some days into the week, I arrive and say I need to talk. He nods graciously as I pour out my impressions – of different ways of dancing, of the roots of the tango, of the social and political meanings as they appear to me. He reaches for a pen and paper and starts to draw. Here is the 1920s, and here the 1930s. Here is the 1940s – the golden age of the tango – dominated by Petrolio. Here is the 1950s, and now in the 1960s the tango is dead. Only the Beatles exist. And in the 1970s it is still dead, but now in the 1980s it starts to come alive again. Copes becomes the king of tango. The tango spreads through the rest of the world and is exposed to other influences. And now it is in a state of transition once more.

I ask him, 'Where does the tango really manifest? On the dance floor, in the process of learning, or on the stage in a theatre?' He replies: 'It was originally in the salon. It came alive in the 1980s again on the stage, and now in the transition we are moving into something else. We are moving towards an unknown.'

His own place in the picture is as a pedagogue, but also as an improviser, probably the best. He has a grasp of a seemingly endless vocabulary of possible moves and variations which make his dancing akin to the most inventively esoteric new music improvisers, but with the visual accessibility of a great variety performer.

His conceptual hunger to examine and test the tango philosophically makes him a tango intellectual, but he is no dry academic – his joy when dancing is infectious, his appetite for dancing seems undimmed; and as a dance partner or teacher he is able to communicate accurately and without words in such a way that one feels seen and appreciated on a primal level.

'You must let yourself go,' he says to me, quietly, as we dance. 'Let your body go where it wants to.'

'Don't think about it too much. Just learn to relax.'

As the lessons sink in, I find that if I relax, I have to stop criticizing myself. I start to feel good – fluid and graceful, on top of things without having to control them. Gustavo's work with me becomes the spine of the experience of Buenos Aires – a place to return to, the essential level of the tango, the place of revelation and transformation.

Graciella

We arrive at Graciella's apartment building in beautiful sunshine and ring the polished brass doorbell. A few minutes later she appears, unlocks the door and ushers us towards the tiny lift. She is diminutive, unsmiling, with long dark hair and ample proportions.

In her small, tiled room she gets Jeff and me to dance for a while while she prowls about watching, smoking a cigarette, staring at my feet.

OK, OK.

She leads me to a wall and the work begins. Slow motion, painful precision. The footwork starts again from scratch. Don't turn out. The knees always touch. She demonstrates, her legs and feet gliding like butter across the floor. And now! – she pulls my hips around – here! Every move of the feet is generated by activity in the pelvis. We graduate to *boleos* (where the hips rotate and one leg swiftly kicks behind, then returns like a Yo-Yo to its original position, sometimes so fast it's like a blur) and *ganchos* (where you hook your leg around your partner's in a sudden, swift embrace. Strong, yet relaxed.)

*

After an hour and a half I am drenched in sweat and my legs are trembling. I stagger out into the light, my body flooded with memories of what it means to *train*. Not since my early twenties have I done this kind of precise, arduous, physical work. And it brings with it a flood of painful memories: of broken dreams and unfulfilled promise as a dancer; of being hopelessly up against my own physical limitations (I did not start dancing until I was twenty-one). But she has also imbued me with hope. She seems completely undeterred by my relatively advanced years (attitude and musicality being much more important than age in the tango), and obviously glories in the attention to detail and pursuit of excellence for its own sake.

I remember suddenly what I always loved about dancing: the combination of vigorous endeavour, present timedness, and dedication to process; the sure knowledge that you never 'arrive', you are instead in a constant process of arrival. It is itself and it is a metaphor: for learning, for living, for being.

Juan Carlos Copes

Jeff and I have been out dancing, as usual, until 4 a.m. At 5 a.m., after reading a couple more pages of 'Heartbreak Tango' by Manuel Puig, I fall into a deep sleep, but wake, ragged and alert before nine. I get up and pad about in my socks in the grey morning light, warming up.

At ten o'clock sharp, the doorbell rings.

The caretaker has recognized Copes; this gives Jeff some pleasure and reinforces his identity as a serious tango-ist, for he has arrived from New York some months earlier to dedicate all his energies to the tango.

We get to work in the tiny empty room, with its shiny dark wooden parquet floor.

'You're leaning on me! Stop leaning!' Copes falls backwards exaggeratedly, as though I were a ten-ton truck mowing him down.

I stumble and stiffen when he leads me into an unfamiliar step. 'No, no, no.'

He shakes me like a sack of potatoes.

'Why? Why you're not following me?'

I can choose to crumble and cry under the barrage of criticism, or rise to the master's instructions. I choose the latter. After half an hour I am apparently more on my own axis, though I *feel* as if I am leaning backwards. He is gliding around me like a panther – sleek, shiny with sweat. I am close to his dyed-brown hair with its famous centre parting. I can see every line in his face, I can feel his worked body.

He demands that I both occupy my own space and take total responsibility for my own balance during all the moves, and yet simultaneously be completely relaxed and responsive to his every move and lead.

'Fifty, fifty – that's how we must be. The man, the woman, fifty, fifty. It's dialogue.'

I realize that in order for him to glide, to glisten, to shine like the star he is, I must surrender my will and give him space. And yet he says, over and over, 'Be yourself!' And so it is. I surrender false controls and find another, more flexible self.

He is a theatrical performer, even in this little room with only Jeff for an audience. He works full out, his expression as concentrated as it ever is on stage.

An hour later he wipes himself down with a towel and packs his shoes away, then turns to me. Suddenly his face shows some vulnerability.

'Did you enjoy it? Did you?'

I reassure him with praise and thanks.

Afterwards, though I am pale and tired, drunk with lack of sleep and steeped in a curious ambitious yearning, I feel suddenly like a girl in early teenagehood, full of the memory of a vital childhood, bursting with fresh female hormones, open and receptive to an exciting world, on my own feet, but longing to be held.

As the week progresses, this feeling grows and grows. I remember that I have a female body, and I love it. I start to glow and feel both rounded and athletic. Muscles that had vanished years ago reappear in my legs; my shoulders fall back into a long-forgotten alignment; my pelvis hangs free and strong from my spine. And the learning curve is virtually vertical.

Ah, I think to myself. If only I could learn to live the way I dance. If only I could learn to work (to write, to direct) without pretension and self-consciousness, strong and sure and vulnerable and open, all at once – sweating, working, at my own limits and yet easy, flooded with pleasure.

Ah, tango, be my teacher, be my guide, and perhaps I will remember who I really am.

Postscript

Towards the end of my stay, I agree to do a couple of newspaper interviews. I had not managed to come over for the opening of *Orlando* in Argentina, and it had been very well received.

In the first interview with *Clarin*, the biggest daily newspaper, after some discussion about the nature of the tango and why I was here, the interviewer asks me, 'But what has this to do with cinema?'

'Someone said the essence of cinema is movement,' I reply, trying to remember who that person was. 'All directorial decisions are also choreographic ones. Where the camera should be, and should it be moving or still; where the bodies are, and what and how they are communicating. Even the flicker of an eyelash in a strictly realist piece of cinema is also a piece of choreography. And film exists only in time – like dance. To understand movement, I must move. And to make a musical – which I want to do sometime – I must immerse myself in a culture which is itself immersed in the language of dance and music. So I am here both for my own pleasure and as a form of research for a film I want to make.'

The relative clarity I am able to muster in an interview disguises the deep crisis of identity I am, in reality, wrestling with. If I love to dance *this much*, does this mean I should be a dancer? Can I be a serious film-maker *and* whiz off to Buenos Aires to dance the nights away? Just exactly what kind of being am I, that I can be so relentlessly, monkishly dedicated to scriptwriting and cinema on the one hand, then so hedonistically, libidinously immersed in the tango a day later?

And how is it that I can be so allergic to forced sentiment and sloppiness on film, but then weep copiously and shamelessly at the tango lyrics which are a sheer over-the-top, melodramatic expression of raw pain and longing?

And how can I fight tooth and nail and with every brain cell at my disposal against female (and all other forms of) oppression, and then delight in wearing the slinkiest, most figure-hugging clothes and highest stiletto dance shoes I can find?

I guess, like every other individual on earth, I am a complex bundle of contradictory identities and am simply fortunate enough to have the means to express some of them.

On my return to London, hallucinating with lack of sleep and the sheer intensity of the experience, I immediately go out dancing – and do so, compulsively, every night for the next few nights in an attempt to come down.

It may not be quite the same in the Welsh Centre in the Gray's Inn Road, or in the back room in a pub in Brixton, but the aficionados dance and sweat together just the same.

I discover that my focus has shifted while I am away. With each new partner I aim to enable him or her to feel more free, daring and able than they have ever felt before.

As I do this, and feel the difference it makes to them, I realize this is the gift I was given in Buenos Aires. They allowed me to feel more free, daring and able than I had allowed myself to experience for a long time.

It's an infectious process.

Farewell

Finally, there are three elegies.

With the death of Federico Fellini, we lost a dreamer who indulged us with images wondrous to behold. Damien Pettigrew takes us into the heart of his creative process.

Viggo Mortensen's poem for Sandy Dennis stands as testimony to her unique talent.

We felt that the most fitting tribute to Lindsay Anderson would be his own tribute to John Ford, whose centenary we commemorate with this edition of Projections.

Federico Fellini (photo by Damien Pettigrew)

15   Creation and the Artist:
Federico Fellini in conversation
with Damien Pettigrew

Introduction

The idea of a long filmed interview with Fellini first came to me in the summer of 1983 during a week-long stay in Rome with Italo Calvino. I was producing a film-portrait of the writer for Canadian television and since Calvino knew Fellini well, having written the brilliant preface 'Autobiography of a Spectator' for the director's *Quattro Film*, it was inevitable that we discuss Fellini's work. Calvino claimed he'd been 'stunned' by *8½* and that it had provoked a revolution in his critical thoughts on film and the novel. Being not only a great novelist but also kind, Calvino encouraged me in my ambition to produce a document focusing on Fellini's unique creative process. It is grace, then, to his influence that I eventually came into *il maestro*'s favour.

The following excerpt is from an eight-hour conversation with Fellini held in Rome in April 1991, recorded on tape using three Betacam SP cameras. I will not pretend that I really knew Fellini or that Federico became a close friend. I didn't know him long enough for that to happen and, anyway, he had a deep distrust of interviewers whose role, as he saw it, was 'to pry open places that ought to remain closed'. But I think he trusted me in the end and understood that I wasn't out to expose him in some way or obtain a scoop because, during a telephone call in May 1993, he seemed content with the work I'd done to date.

It was 7 a.m. when I received a call at my Paris home. I couldn't imagine who'd be pestering me at that hour and when I picked up, I literally barked 'Allo!' There was a second of silence followed by the familiar 'beep' of a long-distance call. 'Federico?' I asked instinctively. 'Damiano!' replied that feminine, unforgettable voice. 'How ees going your project?' I stammered something like, 'Fine, Sgr Fellini! Just fine.' 'Ah,' he said, 'Ees good to know. I dream last night of Calvino . . . So now I call you.'

It was his last message to me and it sounded, even then, like news from another star.

FEDERICO FELLINI: Allora. Corragio!
DAMIEN PETTIGREW: *Corragio! Graziae.*

FF: Are you afraid to ask me questions?

DP: *No, no. Are you afraid to answer them?*

FF: Yes, of course, but everyone knows I'm a big liar so if your questions are too complicated, over-intellectual, riddled with innuendo, I can always invent anything at all. Besides, it's difficult for me to give short replies because of a natural inclination to waffle, like a lawyer.

DP: *Like Ciceron.*

FF: Like a politician, since you have the right to ask me only two intimate questions. So, first indiscreet question – or first very indiscreet question!

DP: *As we grow older, our lives change along with our original identities. You claim you haven't changed from the young man you were when you first came to live in Rome in 1939. How have you managed to preserve this identity in a career that spans almost half a century?*

FF: That's a most engaging question and the kind a psychiatrist might ask. What do I recognize as the most authentic part of myself? I don't know, quite frankly ... I should think it would be the part involved in my work as a film-maker, as it is for artists in general, for whom creation is a unique way of appropriating the shadows, the sounds, the scents, the identity card, and the images that may reveal a man to himself and through which he can recognize a certain continuity over the passage of time. I'm giving you a rather existentialist point of view reduced to simple, concrete and mundane terms. But it seems to me that even as a child – I'm talking about last week – this feeling of suspension, of waiting, the emotion procured in waiting for something to happen, was embodied in a kind of echo, a sound, a suggestion with which I have always identified.

DP: *The sounds and scents, the key images and emotions we carry with us as part of ourselves, are the memories that we all cherish. Why does an artist choose a particular place, a particular memory?*

FF: We need to distinguish between recollection and memory. Recollection can be recalled or invented, as I've done in the majority of my films. Memory, on the other hand, is completely different: we enter here a dimension somewhere between the paranormal and the spiritual, a zone of the unconscious that we have always inhabited. Memory doesn't express itself through recollection. It is a mysterious component, undefinable almost, but which links us to something we perhaps no longer remember having lived, urging us to enter into contact with dimensions, events, sensations we can't name but that we know, however confusedly, have existed before us. An artist – and you must forgive me this somewhat pompous definition – a creator lives in his memory, constantly remembering people, places and situations that may have never really existed in the context of his life.

DP: *Your films are bathed in nostalgia and I would like to examine the reasons behind this need to evoke your own memories.*

FF: Perhaps I'm going to contradict my previous statements on this subject – above all, the critics who insist that my films are born and breast-fed on my own memories – but I don't have a memory made up of personal recollections. It's simply more natural for me to invent my own, inspired by the memory of things that never existed but which feeds on them or calls them into existence. I think I must have invented everything, including my birth. And if I have invented a self, then I recognize my true self reflected in the mirror of my films.

DP: *And the need to invent yourself?*

FF: It's a natural inclination. I invented a youth, a family, relationships with women and with life. I have always invented. The irrepressible urge to invent is because I don't want anything autobiographical in my films. I invented Guido Anselmi and the critics declared he's me. But Guido is not my alter-ego just as I am not Mastroianni. That would be too simple. In *City of Women*, he's my Snaporaz, a representation of myself in a certain sense but I'm also the role played by Ettore Manni. In *Ginger and Fred*, I'm Marcello and Giulietta, Franco Fabrizzi the TV presenter, and the dwarfs as well. I am everything and nothing. I am what I invent.

DP: *During the preparation of a filmed interview with Italo Calvino, the writer read to me a quotation he treasured: 'The Sphinx is a masterpiece in the Sahara desert and cannot be described as anything other than an illusion. The sphinx has not moved but the men who built it have all disappeared without trace, like a midday mirage.' It seems to me that you share this idea that art makes real.*

FF: I do. That's why I can't respond with precision to your request for specific episodes, fragments of events that actually occurred in my life, because the things that are the most real for me are the ones I've invented in my films. Delacroix affirmed that the most tangible things for a painter are the illusions he creates on his canvas; the rest is air. That's what happened to the town I was born in. I can't deny the fact that I was born in Rimini but the real town has faded and been replaced by the Rimini of my films – *I Vitelloni, Amarcord* – down to the last detail. This deconstruction is much more a part of me, of my life, than the Rimini that exists topographically.

DP: *In response to my question, 'Are novelists liars?' Calvino replied: 'Novelists tell the truth hidden at the bottom of every lie.'*

FF: I always knew I had a robust reason for being the liar I am! Truth may be stranger than fiction, but a lie is always more interesting.

DP: *Because it's more entertaining?*

FF: Because of what it reveals about the liar!

DP: *'I feel suspicious about writers who claim to tell the truth about themselves, about life, or about the world. I prefer to stay with the truths I find in writers who present themselves as the most bold-faced liars.' These are Calvino's words and he might just as well have been talking about you.*

FF: Calvino's right. I think lies are the soul of cinema. Why is it necessary that the image we invent be credible? On the other hand, the emotion behind those images, underlying the dialogue, must be absolutely genuine.

DP: *The obligation to express, then, is focused on the invention of memories, of inventing the past.*

FF: I simply don't think it's possible to distinguish past, present and future, the imagined past from recollections of what actually happened, as distinctly as we assume it is. I tried dealing with that in *8½*. I think someone who tries following his vocation as a story-teller can't make this distinction at the moment he's creating his little universe. The creation of his world is a total one. His subsequent identification with it is total as well.

DP: *Why is the identification a total one?*

FF: Because you must absolutely believe in what you're making and when you believe in your creation, you identify with it. It becomes a universe complete in time and not limited to space or the description of characters. You see, my work is to make films and the way I make them is not just a mode of expression, it's a way of being . . . I film and so I am. To arrive at the heart of a story in film is to reach the centre of myself.

DP: *Is Federico dissatisfied being Fellini?*

FF: No, no, I have a good deal of sympathy for myself. I have certainly had more than my fair share of fame and good fortune. The long narrative that a creator threads into the fabric of his work is the search, on various levels, for a style, a coherence, an essence, a greater spontaneity, to be more sincere, less conceptual, to live the expression itself. In the end, it's the search for the truest, the most authentic part of oneself.

DP: *How would you describe yourself?*

FF: I am fellinian.

DP: *Do you think that your decision to settle in Rome in 1939 was the decisive moment when you discovered that an artistic career was your future?*

FF: Well, I could tell you so many different versions of what happened that I no longer remember which one is the most charming of all the hundreds I've made up. But, for once, the shameless liar would like to be absolutely sincere: I do not recognize any particular acts of will on my part that can be said to be decisive. It doesn't seem to me that I ever made a conscious decision that was influenced by the wish to attain something career-wise. I have been extremely lucky in that respect: situations have always presented themselves to me in a spontaneous, generous way and I simply took them up, naturally and with gratitude, as if all of it were somehow predestined. My sole act of will, if you insist, was in not going against a particular situation but following it. Of course, it's obvious I've taken certain decisions in my life as a film-maker – and this is the most curious contradiction of all – to find myself being forced to make a thousand decisions a day during the course of a production, choosing between one actor and the next, between this red or that blue, this jacket with that pair of pants, a certain hairstyle or a plucking of the eyebrows, this bit of dialogue with that tone of voice punctuated by a long pause or a short one or an abrupt silence altogether. It's a profession where you're constantly called upon to make choices. That said, for life in general, it seems I've never decided or chosen anything that was crucial to my career. I didn't seek out Rossellini for *Rome, Open City* – he came to me – and I'm eternally grateful.

DP: *What about the often anguishing problem of deciding which film to make?*

FF: The same for the films I've made. Once the possibility of two projects presented themselves to me, I chose the one I felt most comfortable with. It's as though I were a train – forgive me this ridiculous comparison – and my films the various stations that the train runs through in a familiar, predetermined itinerary. And so I usually found the films I had to make already waiting for me, in a certain sense. I had to go on to direct them, of course, but they were already clear, well defined. I simply pulled into the station of *I Vitelloni* in 1953, another in 1969 that was *Satyricon*, and another in 1990 called *The Voice of the Moon*. I don't recall having scripted with precision any film I made because they were already ripe inside me, already set for production and, to a certain degree, already directed. They simply had to be directed in a concrete way, if you like. I suppose that's why I frighten producers so much.

DP: *What place, if any, does delirium have in your working life?*

FF: I make a film as if I have a disease, suffering hot and cold sweats on an hourly basis, hovering constantly between ecstasy and anguish, lucidity and confusion. Everything is done in a kind of fever. Once the film is over, I fool myself into thinking I'm cured.

DP: *I would like to know if you think creation is similar to variations on a theme, to improvisation?*

FF: I don't think that the word improvisation has any bearing on the creative, artistic process. It's a word I consider utterly inadequate, even irritating. No, I wouldn't speak of improvisation here; I'd use other terms: receptivity, being open-minded. I would say that it's necessary to be receptive, open, responsive to the thing that is struggling to be born but which is still unformed and magma-like, confused, undefined. The creator is there to materialize it, to help shape it, to suggest a certain confused world or a particular emotion that belongs to a particular dimension. Any artist who is called upon to paint a painting, compose an opera, write a novel or direct a film, must maintain a certain availability, what I would call receptivity. That's the word. Not improvisation. He must give himself up entirely to the phantom or creature that slowly begins to appear. An artist mustn't become entangled in the pretension of wanting to shape the creature exactly as he had first imagined it according to the parameters, the rules of his culture or his own ignorance, his political or aesthetic ideology.

No, he must surrender confidently to the suggestions that the creature will offer him – even during the most difficult moments, such as the unexpected illness of a key actor on whom one can no longer depend, or the violent but inevitable dispute with the producer, or the fact that the director falls ill himself. He can interpret all of these events as impeding the vital flow of the film, but also as necessary evils that force him to make changes, transformations, improvements that he would never have thought of had he not been possessed of this receptivity, this particular ear and eye attuned to the process that slowly defines itself day after day. The creature is born by ignoring what you've spent months preparing to film and if you can get the oxygen circulating, nothing else is necessary. The first two weeks, I direct the film; after that, it's the film that directs me. I believe in that profoundly, despite the limits imposed by it and of which I am aware.

DP: *Would you say that your emotional state has a direct influence on your work?*

FF: During the winter, it often happens that I arrive at the studios with a bad cold but even if I'm running a temperature the cold and fever will invariably disappear. I'll warn my assistants who'll suddenly panic and phone the doctor to reassure the producer that work won't be interrupted and I have to insist that all the fuss is unnecessary since I'll be perfectly well in a few minutes, if left alone. And in fact it's the atmosphere in the studio and the kind of work I do, the people I work with – scriptwriters, actors, make-up people, gaffers, grips, cameramen – all of it is profoundly therapeutic for me. In thirty minutes, a fever of 38° will disappear and I can begin working. It's a kind of subconscious yoga practice, that of finding oneself exactly in the place where one ought to be at the right time, and all is well. However, it's not the kind of therapeutic advice I'd want to share with everyone who's caught the flu: 'Come to Cinecitta, Damiano! Soak your feet in a film and you'll be cured!' That would be very costly treatment when two aspirins is all you need. But seriously, even if I can work during an illness, I never allow myself to be conditioned by a particular mood except if it's completely at the service of the game I am directing.

DP: *Do you ever need to isolate yourself during a film shoot?*

FF: No, I don't make films holed up in a monastery!

DP: *What about when you're writing a script?*

FF: I polished the script of *La Dolce Vita* in a hotel in Fregene with Tullio Pinelli and Ennio Flaiano over several weeks . . . I would say that some of my ideas, characters, dialogue, come to me when I'm in a car or on a train. At the time when I had a car – I gave up driving; it's suicidal today – I used to go anywhere at any time just to look at the trees, the sky, the colours, the faces that would pass by me in silence. Once I had two or three ideas, I'd stop by the roadside and write them down.

DP: *Is your method at all similar to a kind of automatic writing in the sense that the scene is rehearsed and then a rush of various ideas and attitudes suggest themselves to you?*

FF: Automatic writing is linked to an unconscious abandon and as far as I know, I'm not a surrealist. The life I depict in *The Voice of the Moon* and the family relationships I established – this fellow was the uncle, this boy the nephew, this girl the daughter – once created, are then observed with enormous attention to detail, a deliberate awareness that leaves nothing to chance. You know from day one where it is you have to go and you discover, in the dark, what you need. It's when everything is clear, defined, laid out in front of you, that you lose your way. This may shock you, but I directed *The Voice of the Moon* by writing each day's scene the night before on a piece of paper.

DP: *A completed scenario would only hamper the vitality you create on the set?*

FF: At the risk of appearing immodest, I have to confess that scripts, ideas, stories, dialogue, the tall dark stranger, his gun and the beautiful blonde are useless to me. I want, need, to take risks in the dream laboratory called Cinecitta. I've always taken risks, even as far back as *The White Sheik*, *La Strada*, *Nights of Cabiria*, when I was using the streets as my lab. Flaiano, Pinelli and I collaborated on a script, a producer was brought in, and I shot the film each day with the aim of being open and receptive to chance circumstances, to whatever and whomever might contribute to the vitality of the scene I was shooting. It's in my nature to take risks. Why would I change at this late stage?

DP: *Anthony Quinn recalls how, during the making of* La Strada, *you devoted an impressive amount of time to obtaining the precise matchbox that someone like Zampano would own. He was amazed at the persistence involved, especially when the accessory was never once filmed.*

FF: Whatever it is you want to express artistically deserves the maximum of rigour possible. Anything less is betrayal. A film-maker's greatest enemy is compromise. Life is meticulous, so how can an artistic expression be otherwise? An artist has the possibility of making something more real than reality itself. Approximation irritates me. Life appears to us as governed by chance, but it is nothing if not exact. A green must be exactly that particular shade of green, just as it is for a painter, and a face must be precisely that particular face, capable of expressing what it must express the moment it appears on screen. Once you begin approximating your vision, there's no end to the damage.

DP: *Would you describe yourself as a perfectionist?*

FF: I would.

DP: *But you seem almost too impatient to be one.*

FF: My closest collaborators tell me I'm impatient, that it's a flaw in my character. I don't agree at all and get very impatient with them.

DP: *Could we talk about magic?*

FF: What can one say about magic? I am curious. Everything interests me and I

believe in all of it. This seems to me the sanest, healthiest way of accom-
modating the irrational. And anyway, how could I be cynical, over-cautious,
sceptical, with the line of work I'm in? I make a living in a high-risk industry
that never ceases to prove that I'm mad! I dream, I imagine something, and
then pull it out of my hat in front of millions of people. Call it what you like,
but for me it's magic. I ask you, how is that possible? How is it possible that I,
for the most part ignorant of politics, philosophy or some other protective
ideology, lacking any true overwhelming passion – I've remained an adolescent
filled with wonder and curiosity at best – how is it possible that I could have
accomplished what it takes to make a film? I'm not talking about aesthetic
results, but rather the operation itself. It all seems beyond me and I say this
sincerely. So, how can I not believe in magic?

DP: *Would this help explain why your films are often self-reflexive, metacinematic?*

FF: In part. I'm genuinely awestruck by what my technicians are capable of
doing, by the very nature of what film is, by the phenomenon of light recorded
on a photographic plate, to the extent that I want simply to stand back and film
what I'm filming, rejoicing in this hall of mirrors that the studio has suddenly
become. However, it's not limited to only that.

DP: *One can't have a conversation with Fellini without bringing up the topic of woman
and women. You've expressed your views often enough on this rather tired subject, but
I'd like you to try and tell me honestly what woman means for you.*

FF: She is the representation of the eternal principle of creation, the yang in
yin, the dark in light . . . I mean, you can't honestly expect me to add anything
new to what I've said *ad nauseam*, can you?

DP: *I'm being unfair. But would you say you understand women?*

FF: No, but then do we ever really understand another person, leaving aside
this problem of the sexes?

DP: *Do you conceive women as a superior force that touches on the vitalistic principle
you outlined earlier? Do you see a link between the two?*

FF: Yes, I do in fact. It seems to me that this concept belongs to the realm of
myth, to legend and to the discovery of certain psychological intuitions, that
women, for men in general and especially for the artist, are a constant
inspirational source that is profoundly nourishing.

DP: *Nourishing like mother's milk?*

FF: It's a very Italian image that I've used once or twice in my films. I repeat,
woman is a mediatrix, an ambassadress and thus a powerful stimulus.

DP: *What role does sexuality play in your creativity?*

FF: For me, directing is a release of creative tension and energy which places
me at the top of my form. I'm blessed, at ease with myself and it seems that all I
need is sex. I exist, I live my dream which is the reality of the film. My tedious,
daily problems return once the film is over and I go on complaining until I'm
back in the studio again.

DP: *Could we say that the fellinian woman is a projection of your own image?*

FF: That's something that I won't admit to! I hear it expressed often enough and you repeat it but, surely as Flaubert said: '*Madame Bovary, c'est moi.*'

DP: *Is narcissism an essential vice for the artist?*

FF: Beyond the element of amusement that is creation, the invention of a world, of characters and situations, and the resolution of an incredible number of technical problems, of craftsmanship, but above all, of expression, there exists a more profound, more secret, more impudent satisfaction that has to do with the myth of Narcissus and the idea of an almost quasi-divine power. A creator almost always has an air of God the Father about him, the exception being that we take a little longer than seven days to make a world. So, a novelist, a storyteller speaks only about himself. He's obliged, forced to speak only about himself.

DP: *Why forced?*

FF: People think that film-making is a 35mm camera and that the reality around us is there to be photographed simply and directly, when in actual fact the director *behind* the camera always puts himself *in front* of it. If not, his cinema offers us a contradictory reality. By expressing his private sphere of emotions and dreams, his proper vision of the world – by not trying to be objective – an artist is more faithful to reality.

DP: *In your view, what is the essential component of film?*

FF: The image, of course! What else could it possibly be? If I were to ask you, 'What is the essential element of painting?' what would you reply? 'Light, tonality . . . '

DP: *Yes, light, tonality, composition, and a lot of other things.*

FF: Well, for film it's the image.

DP: *And the importance of light?*

FF: Without light, you don't have an image and without the image, you don't have cinema. Light is everything. It expresses ideology, emotion, colour, depth, style. It can efface, narrate, describe. With the right lighting, the ugliest face, the most idiotic expression can radiate with beauty or intelligence.

DP: *Does light take precedence over dialogue?*

FF: In my work, dialogue is of little importance when compared to it.

DP: *Wittgenstein, among others, noted that language was a kind of screen between us and reality and the reason why true creativity often begins where language ends. Does this seem absurd to you?*

FF: Not at all. I think we constantly live a contradiction where words mask reality more than they reveal it, like a lighthouse enveloped in fog. Transforming reality into representation is perhaps simply another of the many – albeit more amusing – ways of deceiving oneself and so I think my interest in dreams is due, in part, to their concentration on images independent of words.

DP: *Is it necessary that a film director invent his own style?*

FF: I don't know if someone could feel obliged to be original. Originality is something you have or you don't. You can't go and buy it somewhere.

DP: *Should a film director cultivate his roots in order to make good films?*

FF: I don't think an artist is fully capable of expressing himself except in his own language and that's the reason why I could never accept all the film proposals put to me by American producers. I can't deny the fact that I'm Italian, profoundly Italian, having been educated and lived my whole life here in Italy, which is a country that remains to be entirely told in film. Italian cinema is guilty because it has never managed to really express Italy. The same for Italian literature: we're a completely unknown country because of it. Perhaps Rome has been told a little. Naples, too, but only in a folkloric way. Sicily is forever seen in terms of its truculent Mafiosi history. But the rest of Italy – the real Italy where every fifty kilometres there's witness of another culture, of different myths and customs – goes untold and that's unfortunate because it's really an unbelievable country.

DP: *You can only express yourself, then, in the language and the culture you belong to. You could never go and film, for example, in the American desert like Antonioni did in* Zabriskie Point?

FF: No, never. I can only do it through the filter of memory which decants, decomposes, goes to the heart of things. I don't seem to understand anything in a foreign country and I return weighed down with useless information. Abroad, I'm blind.

DP: *I'd like to talk, if we could, about the relationship between a director and his actors.*

FF: It's part of a game that exists between the puppeteer and his puppets. It's a collaboration: the puppets are happy to be puppets if the puppeteer is a good master. I have never had problems with actors, even with the most temperamental ones, simply because I love actors. I've always loved them. I find them immensely sympathetic. I love their infantile side, their extroversion, their caprices ... Psychologically, they're fascinating. I can be very physical with my actors, but it's not just to get what I want from them. I try to create an atmosphere of confidence on the set and so I'm very affectionate with them.

DP: *How do you go about choosing an actor?*

FF: In a very precise way since the story is incarnated in the faces. I start by making drawings of the characters as I imagine them. Then I audition the hundreds that show up and pin photographs of hundreds more on a large board in my office. As I say, the face has to coincide with the one I have in my head, but I'm also open to new possibilities, to the unexpected, to chance. For example, sometimes I'll choose a face that has absolutely nothing to do with the one which I've drawn and set out to find. But it works in the end because the result is more original than what I'd previously imagined.

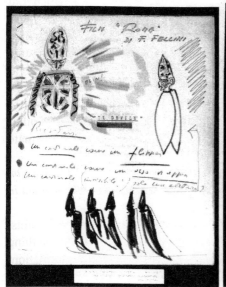

Drawing for *Roma*

DP: *Do you have a particular process that consists of transforming a real person into a fellinian character?*

FF: Well, that's what my work is all about ... I don't have a particular system that I practise religiously. I'm faithful to one thing only: the principle of being receptive by placing myself wholly at the service of the fantasies I want to materialize. I never make the mistake of adapting the actor to a character. I tailor the role to the individual. Every film is different from the next and every moment completely different from every other moment. So, I don't have a system. I couldn't establish a film school. My sole guide is receptivity, open-mindedness. What is an artist, after all? An artist is a medium. In a certain sense, he's only a mind, a network of nerves, a body, hands: a simulacrum destined to be inhabited by a kind of dream, a fantasy, by an idea, a sentiment, which then becomes characters and situations, a story. An artist's sole imperative is to succeed in materializing his story through experience and craftsmanship. A medium-artisan.

DP: *There is the idea that suffering and the lack of financial security are indispensable for the artist. What is the most propitious atmosphere for an artist, in your view?*

FF: When he's obliged to work, period.

DP: *As you get older, do you have a tendency to disagree with what the young do? In* The Voice of the Moon, *for example, you're particularly ferocious with the younger generation.*

FF: The young watch television twenty-four hours a day, they don't read and they rarely listen. This incessant bombardment of images has developed a hypertrophied eye condition that's turning them into a race of mutants. They should pass a law for a total re-education of the young, making children visit the Galleria Borghese on a daily basis.

DP: *Susan Sontag believes that television is worse than heroin.*

FF: Generally speaking, I think television has betrayed the meaning of democratic speech, adding visual chaos to the confusion of voices. What role does silence have in all this noise? *La Dolce Vita* announced the arrival of the consumer society in Italy. *Ginger and Fred* was an attempt to narrate the mutation of our society into one where the myths we need to survive and once had in popular culture have degenerated into game shows where someone with more teeth than a piano spins a wheel shouting, 'My kingdom for a microwave oven!' By replacing experience with this unending flow of obdurate electronic images, we've grown dependent on a virtual reality which is simply a fancy word for an eye laxative. Cinema has the capacity to offer us a high density of meaning by mobilizing each gesture, each colour, each word, each element into a single image. Television, on the contrary, can offer only the meaning of the facts that are being transmitted.

DP: *There's one biographical detail I'd like to clarify. What's the real date of your birth, because apparently it's in dispute.*

FF: When was I born? Why? Are you also an astrologist? *Va bene!* I was born on the 20 January 1920, a lot of years ago now. But as the poet said, 'Nothing is known. Everything is imagined.'

DP: *So that makes you a Capricorn.*

FF: Yes. Capricorns are pessimistic, in general, I'm not, however, in spite of everything: wars, pollution, AIDS ... Curiosity is something to cultivate if we expect to survive. It gives you a kind of alibi, the strength to continue. You know, I once stayed in a large psychiatric hospital as a voluntary patient – I repeat voluntary – to conduct research for a film I wanted to do. This was more than thirty years ago. Enclosed within the four walls of this kind of city of madmen, I felt strangely free. It gave me a sense of freedom impossible to describe, but which was based on the reality created by the imagination, the reality each of us sees peering over the walls of our personal prisons. So, perhaps curiosity can justify a life: to observe and to discover. Are you pessimistic?

DP: *Yes.*

FF: But, in any case, what can you do? What else can we do except observe with affection and irony, and try to do only what we are capable of doing, what we do with pleasure.

(Extract taken from *Federico Fellini: Je suis un grand menteur*, published in France by L'Arche editeur. Translated from the Italian by Damien Pettigrew.)

'I adore interviews!'

16   Missing Sandy Dennis
Viggo Mortensen

There are always moments, sometimes entire scenes and characters, that are cut out of a movie. For anyone who takes an active interest in the story they are helping to tell, whatever their capacity in a production, there is bound to be a degree of mental and emotional adjustment that has to be made between reading the proposed shooting script and viewing the finished work. Often, what is lost – what has been altered or discarded along the way as a result of rewriting, rescheduling, editing, dubbing, or scoring – can play as important a role in shaping one's overall perception of the movie as anything that actually ends up on the screen. Even when one understands and agrees with decisions to change significantly what has been written or shot, the spirit of what was attempted not only lingers in one's memory of the process, but can also colour one's judgement of how well-accomplished the movie finally is. Like it or not, for most of the people involved, their job is completed by others in the windowless rooms of editing bays and sound stages. At times this can be very frustrating. The trick is to find a way of continuing to care about one's contribution and yet be able to walk away when the job is done with a minimum of second-guessing and regret. It can take a long time and many movies to achieve that kind of balance. I know that, as an actor, I am still struggling with this.

Someone who was capable of giving herself completely to a performance and yet still managed to move on immediately, only glancing back at her work with unsentimental objectivity, was Sandy Dennis. Indeed she may have struggled for years to become as self-possessed and pragmatic about her acting as she was when I first met her in 1982, though it is hard for me to imagine that she ever had much trouble in restricting the visible drama of her life exclusively to her performances. Having won critical, as well as a degree of popular success early on, including Tony awards for *A Thousand Clowns* (1961) and *Any Wednesday* (1962), and an Oscar for *Who's Afraid of Virginia Woolf?* (1966), she none the less had a fair amount of trouble getting good roles and making a living throughout her career.

During the last twenty years of her life, though respected by many for her stage work and occasionally given a movie role in which she could shine (such as *The Out-Of-Towners* [1970], *The Four Seasons* [1981], *Come Back to the Five and Dime, Jimmy Dean, Jimmy Dean* [1982], *Another Woman* [1988] and *The Indian Runner* [1991]), she found herself largely marginalized by critics and by those with the power to hire. This was particularly true within the movie industry, where she was generally dismissed – when remembered at all – as a quirky has-been, a benign but overly complicated and totally unbankable actress. She did not complain about this, other than – very rarely – to wonder out loud how she was going to make ends meet and care for the many stray cats and dogs she had taken in over the years. She did not dwell on the past and never claimed to be the victim of injustice, personal or professional, though a case could easily be made for that being so. She was essentially a modest woman with a great gift, one which she enjoyed sharing, as both an actress and a teacher of actors. A professional artist in the best sense.

In 1990, it was my good fortune to work on what would prove to be her last movie. She played the role of the mother to David Morse's 'Joe' and my 'Frank' in Sean Penn's directorial debut, *The Indian Runner*. Charles Bronson played our father, and the cast also included Patricia Arquette, Valeria Golino and Dennis Hopper. When I first met with Sean Penn and his producer, Don Phillips, to discuss the possibility of my playing Frank, one of the first questions I asked them was who, if anyone, they had in mind to play the mother. When Sean answered that he did not want to consider anyone other than Sandy Dennis for the part, I couldn't have been happier, or more in agreement. Aside from my feelings for her as a friend, I believed she would be a great asset to the movie and would inspire us all to do our best. This proved to be true.

As it turned out, however, most of what she did was cut out of the movie. This was not due to any shortcoming on her part. On the contrary, she was brilliant throughout. The bulk of her role was in one eight-page scene in which Frank is taken by Joe to visit their parents for the first time since returning from a three-year tour in Vietnam. Frank is ill-at-ease from the start, and we gather that his relationship with his parents is not a very good one. Joe tries to keep the peace, as is his wont, but Frank rejects their hospitality and attempts at small-talk, insults them and eventually storms out of the house. This is particularly devastating to his ailing mother, who dies not long after. On viewing the assembled footage back in Los Angeles, it was decided that the story would work better if Frank refused to visit his mother and father and, in fact, never saw them again. A subsequent scene was shot in January 1991 to support this plot change.

I agree with the decision; dramatically the movie works better without the home-coming scene. It is perhaps more cruel and a greater source of guilt for Frank that he chose not to see his mother before she died. What I do miss, however, is seeing Sandy's performance in the scene, and having others see it too. She was working on a level far above the rest of us. The concentration and vulnerability that she invested in the scene were remarkable. Heart-breaking. The fact that most of us knew that she was dying of ovarian cancer as she showed us the emotional disintegration of the character made the experience all the more poignant.

I will always remember the three days we spent working on that ambitious scene: the sense of family, the pride in acting with her, the undercurrent of loss. She left Omaha and her native Nebraska, returning to New York the day after completing her job with us. That was the last time I saw her.

Sandy Dennis and Viggo Mortensen in *The Indian Runner* [the scene that was cut (photo by Michael Tighe)]

For Sandy Dennis

1

In an Omaha steakhouse full of indian summer
sunday dinner feasting families you modestly
celebrated what you knew would be the closest
thing to a goodbye glimpse of home by eating
and drinking as if willing the red-robed walls to
fall on our table without a thought for the candle
flame that would surely get sucked out as the
particle board and plywood left the door frames
and windowsills behind and rushed to the floor
with a last gasp of generations of paint and
wallpaper glue swirling into your lungs.

2

No movie can show your eyes as they looked
after completing one last scene playing our
mother, when you limped outside worn out and
uncomplaining to squeeze onto the flimsy,
rusted seat of a child's swingset for a photo
opportunity. Your shaky hands gripped the
chains and I felt your back tense with the strain
of holding onto the unbearably ripe fruit of a
half-stomach, but you allowed your swollen feet –
at last freed of those horrible sandals – to trail
back and forth through the cool September
grass of the unmowed backyard.

3

You're packed and ready to go early the next
morning, sitting on the well-made bed in a fresh
dress and humming slightly out of breath with
the radio, done hours ago with fighting off
dreams.

4

You've pulled apart the heavy hotel drapes to let
in the sun, and exclaim that there isn't a cloud in
all that blue as if you'd never seen such a sky.

5

I carry your suitcase downstairs and we embrace
in the driveway. I worry that I'm holding you too
tight, and start to let go. Refusing to let me take
you to the airport, you kiss me on the cheek and
get in the taxi.

Sandy Dennis in the 1960s (photo by Vytas Valaitis)

17 Meeting in Dublin:
The Quiet Man, 1950
Lindsay Anderson

'I'm a quiet, gentle person.'
John Ford

It is futile to attempt to envisage beforehand what places, people will be like. Inevitably, though, images form in the mind. They certainly had plenty of time to form in mine, for by the time I actually got to see John Ford I had crossed Ireland twice, trusting the telegram I had received to say that the *Quiet Man* unit would be shooting in Cong (in Ford's – or rather his father's – native Galway) till the end of the week. By the time I got there the unit had left. So back I crawled to Dublin, hoping to catch Ford before he flew off to America the next day.

A succession of slowly moving trains and buses had by this time lent to the journey a dream-like quality, not inappropriate to a pilgrimage to the source of a well-loved myth. About Ford himself I felt no temptation to speculate; as my last bus stopped and started its way through the Dublin suburbs I found that I had almost ceased to believe in his existence. What of the setting in which I should find him? I imagined something large, rather formidable; an aloof Georgian or nineteenth-century mansion staffed with a squad of retainers, furnished in mahogany, with soft carpets and tall, dark rooms. I was, anyway, quite unprepared for the trim, very contemporary little suburban home in front of which the conductor set me down; neat front lawn, paved path from the gate, aproned parlourmaid to open the front door. Voices and the clink of knives made it clear that supper was still in progress; I was shown into the front room. But I had scarcely time to sink into a chair and look around me when footsteps sounded outside, the door opened and Ford came in with a rush.

Bypassing the stage of first impressions, we seemed to be plunged straight into familiarity. But let me try. A bulky man, craggy as you would expect, sandy hair thinned and face deeply lined. Eyes hidden behind dark-lensed spectacles. Informal in clothes as in manner; he wore an old sports coat and a pair of grubby grey flannels, his shirt was open at the neck. He flopped into an armchair, in which, as we talked, he shifted from position to position of relaxed comfort – legs crossed, then one up over the arm of the chair, then both. Speech forthright, with a matching ruggedness of vocabulary. Frank; responsive to frankness; a bit impatient, but ready to listen.

He was sorry to have missed me in Galway; they were behind schedule on the picture and, once finished, had no thought but to get away at once, back to

Lindsay Anderson

John Ford

Hollywood to polish off the interiors. He did not seem altogether happy about the experience. 'Something seemed to get into people down there. I guess it must have been the climate.' Had the rain held up shooting? 'No, the weather was all right – that softness is fine with Technicolor. But the unit seemed to go soft too; they started standing about looking at the scenery. I had to start watching for points of continuity – people looking out of windows, that sort of thing, which no one else noticed. Then, of course, our technicians work a lot faster than yours. It was really too big a job for one man to tackle on his own ... I'm just going back to making Westerns.' He looked at me. 'Of course, you're one of the people who think it's a disgrace the way I keep turning out these Westerns.' I protested. 'Yes, you do. You've written that, haven't you? I'm sure I read that somewhere.' One other thing from that article had caught in his memory. 'And what was that you said about me being anti-British?' I told him. ('A true Irishman, Ford has no time for the English.') He laughed, but took pains to deny it. 'I've got more British than I have American friends ... Of course, you must remember I'm Irish – we have a reputation to keep up.'

   About here I made an attempt to pull myself together and be businesslike. I asked if I might get my notebook (which I had left in the hall) and ask some questions. 'Carry on,' said Ford, but with a slight unease. 'I'm not a career man, you know,' he announced defensively. 'I don't suppose I've given more than four interviews in my life. And now two in an evening ...' He did not speak as if the prospect attracted him. 'Christ,' he said, 'I hate pictures. When people ask me if I've seen some actress or other, I say "Not unless she was in *The Great Train Robbery* or *Birth of a Nation*. Then perhaps I've seen her.

Otherwise, no."' I said, 'Why do you go on with them?' 'Well, I like *making* them of course . . . But it's no use asking me to talk about art . . .'

We chatted for a bit about Ford's early days in the cinema. How had he started directing? 'I just started,' he explained. (He had gone out to California at the age of nineteen, after three unprofitable weeks at the University of Maine, to work for his brother Francis – at that time an established star and director.) He began making Westerns in 1917, when he was twenty-two. 'I can't remember much about them, now,' he said. 'We made about one a week. I directed them and Harry Carey acted them. All those early ones were written by Carey and me – or stolen. We didn't really have scripts, just a rough continuity . . .' But he well remembered the making of *The Iron Horse*, his railroad epic of 1924. 'We went up there prepared for routine Hollywood weather – all sunshine and blue skies. We got out of the train in a blizzard and nearly froze to death . . . We lived in a circus train, had to dig our own latrines, build up a whole town around us. Saloons opened up; the saloon-girls moved in . . . The whole thing was very exciting.'

Suddenly we had skipped twenty years and were talking about *They Were Expendable*. Perhaps Ford's attitude towards this film so dumbfounded me that a whole tract of conversation was wiped from my memory. As a matter of fact, we were both dumbfounded. He was looking at me in extreme surprise. 'You really think that's a good picture?' He was amazed. 'I just can't believe that film's any good.' I was amazed. 'But – didn't you want to make it?' Ford snorted. 'I was ordered to do it. I wouldn't have done it at all if they hadn't agreed to make over my salary to the men in my unit.' (Naval, not film.) He added: 'I have never *actually* seen a goddamned foot of that film.' I told him that horrified me. 'I'll use the same word,' he said, 'I was horrified to have to make it . . .' 'Didn't you feel at least that you were getting something into it even though you hadn't wanted to take it on?' He scorned the idea. 'Not a goddamned thing,' he said,'I didn't put a goddamned thing into that picture.' He had been pulled out of the front line to make it, had just lost thirteen men from his unit, and had to go back to Hollywood to direct a lot of actors who wouldn't even cut their hair to look like sailors. I said I found this particularly extraordinary because the film contains so much that needn't have been there if it had been made just as a chore. 'What, for instance?' I made example of the old boat-builder (played by Russell Simpson), who appears only in a few shots, yet emerges as a fully and affectionately conceived person. Ford relented slightly: 'Yes, I liked that . . .' He shifted his ground: 'The trouble was, they cut the only bits I liked . . . Is that scene in the shell-hole still there, between the priest and the boy who says he's an atheist?' 'What priest?' I asked. 'Played by Wallace Ford.' 'There's no priest in the film at all.' This surprised him. I said I found it extraordinary that one could cut a whole (presumably integral) character from a story without leaving any trace. 'MGM could,' said Ford. I said:

They Were Expendable

Rio Grande

'But *Expendable* runs two and a quarter hours as it is . . .' Ford said: 'I shot the picture to run an hour and forty minutes – it should have been cut down to that.' I said that this could not be done without ruining the film. 'I think I know more about making pictures than you do,' said Ford.

He asked me what the music was like; he said he had fierce arguments when the MGM music department had shown him the score they intended to put over it. 'But surely – it's full of just the tunes you always like to use in your pictures.' But Ford had found it too thickly orchestrated, too symphonic. 'I wanted almost no music in it at all – just in a very few places like "Red River Valley" over Russell Simpson's last scene. We played and recorded that as we shot it. Otherwise I didn't want any music; the picture was shot as a documentary, you know. No reflectors were used at any time, and we kept the interiors dark and realistic.' He asked if that last shot was still in, with the aeroplane flying out and the Spanish rower silhouetted against the sky, and what music was over it. He seemed satisfied when I told him it was 'The Battle Hymn of the Republic'.

But chiefly Ford was amazed at the thought that anyone could find *They Were Expendable* an even tolerable picture. 'John Wayne had it run for him just recently – before he went back to the States. And afterwards he said to me: "You know, that's still a great picture." I thought he was just trying to say something nice about it, but perhaps he really meant it.'

I asked him about the music in his pictures generally: how close was the relationship between himself and the musical director on the pictures he had made at Fox? 'Very close – we knew each other very well. I think you can say that I'm responsible for the faults or the qualities of the music we used in those pictures.' (Films like *Young Mr Lincoln*, *The Grapes of Wrath*, *My Darling Clementine*.)

I tried to switch from the particular to a more general view: what was Ford's bird's-eye view of his career; of that astonishing trail? Looking back, did he trace periods of exploration and discovery; the series of pictures he had made with Dudley Nichols, for instance, how did he now feel about them? Ford countered: 'What pictures did I make with Nichols?' 'Well . . . *The Long Voyage Home*, *The Fugitive*, *The Informer*.' 'Oh,' said Ford, 'so Nichols wrote *The Informer*, did he?' He resisted implacably, in fact, any attempt to analyse his motives in picking subjects. 'I take a script and I just do it.' Even when I suggested that there were some films (apart from *They Were Expendable*) that he must have undertaken with reluctance, I got nowhere. He had *enjoyed* making *Wee Willie Winkie*, and was charmed by Shirley Temple, now as then. The nearest he would come to discrimination was: 'Sometimes I get a story that interests me more than others . . .' Such as *The Quiet Man*, which he had wanted to do for ten years. 'It's the first love story I've ever tried. A mature love story.'

Singly, he would comment on films I mentioned. How did he feel now about *The Informer?* 'I don't think that's one of my best,' said Ford. 'It's full of tricks. No, I think that comes quite a long way down the list.' His favourite is *Young Mr Lincoln*: 'I've a copy of that at home, on 16mm. I run that quite often ...' He thought. 'Now let me see ... What other pictures have I got copies of? Not many ... *The Lost Patrol* – I still enjoy that one; and I think I may have a copy of *Yellow Ribbon.*' He is fond of *How Green Was My Valley* and *The Fugitive*. ('I just enjoy myself looking at it.') With some trepidation I asked about a personal favourite – *My Darling Clementine*. 'I never saw it,' said Ford.

We talked for a bit about the Westerns to which he has devoted himself since *The Fugitive*. I asked if they had been undertaken primarily to make money. 'Oh, yes. I had to do something to put my company back on its feet after what we lost on that. And they've done it.' All these films, apparently, from *Apache* to *Rio Grande* have achieved commercial success – particularly (which surprised me) *The Three Godfathers*. Since Ford gave the impression of anticipating attack about them, I made the point that the objection was less to the fact that they were 'just Westerns', than to the carelessness with which, too often, they seemed to have been put together. I asked if it wasn't true that *Fort Apache* was shot deliberately in a hurry and under budget, as it appeared to be. 'Yes, it was,' Ford admitted, then scratched his head. 'Now what was that one about? Oh yes, that was a very concocted story. But very good box-office.' *She Wore a Yellow Ribbon*, he said, was made even quicker than *Fort Apache*, though it was a picture he liked. And so was *Wagonmaster*. 'I really tried to do something with that.' When I instanced crudities that seemed to me to disfigure some of these films, Ford countered with the familiar arguments of finance. 'I think you're being too demanding,' he said. 'These refinements cost money – and all the time there's that tremendous pressure of money on top of you. You do the best you can ... And remember that with all these pictures I wasn't just working to pay off on *The Fugitive*, but to make enough for *The Quiet Man* as well. Of course, it'll probably lose the lot again, but that's the way it always goes.'

Another point Ford made about his recent Westerns, or rather about his reasons for making them, was more personal. Holding up his left hand he said, 'It looks all right, but it isn't.' Injuries inherited from the war give him, intermittently, a good deal of pain; they had put him out of action for a few days on *The Quiet Man* and generally made studio shooting – in the glare and oppressive atmosphere of a sound stage – a penance. 'I was out in Korea before coming to Ireland – I made a documentary there called *This is Korea* – and oddly enough I never had a twinge. But out at Cong it really got me down.' He could even, as a result, envisage *The Quiet Man* being his last picture; at any rate, after it, he would have to take a good long rest.

In the end we talked for about an hour and a half, and I forgot all the questions I had meant to ask. I prepared to take my leave. But first Ford had a question he wanted to put to Maureen O'Hara in front of me. (I had not realized before that this was her family's home where Ford was staying.) 'Now, Maureen,' he said, 'have you ever heard me talk of a film called *They Were Expendable* – or have you ever seen it when we've had a show at the house?' 'No,' said Miss O'Hara, 'I haven't.' 'You see?' Ford said, 'But we'll put it on when we get back. The kids will like the boats anyway.'

We shook hands and Ford went out into the garden to talk. 'He's a great man,' said Miss O'Hara. 'And a wonderful director to work for. In other films you'll be just mediocre; then with him ... ' I asked her how he did it. 'He seems to know just what's necessary to get a good performance from anyone; some people he'll be entirely gentle with, and with others he'll be a brute. But you don't mind because, when you see it on the screen, you realize why.' I asked her about the last scene of *Rio Grande*, Ford's most recent picture. The band plays 'Dixie' as the cavalry rides past – Captain York's olive branch to his Southern wife, received by her not with tears or sentiment, but with mischief and a parasol provocatively twirled. 'Whose idea was that?' I asked, 'Oh, his,' she laughed, 'he told me to do that.'

As the foregoing has probably made plain, Ford is pretty well interview-proof. This is not to say that my hour and a half was not a memorable one, but it was not exactly rich in generalizations, personal pronouncements readily quotable to illustrate the view of John Ford on the film as an art. About other people's films he professed himself uninterested, and certainly it requires a stretch of the imagination to visualize him 'going to the cinema'. Of his own hundred-odd films he was quite willing to talk, or at least to answer questions, but he shied away from any invitation to generalize. They were like, as he spoke of them, stories that he has told, some with more care and enjoyment than others. Some he remembers, some he has all but forgot-ten; all are of the past. 'The best in this kind are but shadows.' At one point, when I broke off for a moment to refer to William Wootten's Index of his films, he reached over and took it from my hand. 'I suppose I ought to have one of these,' he said as he inspected it, but there was no conviction in his tone.

How far this impression of a first meeting corresponds with the truth, I am in no position to say. Any such talk has to be seen in its context: a director in mid-film, at the end of six trying weeks on location, somewhat wary perhaps at being thus pursued to an interview for the first time for a number of years. And at any time (one senses) Ford is a man who speaks by mood, from impulse rather than reflection, and without much concern to qualify – he might very well contradict any of his statements the next day. For instance, it is obvious to anyone who knows his films that his attitude towards his craft has not been always as instinctive, as unconcerned with questions of style and subject, as it pleased him to make out. But in a single interview there was no opportunity of breaking past this firmly held position.

There remained the man. It is natural that anecdotists should concentrate on his wild Irish temper, his fondness for horseplay, the violence of his conflicts with producers and high-stepping actresses; and there is no reason to suppose these stories exaggerated. (Ford has only to protest 'I'm a quiet, gentle person', for one to be quite sure they are not.) But besides the stampedes, the war parties, the knockabout fights, there are those quiet moments in his films, equally characteristic, of tenderness and insight; and these too his presence reflects. This was the Ford I found in Dublin – a man of fascinating contradictions; of authority in no way diminished by a complete rejection of apparatus; of instinctive personal warmth as likely to evidence itself in violence as in gentleness; confident of his powers, yet unpretentious about their achievement. A patriarchal figure, sitting among friends, it was easy to understand the devotion he inspires in those who work for him.

When Ford started talking in terms of his 'last picture', I had the impression that this was not necessarily serious – the momentary result of ill-health and fatigue rather than a real determination to bring his career to a close. And perhaps also a sense that yet another turning point had been reached? Today Ford stands apart, an isolated figure as well as a great one – and the isolation is different from the fierce independence which has characterized his whole career. It is not merely the penalty of remaining true to his own, at the moment unfashionable, vision; his recent pictures have not been consistently of the quality he can give us. The argument of commercial necessity in fact sounds in his mouth far more like the uneasy justification of one who feels himself in some degree guilty, than the callous admission of one who has problems of artistic conscience firmly behind him. It is not necessarily a question of subject; the fresh and vigorous poetry which his often repeated themes evoke from him is more to be valued than the artwork which has sometimes resulted from his tackling of more conveniently ambitious material. It is rather a question of seriousness.

A good deal would seem to hang on *The Quiet Man*, for its success or failure must affect Ford's attitude towards film-making in the future. In any event it is difficult to believe that he will not continue at it for a while yet. 'I want to be a tugboat captain,' he says. But God made him a poet, and he must make the best of that.

Postscript

My Dublin interview with Ford had an epilogue. By the time we had finished talking it was too late to return to London the same day so I took a hotel room for the night: I suppose I gave my telephone number to the publicity man who had arranged the interview.

In the morning, as I was packing my bag, there was a knock at my bedroom door. I was wanted on the phone. I was mystified: who on earth knew where I was? I went to the telephone. It was Ford.

'I want to thank you for going to all that trouble to come and see me,' he said. I was touched and amazed: it was for me to thank him. But Ford went on. 'You were quite right with some of those criticisms you made. Some of that stuff isn't up to standard.' I was humbled, as one is apt to be when people readily admit errors one has charged them with. I hoped I hadn't been too impertinent. 'No – no. It's easy to get careless. Particularly when the financial pressure is so great. But that's not a justification. Thank you for reminding me.' (By now I was speechless. Ford went on.) 'I'm going back now to finish *The Quiet Man*, and I promise you I'll do my best. I'll make it as good as I possibly can.'

I wished him good luck, and he thanked me again – then added, before he rang off: 'I'll see *Expendable*, and I'll let you know what I think.'

He kept his word. Some weeks later I received a telegram. It read: 'HAVE SEEN EXPENDABLE. YOU WERE RIGHT. FORD.'

I carried this around with me for a long time, till my wallet was stolen. The police found it, but of course the money in it had gone. So had the telegram.

[Extract taken from *About John Ford* (Plexus, London)]

John Ford and mailman in Maine in the 1920s

Filmography

1 **Founding Father**

LOUIS LUMIÈRE, along with his brother Auguste, was one of the pioneers of the early cinema, shooting – with his camera/projector – *Workers Leaving the Lumière Factory, Arrival of a Train* and *Lunch for Baby*.

PIÈRRE HODGSON has written screenplays for the Portuguese producer Paulo Branco, produced a documentary series on Northern Ireland for the BBC and has been as assistant director for Raul Ruiz, Olivier Assayas and Jean-Pierre Limosin.

2 **The Burning Question**

MONTE HELLMAN is the director of, among others, *Ride the Whirlwind, Two Lane Blacktop* and *Iguana*.

NORA EPHRON is the writer of *Silkwood* and *When Harry Met Sally*, and the writer/director of *Sleepless in Seattle*.

VINCENT WARD is the director of, among others, *Vigil, The Navigator* and *Map of the Human Heart*.

ROGER CORMAN is the director of, among others, *Masque of the Red Death, The Wild Angels* and *Frankenstein Unbound*.

FRED ZINNEMANN is the director of, among others, *High Noon, From Here to Eternity* and *Julia*.

ANDRE DE TOTH is the director of, among others, *Crime Wave, House of Wax* and *Play Dirty*.

ISTVAN SZABO is the director of, among others, *Mephisto, Colonel Redl* and *Meeting Venus*.

RICHARD LOWENSTEIN is the director, of among others, *Strikebound, Dogs in Space* and *Say a Little Prayer*.

DUSAN MAKAVEJEV is the director of, among others, *Switchboard Operator, W.R. – Mysteries of the Organism* and *Gorilla Bathes at Noon*.

KEVIN BROWNLOW is film-maker and historian. For the past twenty years he has worked with David Gill on a series of documentaries about the silent era – starting with *Hollywood* (1980), the *Unknown Chaplin* (1983) and films on Buster Keaton, Harold Lloyd and D. W. Griffith. They are completing a series on the European silent film for the centenary.

VINCENT SHERMAN is the director of, among others, *Old Acquaintance, Mr Skeffington* and *The Young Philadelphians*.

HUANG MINGCHUAN is a film-maker from Taiwan.

ALEX COX is the director of, among others, *Sid and Nancy, Walker* and *Highway Patrolman*.

MICHAEL TOLKIN is the writer of *The Player*, and the writer/director of *The Rapture* and *The New Age*.

PERCY ADLON is the director of, among others, *Céleste, Bagdad Café* and *Salmonberries.*

3 Anamorphobia
MARTIN SCORSESE is the director of, among others, *Mean Streets, Raging Bull* and *Casino.*

GREGORY SOLMAN is the Senior Editor of *Millimeter* magazine. He also writes for *Film Comment, Daily Variety* and the *DGA News.*

4 Divisions and Dislocations
JAMES TOBACK is the writer/director of *Fingers, Exposed* and *The Big Bang.*

5 Penn on Penn
ARTHUR PENN is the director of, among others, *The Left-Handed Gun, The Chase,* and *The Missouri Breaks.*

TOM LUDDY is the producer of *The Secret Garden,* as well as the co-director of the Telluride Film Festival.

DAVID THOMSON is the author of *Suspects, Showman: The Life of David O. Selznick,* and the *Biographical Dictionary of Film.*

6 Raising the Dead
KEN BURNS is the director of, among others, *Brooklyn Bridge, The Civil War* and *Baseball.*

7 Letters Home
SIDNEY HOWARD is the screenwriter of *Arrowsmith, Dodsworth* and *Gone with the Wind.*

9 Chekhov's Children
LOUIS MALLE is the director of, among others, *Lift to the Scaffold, Atlantic City* and *Au revoir les enfants.*

ANDRÉ GREGORY is the director of theatre productions of *Alice in Wonderland* and *Uncle Vanya.* He has also appeared in *My Dinner With André.*

FRED BERNER is the producer of *Miss Firecracker, The Ballad of Little Jo,* as well as *Vanya on 42nd Street.*

WALLACE SHAWN has appeared in, among others, *Manhattan, My Dinner With André* and *Mrs Parker and the Vicious Circle.*

JULIANNE MOORE has appeared in, among others, *The Hand That Rocks the Cradle, Short Cuts* and *Safe.*

LARRY PINE is a New York actor who has been involved in work on soaps, Broadway, off-Broadway, TV, film – avante-garde and mainstream.

OREN MOVERMAN is an Israeli independent film-maker currently living in New York.

10 Sound Design: The Dancing Shadow
WALTER MURCH was responsible for the sound design on, among others, *The Rain People, The Conversation* and *Apocalypse Now;* he has also edited *Romeo is Bleeding* and *First Knight.*

11 Playing Cowboys and Indians
EDDIE FOWLIE has been responsible for the props on, among others, *Lawrence of Arabia, Doctor Zhivago* and *Beyond Rangoon.*

JOHN BOORMAN is the director of, among others, *Point Blank*, *Zardoz* and *Beyond Rangoon*.

12 Lunch and a Book: Director/Cameraman Relations
JOHN SEALE was the cinematographer of *Witness*, *The Paper* and *Beyond Rangoon*

13 An American in Paradise
GENE KELLY appeared in, among others, *On the Town*, *An American in Paris* and *Singin' in the Rain*.

GRAHAM FULLER is the Executive Editor of *Interview* magazine. He is also the editor of *Potter on Potter*.

14 The Tango Lesson
SALLY POTTER is the director of, among others, *Goldiggers*, *Thriller* and *Orlando*.

15 Creation and the Artist
FEDERICO FELLINI is the director of, among others, *La Strada*, *La Dolce Vita* and *8½*.

DAMIEN PETTIGREW is the director/producer of the documentaries, among others, *Eugene Ionesco*, *Italo Calvino* and, most recently, *Federico Fellini*.

16 Missing Sandy Dennis
VIGGO MORTENSEN has appeared in, among others, *The Indian Runner*, *The Reflecting Skin* and *Carlito's Way*.

17 Meeting in Dublin: The Quiet Man, 1950
LINDSAY ANDERSON is the director of, among others, *This Sporting Life*, *If...* and *Britannia Hospital*.

Faber Film List

New and Forthcoming

The Centenary:

Letters: Inventing the Cinema
Auguste and Louis Lumière

Flickers: An Illustrated Celebration of 100 Years of Cinema
Gilbert Adair

Projections – Special Edition
In association with the French film magazine, *Positif*, Projections presents essays by film-makers around the globe about their favourite film, director or actor.

Film-makers on Film-making:

Almodovar on Almodovar
Edited by Frederic Strauss

Burton on Burton
Edited by Mark Salisbury

Fellini on Fellini
Edited by Constanzo Constantini

Hitchcock on Hitchcock
Edited by Sidney Gottlieb

Images: My Life in Film
Ingmar Bergman

Magic Hour: An Autobiography
Jack Cardiff

Notes: On the Making of Apocalypse Now
Eleanor Coppola

Projections 1

Winner
British Film Institute
Michael Powell Award
Best Film Book of 1992

Projections is a forum for practitioners of the cinema to reflect on the year in cinema and to speculate on the future. The first issue contains:

Bright Dreams, Hard Knocks
a journal for 1991 by John Boorman

Film Fiction
an essay by Sam Fuller

The Early Life of a Screenwriter
from the Berlin diaries of Emeric Pressburger

Demme on Demme
a comprehensive survey of the career of
1991's Oscar-winning director

Matters of Photogenics
an essay on photographing the human face by
Oscar-winning cameraman Nestor Almendros

My Director and I
a conversation between River Phoenix and
Gus Van Sant during the shooting of River
Phoenix's most memorable film, *My Own
Private Idaho*.

Surviving Desire
a screenplay by Hal Hartley

Making Some Light
Michael Mann discusses the making of *The
Last of the Mohicans*.

There are also contributions from: Denys
Arcand, David Byrne, Jane Campion, Costa-
Gavras, Terry Gilliam, Mike Figgis, Tony
Harrison, Kzysztof Kieślowski, Richard
Lowenstein, Louis Malle, Claude Miller,
Arthur Penn, Sydney Pollack, Kevin
Reynolds, Francesco Rosi, Ken Russell,
Ettore Scola, István Szabó, Paolo and Vittorio
Taviani, Michael Verhoeven, Paul Verhoeven,
Vincent Ward and Zhang Yimou

Projections 2

The second issue contains:

Shadow and Substance
George Miller charts the journey he has made
from the *Mad Max* trilogy to *Lorenzo's Oil*.

Movie Lessons
Jaco van Dormael discusses the creative
process that led to *Toto the Hero*.

Searching for the Serpent
New Zealand director Alison Maclean
discusses her work.

Freewheelin'
A free-ranging phonecall between Derek
Jarman and Gus Van Sant.

Acting on Impulse
Willem Dafoe describes his approach to
acting.

The Early Life of a Screenwriter
Veteran writer/director Sydney Gilliat relives
the early days of British cinema.

Altman on Altman
From *M*★*A*★*S*★*H* to *Short Cuts*, Robert
Altman discusses his career.

Bob Roberts
Tim Robbins's stunning, incisive political
satire

I Wake Up, Dreaming: A Journal for 1992
Bertrand Tavernier's diary records the
evolution of his controversial film *L627* against
the shifting European cultural landscape.

There are also contributions from:
Denys Arcand, David Byrne, Monte Hellman,
Richard Lowenstein, Jocelyn Moorhouse,
Arthur Penn, Nicholas Roeg, Philippe
Rousselet, Paul Shrader, Ron Shelton, Roger
Spottiswoode, István Szabó, Michael
Verhoeven, Vincent Ward and
Fred Zinneman.

Projections 3

The third issue contains:

Journals 1989–1993
Francis Ford Coppola
An intensely personal and highly revealing
documentation of the creative processes of
one of America's greatest directors.

The Narrow Path
Chinese director, Chen Kaige, discusses his
life and work, culminating in his Cannes-
winning success, *Farewell My Concubine.*

Acting Is Doing
Veteran director Sydney Pollack discusses his
approach to working with actors.

Art Direction: Wajda to Spielberg
The Oscar-winning art director of *Schindler's
List* describes his approach to his craft.

Making Music for *Short Cuts.*
Hal Willner discusses how he created the rich
musical texture for Robert Altman's film.

Pixelvision
Michael Almereyda reveals the mysteries and
beauties of this video medium.

Kasdan on Kasdan
From *Body Heat* to *Wyatt Earp*, Lawrence
Kasdan discusses his career.

Screenwriting
Michael Tolkin, the author of *The Player*,
discusses the struggles of the screenwriter in a
town where writers are treated with
ambivalence, if not distain.

Producing
Art Linson discusses his tussles with David
Mamet on *The Untouchables.*

Answers First, Questions Later
Quentin Tarantino traces the journey that led
to *Pulp Fiction.*

On Tour with *Orlando*
Sally Potter's diary of her promotional tour for
Orlando.

The Hollywood Way
An excerpt from Gus Van Sant's 'biographical novel, with a few movie hints'.

'I Wake Up Screaming'
Richard Stanley's diary of the trials and tribulations of shooting *Dust Devil* in Namibia.

Flirt
The script of Hal Hartley's latest exploration of love and manners.

Cry from Croatia
Croatian film-maker, Zrinko Ogresta's lament for the destruction being wrought on his country.

And the Dreams of:
Denys Arcand, Monte Hellman, Richard Lowenstein, Sally Potter, Paul Schrader, Steven Soderbergh, Jaco Van Dormael and Alex Van Warnerdam.

EDUCATION

With the ever increasing interest in the use of film and television within the National Curriculum and the continuing development of Film & Media Studies examinations at all levels, arguably the most prominent art forms of the twentieth century are finally gaining the recognition they deserve within the education system. Since its inception in 1986, Film Education is proud to have been at the forefront of this development.

FILM EDUCATION

Film Education is a unique, charitable organisation with an unrivalled reputation for promoting the study of cinema and film in schools and colleges whilst meeting the demands of the National Curriculum. To this end, we publish a variety of free teaching materials, offer specialist in-service training for teachers and organise cinema visits, lectures and seminars for schools.

Over the last 9 years we have established an extensive database of over 10,000 named teachers throughout the UK, all of whom now regularly incorporate the use of film into a large variety of different subject areas across the curriculum.

Our special relationship with the film industry enables us to access 'inside' information on producers, films and release schedules; in short, the entire production, distribution and exhibition process.

We provide the vital link between the film industry and education.

Our extensive back-list of over 200 study guides are geared towards both primary and secondary students and cover a wide variety of subject areas.

ALL STUDY GUIDES ARE AVAILABLE **FREE OF CHARGE** TO TEACHERS

If you are a practising teacher who would like to become a member of our mailing list, please write to us at: Film Education, 41-42 Berners Street, London W1P 3AA.

TARTAN VIDEO

The First Choice in Independent & World Cinema for 1995

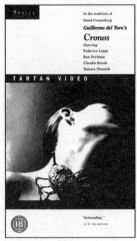
In the tradition of David Cronenberg
Guillermo del Toro's
Cronos
Starring
Federico Luppi
Ron Perlman
Claudio Brook
Tamara Shanath
"Astounding."
KIM NEWMAN

From the director of Vacas
Julio Medem's
The Red Squirrel
Starring
Nancho Nova
Emma Suarez
"Bold and mesmerising ...sexy."
THE GUARDIAN

From the award-winning director of Aguirre, Wrath of God & Stroszek
Werner Herzog's
Fitzcarraldo
Starring
Klaus Kinski
Claudia Cardinale
"Terrific entertainment... has to be seen to be believed."
THE GUARDIAN

CRONOS   **THE RED SQUIRREL**   **FITZCARRALDO**

Tartan Video offers you the finest in independent and world cinema. Films of distinction and enduring excellence digitally remastered for superior quality and presented with extensive liner notes.

Following the record-breaking success of **Hard Boiled** and **Cinema Paradiso The Special Edition** Tartan Video are proud to announce a line-up of sizzling new product for '95. From the director of the highly successful **Golden Balls**, Bigas Luna, comes the sensual and bawdy, **The Tit and The Moon** and the provocative **The Ages of Lulu**; the twin hits of the Cannes Film Festival, the eerie and intriguing **The Red Squirrel** and Alison Anders controversial **Mi Vida Loca**. From France, the acclaimed thriller **Love in the Strangest Way** and from Canada the startling and gritty **I Love A Man In Uniform**. Further releases from the master Ingmar Bergman will include **Smiles of a Summer Night** and his classic **Scenes From a Marriage**. From Alan Rudolph, the evocative **Equinox** and later in the year the acclaimed festival hit, **Strawberry and Chocolate**. Australia offers Paul Cox's **Exile** and from Mexico the film acclaimed as the best horror movie of the year, **Cronos**, a startling reinvention of the vampire myth.

Future releases will include the definitive collection of the films of Werner Herzog including the epic **Aguirre, Wrath of God** and the stunning **Fitzcarraldo**, and from the late great Derek Jarman, the seminal **Sebastiane** and the anthem for the punk generation, **Jubilee**.

All these and many more comprise an outstanding and beautifully packaged collection of the finest in international cinema. Now available on both high quality VHS and Laserdisc* in their original widescreen format**.

Available to buy from HMV, Virgin, Our Price, Tower, WH Smiths and all good video retail outlets.

TARTAN VIDEO - COMMITTED TO EXCELLENCE

*selected titles only   **where available

"MALLE'S MANHATTAN MASTERPIECE...
A FEAST OF FINE ACTING"
QUENTIN CURTIS, INDEPENDENT ON SUNDAY
"UTTERLY MAGICAL,UTTERLY MEMORABLE"
FINANCIAL TIMES
"AN ASTONISHING PIECE OF THEATRE AND
AN AUTHENTIC CINEMATIC EXPERIENCE"
PHILIP FRENCH, OBSERVER
"★★★★ THIS FILM WON ME
OVER, IT'S SO WELL
PERFORMED"
RACHEL SIMPSON, DAILY EXPRESS
FROM THE CREATORS OF
"MY DINNER WITH ANDRÉ"
A FILM BY
LOUIS MALLE
VANYA
ON 42ND STREET
U
STARRING
WALLACE SHAWN JULIANNE MOORE
ANDRÉ GREGORY'S ACCLAIMED PRODUCTION OF
CHEKHOV'S "UNCLE VANYA" ADAPTED BY DAVID MAMET
A Mayfair Film Released by Artificial Eye
OUT ON VIDEO SPRING 1995